"In a time of taking two steps back, *Revolutionizing World Trade* makes a bold leap into the future and the verdict is there is nothing to fear! Suominen provides a thorough review of what's to come for the global economy and while not shying from the real challenges facing consumers, governments, and businesses, generates a sense of promise and optimism sorely missing from today's discourse on global affairs."
—Susan F. Stone, Senior Trade Advisor, OECD

"An important new book, highlighting the trading opportunities that come with new technologies. It analyzes the challenges that need to be overcome, including cross-border procedures, and makes the key point that beyond digitizing trade, we also need to digitize customs, borders, and ports."
—Jan Hoffmann, Chief, Trade Logistics Branch, Division on Technology and Logistics, UNCTAD

"Suominen introduces this book as a roadmap for the far-sighted entrepreneur, but it is much more than that. She explores the opportunities and challenges facing businesses, policymakers, regulators, and society in general before setting out her manifesto for using e-commerce as a key enabler for inclusive trade. Whatever your role or interest in e-commerce and trade, this book will help you better understand how e-commerce is shaping our world and the benefits that it can bring today."
—Steven Pope, Vice President of Customs & Regulatory Affairs, DHL Express Europe

"Kati Suominen 'gets it.' Globalization, technology, and mass affluence have changed the rules for international expansion. In *Revolutionizing World Trade*, Suominen walks us through how these changes have upended the traditional trading world, driven by ecommerce and the Internet. Every international business should read this book. Then they can 'get it' as well."
—Frank Lavin, Chairman, Export Now, former Undersecretary for International Trade, U.S. Department of Commerce

"*Revolutionizing World Trade* provides an in-depth look at forces changing trade and global business and makes important recommendations for bold policy ideas which would enable outsized economic growth across global markets. A must-read for anyone driven to solve these big problems."
—Brenda Santoro, Head of Global Trade, Silicon Valley Bank

"Kati has a wealth of experience in international trade from both a private sector practitioner perspective as well as a public sector policy perspective. Her work has taken her to the forefront of the evolving trade landscape. This book elucidates this evolution and is a great contribution to the debate about the future of trade and our ability to shape its course for the betterment of the global community."
—Steven Beck, Head of Trade and Supply Chain Finance, Asian Development Bank

REVOLUTIONIZING WORLD TRADE

Emerging Frontiers in the Global Economy

Editor J. P. Singh

Series Board Arjun Appadurai, Manuel Castells, Tyler Cowen, Christina Davis, Judith Goldstein, Deirdre McCloskey

SERIES TITLES

Globalization Under and After Socialism: The Evolution of Transnational Capital in Central and Eastern Europe
Besnik Pula, 2018

Discreet Power: How the World Economic Forum Shapes Market Agendas
Christina Garsten and Adrienne Sörbom, 2018

Making Money: How Taiwanese Industrialists Embraced the Global Economy
Gary G. Hamilton and Cheng-shu Kao, 2017

Sweet Talk: Paternalism and Collective Action in North-South Trade Relations
J. P. Singh, 2017

Breaking the WTO: How Emerging Powers Disrupted the Neoliberal Project
Kristen Hopewell, 2016

Intra-Industry Trade: Cooperation and Conflict in the Global Political Economy
Cameron G. Thies and Timothy M. Peterson, 2015

REVOLUTIONIZING

WORLD TRADE

HOW DISRUPTIVE TECHNOLOGIES

OPEN OPPORTUNITIES FOR ALL

KATI SUOMINEN

STANFORD UNIVERSITY PRESS ▮ STANFORD, CALIFORNIA

Stanford University Press
Stanford, California

Printed in the United States of America on acid-free, archival-quality paper

Library of Congress Cataloging-in-Publication Data

Names: Suominen, Kati, author.
Title: Revolutionizing world trade : how disruptive technologies open opportunities for all / Kati Suominen.
Description: Stanford, California : Stanford University Press, 2019. | Series: Emerging frontiers in the global economy | Includes bibliographical references and index.
Identifiers: LCCN 2019007912 (print) | LCCN 2019010050 (ebook) | ISBN 9781503610729 (ebook) | ISBN 9781503603608 (cloth: alk. paper) | ISBN 9781503610712 (pbk.: alk. paper)
Subjects: LCSH: Technological innovations—Economic aspects. | International trade. | Globalization—Economic aspects.
Classification: LCC HC79.T4 (ebook) | LCC HC79.T4 S875 2019 (print) | DDC 382—dc23
LC record available at https://lccn.loc.gov/2019007912

Cover design: Tandam Creative

CONTENTS

Prologue ix

PART I. THE OPPORTUNITY

1   Introduction   3

2   World Economy Goes to Heaven   14

3   Killer App for World Trade   38

4   When Six Billion People Go to the Mall   61

5   Driverless Delivery, Door-to-Door   77

6   Finding $1.7 Trillion   102

7   The Big Query   118

PART II. THE CHALLENGES

8   Offline   137

9   Stuck in Customs   160

10   Splinternet   176

11   Credit Crunch   199

12   Techlash and Trade Wars   220

13   Better Trade by More People   250

Notes   281

Index   331

PROLOGUE

In 2005, Thomas Friedman's *The World Is Flat* defined the third wave of globalization and its meaning to our lives. "The Flat World" was shorthand for global supply chains run by major corporations: riding on the IT revolution and trade and investment liberalization, corporations such as Apple, Dell, and General Electric offshored manufacturing to low-cost economies, outsourcing parts and components from suppliers around the world. China became the world's factory, mass-producing computers, clothes, and gadgets for Western consumers; developing and developed nations alike prospered as China's parts warehouse. World trade tripled between 1990 and 2010, while trade in parts and components shot up almost five-fold. As a fitting example of fragmentation in global production, Friedman famously catalogued the making of a computer from parts that originated in seventeen different countries.

The global trade and development communities have operated from this paradigm of globalization for three decades, negotiating trade deals that cut tariffs on products at borders and protected foreign investors behind the border, helping developing countries transform into global production platforms, expanding roads and ports and streamlining customs clearance, and training small businesses to become suppliers to large multinational companies. But this paradigm of globalization started to unravel in my mind in the fall of 2013, as my company Nextrade Group was working on a flagship report for the Inter-American Development Bank on small business exports in Latin America. We found that only 13 percent of the region's companies had export activities, and that companies that did export did so typically to only one or two markets and had little staying power: over 70 percent of companies that started exporting in one year no longer exported the following year.

One question we sought to answer was how to expand the number of exporters in the region. As fate would have it, at the same time eBay published two studies based on the company's transactional data that showed that across markets as diverse as the United States, South Africa, and Chile, ecommerce was turning everything trade economists knew about small business trade on its head. For example, eBay's data showed that while 18 percent of Chilean companies exported and typically only to two or three markets, of Chilean eBay sellers, 100 percent of companies exported to twenty-eight markets, and 70 percent continued exporting the year following their first inroads into exporting—and most continued exporting five years after they first started.

That was a eureka moment—eBay's data suggested ecommerce could be the silver bullet the trade and development communities had been looking for to enable small companies to grow into exporters and become what eBay termed "micro-multinationals." This realization made me consider how a range of other technologies such as 3D printing, cloud computing, the Internet of Things, and blockchain might be having an impact on trade and firms that trade. The more I thought of the implications of these technologies for trade, the more I started to gain a sense that globalization as we had known it was coming to an end. A new globalization was taking form right before our eyes.

This led me to pursue empirical work on how new technologies are driving trade and what policy mixes optimize their adoption; to ideate and build new global initiatives and public-private partnerships to accelerate the adoption of technologies to fuel trade in developing countries; to help leading technology companies bring their technologies to serve various parts of the global trade ecosystem; and to apply new technologies, particularly AI and machine learning, in my company's work on trade and economic development. It also led me to write this book.

Revolutionizing World Trade argues that globalization is undergoing a quiet revolution, one that is critically reshaping the patterns, players, and possibilities of world trade. The unfolding wave of globalization can be the most dynamic, prosperous, and inclusive wave yet. It can be globalization for all.

Yet this book will also show how the promise of the next wave of globalization is fraught with challenges, such as policy barriers and legacy institutions that stifle the transition to twenty-first-century, technology-powered trade. If we overcome these challenges, twenty-second-century economic historians will look back on this period as a global economic renaissance and a transformation that enabled people around the world to gain from trade as producers and consumers, sellers and buyers. If we fail, the global economy can balkanize just as in the nineteenth century, when countries used tariffs to collect revenue and nurture infant industries. This was a self-defeating approach that took over a century to correct. The book shines a light on the clash between an emerging wave of possibilities and outdated policies that arrest us.

Revolutionizing World Trade is not motivated by recent U.S. trade policies—I started writing this much before President Trump was even a candidate. It is about a technological change that can reinvigorate economic growth and entrepreneurship around the world—if we just end our myopic focus on trade as it has been, on factory jobs that will never come back and tariff wars that no one will win, and instead focus on building the bases for thriving in the twenty-first-century global digital economy. I critically discuss the Trump administration's trade policies—but mostly this is a book about longer-term trends and bigger, more compelling solutions that this and future administrations all must drive.

Granted, this has been a tough book to write. The patterns described here are nascent, data on them are only starting to come in, and technological change is rapid. At times I fret that this book is appearing only now, after many of the technologies are already mainstream—back in 2013 most trade economists had not even heard of 3D printing or the power of ecommerce to drive trade. *Blockchain* was a fringe term never used in trade policy conferences. At the same time, the book feels timelier than ever, now that the global trade policy community has awoken to the opportunities technology offers. In a time of much chatter and trade tussles among nations, but scarcity of compelling, big ideas, we risk squandering a historic opportunity for hundreds of millions of people to realize their economic potential. And so, *Revolutionizing World Trade* is also about setting out bold ideas to undo these obstacles and unleash the next era of globalization. And it is a book about the pioneering men and women who are developing and using new technologies to transform globalization and open opportunities for all.

I am particularly grateful to former Stanford University Press editor Margo Fleming and Don Fehr of Trident Media for taking a chance on me, and Stanford current editor Steven Catalano as well as Sunna Juhn, Tim Roberts, and David Horne for outstanding editing and management of the book project. I dedicate this book to my many colleagues and clients, who are tirelessly working for a more vibrant world economy.

Kati Suominen, Los Angeles, November 2018

PART I

The Opportunity

$$\boxed{1}$$

INTRODUCTION

Consider two very different worlds only a few miles from each other. One world is that of Jennifer Shanklin-Hawkins and Nicole Hargrove, featured in November 2016 in *The New York Times*, who have worked all their lives at the Carrier air conditioner factory in Indianapolis and eagerly expected President-elect Trump to impose tariffs on air conditioners to prevent their factory from moving to Mexico.[1] The other world is that of Travis Baird, who lives 150 miles away in Elkhart, Indiana. In 2004, Travis started his motorbike gear business with $3,500, and today, selling on eBay, sells gear to 131 countries and derives 41 percent of his revenue from exports riding on free trade and prosperity in other countries.[2]

Which is the world you want to live in? One in which low-skilled, disillusioned factory workers call for protectionist barriers against international trade? Or one in which entrepreneurs—using their ingenuity, state-of-the-art technology, and the open market access that American trade negotiators have secured over the past eight decades—sell their products and services to customers across the planet, grow their businesses, hire new people, and realize their potential? If you choose the latter world, this book offers a roadmap. For it won't come about on its own.

Globalization—growth of cross-border flows of products, services, data, capital, and people—has unfolded majestically around the planet over the past 150 years, sweeping over just about every country, city, and household. Ravaged by wars, recessions, and protectionist pressures, globalization has gone undefeated, time and again rebounding with new vigor and reach. In the past three decades, a period of the greatest wave of globalization yet, globalization has been driven by multinational corporations and their global supply chains. In this model, companies sourced parts, components, and raw materials from suppliers around the world for assembly into final products in low-cost manufacturing hubs in Mexico and China and Poland, and exported the final products to shoppers touring Walmarts in St. Louis and Apple stores in San Francisco. Describing the globalization of production, the World Trade Organization declared products were no longer made in China or made in the United States—they were now "Made in the World."

As global production disintegrated, national economies integrated. In the United States, trade soared to 24 percent of GDP, up from 2 percent in 1980; in Korea, to 87 percent of GDP, in Germany, to 75 percent, in Mexico, to 63 percent, in China, to 47 percent. Even economies that have long been closed to trade such as Cuba and Myanmar have embraced foreign trade and investment. Trade grew almost twice as fast as the world economy in 1980–2015, from 35 percent to nearly 60 percent of world GDP, and foreign direct investment stocks soared from 5 to some 35 percent of world GDP.[3]

Attesting to the rising relevance of trade in national economies, global companies and import-competing lobbies clashed in fierce battles over the direction of trade policy. Threatened by low-cost labor in emerging markets, American unions fought each new trade deal; dependent on their subsidies, farmers from France to Korea mounted violent street protests. Rock-throwing protesters hounded WTO's biennial ministerial meetings, claiming corporations were exploiting workers in developing nations. At the same time, gains from trade quietly expanded around the world. Every American household is found in several studies to be roughly $15,000 richer each year because of the cost-savings created by the fact that America is open to imports.[4] Opening to foreign investment and trade, backward-developing countries got on a growth escalator, transforming into booming emerging markets. From the 1990s onward, countries around the world have negotiated dozens of free trade agreements (FTAs) with each other; every WTO member belongs to at least one FTA. Most recently, African nations have come together to negotiate a historic continental trade deal. The recent U.S.-China trade warring aside, the free trade coalition has held: there have been no major reversals in trade liberalization since the Great Depression.

Yet there are few reasons to sit still.

First, productivity growth has sagged in just about all major economies. Economic growth is the engine of prosperity and income growth, and behind economic growth is productivity growth. Rise in productivity is why we make much more by working less than our great-grandparents did. There has been a great deal of concern about the recent deceleration in productivity growth in the United States and advanced economies. In most emerging markets, with the exception of China and a handful of Eastern European countries, productivity has been growing more slowly than in America.[5] Granted, the first few months of 2019 saw a jump in U.S. productivity growth, hopefully a sign of things to come.

Second, one key driver of productivity growth, world trade, is only cautiously rebounding since plunging and then flatlining after the 2008–2009 global financial crisis. In the post–Great Recession years, globalization has lost some of its vigor. Shackled by economic cooling and slowdown in liberalization, trade has grown more slowly after 2008 than at any time since the recession of the early 1980s. Still upbeat about its prospects in 2015, by 2016 the global shipping giant Maersk had declared that the shipping industry faced conditions—such as the crude oil price crisis and sluggish demand in Brazil, Russia, and Europe—that were much worse than those that preceded the 2008–2009 crisis. It is no coincidence that productivity growth around the world has sagged as trade growth has slowed. Growth of world trade improved in 2017 to 4.6 percent but fell in 2018 to 3 percent, still too low to drive economic growth.[6]

Third, all the talk about globalization notwithstanding, the world economy is still far from globalized. Trade economists have long known about "missing trade"—the fact that there is far more trade within than between countries, than would be expected on the basis of economic fundamentals. Almost one half of all pairs of countries in the world, some fifteen thousand pairs, are tradeless couples. Much of world trade is carried out among countries that share a border: for Latin American countries, trade with land neighbors is 20 percent of total trade, for European and North American economies, it is up to 35 percent. And what economists call "home bias" persists. For example, only 5 percent of U.S. companies, 6 percent of Mexican companies, and 20 percent of Swedish companies export. Empirically, most of world trade is still generated by "export superstars," the top 1 percent largest exporters, such as GE, Boeing, and Walmart in the United States. Most of their trade is intra-firm, among their own subsidiaries. The world is not yet as flat as we might believe.

Fourth, free trade has become a curse word, and trade politics have soured.

At the time of writing, Washington and Beijing are raising tariffs on each other's exports, engaged in a futile, counterproductive trade war that neither can win. For many Americans, the image of globalization is still one of American factories fleeing to Mexico or China in search of low-cost labor. While bilateral trade agreements have flourished in the past several years, the multilateral Doha Round is dead, the United States has pulled out of the Trans-Pacific Partnership, and Brexit has been evoking fears about a balkanized world trading system. Except for a flagship agreement on trade facilitation reached in 2013, the WTO membership has failed to make any significant progress since the institution was launched in 1995. The WTO will not rebound as a venue for multilateral trade deals inked by its 164 members. Trade deals will continue to be plurilateral and bilateral, negotiated among coalitions of the willing.

This book regards trade as a force of great good, one that improves lives around the world. It also sees trade as but a voluntary, mutually consenting exchange of goods and services between a buyer in one country and a seller in another country. No one forces an American business to import computers from China or French online shoppers to buy Argentine Malbec: they do so because they want to, enjoying their freedom to trade. However, I also recognize that trade has distributional impacts. If not coupled with efforts that ease the transition of uncompetitive businesses and workers to a world of freer trade, trade liberalization can hurt them, while making good companies even better and more productive, and decidedly benefiting consumers and businesses that import. I personally failed to understand how viscerally these distributional effects would be transposed into American politics and how they could brew to help bring about the election of President Trump. But I am an empiricist and espouse the view that most job churn, unemployment, and inequality are not driven by trade—or imports, more specifically. Empirically, these troubles have many drivers, from technological changes such as automation to gaps in skills development in the workforce.

But this book is not about trade as it has been or as it is—it is about trade as it is becoming.

Not Your Grandpa's Globalization

During the one minute it takes you to read this sentence, 17,200 parcels are being ordered and delivered across the largest markets in Europe, 476 people will become new netizens and start using the Internet, 380 people will get a smartphone with which to connect to the global online shopping mall, 162 new users will register on Alibaba to browse and buy products, eBay and Amazon sellers collectively will gross $228,064, and the amount of video uploaded globally on the Internet would take you twenty-three years to watch.[7]

This is globalization in the twenty-first century. It is a world in which disruptive technologies—3D printing, ecommerce, blockchain, AI, 5G, and so on—are quietly revolutionizing the economics of global production and trade. They are empowering businesses of all sizes to cut costs and make, move, and market products and services worldwide with greater ease than ever before. They are encouraging millions of solo entrepreneurs to grow into multinational sellers. They are enabling consumers and companies to access and choose from a global catalogue of products and services. They are slashing the costs companies have paid to intermediaries such as banks, freight forwarders, customs brokers, trade lawyers, and shipping lines, by automating and accelerating the flow of goods from door to door and payments from bank to bank, and by digitizing the piles of documents, data, and information that accompany the billions of trade transactions that crisscross the planet each year. They are helping us close in on the Holy Grail of world trade: seamless integration and automation of the informational, financial, and physical supply chains that undergird trade transactions.

The best part: the emerging technologies change the possibilities of trade to do good—to reignite productivity growth of economies, raise incomes, and empower people around the world to realize their full economic potential.

The technologies discussed in this volume are undoing every major cost hampering world trade. Ecommerce and online payments are lowering the search and transaction costs that have for centuries limited transactions between geographically distant buyers and sellers. 3D printing, robotics, blockchain, and new delivery models are obliterating transport and supply chain management costs. Expanding companies' abilities to forecast trends with customers, markets, and prices, massive data and computing power are lowering the informational costs that have kept companies driving in the fog in world markets—and hesitant to even get on the road.

Globalization as we have known it is fading into the rearview mirror. This book tells how this is happening and what it means. It is written because the ongoing technology-driven transformations are not trivial or piecemeal. They are changing an entire paradigm of globalization, a set of long-standing "facts" or conventional wisdoms held by an entire generation about what globalization is and what effects it has. Among these wisdoms: that products are "Made in the World" in giant global supply chains, that small businesses struggle to export because of high fixed costs of doing so, that trade facilitation at the border is key to boosting trade volumes. These and other wisdoms—all of which are certainly correct and widely studied—have shaped hundreds of major trade policy decisions, thousands of academic and policy papers, countless policy careers, and hundreds of billions of dollars in development assistance over the past three decades. I argue, though, that these "facts" may not be facts any longer in five to ten years—that an entirely new paradigm of globalization is emerging. In the new paradigm, new technologies are transforming the patterns, players, possibilities, and even the politics of trade.

This new wave of globalization, let's call it Globalization 4.0, has already started. Only it isn't your grandpa's or even your dad's globalization. This globalization is not driven by global corporate supply chains but by online platforms such as Alibaba, Amazon, MercadoLibre, Jumia, and eBay that connect hundreds of millions of individual buyers and sellers to transact with each other. This globalization is not directed by giant retail chains but by hundreds of millions of smartphone-wielding consumers ordering goods to their doorsteps and services in their inboxes. This globalization is not measured by trade in physical products as much as in cross-border flows of bits and bytes—sales and purchases of digital designs, digital services, and data. This new era of globalization is not about perfecting mass production of standardized goods in a low-wage country; it is an era of mass personalization of products ideated and made on-demand in small production units running on 3D printers and robots near end consumers. The next wave of globalization is not jammed by paperwork and bureaucracy at countries' borders—but by the costs of last-mile delivery, cybersecurity challenges, and arcane digital regulations that raise the cost for companies to offer, buy, and pay for goods and services from other countries.

Of course, our era is but old trends in new clothes. Technology and trade have through the ages conspired to create new supercycles of globalization. Each cycle—in the 1850s, in the 1950s, and in the 1990s—has been started by technological changes that transform how and where companies make, move, and market products and services. Much like its predecessors, the coming cycle, Globalization 4.0, is fundamentally driven by technological changes, a new industrial revolution often dubbed Industry 4.0. And it can be the most transformative and exciting wave of globalization yet: it opens opportunities for people around the world to gain from trade, as producers, online sellers, exporters, importers, and micro-multinationals.

Granted, the conventional wisdoms of globalization are still valid and still matter. It is still useful for governments to reform and modernize customs. It is still meaningful to facilitate corporations' global supply chains by upholding open trade policies and robust protections for foreign investors. It is still useful for governments to offer export promotion services and working capital to help small businesses export. But we must get ready for the new era of globalization and help it come about, for it can improve the lives of many but it can't come about on its own. Many challenges stand in the way. Adoption of technologies that transform trade opportunities is still incipient. Policies from old, arcane customs procedures to new, stringent data transfer regulations hamper businesses' ability to translate technologies into trade opportunities. A range of inefficiencies bedevil trade transactions: players don't interoperate well, companies' visibility into their shipments is low, sudden tariffs and trade barriers complicate business planning, and the regulatory paperwork involved with moving goods from country to country is endless. In this giant system in which goods and services are bought, sold, shipped, insured, inspected, and increasingly returned, the whole is in many ways still less than the sum of the parts.

Imagine if we could go farther. Imagine if small businesses could within minutes secure the working capital they need to deliver an export shipment that enables them to hire new workers. Imagine if companies did not have to wrestle with complicated and divergent national regulations when selling and operating across markets. Imagine if people in poor developing countries were armed with 5G connections and knowledge on how to use technologies such as ecommerce and AI to make their businesses more productive. Imagine if large cross-border payments could clear in seconds. Imagine if international trade transactions were fully digitized and automated end to end, with the movement of a product from market A to B triggering the various events required for the transaction to complete, such as cross-border payments from buyer to seller and regulatory filings to national border agencies. Imagine if the world economy was one giant marketplace, a medieval town square, in which buyers and sellers regardless of their location, nationality, currency, or language could buy and sell just about anything, from and to anyone, anywhere, any time. Imagine how people in such a world could realize their full economic potential and build their businesses and a better life for their children. That world is for the first time within reach—but it will take work for us to bring it about.

As the patterns and players of world trade change, so change the constraints to trade. The global trade and development agenda must therefore also be realigned across the many areas of policy action. *Revolutionizing World Trade* also tells what needs to get done. Governments need to realign trade policy, trade enforcement, trade facilitation, trade finance, trade adjustment, and export promotion, and educational and economic policies, to bring about the next era of globalization. Trade policy should no longer be what it has been for decades, tariffs and non-tariff barriers at the border or protections for foreign investors behind the border; it should be about digital regulations such as free cross-border flows of data, duty-free access for digital products to countries' markets, and fluid access for ecommerce and payment platforms to service customers in new markets. International trade development is no longer about building wider roads, better manufacturing plants, or more productive rice paddies; it is about accelerating the diffusion and use of leading-edge technologies among developing-country companies, citizens, and governments. American trade politics should no longer be focused on recovering factory jobs from China—future production is not done by American or Chinese manual labor but by 3D printers and robots manned by a handful of humans.

The best U.S. trade policy has no word "trade" in it at all: it is about educating and equipping our workers and next generations to thrive in the global digital economy as entrepreneurs, business leaders, employees, and freelancers. It is about enabling Americans of all walks of life to use their ingenuity and build and apply technology to solve major business and economic problems. For it is those who know how to use technology that extend their capabilities and grow their incomes.

Why This Book Now?

Policymakers and analysts might have three objections to a book like this. One is that "things will still take a long time"—that the technologies discussed here will take time to mature and truly transform industries and trade patterns. Another is that technology is not a panacea—technologies all have their problems and bring new ones, from fake news to cybersecurity threats and privacy concerns. Still another is that technologies exist, but their adoption and use for cross-border economic exchange is stifled by many challenges, such as inertia in C-suites and outdated policies and institutions created for a bygone era.

I say no to the first objection—I believe change is happening much faster than most appreciate. Just looking back a decade suggests that technologies will transform trade the way Mike went bankrupt in Hemingway's book *The Sun also Rises*: "First gradually, then suddenly." In 2008, among the global platforms that today shape everything from personal branding to political discourse, Twitter was turning two and had 6 million users when it in 2018 had 335 million, and Facebook had only 100 million users, when it in 2018 had 2.3 billion users.[8] The nascent ecommerce empire Alibaba had 4 million users when in 2018 it had 500 million.[9] The device that transformed how we order products, services, and information, the iPhone, had come to market for the first time just ten months previous and had been bought by 7 million people—when in 2018, 218 million iPhones were sold worldwide.[10]

It is easy to forget how incipient the global digital economy was in 2008. Ten years from now, in 2028, we will realize how nascent it was today. This book is about the next ten years—how the technologies that are emerging today will reshape globalization, and what business and policy leaders need to do today to harness them to fuel trade, inclusion, and economic growth worldwide.

To the second objection, that new technologies bring new problems, I offer a qualified no. Of course there are problems, and new ones will emerge— Facebook's travails with Russian trolls are just among a handful of such enormous challenges. Readers who have studied quantum computing see an array of stomach-wrenching national security risks the technology can bring, right alongside its mindboggling possibilities to cure disease and unlock the elusive secrets of the universe, including the mysteries of economic growth. But there is also a wide range of solutions, both technology and policy, to address these risks—an imperative of our era, given the payoffs discussed in the subsequent pages.

To the third objection I say, yes, uneven and slow adoption of new technologies and policies that stifle them are problematic, and thus this book. While transformative technologies exist, outdated policies, zealous regulations, legacy institutions, and digital divides arrest their power to boost trade and bolster productivity, and risk squashing the opportunity for hundreds of millions to realize their full potential in the global digital economy. *Revolutionizing World Trade* highlights and dissects these challenges and prescribes policies to remove them.

The very point of writing this volume is to drive policy and business leaders to create a better future. A better future will not come from "there are so many new problems" or "it's too early to tell" conversation killers. It will come if we are willing to look at the opportunity before us right now, take what we have, and build on it, and create a new era of globalization.

Academics might object to this book by saying there are not enough data or evidence yet to ascertain technologies' impacts or whether causal patterns are real. But this book is not a conventional academic book that draws on decades of data and hundreds of papers to explain a phenomenon and recount what happened. The technologies I discuss are new, their impacts are only coming into focus, and data are incipient. Studies about causal relationships are nascent and will be scrutinized for years to come—an entire field is emerging on the drivers and impacts of digitization on trade. This book is akin to a book about the rise of outsourcing and offshoring written not in 2006 when Friedman wrote his or 2018 when there is already an enormous amount of data and empirical studies on the phenomenon, but in 1990, when that trend was only starting. I take the data and studies we have, relate them to the past two hundred years of globalization to show what is changing and with what impacts, and project out to tell about a future that what could be, if we play our hand right.

So why write now? Why not play it safe and wait until we have more data, more papers, more evidence—write only when trends described here have become the widely accepted conventional wisdoms? I write because I am compelled—I believe we are on the cusp of historic opportunities to fuel trade, inclusion, and economic growth, and that someone has to stand up and say it. I write to catalyze realignments in various policy areas that are needed to seize the emerging opportunities. I write to inspire young executives to see the great opportunities in the changing global economy for their businesses and careers. I write to shape the research agenda of a field that is now expanding rapidly and I believe will be front and center for trade economists and trade and development policy communities over the next decade. And I write to offer what is still often missing in policy debates—big, bold ideas.

The following six chapters detail how technologies are transforming trade and improving economic prospects. I have made hard choices and address a handful of technologies that I believe can have a particularly meaningful role in reshaping big, widely held facts in world trade—how additive manufacturing and 3D printing are disrupting supply chains; ecommerce is bringing new players to world trade; the smartphone revolution is globalizing globalization; blockchain is accelerating global logistics and companies' access to trade finance; and cloud computing is opening entirely new possibilities for analysis, prediction, and precision for companies operating in world markets. I show how world trade, powered by emerging technologies and paired with good policies, can create a global economic renaissance—one that is rifer with opportunity for businesses to prosper, consumers to gain, and nations to thrive than ever before.

The second part of the book considers challenges. Technology and trade can conspire to drive productivity in the twenty-first century, but trouble looms. A thicket of taxes, tariffs, red tape, regulations, and other challenges must be cleared if technology-powered trade is to run free and catalyze economic growth. Chapters 8 through 12 detail the various challenges, such as widening gaps in the adoption of technologies among and within countries; arcane customs procedures and congested cities that still regularly grind trade to a halt; creeping digital protectionism that stunts businesses' scalability; small companies' limited access to finance for growing their global business; and the acrimonious politics around trade and the impact of automation and AI on jobs.

The final part in Chapter 13 offers a bold policy agenda to bring about an era of unprecedented prosperity, innovation, and opportunity for people around the world to realize their full potential in the world economy.

2

WORLD ECONOMY GOES TO HEAVEN

In his 2005 best-seller *The World Is Flat*, Thomas Friedman described a new era of globalization, one of vast global supply chains run by major corporations.[1] But this popular characterization of globalization is no longer prescient. Global production is on the verge of its third inflection point since World War II.

The first inflection point was reached after World War II and turned on vertically organized companies. Making a product, from design to production, marketing, branding, and sales, took place within the same firm. Home to leading corporations, the United States, Europe, and Japan powered global manufacturing and trade, importing raw materials and exporting products—mostly to each other.

The second postwar economic system was the "Factory World," also known as the "Flat World." Breaking out in the 1990s as governments liberalized trade regimes and the IT revolution lowered communications costs, this system was about the unbundling of production—outsourcing production to low-cost locations, and sourcing components around the world. World trade in parts skyrocketed; companies from Dell to Apple became built on the global supply chain. The victors were countries with cheap labor and their eager sponsors—Western shoppers enjoying cheaper computers, clothes, cars, and call center services.

We are now verging on the third postwar economic system. In this system, the world economy goes to heaven: supply chains run in the cloud. Trade is less about the shipments of physical goods across borders and more about the cross-border flow of bits: digital goods, designs, and data. The driver of trade in the Flat World, imports of parts and components from around the world for assembly into iPhones, BMWs, and Sony TVs in China or Mexico or Poland, is yielding to a new model in which parts are 3D-printed right where they are assembled into final products.

In the coming era of global making, there is no need for trade to bring intermediate products to assemblers. Regionalized production hubs in East Asia, North America, and Europe, the Flat World's hallmark, are transforming into virtual and genuinely global supply chains—yet ones that are no longer than the distance between a man and his laptop. Cars and gadgets can now be sold to Kansas City shoppers on demand one day, and assembled the next in a local mini-factory from 3D-printed parts by intelligent robots using the Internet of Things to confer with each other and with the odd iPad-carrying human manager. In a world in which time to market and customization are key to competitiveness, production will increasingly be done by mini-factories near the end-consumer, whether in Beijing, Atlanta, or New Delhi. What's left to trade?

The Great Rebundling

At 3:30 a.m. one May morning in 2011 in California, Tony Prophet, senior vice president for operations at Hewlett-Packard, was awakened and told that an earthquake and tsunami had struck Japan, a vital supplier of parts and equipment for major industries such as computers, electronics, and automobiles.[2] Soon after, Prophet had set up a virtual situation room, so that managers in Japan, Taiwan, and the United States could rescue HP's global supply chain, which feeds its huge manufacturing engine churning out two personal computers a second, two printers a second, and one data-center computer every fifteen seconds. HP managed, but not everyone fared as well: a General Motors truck plant in Louisiana temporarily shut down for lack of Japanese-made parts, and Toyota and Sony suspended production on several plants. Korean shipbuilders, European cell phone companies, and U.S. solar panel makers too were hit.

Prophet's problem epitomized the fragilities of globalization as his generation had come to know them: a system with a tremendous array of moving parts—dozens of suppliers and service providers sending inputs and services to manufacturing hubs on ships, trains, trucks, and express shippers spanning the globe, to bring to the consumer gleaming printers, smartphones, and TV sets. The system was fragile: the failure of any one player in this global orchestra would debilitate the others too.

In 2006, trade economist Richard Baldwin conceptualized the wave of globalization Prophet was part of driving as the "second unbundling."[3] The first unbundling was the great geographic unbundling of production and consumption in the late nineteenth century. As ships got faster and railroads expanded across the United States and Western Europe, towns and villages no longer had to make most of what they would consume. As if taking their cues from the theory of comparative advantage fashioned by David Ricardo in 1817, they could focus on goods they produced best and exchange those for goods made and transported from elsewhere. English cities endowed with water power could use new technologies such as steam-powered mechanical assembly and focus on making textiles and other manufactured goods, and, thanks to better transport systems, exchange them for food, wine, and raw materials made in Spain and France, which are endowed with ample arable land.

While farmers in France could now more easily buy Sunday suits from England, the making of a product, from R&D to design, branding, manufacturing, marketing, and sales, remained within the confines of the same company well into the postwar era. The reason was simple: production from start to finish is a complex process involving several steps as well as assets—people, information, and investments—all of which are easiest to coordinate in one place. For the European, U.S., and Japanese companies that ran the world's manufacturing industry, there also was nowhere to offshore—developing countries such as China were still rural economies farming rice and mining ores.

This equation was disrupted by the 1990s IT revolution and trade and investment liberalization. Companies could use information technologies to manage suppliers and manufacturers regardless of their location, and unbundle their production processes to where they were most efficiently done: Chinese, Czech, and Mexican manufacturing hubs brimming with low-cost labor. The wage differential was phenomenal. In 2002, a Chinese factory worker earned 60 cents per hour, about 14 percent of her American counterpart.[4] The promise of deep savings in making products led Apple, Dell, GE, Sony, IBM, and hundreds of other companies to offshore manufacturing to low-cost economies, and outsource parts production to suppliers around the world. The modern-day global supply chain was born.

China became the world's factory, mass-producing computers, clothes, and gadgets for U.S. consumers; East Asia prospered as China's parts warehouse.

Comparative advantages sharpened. Developing economies specialized in manual assembly, advanced economies focused on their forte—R&D, design, marketing, and sales. Economist Stan Shih famously pictured global production as a "smiley curve."[5] At both ends of the U-shaped smile are high value-added activities: idea creation, R&D, branding, and design at one end, and distribution, marketing and sales, and service contracts at the other. In the low middle is the low value-add part of manufacturing and assembly. The point of offshoring was to shift the low value-add part to where it is done most economically, countries with ample manual labor and low labor costs.

Such production migration was not completely new. In the 1960s, Japanese scholar Kaname Akamatsu branded the phenomenon of lower-end production shifting from more advanced countries to poorer ones as "flying geese."[6] The lead goose—a Japanese conglomerate—flies farther and farther from manual assembly into knowledge-based activities, delegating production to the four tigers, which are then followed by Indonesia, Thailand, and Malaysia, which in turn are followed by China, Vietnam, the Philippines, and so on. But it was in the 1990s when the offshoring phenomenon truly jumped out of economic data: in the 1970s, 70 percent of global manufacturing was in the United States, Japan, and Western Europe; by 2010, this share had dropped to 47 percent, with East Asia, Mexico, and Eastern Europe claiming much of the rest.[7]

The winners in this economy were countries with vast amounts of cheap labor and their eager sponsors—Western shoppers touring the aisles of Walmart, testing flat screen TVs at Best Buy, and fixing their desktops with long-suffering staff at Indian call centers. As countries specialized in what they were best at and exchanged their products and services with each other, economies grew. The exacting quality standards of global companies forced little suppliers to get better; those that performed got a chance to sell into Daimler or Sony or Apple's supply chain, even if as second- or third-tier suppliers supplying suppliers in the tier above them.

Yet for multinational companies, efficiencies from offshoring and outsourcing had a price. Companies such as Prophet's HP spent billions in supply chain and inventory management—for example, searching for high-performing suppliers; navigating trade policy barriers and shipping costs; and dealing with the heartburns of international logistics, transport costs, defective products, and just-in-time inventory management. A nonprofit funded by selected American assemblers, the Reshoring Initiative, calculated the "total cost of ownership" of making goods in China as far outweighing what production might have cost in America that had far fewer problems with underperforming suppliers, disruptions in transport, or precarious enforcement of contracts. It claimed American companies had failed to take into account over 20 percent of the real costs of making things in China.[8] Foreign labor costs also were not what they used to be—by 2011, Chinese wages hit $2.20 per hour, almost four times 2002 levels, and rose further to $3.60 per hour in 2016. American companies started to have second thoughts about China and many reshored production—often to Mexico, but also back to the United States. Stalwarts such as 3M, Boeing, Caterpillar, General Electric, Hanes, and J Crew, among many others, reported some repatriations. The trend did not have an overwhelming impact on the U.S. economy. Now, however, new technologies are on the cusp of overhauling the very equation behind the global supply chain.

Globalization in 3D

In the early 1980s, an engineer named Chuck Hull in a small California business, UVP, Inc., that made tough coatings for tables using ultraviolet lamps, approached his boss with an idea: to use the UV technology to quickly turn computer designs into prototype products one could hold in one's hand.[9] Focused on the company's core business, Hull's manager shot down the idea. But eventually the two men reached a compromise: Hull would dedicate his days to making UV lamps, and craft his dream machine at night.

In 1986, Hull's nighttime toiling paid off: he obtained the patent of stereolithography apparatus and co-founded 3D Systems with Raymond Freed in Valencia, California. Within two years, theirs became the first company to sell 3D-printing systems. The company went public in 1990.

Nearly a quarter century later, the 3D printer broke through at the 2014 annual Computer Electronics Show in Las Vegas. TechRepublic hailed 3D printing as an industry "poised to transform nearly every sector of our lives and jumpstart the next industrial revolution."[10] Martha Stewart was reported to review 3D printers as a new means to craft her Easter wares.[11] Experiments spanned the spectrum: stilettos, President Obama's bust, human organs, pizzas, and even entire houses have been 3D-printed.

The fascination was not unfounded: 3D printing opened mindboggling possibilities for both deep cost savings and infinite customization. With software guiding the printing process, 3D printing makes it possible for each item to be made differently without any retooling. The 3D printer then patiently adds only as much material, razor thin layer by layer, as is needed for the product. This additive manufacturing contrasts with the old, "subtractive" production of cutting, drilling, and bashing metal. The savings are phenomenal. The 130-employee Houston-based ClearCorrect, a maker of invisible braces, previously used milling machines to make models of customers' teeth that were thermoformed with a thin, clear plastic to make braces. Only one model could be made before the expensive machinery had to be reset. The machine also often broke down. With 3D printing, the company could run batches of sixty to seventy models at once, taking five minutes each, as opposed to one model at thirteen minutes in the past.[12] What still in Hull's time was a machine from *Star Wars* by 2015 had made ClearCorrect 130 times more productive. The company could downsize from its eleven-thousand-square-foot hub with ten to fifteen people manning its machines to a four-thousand-square-foot facility with three people.

Major companies are scoring similarly astounding gains from 3D printing. Using 3D printers, Volvo reduced the number of days to make engines or Volvo Trucks by 94 percent, from thirty-six to two.[13] Aircraft parts 3D-printed by Airbus reduced raw material needs by 90 percent and halved the weight of the parts. GE reports that 3D-printed components cost 25 percent less than components made with traditional manufacturing methods, due to the changes in the product design and reduction in raw material.[14] IBM projects that by 2022, hearing aids made with 3D printers will be up to 65 percent cheaper than those with traditional manufacturing approaches. Inventory costs are plunging as parts can be printed right when they are needed.

3D printing puts innovation on steroids. Just about any company can now design and print a variety of rough-and-dirty prototypes at a rapid pace, test them out with buyers and go back to the drawing board, perhaps apply for a patent, and then start mass production. In his manufacturing company's lab in Temecula, California, Roy Paulson, one of America's leading small business manufacturers, has a software engineer specialized in 3D printing and two 3D printers with which his team prints eye and face-protection products such as medical splash protection gear and ballistic shields for soldiers and law enforcement, then tests their durability, following this by replicating the most resilient ones. The lab can test several models a day, an impossibility in the analog world when creating a new model took weeks. Paulson's dad, who founded the business in 1947, tested new designs by handcrafting patterns and designs, a slow process requiring great skill. Now a machine makes the adjustment to the mold within seconds. Paulson sees the rapid prototyping process as a method of communicating: it supplies physical parts to express a new product concept.

3D printing helps bring better products to market faster. For example, Ford uses 3D printing to quickly produce prototype parts such as cylinder heads, intake manifolds and air vents, and engine covers, shaving months off the development time for individual components. Nike and Adidas have both introduced 3D-printed running shoes.[15] The Egyptian fashion designer Sara Hegazy experiments with 3D printers to produce prototypes of evening gowns.[16] Right outside New Delhi, India's largest two-wheeler maker Hero MotoCorp uses 3D printers, robotic arms, and computerized warehouses to make almost seven million motorbikes a year in three factories, and hopes to copy-paste its model into twenty world markets by 2020.[17] Apple's iPhone supplier, the million worker Foxconn factory in China, is no longer only targeting American shoppers—rather, it is selling more and more phones and accessories on ecommerce channels to Chinese consumers, and announced in 2016 plans to operate fully without people.[18]

Additive manufacturing is entering the mainstream of manufacturing. Some 68 percent of U.S. manufacturers—which are the global vanguard in 3D printing—have adopted 3D printing for prototyping, and 52 percent believe it will be used for high-volume manufacturing by around 2020–2022.[19] McKinsey believes the overall economic impact created by additive manufacturing could be up to $250 billion by 2025, if adoption across industries continues at today's rates.[20] The sectors in which 3D printing will have the greatest impacts include aerospace and defense, automotive, medical, and consumer goods. A manufacturer does not even have to invest in a printer to generate products. She can now send designs to nearby 3D printing shops, just as she might have got documents and banners done at Kinko's fifteen years ago with 2D printers.

The technology is also superb for making customized goods in remote regions. Within a few hours in the wake of Nepal's earthquake, 3D printing was used to create new water pipes that fit with the local infrastructure.[21] In Myanmar, farmers are using a 3D printer of the social enterprise Proximity Designs to create parts for sprinkler systems and solar pumps.[22] The military is an obvious beneficiary, as are car, computer, and TV repair shops. 3D printing can be especially useful for creating slow-moving parts and unique parts that are expensive to source and stock.[23] Aftersales service teams and end-users, such as mining and agricultural firms, are already hitting "print" to create dozens of part right in front of their eyes.

The benefits and cost-savings from 3D printing are so compelling that it is hard to see why 3D printing would not proliferate and revolutionize not only the making of products, but also trade and globalization. After all, no more do parts and components need to be shipped from the supplier in country A to the manufacturer in country B: they are now digital designs made in-house or traveling in the cloud and printed right where they are assembled into final products.

What, then, will be the impacts on world trade? The most immediate impact of 3D printing on trade is on parts and components—or "intermediate products." GE has invested millions in 3D printers to produce eighty-five thousand fuel nozzles for its Leap jet engines in-house—a part that used to be assembled from twenty different parts sourced from around the world.[24] The fully 3D-printable car Strati made in Nevada uses only forty-nine parts, as opposed to a typical car stacked with some thirty thousand parts and components shipped in from around the planet.[25] Boeing and Ford have for years been designing and 3D-printing jet and car parts right where they are assembled into final products—Boeing's Dreamliner uses 3D-printable parts that weigh less than traditional parts, saving airlines as much as 50 percent of fuel costs.[26] In the process, Boeing and Ford are escaping the many hazards of global supply chain management, such as excess inventories, tight delivery times, and high carbon footprints.

3D printing can have an impact on trade in intermediates and reverse the unbundling of production that started in the 1990s: it is rebundling production, pulling global supply chains back within the four walls of a company. Intermediate goods production localizes, and supply chains become short, simple, and local, rather than elaborate, long, and global. International trade in intermediates has already been slumping, as Chinese manufacturers have opted for Chinese suppliers instead of foreign ones. In 1995–2015, the share of imported parts and components in China's exports dropped from 60 percent to 35 percent, suggesting that China was making more parts and components at home.[27] Also, Latin American and European manufacturing hubs Mexico and Poland are using somewhat fewer imported intermediates today than in the early 1990s.

3D printing can also bite into trade in certain types of final products. Imagine, for example, women's high heel shoes designed by a Parisian entrepreneur whose 3D design is viewed by a busy businesswoman in New York on her iPhone at 8:30 a.m., who subsequently subscribes to the design, customizes the shoes to her feet and preferences (lavender, two-inch heel, size 6.5) and sends the preferences with a 3D model of her feet to a Manhattan 3D-printing shop that will finalize the shoes, perfect for her feet, by 5 p.m. No parcel traveled across the Atlantic, and there were no customs duties or shipping costs, yet the lady got her perfect shoes designed in Paris in eight short hours, literally fresh from the oven. If this sounds utopian, it is already happening: Nike has partnered with HP to make custom shoes for NFL players, and Adidas is working with Foot Locker to 3D-print running shoes to respond to demand, as much as thirty-six times faster.[28]

How much of world trade will 3D printing replace? Consulting firm PricewaterhouseCoopers found that 3D printing will reshape, and replace, trade in aircraft and auto parts, electronic equipment, ceramic products, toys, footwear, and computers. In these categories, 3D printing puts as much as 41 percent of air cargo, 37 percent of ocean-container trade, and 25 percent of trucking at risk.[29] Insurance company ING has reached similar conclusions, calculating that by 2060, 3D printing will demolish 25 percent of world trade, particularly in automotive, industrial machinery, and consumer products; if investment in the technology is doubled every five years, ING claims, these impacts would be felt already by 2040.[30]

3D printers do need materials, and raw materials may have to be imported—but they may also simply be taken from a local recycling facility. 3D printers that use plastics are already using ocean plastics to print shoes and shirts. In the 3D era, international trade does not end, but it does change.

Skeptics argue that this future is not within sight. This is a reasonable statement with empirical basis—3D printing has yet to succeed at mass production; rather, it has for three decades been used as a prototyping technology among multinational manufacturers, while other mass manufacturing methods have evolved to enable economies of scale in production. But there are four reasons to think this time is different.

First, a number of technological advances are making 3D printers more capable of mass production. Second, the entire paradigm of manufacturing is shifting: the future is not about mass manufacturing as much as about mass customization and on-demand production, something 3D printing makes possible. Third, robotics is improving and becoming much more affordable for businesses to adopt, enabling makers to pair 3D printers with intelligent robots and print parts and assemble them in one place. And fourth, policy is making a difference. Enlightened governments are already supporting 3D printing to increase innovation in their economies, reduce stress on the environment, and lower costs to consumers. Let's explore these trends next.

Mass Printing

3D printing has been a prototyping technology for thirty years. Many astute observers believe it is bound to stay that way for the foreseeable future—and there is a good reason. While the gains for innovation and prototyping enabled by 3D printing have exceeded the costs, the gains in production processes—in terms of materials saved, transport and supply chains management costs averted, and so on—still tend to be exceeded by challenges. The challenges have largely been technical: high cost of printers; limitations of quality; manufacturers' limited in-house design expertise; difficulty working with metal components; cybersecurity concerns; and lack of industry-specific testing procedures and specifications, again especially on metal components.[31] Yet today a number of forces are pushing 3D printing toward prime time in mass manufacturing.

First, materials technology and 3D printing have evolved to a point at which several companies see an opportunity to create 3D-printable lines for mass production. In 2018, the German sportswear giant Adidas, which manufactures most of its running shoes in China, Turkey, India, Indonesia, and Thailand, announced a line of running shoes with a 3D sole called Futurecraft 4D, starting with a hundred thousand pairs in 2018 and aiming at ten million pairs over time.[32] The shoes are made in Adidas's Speedfactory outside of Atlanta with 160 high-skilled workers and robots via "digital light synthesis," a process developed by the California-based tech company Carbon that enables printing of high-resolution parts (such as complex, high-performance monolithic designs that typically require the assembly of multiple parts to create varying performance zones within a single midsole) dozens of times faster than with typical additive manufacturing processes—something experts call a night and day difference to existing techniques. The $300 shoe flew off the shelves, and resale prices of the collectors' items reached $20,000.

Ultimately each shoe can be customized to the user, optimizing fit and reducing waste. Nike followed with the debut of Flyprint, a 3D-printed running shoe that has also a 3D-printed textile upper, using a novel process called solid deposit modeling. The first hundred Flyprints went to market at $600 a pair.[33] All shoe majors—Nike, Adidas, New Balance, ASICS, and Under Armor—have their own 3D production lines.

In France, the fashion icon Chanel started mass production of 3D-printed mascara brushes in 2018 with six industrial 3D printers able to make fifty thousand brushes a day, to meet Chanel's target of one million brushes a month.[34] The company has held the patent for 3D-printed brushes since 2007 and used 3D printing to create and perfect a hundred prototype brushes whose granular texture and microcavities maximize mascara application to lashes. The finesse would not have been possible under traditional injection molding methods. After a decade of work, Chanel now has the product and technology to go to mass market.

These cases are a sign of things to come: mass production of various consumer products using additive manufacturing techniques. Another area in which 3D printing is becoming mainstream is dental care: for example, Align Technology Inc. is 3D-printing eight million orthodontics a year in Juarez, Mexico.

The second reason why 3D printing is readier for mass production is the improved prospects for 3D printing of metal parts. Metal 3D printing at a mass scale would likely make a major dent in world trade. In 2018, Hewlett Packard launched HP Metal Jet, a 3D-printing technology that is hailed as a leap forward in making production-grade metal parts at high volumes.[35] The market is huge: vehicle, industrial, and medical sectors use billions of metal parts each year. So far, metal has been hard to bend to the will of a 3D printer. For example, it requires higher temperatures than plastic to be worked on—high-carbon steel melts only at infernal 1,370 Celsius and titanium at 1,668 Celsius (in comparison, water boils at 100 Celsius, a temperature that tends to force even the most seasoned sauna bathers to head for the exits). HP's printer uses new methods to melt the steel, promising up to fifty times higher productivity rates than offered by current 3D printing methods. With an initial price tag of $400,000, the printer is available for multinationals and mid-size companies. HP has also produced a lighter version that retails at $130,000 and is considered the most competitive product yet.

Enamored with the light weight and elegance of the Metal Jet's 3D-printed components, Volkswagen engineers believe the printer can enable mass production of all vehicle parts up to the size of a soccer ball, each with a hundred thousand units per year.[36] VW is already using 3D printers to make small, customizable parts such as tailgate lettering, gear knobs, and personalized keys. GM's engineers have similar dreams. Take GM's seat bracket, the piece that provides a firm base for car seats and seat belt buckles.[37] It previously required eight separate parts, purchased from several different automotive suppliers. Now it can be 3D-printed as one big piece—which is also 40 percent lighter and 20 percent stronger than its predecessor. These numbers translate into faster cars with higher gas mileage, an idea that should appeal to just about any consumer. GM believes it can initially 3D-print a thousand of the thirty thousand parts going into any one of its eight thousand cars made each day.

Newcomers also shape the field of mass printing. For example, the Italian 3D-printed X Electrical Vehicle, a little car with maximum speeds of fifty miles per hour that are rather perfect for busy and dense urban areas, is closer to mass production.[38] The visible parts are 3D-printed; windows, tires, and chassis are still made in traditional ways. The car sells at below $10,000 and has received seven thousand orders from businesses and postal service providers. As small as the market for such tiny, slower moving electric cars may seem to many Americans, the demand in China is reportedly sky high: 1.75 million of them were sold in China in 2017, more than twice the sales of regular electric cars.[39] One can easily imagine the appeal for European urbanites navigating the narrow streets of Rome or Paris. In China, electric vehicle companies are seizing on the opportunity in a market where EVs are expected to make up 50 percent of cars in 2025—and typically also using 3D printing for their parts.[40] As production volumes grow, the company expects scale economies to kick in and the cost of cars to be cut in half. While this is not exactly GM volumes, it may point to a future when smaller companies leverage additive manufacturing methods to earn their place in major industries.

The third driver of 3D mass printing is the recent entry by major players such as HP and GE in the sector. This is also firing up industry incumbents such as Stratasys and 3D Systems. After IPOs and hype, Stratasys's stock price dropped by a good 50 percent, settling at a much lower equilibrium over 2015. Dreaming about putting a 3D printer in each home, Stratasys ran into problems of cart abandonment as consumers assessed other alternatives such as HP printers, and as purchases of printers for prototyping slowed down.[41] As HP, GE, and Siemens all entered the printer market in 2016 through acquisitions of major European companies, Wall Street analysts started to see the making of printers for mass manufacturing of metals as a way for Stratasys too to rebound. The hope was revealed in the spiking of Stratasys share prices upon the announcement of U.S. tariffs on products made in China—which Wall Street interpreted as catalyzing 3D-printed mass manufacturing in the U.S.[42]

As more players battle for preeminence in mass 3D printing, competition ought to drive printers' prices down, addressing the main bottleneck. Consolidation among printer makers and growing global demand for printers, for example from China, could deliver further scale economies in making 3D printers. Experts agree that the industry will be further boosted by patent expiration and reduced needs for postprocessing. Additive manufacturing machine makers are now at work on what manufacturers have been asking for: perfecting machines' in-process control, quality diagnostics, and data storage along with the production process needed for eventual product certification.[43] What is still needed are 3D printers that can produce metal parts at the pace of final goods production, and, important for industrial-scale production, the digital backbone to transfer files of parts and components.[44] We are not there yet, but there is a market for them, propelled by consumers that like elegant design, low carbon footprints, and better gas mileage, and companies that see them.

Markets of One

Global supply chains have been motivated by what the Ford Model T was motivated by: standardization and scale economies. The recipe for manufacturers has been to standardize parts and final product; find an assembler and standardize the production process; use thousands of worker bees, each specialized in his or her respective repetitive task to collectively make large volumes of a product; and you will drive down the unit cost of the widget and increase your per-unit profit. The bigger the production run, the lower the cost; the dream is to make a million units with the cost of one. The tendency to operate from this old paradigm is a leading reason for skepticism about the impact of 3D printing on the global geography of production and trade. It is time to upgrade the paradigm: mass customization.

The demand for customized products has grown since the 1980s, and the trend continues. In a 2015 survey in the United Kingdom, 36 percent said they want customized products, 48 percent expressed willingness to wait if that was necessary to get their custom product, and 20 percent were ready to pay 20 percent extra to get a custom product.[45] Most eager for customized products were the emerging consumers, sixteen-to-thirty-nine-year-olds. Customization also leads to brand loyalty. Bain & Company found that customers who had customized a product online with a certain company visited the company's website more frequently and stayed on the page longer, and were likelier to come back to buy.[46] Customers who designed their own shoes gave companies a 50 percent higher Net Promoter Score used to measure customer loyalty than customers who bought regular products.

Companies are already responding to these "markets of one" with personalized digital advertisements and emails and with a range of consumer products, such as customized soups, shampoos, makeup, and pizza. The main enabler that was still missing in the 1980s is technologies that enable customization: algorithms. For example, L'Oreal is using machine learning to help women, and perhaps many men as well, find the right foundation shade to match their skin tone. All that is needed is a spectrometer, a handheld machine that shoots a light on the shopper's face to measure her skin tone (on the basis of how much light reflects off the skin). The information is entered on an app for algorithms to produce the solution set: the right shade. The wizardry is then fed to a mixer that uses the right ingredients to mix the customized serum, which is packaged into a bottle containing a sticker with an individual ID number that makes it easy to reorder. Voilà. Next, the shopper can log onto the Function of Beauty website to take a personalized hair quiz, pick a color to match her shower aesthetics, and choose a scent—and in a day or two get a customized shampoo kit. And next she can go on the 2017 IPO sensation StitchFix and click on images of clothes she likes and answer a few short questions, and soon enough receive in the mail personalized packages of different types of pants, suits, jackets, and scarves that algorithms decide will look great on her, especially in combination with one another. She can then log back in and comment on the shipments, to tighten StitchFix's algorithms.

Can hard physical products such as shoes, gowns, tennis racquets, and so on be profitably mass customized? Companies from Nike to Dell and Levi's have responded to the demand for customized products for years, many of them successfully. But the convergence of demand for personalized products and the profitability of making them even at small scale—something enabled by machine learning and 3D printing—is newer. Thanks to additive manufacturing, the time and cost to produce a hundred different variants of one product versus a hundred exact same units of the product is shrinking, possibly dramatically. IBM estimates that 3D-printing costs will fall by 79 percent between 2017 and 2022 and by 92 percent between 2017 and 2027. Companies can become cost-competitive with production volumes that are 75 percent lower by 2022 and up to 98 percent lower than traditional supply chains by 2027.[47] In other words, it is becoming completely possible to run a profitable manufacturing business with small production runs. The minimum efficient scale is tiny, compared to the Ford Model T or the time Paulson's dad made his first molds.

So far, mass customization and personalization have been executed successfully by digital natives that are used to digital technologies. The use of additive manufacturing by Adidas and Chanel, among others, suggests that also the traditional brick-and-mortars are looking for more ways to personalize their products. The big question is to what extent larger products such as vehicles and white goods can be mostly or fully customized. Car companies such as BMW and VW are already enabling personalization using 3D printers of certain car parts, such as cockpit facia and side scuttles. The industry is paying attention: 3D printing technology developed between BMW, Hewlett-Packard, Carbon Inc., and EOD GmbH was awarded a gold medal in the Excellence in Business to Customer category by the German Design Council.[48] Another vehicle wunderkind, Daimler, is using 3D printers to produce on-demand interior parts for its Daimler Buses division.

Mass customization is also helped by the expanded possibilities for customizing materials that go into a product, such as for the shopper to use environmentally friendly materials. In the Netherlands, two designers have developed an algae-based polymer that absorbs carbon dioxide so well it can make the 3D-printing process carbon negative—that is, to suck carbon dioxide as goods are made.[49] In contrast, the production process of plastics releases significant amounts of CO_2. Their bioplastics and process could be applied in countless areas of making, from shampoo bottles to building facades. Imagine a shopper going to the neighborhood 3D-printing store to order an algae-based chair or a Tupperware collection made with mycelium, potato starch, or cocoa bean shells. Bioplastics are also much easier to recycle and degrade more quickly than synthetic plastics. Surveys suggest that strong majorities of shoppers, especially among Generation Z, in the advanced economies would pay a premium for 3D-printed, customized products and packaging made with bioplastics and other sustainable materials.[50] So might the many brands such as Starbucks that are shedding plastics: already, an L.A. company, FinalStraw, is making reusable foldable 3D-printed straws from silicon and steel, grossing at the end of 2018 almost $5 million.[51]

It is no stretch to think Chanel might be a bioplastic brush convert. But where exactly will it print these brushes—how is the geography of production shifting in response to 3D printing and robotics?

The Incredible Shrinking Supply Chains

In her book *Where I Was From*, Joan Didion describes the end of one golden era of California—the later 1980s, when airspace companies left California and went to the South and Washington DC.[52] The lure of the Sunbelt owed to lower rents; cheaper, less unionized labor; and lower taxes. In the 1990s, scholars in the United States started to explain the empirical fact that industries moved in a flock and clustered in certain regions, such as Detroit or Dallas. The idea was that as many firms in an industry cluster in the same geography, their production costs decrease. After all, clustering with their peers enables companies to tap talent in the industry, access a wider range of suppliers and inputs, spy on the latest technologies and ideas in the industry, and poach talent next door. Job-hopping workers are like bees, cross-pollinating ideas and information across firms and injecting dynamism in the industry by moving out of low-performing firms to high-performing ones. (Sound like Silicon Valley yet? This was also Detroit in full manufacturing swing, Hollywood through the ages, and Washington's government contracting world). In Paul Krugman's classic formulation of "agglomeration economies," further savings come from the fact that input suppliers locate in these hubs, to be next to the final goods producers in their industry, which lowers trade costs for parts and components to almost zero and makes both firms more productive.[53]

Over time, each firm specializes more narrowly, together producing new productivity gains. And when labor costs and taxes rise too much, the entire industry migrates to a new place—such as the aircraft industry did from California to the American South, or the Japanese electronics industry to the four Asian tigers. Yet agglomeration was long amazingly persistent: once industries were in a place, they were in no mood to move. One reason was the relatively high cost of moving people—after all, they had houses, children at school, friends and neighbors, potential further employers, and spouse's job all tied to a place. It took a lot to get them pushed out.

In the 1990s, however, two things started to reshape companies' thinking about location of production: the Internet, which enabled information and knowledge spillovers far outside their origin, and reduction in the cost of moving trade, or trade costs, which enabled cost-effective shipping from distance. Globally, trade costs dropped by 15 percent in 1996–2008 in high-income countries and by almost 10 percent in upper-middle-income ones in 1990–2010, as countries liberalized and modernized their customs, and as shipping grew more efficient.[54] Companies' needs to be co-located with each other and with certain workers and input providers decreased as the 1990s wore on: they could now find workers in China or Mexico and suppliers around the planet, and ship goods economically from market to market. Economists at the time found that firms optimized their production according to their trade costs: if the costs of shipping parts into China and the final product from China did not defeat the purpose of making the product in China with low-cost labor, then why not make it in China? In the early days of NAFTA, trade economist Gordon Hanson showed that as better transport systems and trade liberalization lowered the trade cost constraint, the Mexican northern border gained in production facilities.[55]

Together with the IT revolution that enabled companies to orchestrate and oversee production from a distance, the decline in trade costs activated the supercycle of globalization, one of outsourcing, offshoring, and global supply chains, and the hunt for low-cost labor.

In the next supercycle, 3D printing and robotics relax companies' need for low-cost inputs sources from around the world and low-cost labor in developing countries: the marriage of 3D printing and intelligent robotics will again disrupt companies' locational decisions.

Robots have been around and ready to work for quite some time—but at $200,000 a piece, they could not easily beat the cost of human labor. Now the equation is changing: some of the newest generation of intelligent robots cost as little as $25,000.[56] They are also better, with greater dexterity and abilities to operate in free-wheeling unstructured environments than their ancestors possessed. And they do not need to be interviewed or contracted or provided medical insurance: they are programmed and ready to start work in just one day, show up to work every day, and can work without complaints or coffee breaks 24/7. Like piano players that practice hard, they are becoming more agile; unlike capricious artists, they are also growing more obedient with safety practices. These robots also nano-manufacture, when tiny nano-scaled materials are used to make such unsung heroes of the product world as scratchproof eyeglasses, crack-resistant paints, anti-graffiti coatings, stain-repellent fabrics, and self-cleaning windows.

With 3D printers increasingly able to produce components and robots capable of assembling even complex final products, manufacturers' constraints change. No longer do they need to hunt for low-cost labor around the planet: they can design and procure parts and assemble products within the same four walls. This does not necessarily entail a mass wave of reshoring to the United

States or spell an end to Asian manufacturing. What it does mean is that the constraint of input and labor costs is gone: all other things equal, parts production, assembly, and demand can increasingly be co-located.

Located where exactly? The knee-jerk answer is, next to customers, to optimize responsiveness and minimize transport costs on final products. A number of theoretical academic papers on the question have arrived at this answer, as have industry surveys.[57] If these forecasts hold, we should be seeing manufacturing plants sprout by the world's megacities. But will companies decide to set up a production facility near every major city, or will they focus on fewer locations that produce for broader regions or even for a set of smaller countries, for example?

The choice ultimately turns on many variables, such as local taxes, office lease and real estate costs, and transport costs. Of course, the constraints vary by sector and firm, and may well include considerations as to whether the owner is loath to leave because she has kids at a school they love. But mostly the answer will turn on transport costs. In the era of robotized additive manufacturing, the question becomes, Would you rather set up a car plant using 3D printers and robots in tax-light Nevada and ship cars from there, or in tax-heavier Southern California that is home to one of the world's largest auto markets?

The answer likely boils down to transport costs of cars from Nevada to Los Angeles County. If we assume that transport costs are what the choice will turn on, the result is clear: if transport costs are zero and labor costs irrelevant, companies would likely want to centralize production; if transport costs as share of final goods are meaningful and labor costs irrelevant, companies will likely produce where they sell. Or they could contract production out to specialized additive manufacturing firm.

What impact does 3D printing have on total transport costs in global supply chains? In a simulation of 308 different industries, a team of German researchers found that the total miles products travel and their transport costs decrease possibly up to 30 percent in the leg between factory and consumer, and also between the source of raw materials and the factory (as 3D printing reduces waste in the use of raw materials).[58] However, there are some caveats to this story. For one, these impacts depend on how close to the customer a company is already making its products: if the number of production sites remains rather fixed upon the introduction of additive manufacturing, total transport costs in a supply chain still go down but the share of costs stemming from the leg between factory and consumer becomes proportionately higher.[59] If the economics of production are amenable to decentralized micromanufacturing, then it becomes possible to establish new production units next to customers, and overall transport costs drop. This flexibility and interest in decentralized networks is higher in products with low buy-to-fly ratio—weight between the materials used for a product and the weight of the product itself, which is a proxy for the efficiency of material usage in a production process. In other words, firms in highly efficient industries are likelier to co-locate production near consumers.

Now take a step back: in any of these cases, you will see that labor cost differentials across countries and opportunities for scale economies no longer dictate the geography of production; the geography of consumption does. And this is where the paradigm of globalization we have known for three decades shifts: it is not about global supply chains, it is about localized production. If this is true, we should empirically start seeing production units commensurate to the size of a city they are serving near major cities such as São Paulo, Chicago, and Bangkok—and gradual erosion of trade in parts and, eventually, final goods.

Empirically, a clear pattern has yet to emerge—partly because a great many variables go into firms' locational choices; partly because investments in 3D printers and robot-run factories take time to make; partly because companies will unlikely make abrupt breaks, abandoning all traditional making when adopting 3D printing; and partly because each industry is different, making generalizations harder. What additive manufacturing and robotics do create is an increased *tendency* to make goods locally and in smaller batches—a tendency whose economics are becoming compelling enough for it to become a paradigm-changer similar to what outsourcing and offshoring once produced. The hub-and-spoke regional production hubs in East Asia, Europe, and North America will be yielding to a more colorful map of global making.

What Does This Mean for America's Trade Deficit?

Could additive manufacturing over time be a solution to the Trump White House's obsession with closing America's trade deficit? While just about any economist including your author considers trade balance the wrong measuring stick of our success in trade and our well-being, the question is interesting. Could America, for example, stop importing products from Mexico and China and simply 3D print and assemble them at home?

Unlikely. Most of the U.S. trade deficit is in final goods rather than in parts and components, so that a global 3D-printing-induced reduction of trade in intermediates could in fact increase America's trade deficit, by undermining U.S. intermediates' exports. In U.S.-China trade, for example, in 2017 the United States exported about $22 billion in intermediates to China and imported $36 billion in intermediates from China, whereas it exported "only" $24 billion in final consumer products to China while importing almost ten times as much, $227 billion in final consumer products from China. The U.S. has a $22 billion surplus in intermediates exports to Mexico, such as motor vehicle parts, petroleum and coal products, computer equipment, semiconductors and other electronic components, and basic chemicals, while U.S. imports from Mexico are mostly final products made with these inputs, such as motor vehicles, computers, TVs, stereos, and communication equipment.[60] Mexico has a hefty surplus in consumer and capital products with the United States, but a deficit in intermediates.

What might narrow the U.S. trade deficit is increased production of final goods at home. But even if America made everything it consumed domestically, manual factory workers' jobs will not be brought back in the era of 3D printing and robotics. The National Association of Manufacturing projects 3.5 million new jobs in American manufacturing in 2018–2027—but its president, Jay Timmons, explains the jobs in demand will be for skilled workers able to leverage the latest technologies, such as software engineers and data scientists.[61]

What can cut into the U.S. trade deficit is services exports. The United States has had a trade surplus in services for years and is unquestionably the world's largest services exporter, with four times as many services exports as China and five times as many as India in 2016. Technologies can sharpen America's edge in services further.

Services Unbundling

In 1776, Adam Smith visited a pin factory and famously found that if workers specialized in one of eighteen specific functions related to making the pin, rather than each making the whole pin alone, output per worker increased a staggering 24,000 percent, from 20 to 4,800 pins per day.[62] Such specialization is now happening in services, globally, with tremendous potential for efficiency gains.

Since the 1990s, companies have outsourced non-core services, such as legal, financial, human resources, advertising, consulting, business process outsourcing, IT, accounting, medical, travel, architectural services, and software development and maintenance, to vendors at home and abroad. World trade in services tripled in the past fifteen years, with India, the United States, the Philippines, Eastern Europe, and Costa Rica emerging as services hubs. Some of the services were delivered in person: for example, Americans could go to India for a hip surgery. But another simple reason for the growth in the so-called "trade in tasks" was the Internet, which made vendors easier to find and email, which digitized the delivery of service and thus made it easier to deliver services efficiently from afar. Next came such useful tools as DropBox and its many variants for the sharing of large and multiple files securely online. Today, over 60 percent of U.S. services are digitally deliverable. We don't know, nor do trade data show, how a given lawyer or an architect or a lender ultimately delivers legal, architectural, and financial services, but we know that these sectors are highly susceptive to digital transfers of outputs such as documents, images, drawings, and money—that is, sectors where services can be "digitally deliverable".

In the early 2000s, the rise of trade in tasks sparked fears in the United States of a loss of at least three million white collar American jobs to India and other developing economies. Yet services trade was still limited, given that major corporations wanted to keep most services in house where they were easier to coordinate. Companies particularly wanted to do internally work that involved high levels of information and face-to-face interactions, often with each other, such as selling, working with others, negotiating, innovating, solving complex problems, and thinking creatively. Outsourced abroad was the more standardized information-processing work that supports the soft-skilled information workers.[63] If outsourced to outside vendors, the higher-value-add services were often closely co-located with the client, as expected in the agglomeration economic literature. As one example, in Brazil, a country with the world's second largest general aviation fleet, the Aerospace Cluster in the Technological Park São José dos Campos has grown to encompass ninety companies, including eighteen services firms, which can together share knowledge, develop new products, and perfect processes. Such clustering of services with good producers is particularly prominent among R&D-intensive manufacturers with non-standardized products; these types of firms have also been most prone to reshore services if they at some point offshored them.[64]

But now things are changing: if global manufacturing is rebundling, services are unbundling. Trade data indicate that trade in knowledge-intensive business services (KIBS)—a rather broad category of services that are intensive in their inputs of technology and/or human capital and that are provided for other businesses—has been growing particularly rapidly as part of world trade and in emerging markets' trade.

For example, in Argentina, KIBS grew from 5 percent of all exports in 2005–2007 to over 8 percent in 2015–2017, driving the share of services of all exports from 14 to 18 percent.[65] KIBS grew also in Brazil's exports from 6 to almost 9 percent during that time, to make up three-quarters of Brazil's services exports. Computer and information services exports from developing countries, a subcategory of KIBS, have been growing particularly fast, at 22 percent in 2000–2013 from developing economies, 35 percent from transition economies, and 22 percent from Latin America.[66]

A key driver of services unbundling is cloud computing, which has opened up new opportunities for performing and delivering B2B educational, financial, logistics, business, and other services. For example, in India, cloud-based software company Freshdesk (now Freshworks) has grown from two employees in 2010 to nine hundred today by helping two hundred thousand companies such as Cisco, Honda, and 3M worldwide to offer better customer experience.[67] Brazilian company Samba Tech, which established a Seattle office in 2016, has built a "corporate SnapChat," where CEOs and directors can record videos and share these internally with individuals possessing corporate email accounts within the same company.[68] The feature is being used by major companies such as LATAM, Microsoft, and IBM. Chilean company Mediastream enables multinationals such as BBVA and Claro to manage the creation, publication, and classification of their video content to more than seventy million users worldwide.[69] Argentina's unicorn Despegar helps Latin American travelers book flights and hotels online much like Orbitz does for American travelers. Mexican company Softek offers cost-saving niche IT solutions—such as for the aircraft industry or the media—to Fortune 100s.[70]

Services vendors are also in greater demand due to what economists have awkwardly termed "servification" of traditional manufacturing in such sectors as vehicles, food processing, aerospace, manufacturing, and agriculture. The inputs and outputs of many manufacturing and agricultural businesses are now services, and manufacturers and farmers are hiring mathematicians, computer scientists, IT managers, environmental managers, and AI-powered meteorologists. Services outsourcing can benefit especially countries such as Argentina that struggle with high trade costs, yet have a pool of digitally savvy businesses able to produce quality services at lower cost than advanced economy firms. Governments understand that services firms' vitality is critical for various sectors in the economy, including and in particular manufacturing and the public sector itself, and a growing export opportunity. For example, in Mexico, the world's third largest IT services outsourcing hub, the $250 million, government-backed Program for the Development of the Software Industry (PROSOFT) has boosted the capabilities of more than seven hundred services firms that supply services to traditional manufacturing sectors and to emerging sectors such as biotech, and export IT services to multinational and foreign enterprises.

While more data are needed on the specific services provided in these broad categories, the growth of KIBS in trade suggests that corporations are no longer slicing mind-numbing standardized services off to emerging markets; they are increasingly using emerging market firms in the more sophisticated tasks such as software consulting, market research and polling, and data science.

Still another driver of services unbundling is the proliferation of online work platforms such as Freelancer and Upwork, which make it efficient for firms of all sizes to vet and hire service providers. Workers specialized in web design, coding, search engine optimization, design, translation, marketing, accounting, and twenty-seven hundred other occupations from such countries as Ukraine, China, India, the Philippines, Pakistan, Bangladesh, Kenya, and Argentina use these platforms to service clients worldwide. Annually, some forty million users get on these platforms alone looking for jobs or talent. Uruguayan company Codigo Del Sur has worked on more than 150 projects on Upwork for companies such as U.S.-based Skout, a dating app with more than two hundred million users, and Kindara, a popular health startup.[71] The company grew from two employees in 2008 to forty-eight employees in 2016, working over fifty thousand hours and earning more than $1 million over the period.[72]

Local work platforms too have taken off: Argentina's Workana enables four hundred thousand Latin American freelancers to connect with small businesses looking for part-time remote staff. Platforms are differentiating: for example, Toptal brings seasoned, highly skilled freelancers to global corporate clients such as J.P. Morgan. McKinsey projects services job platforms will have 540 million employees by 2025.[73]

Unbundling of services sharpens global division of labor and induces firms to specialize, which, like specialization in the pin factory Adam Smith visited, is good for output growth. The main bottleneck for knowledge-intensive services exports in countries such as Mexico and Argentina is availability of talent. IADB economists Carmen Pagés and Graciana Rucci have with their team plowed through millions of rows of LinkedIn data to highlight the gap between HR managers' wishlists—topped by software developers, creative designers, business strategists, and social media consultants—and the skills of workers in Latin American economies.[74] They find that the lower skill content of workers in Latin America than in the United States makes it harder for, say, Argentina to leap from a declining occupation such as IT consultant or accountant to an expanding occupation. Americans, in other words, have better and more transferable skills and are thus better placed to withstand labor market disruptions in the digitizing world economy, something that cements America's edge as the superstar services exporter.

Conclusion

The manifestation of globalization in the twentieth century, global supply chains are being inverted from within. In products, 3D printing and robotics are helping companies rebundle production and free themselves from the constraints of relative labor costs, quality of suppliers, standardization, and economies of scale. The economics of making are changing: it is entirely possible to make a profit on small runs of on-demand customized products. Trade costs can be increasingly obsolete: in lieu of physical supply chains vulnerable to trade wars, natural calamities, transport costs, and underperforming suppliers, companies now have software-driven supply chains as long as the distance between a laptop and the 3D printer next to it. Trade will not end but its composition will transform—products traded will increasingly be digital designs and unique customized final goods, and grains and raw materials.

The reverse is happening in trade in services: unbundling of services from corporations to domestic firms and foreign service providers. This is poised to sharpen global division of labor: in its new era, globalization can play at the higher resolution yet. As a result, just like in the pin factory, players gain in productivity and end-consumers get a wider variety of products and services at a better price. And directly stacked up against their international competitors, specialized vendors have incentives to specialize even further—and spawn entirely new industries.

KILLER APP FOR WORLD TRADE

In 2005 Urmex, a dusty storefront company producing customized USB drives and serving passersby in Toluca, Mexico, still promoted its products with flyers and cold calls. Then the founder decided to test traction online. Urmex invested a full $10 in online advertising, targeting customers in Mexico City. Realizing an immediate return on investment, it invested in further online campaigns across Mexico and other parts of Latin America, using Google AdWords, YouTube, and Twitter, as well as selling on MercadoLibre and Alibaba. By 2012, 60 percent of Urmex's profits were generated by online sales to Peru, Colombia, Chile, Brazil, and other markets in Latin America and to such companies as Coca-Cola, HP, BMW, and DHL.

Urmex's story is one of millions unfolding around the planet. It epitomizes the revolution in world trade: even the smallest businesses, once setting up shop on major global ecommerce platforms, can gain global customers from multiple markets without the types of up-front costs as required in the world of brick-and-mortar stores. This is transforming the long-held conventional wisdom that small businesses cannot export because of the high fixed costs for them to find global clients. Ecommerce is changing the face of world trade—and with it, companies' growth prospects and global economic geography.

Everyone's an Exporter

The seven years after the Great Recession of 2008–2009 will in international trade circles go down as the long slog through dreadful drought. Trade growth flatlined to less than 3 percent annually, with 2016 infamously becoming one of the few rare years that trade grew more slowly than the world economy. But this depressing picture has disguised a trend of stunning growth—the explosive growth of cross-border ecommerce, still a fraction of world trade. Globally, B2C ecommerce is surging at almost 30 percent per year, and will in 2020 make up almost 30 percent of all B2C transactions, up from 15 percent in 2014.

Online sales in advanced ecommerce markets such as the United States, the United Kingdom, and China are already about a fifth of all retail sales. In the United States alone, total online transactions grew from $3 trillion in 2006 to over $6 trillion in 2013, equivalent to a third of the U.S. economy. China is the world's top online market: it has seven hundred million net users, almost twice as many as the United States and Japan combined. China's ecommerce soared from 3 percent of retail in 2010 to almost 21 percent in 2017. This owed in part to the fact that the country's Internet penetration rates grew rapidly during the time and physical retail infrastructure was much more well-developed than those of Europe or the United States, so that companies did not have to re-gear legacy offline systems for online channels. They were born digital.

A good share of ecommerce is cross-border trade. As much as 40 percent of ecommerce in Asia-Pacific, Europe, and the United States already consists of transactions with foreigners. While China is the undisputed king of ecommerce exports to the United States and Europe, the United States and the United Kingdom too have a voluminous ecommerce trade with each other: 70 percent of U.K. ecommerce shoppers use U.S. ecommerce sites, while 49 percent of Americans buy from U.K. sites.[1] The most explosively growing part of global ecommerce is not exactly container loads: it is parcel-based trade in low-value items below $100, such as used running shoes and machine parts, whose trade grew ten times faster than world trade in 2011–2015.[2]

The biggest story in the digitization of retail and trade is the change in the face of trade. For most companies on the planet, exporting goods or services to other countries has been like going to the moon. Only 10 percent of businesses in East Asia and sub-Saharan Africa export, 13 percent in Latin America, and, generously counting, 5 percent in the United States. The vast majority of companies are small businesses with fewer than 250 employees, and the vast majority of small businesses sell only to buyers in their own domestic market.

Those that export tend to be sporadic and narrow exporters—companies that export only periodically, typically only to one or two foreign markets. Most companies that start to export do not however last long: over 70 percent are no longer exporting after a year.

For some companies that do export, exports are a big deal—for example, about 50 percent of sub-Saharan African exporters' revenues stem from exports. But small business exports put together are not that big of a deal for any one country. Practically every country's exports are driven by "export superstars," or a few large companies such as GE, Boeing, Embraer, Samsung, or Sony that have had the staff, capital, and scale economies to go global, cut costs, and compete. In most countries, the largest 5 percent of exporters generate over 80 percent of exports. They, in other words, were the face people thought of when thinking of world trade. In Chile, the top 5 percent largest exporters, many of them companies associated with Chile's copper industry, generate over 90 percent of Chilean exports—such that 95 percent of all exporters are the source of less than 10 percent of exports in Chile.[3] Trade has long been a long-tail business, run by a few big players.

What is common among the few companies that export? Data tell us that the few businesses that do export are standouts: they are typically larger and more productive than non-exporters. In a series of rich and seminal papers, Andrew Bernard of Dartmouth and his colleagues showed that exporters outperform the broader market across several metrics. Small and medium-sized enterprise (SME) exporters employ significantly more workers, pay higher wages, are more skill-intensive, and have higher sales and labor productivity than do SMEs that only target the domestic market.[4] There is a pecking order of companies that Bernard found in the U.S. and I also picked up in econometric work on Latin American businesses: importers did better than non-importers; exporters did better than non-exporters and importers; and two-way traders, companies that export and import, were more productive than exporters or importers.[5] Exporters also sold a wider range of products than non-exporters. Other work has found that companies that had investments overseas—that is, had incurred very significant sunk costs to internationalize—were most productive of all.[6]

In 2003, Marc Melitz of Harvard sought to explain this empirical regularity—why exporters are more productive than non-exporters—by arguing that exporters are better *to begin with*.[7] In other words, it is the cream-of-the-crop companies that self-select into exporting—laggard companies do not make it in the rough and tumble of world markets and seldom even try. Melitz argued that as more productive firms, today's exporters were, when they started exporting, able to do one thing non-exporters could not, namely foot the high sunk costs that a company incurs before being able to sell a thing on foreign soil, such as finding foreign customers, locking in contracts, adjusting products to meet foreign product standards, dealing with the red tape of trade compliance, and so on. These tasks are of course easier for large companies than small ones to handle: the fixed costs of starting to export are a smaller share of large companies' revenues, but often overwhelmingly large for a ten-person business. And they multiply with each new product—which helps explain why the better companies not only export, but have more export products. This suggests that small business exporters that do exist are high-productivity firms led by exceptionally intrepid entrepreneurs willing to take a chance on international markets.

Ecommerce is now breaking these supposed "iron laws" of international trade.

In contrast to the 5 percent of American companies that export and the about 20 percent of American manufacturers that export, as many as 97 percent of American micro- and small businesses that sell on eBay also export—and export on average to twenty-eight markets, as opposed to the typical U.S. brick-and-mortar exporter that sells to either Mexico or Canada. And, unlike offline exporters, online exporters have staying power: of even the very smallest companies, 54 percent still export five years after starting.[8]

These figures play out worldwide. While only some 5 percent of brick-and-mortar Thai companies export, those that do, derive 56 percent of their revenue from exports. Meanwhile, 100 percent of Thai eBay sellers export and derive 98 percent of their eBay-enabled revenue from export markets. The average number of export markets per online seller is staggering: 46 in Thailand, 56 in Korea, and 63 in China, as opposed to 2.6 markets for the average developing-country brick-and-mortar exporter.[9] Similarly, Chinese micro-, small, and midsize businesses selling on Alibaba reach up to 98 export destinations and sell a wider range of products than their offline peers.[10] In other words, data suggest that ecommerce is helping small sellers become micro-multinationals, in the process turning all data we know about firms in international trade on their head. It is the killer app for small business trade.

The app works especially well for firms in developing countries. In a report for USAID, examining transactional data from global online platforms, I find that in small developing countries, 90 to 100 percent of platform sellers export on platforms, 90 percent of them export to more than ten markets, and companies that export on platforms derive on average 96 percent of their platform revenues from exports.[11] Meanwhile, some 70 percent of developed-market platform sellers export, about 50 percent sell to more than ten markets, and sellers that do export derive 50 to 60 percent of their sales from exports. In other words, while platforms are a very important means for developed-country businesses to expand their sales across borders, they are an extraordinarily useful means for developing-country companies to expand their export sales.

Developing-country company sales on platforms are also not one-off tiny transactions every now and then. Developing-country companies that export on platforms, particularly companies in middle income countries, tend to have export sale volumes very similar to platform-based exporters in developed countries.

Today, the best means for small companies to find global customers and grow is to get on a global platform such as eBay, TradeKey, or Alibaba, which are used by gigantic pools of buyers worldwide—eBay alone had 170 million buyers at the end of 2017. Platforms are for small merchants what greenhouses are for plants, nurturing environments systematically geared to growing sales at home and especially across borders. But the differences between online and offline businesses are obvious even outside global platforms, such as for businesses that have their own online stores or are selling on regional platforms such as MercadoLibre in Latin America or Lazada, now owned by Alibaba, in Southeast Asia. In 2017, my company cast random samples with thirty-five hundred businesses in sixteen developing economies such as Ghana, Kenya, Chile, Colombia, Bangladesh, and Brazil, and found that companies with online sales capabilities are three times likelier to export than small companies or companies that do not have online sales.[12] While only some 20 percent of small businesses that neither buy nor sell online have export activity, over 60 percent of small businesses that buy and sell online also export. Fewer than 30 percent of large companies that do not transact online export, but almost 90 percent of large companies that buy and sell online export. And they did not just export once in a while: they got 26 percent of their revenue from exports, and over 60 percent of them sold to three or more markets.

Now you might ask, did the online exporters export before they were selling online, or did selling online really help them become exporters? Survey data would confirm both ideas. Data from Central America, Southeast Asia, and the Middle East suggest that 40 to 50 percent of online sellers started to export only after starting to sell online. The most important impact of online selling tend to be export diversification. In a survey of Latin American firms, we found that two-thirds of companies that start selling online score entirely new customers—in other words, selling online enables companies to score foreign buyers they otherwise may not have reached.[13]

Ecommerce is also enabling firms to access the global supermarket of supplies and import. A Boston Consulting Group study shows that companies that use the web intensively are 69 percent likelier to import from global markets than those that do not.[14] In Latin America, where businesses in small countries seldom have quality supplies and inputs available domestically, the Internet is helping companies access parts and components beyond borders. Latin American companies that report making online purchases, 85 percent also import, while "only" 58 percent of companies that do not report online purchases import. In turn, companies that import also tend to be two-way traders—80 percent of online importers also export, possibly precisely because imports of foreign parts, components, and services make them more efficient and competitive in global markets.

If before companies needed certain scale to engage in trade, in the ecommerce era it is trade that enables companies to scale. How exactly does this magic work?

New Economics of Trade

In 1962, Dutch economist Jan Tinbergen pioneered in using what would become trade economists' workhorse: the gravity model. The model explains the volume of trade between countries as a function of their respective GDPs and distance. Thus large countries that are close to each other trade much more than small countries that are distant. Empirically, distance has been a huge deal breaker for companies to engage in trade: trade between neighboring France and Germany is about ten times the volume of trade between Germany and Brazil, whose economy is just about the size of the French economy but is 5,850 miles farther from Germany. Yet when economists analyze online trade, distance has much less explanatory power: the Internet drastically reduces the geographic distance which for centuries has curtailed visibility, trust, and trade between buyers and sellers located far apart and made it expensive for small businesses to find foreign customers.

Enabling buyers to find products online from sellers all over the world, ecommerce is lowering the wall over which sellers need to jump to get to global markets, even distant ones. Today, a small-business owner looking for customers in Brazil will no longer have to travel on costly trade missions, sit in endless negotiations, try to pick up some Portuguese, or lose sleep over whether buyers will pay. Rather, she can place her products online to be instantly visible to shoppers in São Paulo, go on to figure out her optimal customer segments by analyzing inbound traffic, and earn her stripes as a global seller by shipping the right item in a timely manner to each customer, over and over. She can also advertise on the global billboard called YouTube for much less money than would have been needed for the same visibility offline. As a fun example, one of the first of the three-hundred-employee Utah company Blendtec's "Will It Blend?" YouTube videos, in which its high-end blender pulverizes an iPad, received 135 million hits from around the world; the company's global retail sales spiked by 500 percent in 2007 following the quirky campaign.

Online sellers have at times been characterized as "accidental exporters" that begin to sell abroad not because of their own efforts but after being discovered by foreign buyers. This is not completely accurate: owners of companies get on major ecommerce platforms *because* they know that a global platform will help them get in front of buyers around the world and win buyers over through performing. After all, platforms' star ratings systems and customer reviews instantly signal to potential buyers things about the seller that offline would take time to communicate—such as if the seller's product is indeed of great quality or if the seller ships in a timely manner.

For example, rather than divining an Argentine wine seller's trustworthiness from indirect information such as his country image, a Korean buyer can now ride on the opinions of his fellow online shoppers and perhaps a few Instagram influencers, in the process freeing the Argentine seller from preconceptions about Argentina. Such reputational signals work in many sectors to persuade buyers. In a natural experiment, a team of economists compared an experienced eBay seller using its own eBay seller identity and seller reviews with a version of the same seller using a new eBay seller identity without any buyer feedback history.[15] The former version received bids that were 8 percent higher. In some categories such as collectable Corvettes the power of seller ratings vanishes.[16] But overall, it seems to drive buyers and values.

Ecommerce is in some ways akin to what ethnic diasporas have done for trade for centuries. Jim Rauch, a University of California, San Diego economist and his co-author Vitor Trindade famously showed that the Chinese diaspora encouraged trade—that there was much more trade than otherwise expected among countries with significant ethnic Chinese populations.[17] Their interpretation was that ethnic Chinese share business and social networks spanning borders help match buyers and sellers in different countries, reduce informational costs for both sides by informing buyers of the credibility of sellers, and deter opportunistic behaviors by throwing buyers and sellers who do not live up to their contractual obligations out of the network. Now these tasks crucial to trade are done by global online platforms such as Etsy or eBay. And you don't have to master Chinese to make sales and earn your stripes. Some econometric studies show that a common language between buyers and sellers is also less important online than in traditional, offline trade—online transactions simply involve less talking and contracting.[18]

Growth Alchemy

Ecommerce is a remarkable way to obliterate distance and turn businesses into exporters. But even better things may follow: business growth and economic progress.

Small-business growth matters: in most economies, small businesses employ over 90 percent of the workforce. While many studies concur that it is better companies that start to export, research since then also found that the very act of exporting makes companies better. Compared to non-exporters, exporters have higher revenue and productivity growth rates. For example, a 1997 study of German exporters found that the labor productivity of export starters is up to 7 percent greater than for non-exporters in the year *after* exporting starts.[19] A study of Colombian companies found that compared to non-exporters, exporters' labor productivity grows 1.5 percent faster annually for five years after export entry.[20] Studies on Italian, British, Canadian, Chinese, and Sub-Saharan African companies all yielded similar results.[21] In 2012, U.S. ITC showed that American small and medium-size enterprises manufacturing exporters grew by 37 percent, while non-exporters' growth declined by 7 percent—a difference that putatively is caused by the fact that exporters were less exposed to the economic calamity that hit the U.S. economy harder than most emerging markets.[22] In a rigorous econometric exercise I ran for Latin American firms, exporters outperformed non-exporters across key business metrics: by over 50 percent in sales and value added by workers, over 40 percent in wages, and almost 10 percent in skill levels, controlling for firm size and sector that can also shape these outcomes.[23]

There are at least five channels through which exporting makes companies better. First, exporters learn by doing: they gain new information from their international buyers, distributors and competitors, which leads to discovery of new market opportunities and improved management decision making.[24] Second, exporting can increase companies' propensity to innovate and invest in R&D, as exporters seek to improve products and processes in order to respond to customer demands and competitive pressures.[25] Third, exporters diversify their revenues across different international markets, which often reduces the volatility of the company's sales along with vulnerability to downturns in any one market. Fourth, selling in international markets increases companies' capacity utilization and reduces average costs, helping them scale. Fifth, exporters are generally exposed to intense foreign competition, which forces them to become more efficient in order to survive in the global marketplace.

Still another reason why online sellers do better is that they often also buy online, where they can quickly access a vast variety of products, hunt for the best deal, and save on input costs—which in turn helps them offer better prices to their customers and compete harder.[26] Importing is particularly crucial for firms in developing countries with limited domestic supplies; ecommerce enables firms to find the right suppliers and screen their quality.

Whichever the causal mechanism by which trade makes companies better, the ultimate proof in the pudding is growth in the company's businesses, which can in turn yield many desirable outcomes: as the business owner grows her business, she earns greater profits, hires more people, and may be able to put her children through a great school that makes them into high-earning knowledge workers who build their own businesses or get high-paying jobs. She transforms her and her family's life, and in the process adds to her country's and global economic growth.

Even better for exporters and online sellers is if the exporter's country also liberalizes trade and allows more imports. Why? Because when governments open their economies to imports, competitive, high-productivity firms expand, while low-productive ones struggling to compete with more efficient foreign firms and incoming imports shrink and even die. If this sounds harsh, it makes economies grow faster and consumers be better off: resources such as workers and investments in an industry shift to the expanding high-productivity firms, which raises the industry's productivity and generally also lifts all boats in the economy, improving, as it were, the economy's batting average. In 2002, Dartmouth economist Nina Pavcnik made waves showing that about two-thirds of the 19 percent increase in Chile's productivity following its aggressive trade liberalization of the late 1970s and early 1980s was due to the survival and expansion of high-productivity firms.[27] And this is the charm of free trade: it increases long-run economic growth precisely because of these sifting-and-sorting effects that go on in the economy when it opens to trade.

It seems to be no stretch to say that by helping companies export, ecommerce also makes companies more productive and helps propel economic growth. Survey data show that online sellers indeed do grow faster. For example, companies in the Southern Cone of Latin America tend to have higher growth rates: over 40 percent of companies in the region that buy and sell online grow at 10 percent or faster each year, while only 28 percent of offline sellers are such higher-growth companies.[28] The World Bank finds that companies that have an online presence have almost four times greater labor productivity than companies that do not, and companies that are online and have online stores are more productive yet. For example, Vietnamese online sellers have 50 percent higher labor productivity growth and 75 percent higher overall productivity growth rate than Vietnamese companies that use the Internet but do not sell online, all other things being equal.[29] In other words, it is not just being online that spurs growth; it is selling online that seems to do so. It appears then that a good share of online sellers are firms that have entered the virtuous cycle of online sales, trade, and growth.

Engineering an Ecosystem

If you plant an apple tree today, you will get your first apple in three to six years. The same goes for ecommerce markets: they typically expand quickly in years three through six after the first transactions are made, word spreads, and a critical mass of shoppers buy successfully online, learning to trust the new channel. In the ladder of consumer demands for online shopping, trust is the first rung. In advanced economies, people trust Amazon to bring the package to their door the next day—because Amazon has brought it millions of times to doors the next day. In most developing countries this trust has yet to be attained. Most sellers are also so-called Facebook merchants that market their goods and services on Facebook or some other social media platforms, the tool they adopted when first accessing the Internet and that they are familiar with, as typically are their customers.

Ecommerce platforms in emerging ecommerce markets, such as Kenya's

KiliMall and Bangladesh's Chaldal, are inherently incentivized to build trust with buyers, both to secure customers and to build a good reputation among consumers venturing to make their first online purchases. Their owners stress the importance of timely delivery, double-checking that a customer gets what he or she ordered, and promptly replacing or refunding items if the customer complains. Prompt dispute resolution is another key to building trust. For example, eBay has a semi-automated online dispute resolution system that resolves some sixty million minor disputes between small merchants and buyers annually, inspiring lawyers to assess its feasibility for courts around the world.[30]

Governments in markets where ecommerce is booming are already bridging online economy's trust gaps. The Mexican government started early in 2008 to create an online dispute resolution system called Concilianet that enables consumers to go online and initiate and resolve complaints or claims against companies and get justice via an efficient online court video proceeding. By 2017, more than ninety companies had participated in the system, including major airlines and retailers such as American Airlines, MercadoLibre, and Walmart.[31] In China, where the volume of ecommerce consumer complaints has overwhelmed courts, the government has created a "cyber court" to solve cases on product liability in ecommerce, Internet service contract disputes, and online loan and copyright issues. The court is armed with high-tech devices that allow plaintiffs to file cases and upload evidence online in five minutes, with their identity verified by Alipay, and court hearings are conducted via online video sessions lasting only twenty minutes.[32]

When the trust deficit is filled, an ecommerce market has more air to grow and diversify. In Brazil, online shoppers are going for a wide range of products and services on their phones, from fashion to cosmetics, home appliances, home décor, perfume, beer, and books. In America, Amazon has offerings in just about every product category except prescription drugs, a market of tremendous regulatory complexity that Amazon is now tackling. China's ecommerce market is the most diversified yet. Everything from fresh imported cherries to luxury BMWs is sold online—while 40 percent of U.S. online sales are made up by only five categories such as electronics and clothing, in China the same 40 percent is split into fifteen categories.[33]

Individual shoppers themselves become online sellers as ecommerce takes hold. First they may be Facebook sellers marketing their used or home-made products online. Then they may graduate to sell on ecommerce platforms for the same reason they might drive Uber, as a side hustle to supplement their incomes in high-cost cities. Many of them may also be particularly active participants in the circular economy—people who might be Amazon Prime buyers that like to use a product for a while, sell it perhaps on eBay, only to buy new products.

In the growing field of online sellers also start sprouting digital natives and niche brands. Think of those hundreds of times you pushed your cart through a grocery store, the few occasions you walked through a showroom to test different kinds of mattresses or new glasses, or the time, that hopefully never arrives, that you go to your dentist for implants. Businesses such as Grubhub, Caspar, and Warby Parker have years ago taken these categories online. Now specialized online retailers are also emerging in the developing world, helping shoppers access a wider variety at better prices while saving time. The Bangladeshi grocery e-tailer Chaldal is solving a problem for shoppers exasperated with the time it takes to buy groceries in Dhaka, the capital of Bangladesh, which has an enormous congestion problem. Operating from residential buildings in different parts of the city that double as warehouses, this Y Combinator company fields hundreds of orders from five locations in the city, monitoring inbound orders and deliveries in real time on an online platform that enables Chaldal to streamline processes and route choices.

As ecommerce markets mature and diversify, they spawn local services ecosystems to support online sellers and buyers. As the Bangladeshi ecommerce economy has grown, entrepreneur-founded online payments companies such as Bkash have sprung up to solve the payments bottleneck that arrested the market's development. In Kenya, Sendy is unlocking last-mile logistics through a marketplace that connects customers in the Nairobi region wanting to send packages and documents with motorbikes, vans, and pickup trucks. In Jakarta, FinAccel has created credit lines for Southeast Asian online shoppers, using over eighteen hundred data points to assess applicants' credit worthiness within two minutes.[34]

In many countries and regions, ecommerce players are transforming the ecosystem themselves. Latin America's leading B2C ecommerce firm MercadoLibre has created an entire ecosystem of shipping, online payments, and financing. Mercado Envíos was set up for buyers making a purchase on MercadoLibre to instantly organize shipping and track the packages in real time. MercadoLibre's Mercado Pago secures the money until the delivery of the product.[35] Mercado Envíos has been growing fast; in 2017, 150 million articles were sent through the platform, about 60 percent of all MercadoLibre orders, with 74 percent growth compared to 2016.[36] MercadoLibre's Mercado Crédito provides access to fast-disbursing working capital loans to MercadoLibre sellers who have over $5,000 in monthly sales and uses its own transaction data to assess their credit worthiness.

Once built and proven by local entrepreneurs, ecommerce markets become battlegrounds for the Goliaths of commerce. This is certainly the case in Mexico, a booming market contested by Amazon, eBay, Walmart, OLX, MercadoLibre, and Alibaba, among others. In India, a market of over a billion where ecommerce sales are growing at over 30 percent annually, buyers are wooed by the likes of Amazon, Alibaba, Rakuten, and local giant Flipkart—a sea change for people long locked into buying from inefficient mom-and-pops at high mark-ups and lining the pockets of middle men. The winners of countries' journeys to the ecommerce era? Local consumers that get a wider variety of goods at a lower cost; companies riding to new markets on the back of Amazon, vTex, or Alibaba; and millions of logistics, IT, and management workers toiling in the ecommerce ecosystem.

As the industry blossoms, platforms and their support companies become more sophisticated. Three technologies are driving the industry to its next era, at least in three ways.

First, AI is producing ever more perfect matches between a company's products and shoppers. The machine already knows your wants and desires better than you do: several businesses are using a prospective shopper's data across platforms to build a complete profile of that shopper, helping platforms lock in new clients and win back defectors, typically at higher rates and at vaster scale than the best Nordstrom's store associate. Alibaba offers its merchants spot-on data on consumer needs, enabling highly accurate recommendation of best-fit products and best-fit adjacent ones, such as socks with running shoes or scarfs with jackets. According to Neel Patel, an online marketing wizard, ecommerce merchants score 15 percent higher returns by showing to shoppers adjacent products (great silk socks to match the recently bought leather shoes) the shopper likely most desires.[37] Better matches, more sales.

Second, blockchain helps build trust among online buyers and sellers conducting transactions online. In China, a hotbed of food safety scares, ecommerce giant Alibaba is launching a blockchain initiative in partnership with PricewaterhouseCoopers, Blackmores, and Australia Post, aimed at helping Chinese consumers separate legitimate, good-quality foods (such as Australian health supplements, beer, wine, honey, and cherries) from counterfeit products online.[38] China's other major ecommerce platform JD.com uses blockchain to track the production and delivery of frozen beef by Kerchin, a Mongolian-based beef manufacturer.[39] Alibaba's Tmall has adopted blockchain to help Chinese netizens track provenance and logistics data on their smartphones for thirty thousand goods from fifty countries.[40]

Third, 5G is transforming online shopping yet again. With download times that are a thousand times faster than those on 4G LTE phones, 5G gives sellers superpowers to appetize buyers. Clothing makers such as Adidas have used augmented reality to enable customers find the right fit. The Swedish household product and furniture retailer IKEA has created an augmented reality catalog app that works especially well on 5G, to help customers visualize how their selected IKEA furniture would fit and look in their own homes, enabling them to explore designs and colors that suit their home before purchasing the furniture.[41] Economies with 5G and deep pools of talent to use blockchain and AI—the United States, Korea, Singapore, the United Kingdom, Japan, and so on—will be spearheading the next era of ecommerce.

Does Ecommerce Create Jobs?

Ecommerce is often hailed as a means for small businesses to engage in trade and create new jobs. However, the empirical evidence on firms' use of ecommerce and job creation in those firms is still limited. Survey data strongly suggest that online sellers are likelier to export and grow faster than offline sellers and thus hypothetically also likelier to create new jobs, but whether that is correlation or causality is still not clear—it may well be that high-growing firms self-select into becoming online sellers. Early evidence suggests that probably a bit of both is going on: better, more productive, more creative, and indeed more export-driven companies are probably likelier to get into ecommerce, but once they do, ecommerce does to them what exporting does—increases their margins and makes them better.

Anecdotal evidence suggests that firms that establish online sales capabilities create more high-paying jobs and shed low-paying ones. While on a visit to El Salvador, I heard of a success story that policymakers should replicate. This was a B2B baby apparel company that had previously sold to a distributor in the United States, but that decided to use ecommerce and sell directly to American consumers instead. The company spent about $150,000 to develop digital marketing and sales capabilities, train staff to do ecommerce, and develop reverse logistics, and possibly another $50,000 to set up reverse logistics and deal with related issues such as trade compliance. It ended up succeeding at selling directly to consumers. As a result its volumes decreased but margins increased: it became more profitable. It also hired more high-wage employees, while cutting back on low-wage labor. In other words, it did what most governments would want firms to do: create well-paying, high-skilled jobs and become more profitable and productive.

At the same time, it could be that firms engaged in ecommerce are also more technology-intensive and more prone to substitute technology for labor, so that their job-creation potential is limited even if they were to grow fast. This is a hypothesis that, as discussed in Chapter 12, will depend on many variables such as relative demand and cost of technologies versus human workers, and an equation that varies extensively across countries and sectors. To be sure, ecommerce employment is also not a clear-cut category: online seller jobs are created more organically rather than overnight. For example, platform sellers typically start out as part-timers who after getting some traction quit their jobs to become full-timers. Althea Erickson, the public policy head of platform Etsy, the staple seller of which is a woman making and selling crafts and clothes from her living room, characterizes sellers as part-time "amateurs" who grow into full-time "makers."[42] These people readily create at least one new job (provided their ex-employer hires for their slot). Upon expanding their business, they tend to hire online marketers and social media managers, in order to (perhaps literally) stick to their knitting.

There are of course further questions about the indirect effects—such as whether the rise of online sellers also induces growth and job creation in adjacent industries such as in logistics and knowledge-intensive legal, business, and IT services. This is where there is bang for the buck. For example, KPMG calculates that in India, each new ecommerce merchant creates 10 jobs and 4 jobs in downstream industries, such as logistics and warehousing.[43] India is expected to add 10 million ecommerce jobs by 2021, of which 1.45 million are in e-tail, and some 1 million logistics jobs, most of which are in last-mile delivery—that is, which require no formal training.[44] Some 400,000 tech, IT, and traditional corporate jobs such as in HR and finance will also be created. The Chinese government arrives at similar numbers for their country: it estimates that ecommerce had by 2016 created 10 million jobs in online stores and related services, making up some 1.3 percent of the country's employment.[45]

In the United States, the number of ecommerce economy jobs has been growing—in 2014–2017, warehousing jobs, light delivery services, and non-store retail all grew at about 5 percent a year (warehousing jobs boomed by over 10 percent in 2015–2016), as opposed to general in-store retail, which grew at about 1 percent annually. Ecommerce sector workers, including in fulfillment centers, also do better: they earn an average of $17.41 per hour, 26 percent more than the average $13.83 per hour in brick-and-mortar retail, and overall wages paid to ecommerce workers have increased by $18 billion since 2007, as opposed to $1 billion for traditional retail.[46] And this is not even counting for managers, IT services, and data scientists in companies that also benefit from ecommerce.

These numbers lead to interesting hypotheses. One is whether ecommerce could substitute for losses in manual manufacturing jobs by spawning new jobs in logistics and warehousing, often among low-skilled males. Another is whether the fact that ecommerce enables working mothers to order groceries, household supplies, meals, and cleaning services online enables women to fully specialize in their salaried jobs and even spend more time in the office—and thus power them to the top of organizations and improve allocation of labor in the economy. There are several such policy-relevant questions about ecommerce's second-order impacts that we have yet to even start tackling. Does ecommerce help firms scale and create jobs in developing countries? Does it increase the incomes of people working in ecommerce firms or adjacent industries? Does it reduce or widen geospatial disparities in firms' labor and total factor productivity? Let's explore that one next.

New Economic Geography

Remote rural companies have traditionally had a raw deal, especially in developing countries. They face much higher costs of bringing products to markets than companies in port cities, and have more limited access to the Internet, credit, and talent. Research by the Inter-American Development Bank (IADB) shows that most Latin American exports tend to originate from regions where the costs of reaching large markets or export are lowest. For example, companies in northeast Brazil and southern Mexico export relatively little, compared to those in southwestern Brazil and Northern Mexico. This fact alone accentuates disparities between firms near export ports and firms in remote regions.[47] The IADB at one point concluded that companies in these remote regions are simply "too far to export." Rural shoppers surrounding rural firms are typically much poorer than they are in cities—people in the Chinese countryside make a third of the wages their urban peers make. Rural companies are in essence penalized in world trade for being rural, and this is one of the reasons industrial activity has agglomerated in major cities and near major highways and ports. Even knowledge-intensive services companies, which in principle are footloose and could use the Internet to service customers from a distance, have tended to find it better to be in cities, in the vicinity of their clients.

Granted, prosperous, busy cities are where there are also a lot of ecommerce sellers, including small businesses and individuals who sell their ill-fitting yoga pants or old bookshelves online. But where online seller *growth* is coming from suggests that ecommerce and digitization could be closing in-country disparities between rural and urban areas, at least in advanced economies. For example, a study by the Economic Innovation Group and eBay shows that while half of new enterprise formation in the United States in 2010–2014 was concentrated in the twenty largest counties in seven states, such as Los Angeles or New York counties, which represent 20 percent of Americans, the world of the six million eBay sellers was much flatter.[48] Only 38 percent of new sellers on eBay are in the major counties; one-half of the net increase in eBay sellers came from seventy-five counties spread across twenty-four states, accounting for 36 percent of Americans. Of these counties, many have larger cities such as Dallas or Atlanta, but eBay's data also suggest that a substantial share, 36 percent, of its sellers are not in large cities, but in rural areas or small towns. Thirty-two of the hundred counties with the highest number and revenue of eBay commercial sellers per capita are rural counties such as Essex County, Vermont; Clay County, North Carolina; and Flagler County in Florida.

Etsy sees a similar pattern: in its Seller Census, 99.9 percent of U.S. counties have Etsy sellers, and 28 percent of Etsy's 1.7 million sellers live in rural communities, compared to 17 percent of non-farm business owners nationwide.[49] Upwork's Freelancing in America analysis also finds that freelancers are also somewhat likelier to live in rural areas than other workers: 18 percent of freelancers live in rural areas.[50]

Another way to look at the data on the geography of ecommerce is to ask which of the 3,143 counties grew in the wake of the Great Recession. For the overall economy, the number was only 41 percent in 2010–2014—while 71 percent of the counties comprising 95 percent of Americans saw a net increase in eBay sellers.[51] EBay's Hanne Melin Olbe finds similar patterns in Europe. For example, while London and the southeast region of the United Kingdom claimed 45 percent of all enterprise growth in the U. K. in 2011–2014, and the poorer Wales, West Midlands, Yorkshire, the northeast region, and Northern

Ireland collectively made up 8 percent, the share of eBay sellers in the wealthier regions was less than in the traditional economy, at 30 percent, and in the poorer regions higher, at 16 percent.[52] In the former East Germany, excluding Berlin, traditional firms contributed only 3 percent to the total German enterprise growth in 2011–2014, while eBay sellers in East Germany contributed 20 percent to all eBay sellers' growth in Germany during the time. These trends may well reflect the idea that many sellers are individuals who use ecommerce to supplement their incomes.

Ecommerce seems to be reshaping economic geography in India, where 70 percent of online sellers are poised to come from "rurban" (rural/urban) small, more remote cities by 2020.[53] Etsy is nudging rural Indian crafts people whose families have for generations made distinct products such as sharis to sell online by helping them use the Internet and providing them an online store on Etsy, high-quality photos of their products, and a professionally crafted narrative of their story. This work has many exciting benefits: these sellers are overnight able to showcase their products to shoppers in New York or London, something next to impossible in the analog world, and they can increase their margins and incomes by selling directly to the consumer, escaping the many middle men who would otherwise take hefty cuts before the product is in the hands of a foreign buyer. The best part is that this model is commercially viable: wealthy shoppers from around the world get access to what they want—highly differentiated, unique products—thereby supporting the businesses and incomes of developing country sellers.

If the second unbundling discussed in Chapter 2 enabled millions of rural developing-country workers to become urban dwellers employed by megafactories, the ecommerce revolution can make them into entrepreneurs and online sellers.

Rural ecommerce is gradually becoming a reality in Africa, in part because ecommerce is a vehicle for African firms to import products that they simply do not have access to in their own countries. In the survey "Use of the Internet in Burundi" conducted by Burundi Internet General Applications Network in 2010, more than 70 percent of respondents in rural communities felt that ecommerce can significantly address their business challenges, such as difficulties accessing urban buyers and inadequate supply of seeds, fertilizers, and parts and components.[54] Local platform Burundi Shop has responded by enabling rural buyers to access goods and services from across East Africa, track their shipment by text messages and tap affordable courier services running door-to-door, and use a creative workaround with local banks to enable cross-border payments. It is going against daunting odds—broadband barely exists and cross-border logistics to import can be a nightmare. But the demand is there, and if filled, Burundi Shop may end up making rural firms more competitive and prosperous.

These patterns suggest that ecommerce may enable remote firms to thrive and thus enables them to stay where they already are, doing what they do, limiting outmigration for rural areas. Of course, merely dropping ecommerce into a digital desert devoid of the Internet and people able to use it won't do: also needed are better broadband, good logistics services, and people who know how to use ecommerce. An even more interesting question for economic development is whether ecommerce might induce urban firms to relocate to literally greener pastures. One hypothesis is that while the technological shock of 3D printing and robots may induce manufacturing of products near urban centers where a customer can stop by to co-customize his new car and get it sans the costs of transporting the car from a distant manufacturing plant, the ecommerce shock could incentivize entrepreneurship in more remote areas in lighter products and services. After all, Americans at least are sick and tired of expensive and clogged cities, with a record 27 percent wanting to live in rural areas (when 15 percent actually do) where they can have bigger houses, greener lawns, and peace and quiet.[55] Does ecommerce enable them to take their jobs and businesses to the countryside?

One might certainly expect that firms and freelancers, particularly ones that do not sell products and are thus free from logistics costs considerations, would be increasingly footloose and able to move away from cities. After all, all that is needed is a laptop, a great work product, and, critically, great Internet access. The online work platform Upwork has birthed quite a few digital nomads, who not only go rural but go global, wandering around the planet. For example, Indian-born Upwork freelancer Radhika Basuthakur has been working as a node in global supply chain on social media and content marketing all the while enjoying a peripatetic lifestyle, living in various countries such as Thailand and Colombia for a few months at a time.[56]

However, public sector intervention is needed to sweeten the deal for urbanites to move to rural areas. In America, a 2010 study found that improvements in rural broadband connections have fueled some immigration into American rural areas, though it has not stopped outmigration to cities.[57] A more granular zip-code-level study suggests that the impact of improvements in broadband on relocation of firms is greatest in semi-rural areas adjacent to larger cities, where businesses enjoy the best of both worlds, cheaper and more spacious living but with a short drive away to their urban customers.[58] Meanwhile, very remote areas have to do much more than establishing last-mile broadband to keep businesses around and prevent an exodus of capital and talent to cities, let alone get them to relocate from cities.

What's a Better Gender to Use Online?

Is there a gender gap in ecommerce? The question is timely, as promoting women's economic opportunities has become a major global development tenet, and that permeates the United Nations 2030 Sustainable Development Goals.[59] It has also become fashionable among governments and businesses to promote women in international trade and ecommerce. This is positive for three reasons. First, while there are some studies on the impact of trade liberalization by gender, there is rather little data on how particularly *women-led firms* do in international trade. Second, since women are becoming more prominent in many economies as employees, employers, business owners, consumers, and investors, it is useful to know about their choices and constraints. Third, women's economic empowerment helps optimize a society's productive resources; expand the tax base; and improve economic growth, households' welfare, and intergenerational wealth transfer. Thus, it is useful to know more about what women do and prefer, and what challenges they face, including in trade.

Given the growing attention on women in trade and development policy circles, one might expect to find a notable differences in the performance and barriers facing women-led firms versus men-led firms in trade or ecommerce. To date in several surveys of over seven thousand firms in Africa, Asia, and Latin America, a finding striking to me is how similar the online sales, export, and growth performance of women-led firms are when compared to those of men-led firms of similar size categories, sectors, and countries, and how similarly men and women business leaders rate their barriers to ecommerce. I have not found any major differences between genders in participation in ecommerce or in the severity of regulatory challenges facing companies, after controlling for firm size and country.

Where the gender gap does exist is among CEOs. Data on the breakdown of women versus men CEOs online reflect the breakdown in the broader economy. Significantly fewer women run and own companies in most countries than men—15 percent of Latin American firms, 13 percent of African firms, and 19 percent of Asian firms had a female CEO in 2015, and women held slightly over a third of management positions in firms.[60] In OECD economies and China, 25 percent of CEOs are women.[61] Online, data are very similar—to a good extent because many companies that sell online are the same ones that sell offline. While data are sparse on the gender distribution of firms that are digital pure-plays or "born digital" companies, however, one proxy is capital raises by tech startups: tech companies that raise capital are in 90 percent of cases founded by men.[62]

If we believe data that say there are disparities between women and men in running businesses in the traditional offline economy, ecommerce may be leveling the playing field for women-led firms. Yet few firms that sell online are run by women. What this then suggests is that getting more women into business and selling online may help level the playing field between women- and men-led firms.

Besides, women may prefer being online sellers. For example, a 2015 survey Alisa DiCaprio of the Asian Development Bank and I ran in the Pacific Islands in places such as Fiji and Samoa showed that businesses that are active online are smaller, newer, and have a greater concentration of female executives under forty-five years of age.[63] These women stated they like doing ecommerce because of the flexibility—they can run their online businesses while also handling household obligations—and because ecommerce enables them to expand their reach to wealthy markets such as Australia and bolster their earnings. Indeed, the World Bank thinks that ecommerce can be particularly empowering of women in cultures in which they are expected to stay at home and they lack the professional networks and resources men have. As one piece of evidence, the Bank finds that there are proportionately many more women employed on Upwork (44 percent of total) than there are in the offline non-agricultural labor market (25 percent).[64]

Of course, the web is not completely free of bias. A team of Israeli analysts found that women get a lower number of online bids and make only 80 percent of what men do for the same new product and 97 percent from used products—even if women are perceived to be more honest and reliable as sellers than men.[65] They suggest this is because people perceive goods owned by men as having more value, especially if the goods are army knives or car seat covers. Perhaps women selling these products did better posing as Johns and Steves. But in the main, early evidence suggests that ecommerce is helping women, including vis-à-vis men. Online, women can bypass old boys' clubs that were previously gatekeepers of customers and capital, find and vet vendors, tap real-time information and data for marketing and pricing their products and services, and even perhaps have it all—multitask and juggle work and family.

However, much more work needs to get done: samples of women-led firms are small and generalizable findings are still scarce. There is a great deal of work ahead to understand how women-led firms perform as online sellers and online exporters and importers, and whether and which types of women-led firms—or any firms for that matter—grow faster, create more jobs, and do more to reduce poverty among their employees and communities than firms that do not sell online.

This means that policymakers need to be careful about how to interpret data on gender differences, and to not read too much into descriptive statistics when assessing them. Before deciding that women face higher hurdles or that women-led firms do better or worse than male-led firms, it is imperative to control for the many other variables that consistently shape firms' performance, engagement in ecommerce, export participation, job creation, and growth. Gender (of the CEO or management team) may be one of the factors that makes a difference, but it is hardly the only one, probably seldom the main one, and may not matter at all. The familiar basics like firm size are still the key determinants of companies' performance.

Conclusion

Centuries ago, open air markets in Ancient Greece, classical Rome, and medieval town squares transformed on Saturday mornings into bustling markets. They were also tremendously efficient markets: all sellers, products, and prices were fully visible and comparable to all buyers, and any transaction could be consummated instantly without friction. There were practically no search, informational, or transactions costs on either side. The square was also a place that encouraged entrepreneurship—a channel for people with something to sell to reach much of the population; a great way for people with ideas to test them out. And it was democracy's playground. Drawing everyone together, buyers and sellers, rich and poor, old and young, town squares encouraged dialogue and self-government.

For the first time in history, we have a chance to mount the medieval town square globally. Ecommerce bridges geographic distances between buyers and sellers located far apart, enabling small businesses to export. It is also jet fuel for small businesses looking to scale global sales, an equalizer between businesses in urban and rural regions, and an opportunity for youth employment and for women to start businesses and export. It tears down brick-and-mortar stores and creates new vibrant ecosystems of payments, logistics, IT, and financial services, and millions of jobs in these industries. It has birthed millions of new sellers and exporters—people who in the analog era would have a Saturday garage sale and on Monday report back to their day jobs. Today, it turns out, garage sales can be global and people can do them for living. The best part: ecommerce is still only in beta. In Brazil, which is among the top ten ecommerce markets, only 4 percent of retail is online. In much of Asia and Africa, these figures are even lower, suggesting a massive online growth opportunity. Let's look at the other side next, the rise in the number of online shoppers.

4

WHEN SIX BILLION PEOPLE
GO TO THE MALL

You will in all likelihood have today held the tool that is globalizing globalization: the smartphone. While the richest segments of mankind are already connected to the worldwide shopping mall many times over via phones, tablets, computers, and TV screens, most developing-country citizens still shop in the physical rather than the virtual world. But now this is changing—radically. According to the network and mobile company Ericsson, there were 2.6 billion smartphone subscriptions globally in 2015; by 2020, Ericsson predicts, 6.1 billion people, or 70 percent of the global population, will have smartphones and 90 percent of the planet's people will be in areas with a mobile broadband network, thus with a chance to get online.[1] The Asia-Pacific area alone will birth 1.6 billion new netizens; in Africa and the Middle East, 740 million will come online. In Latin America, an estimated 270 million people will be using smartphones by 2021, twice as many as in 2015. While some forecasters have attained somewhat lower predictions, everyone is seeing dramatic growth in the use of smartphones and mobile services—and the time we spend on mobiles as a share of total Internet time, which is climbing steadily from 26 percent in 2014 to 48 percent in 2019.[2]

The smartphone revolution is unlocking mega-markets at the nexus of newfound connectivity and income growth. Individuals increasingly direct global distribution of just about everything, from designer shirts to appliances and food. Soon just about anyone can sell almost anything to almost anyone, any time: garage sales can be global. How exactly is the smartphone reshaping world trade and prospects for prosperity?

Digital Divas

Previously run by giant retail chains, distribution channels now lead straight to individual consumers leveraging their smartphones, tablets, and laptops to buy, make, modify, and return goods and services from around the world. No more are consumers driving to the Flat World's superstar Walmart to buy shirts and toys made in China or wandering around Nordstrom for Alpaca blankets made in Peru; they now shop online, be it at Walmart.com or an online Alpaca shop with a storefront in Cuzco, and have products delivered to their doorstep. Ecommerce has roared into living rooms: in 2018, it made up a tenth of U.S. retail and 18 percent and 28 percent of U.K. and Chinese retail, respectively, up from less than 3 percent in 2008.[3] Online shopping is growing globally, from 7 percent of retail in 2015 to 15 percent in 2020.[4]

Wealthy women are especially voracious online shoppers. In the United States, boomer women—women born between 1946 and 1964—have earned the label "digital divas." They have an estimated net worth of $19 trillion and spend on average 250 percent of what the general population spends online.[5] At least in the United States, women also spend more online relative to their incomes than men, and they get each other to buy: as many as 92 percent of digital divas pass along information about online deals to others, boosting sales and bolstering brands.[6]

Research suggests that the first adopters of online shopping were well-educated and wealthy. Ethan Lieber and Chad Syverson of the University of Chicago show that education levels are a particularly important driver of ecommerce purchases in the United States.[7] Having graduated from high school reduces the probability of using the Internet by 8 to 9 percentage points while having a college degree raises it by 6 to 8 points. Education is of course correlated with incomes—the prime Amazon Prime users are urbanites with $150,000 or more in annual income.[8] Age played a role too. A thirty-five-year-old in the study was 5.5 percentage points less likely to be online than a twenty-five-year-old, while a sixty-year-old was 6.8 percentage points less likely than a fifty-year-old to use the Internet. Race defined online shopping patterns, likely because it tends to be correlated with education and income levels. Blacks were about 4 percentage points less likely to be online than whites, while Asians were 3 percentage points more likely. These patterns are echoed in some of my company's work on the geospatial determinants of ecommerce activity with leading platforms.

Digital divas and wealthier Western shoppers will carry global online commerce to the future. In 2020, 80 percent of the world's shoppers and 91 percent of the growth in consumption is expected to come from 430 cities.[9] While one might think these would be the sprawling Lagos, Rio, or Mumbai, most urban consumption in absolute numbers in 2030 will still be in North America, where 315 cities make up 40 percent of global consumption growth. In 2015–2030, consumption in New York, Los Angeles, Osaka, and Tokyo will grow a stunning four-fold, and it will triple in London. These five cities alone will by 2030 have purchasing power of nearly $6 trillion, roughly equivalent to today's Japanese and Korean economies combined.[10] And much of their shopping by that time will be done online.

Granted, wealthier segments in emerging markets have also been spending heavily online. China—where most ecommerce spending is made by so-called "super-heavy spenders" who splurge more than $1,500 per year online, making up 7 percent of all online consumers but 40 percent of sales—will by 2020 have a hundred million people that are making $24,000 or more per year. This segment alone will in 2020 make $1.5 trillion in incremental spending, a market the size of the Spanish economy.[11] They are already buying Western brands and foods online. Worried about the safety of local food, Chinese consumers are placing online orders for Mexican avocados, Alaskan lobster, and Scottish mackerel. Ecommerce purchases have grown also in other emerging markets—for example, forty-five-fold between 2000 and 2015 in Brazil, where online buyers devour electronics, books, appliances, clothing, and footwear.[12] With professional women increasingly using ecommerce in Brazil, online sales of beauty and health products are soaring. In India, shoppers from 2,638 cities are opening their wallets to eBay entrepreneurs in 141 countries, buying electronics, lifestyle products, and high-end chocolates.[13]

Emerging ecommerce markets typically have had a flat tail—a relatively small share of shoppers make most of the ecommerce purchases while the majorities spend just a little. But at least in China, Millennials are making the tail fatter: over a half of China's online shoppers are Millennials who are 40 percent likelier to buy online than people in the same income bracket—and make truly eye-popping purchases. For example, Chinese Millennials are known to buy overseas properties "sight unseen" on their mobile devices, to combat weakening currency, escape pollution, and pave the way for their children to have residences where they can live while studying abroad.[14]

Mobile-First

The wealthier segments of the global citizenry have many tools to shop with online—iPads, laptops, desktops, and the latest generation smartphone. But a new marketplace is soaring: that of the low-income, developing-country smartphone shopper. This person will have only his phone to get online to visit the worldwide shopping mall. For example, India has three hundred million mobile users, none of whom owns a PC. By 2014, web views from mobile phones had outpaced views from PCs in forty countries, including India, Nigeria, and Bangladesh, and other developing economies.[15] Even in emerging economies such as Argentina, where PCs are adopted quite widely, the emerging wave of consumers such as Millennials are likelier to own a smartphone than a PC.[16]

With low PC adoption rates, Africans are the world's most committed smartphone shoppers: 63 percent of Kenyans, 65 percent of Nigerians, and 73 percent of South Africans already use a mobile device to make their online purchases, as opposed to 10 percent of Australians and Americans, of whom 80 percent purchase via computers.[17] With almost a billion Africans expected to get a smartphone by 2021 and many to use it to access the web, online spending is expected to grow seventy-five-fold in 2016–2025, from $1 billion to $75 billion.[18] Smartphone shopping, as opposed to PC shopping, is quite systematically negatively correlated with incomes in cross-country and in-country data. In Brazil, for example, 53 percent of people do their online shopping on smartphones, but 68 percent of low-income people do.[19]

The drivers of the smartphone revolution are straight-forward: dropping cost of devices and connections, and growing incomes. While in some countries such as the Congo and Niger mobile broadband still costs more than a consumer's annual disposable income, in most of the world, including in eighty-three developing countries, mobile broadband costs have come down to 5 percent or less of annual incomes.[20] This is caused by the drop in the cost of devices and connections and by growth in incomes. There is a strong correlation between incomes, Internet connectivity, and of course online shopping. The share of people that are online in a country rises from 20 percent to 70 percent when per capita incomes shoot from $10,000 to $20,000. Latin America and much of the Middle East and North Africa are hitting $20,000 in incomes in 2020; emerging and developing Asia, where incomes are at around $10,000 in 2016 and $15,000, will get there somewhat later.

That the newest netizens are only using phones to get online and the existing netizens, especially Millennial ones, primarily use phones to buy online has birthed the term *mobile-first* among retailers' marketing and sales teams to prioritize the needs and wants of mobile shoppers. Pioneering companies are well on their way. India's largest ecommerce marketplace Flipkart has an app for the tens of millions of Indians who rely on mobile devices to search, share, compare prices, and shop from thousands of third-party vendors in more than seventy categories. Mobile apps today make up 90 percent of Flipkart's business.[21] Unilever, one of the pioneers of serving bottom-of-the pyramid markets with small-pack product lines and whatever-it-takes logistics, is now getting its personal care products in front of Pakistan's nine million smartphone shoppers, many in rural areas, through a partnership with Daraz, the country's leading ecommerce platform optimized for mobile phones.[22] Since a growing share of sellers themselves have nothing more than a smartphone either, ecommerce platforms are adapting—the Singapore-based mobile-to-mobile commerce platform Shopee helps sellers display items with a line of text and a couple of pictures taken on a smartphone. Shopee reached three million users six months after its launch in Taiwan and Southeast Asia.[23]

Granted, even though enjoying higher incomes, most new netizens are not your Gucci shoppers—they are closer to the bottom of the income pyramid. While the world's poorest of the poor living on less than $1 a day will continue living offline and essentially in the dark, the global "bulk bracket"—the two billion people making $10 to $60 per day and the three billion making $1 to $8 a day—are emerging as a $7 trillion, underserved digital market. One might of course argue that this group of people will not buy online—after all, don't their purchases consist of foods and undifferentiated goods like paper towels or canned foods readily available in the kiosk next door? But data suggest that in each income group, a growing share buy online. For example, in Europe, some 56 percent of low-income Internet users bought online in 2017, up from 32 percent in 2013, while some 74 percent of the wealthiest quartile buy online, up from 67 percent in 2013.[24] Both high-income and low-income shoppers are also spending more online per person. And interestingly, the prevalence of online purchases among all purchases grows especially among low-income shoppers, even if at first they might not buy a lot online.

In other words, online shopping seems to be an acquired taste: rich people got connected to the Internet first and have over time been spending more and more on consumption online; now it is the newer netizens in the poorer segments that are raising their share of online purchases of all purchases.

Both income groups buy more online, but they buy for different reasons: poorer segments buy online to find the best fit; the higher income categories to save time.[25]

The smartphone revolution has surfaced new simmering segments with expanding spending power. Removed from big-box retail, rural shoppers armed with smartphones are a segment leapfrogging to online supermarkets. In India, Amazon, Flipkart, and Snapdeal enable rural shoppers to access retailers that were previously visible and accessible only to urban shoppers. The third of Indians that live in rural regions are creating an ecommerce boom: by 2020 almost one-half of India's online shoppers are expected to come from rural areas.[26] Big Box retail is coming to Indian farmers via smartphones and India's postal service—and without expensive middle men.

Developing-country women armed with smartphones may offer the biggest gain yet to commerce companies. Globally, women collectively own two hundred million fewer smartphones than men and hold only 30 percent of wealth worldwide, but these gaps are narrowing. More women are getting online, and by 2020, women will have $5 trillion in disposable income in China and India, up from $1.5 trillion in 2015.[27] They also direct their families' online dollars: for example, tiger moms in Asia already dictate their household spending on groceries, clothing, and cosmetics. Accounting firm Ernst & Young believes women will hold 75 percent of the world's discretionary spending power by 2028.[28]

Mobile-first is becoming key in B2B sales as well. Google's search statistics show that Millennials account for nearly half of all B2B purchases, and 42 percent of searches for B2B purchases come from mobile phones—a three-fold increase from 2012.[29] Now add two plus two. Some 85 percent of the world's workforce will be Millennials by 2025. Socialized by B2C social media, ecommerce, and the sharing economy into mobile purchases, Millennials will also make B2B searches online. They already account for nearly half of all B2B purchases. One can imagine a new, vibrant shopper for B2B mobile marketers: Millennial Chinese corporate women. Smartphone is the new shopping mall and warehouse alike—and heralds significant economic gains.

Handheld Economics

In 2003, Nokia introduced Nokia 1100, a crafty $100 mobile phone. The rugged, dust- and waterproof device with a flashlight went viral, selling over 250 million units and becoming the world's best-selling handheld of all time and the world's best-selling digital product. Nokia 1100 unlocked the mobile revolution—by 2013, seven billion SIM cards had been sold worldwide.[30] Hundreds of local repair shops in Africa thrived on sales of spare parts for the 1100.

The Finnish "Kalashnikov of Communications" also caused an explosion of analyses on the impact of handhelds on economies. Early work found good things all around: mobile phones were found to speed communications and information-sharing, and to accelerate economic activity across sectors, from finance to health care and agriculture. For example, intrepid Pakistani farmers armed with price data from their smartphones could learn about and shift to higher-return perishable cash crops in high demand in the market and cut post-harvest losses from perishable crops by 35 percent.[31] Econometricians advised us that when ten new people of every one hundred adopt a mobile phone, GDP per capita growth increases by 1.2 percentage points.[32] Further studies showed that 10 percent growth in the use of 3G systems, when upgraded from 2G systems, boosted per capita GDPs 0.15 percentage points.[33] And a 10 percent increase in mobile penetration in countries was found to expand long-term productivity by a whopping 4.2 percentage points. The prime Nokia 1100 users, Africans, simply felt the portable phone made their lives better: 76 percent said mobile phones helped them save on travel time and costs and 62 percent felt mobile phones made them more secure.[34]

What then happens when mobile phones in the third world also connect on the Internet?

The short of it is access to more and better services by domestic and foreign providers, and more commerce in goods, including cross-border. To put a number on these gains, economists have turned to the concept of consumer surplus—the difference between the price that you pay (such as a $2 cup of coffee at Starbucks) and the value that you place on the product (perhaps $20 in an early morning when you really need that coffee).

The typical method to quantify the Internet's consumer surplus is to ask, how much would you pay for Google Search if you had to pay for it? Americans answer $500 per year, according to Google chief economist Hal Varian. But such numbers may not get at the many gifts of the Internet, such as the expansion in choice, convenience, knowledge, and leisure time (and the dramatically accelerated research for a book); they may still underestimate the gains. Another method embraced by such scholars as President Obama's economic advisor Austan Goolsbee and his co-author Peter Klenow is to ask, how much of your free time do you spend on a digital product and what value (or "utility") do you gain from it? Taking into account the cost of an Internet connection, the time consumers spend online, and the opportunity cost of their time makes Goolsbee and Klenow conclude that Americans' consumer surplus from the Internet was $3,000 on average in 2005.[35] Another global study estimates that the annual economic value generated by the Internet in 2012 was $1,488 per capita in developed countries that were already highly connected at the time, and $119 at the time in the much less connected developing economies.[36]

Still another method is to ask, what is the cost saving for consumers from buying the same product online versus offline? Turns out that online there is both more competition and more choice, and it is especially the choice that drives the surplus. In 2003, according to a team of MIT and Carnegie Mellon economists, Americans increased their welfare seven- to ten-fold when buying books online as opposed to buying offline. And this was not counting the time it takes to go to the physical store and find the book there, versus the time spent on finding the book on Amazon.[37]

Of course, there may be some welfare losses in that online shopping may not be as romantic or fun as browsing books in book stores. But some apps are changing that. For example, Instacart, the online grocery delivery company, enables friends located in different places to fill a virtual shopping cart together. Another negative side effect of one-click online shopping is impulse buying. Online buyers' remorse got worse, surprisingly many scholars of the subject say, after smartphones rolled out.

Overall, the smartphone compounds the consumer surpluses the Internet creates. If you are a Millennial, you have likely exploited the Internet's rock-bottom information costs just recently on your (increasingly smart) smartphone. Research firm Alliance Data found that 84 percent of Millennials use smartphones in stores to assist with their shopping, 53 percent use their phones in a store to search for a discount or coupon, and 34 percent use their phones for looking at product reviews.[38] Compare that to your grandma, who in her youth battled information asymmetries by gathering product and price data from the woman next door, clipped coupons from the paper each Sunday, and then went to the store to gather the last bits of information by inspecting the product first-hand and typically concluded her shopping there.

In an exciting study, Stephanie Lee uses Korea as a laboratory to analyze the increase in consumer surplus in 2010–2014 when the share of Koreans using the Internet skyrocketed from 10 to 70 percent, mostly thanks to the proliferation of smartphones.[39] She finds that average annual consumer surplus per person from a smartphone is $492, of which $276 is from expansion (impact from consumers' use of a smartphone for digital activities that were previously inconvenient, such as searching for information online while on a bus to go to work) and the rest from substitution (how consumers may use a smartphone for activities previously done on other devices, such as dialing a taxi from a phonebooth instead of ordering an Uber from a smartphone app). Lee also finds that free WiFi on public transportation in Seoul increases consumer surplus by $117 million per year, a gain that well exceeds the annual budget to provide the digital service.

These findings echo the idea that PayPal, Airbnb, Lyft, and other such "Internet intermediaries" boost consumer welfare and firms' competitiveness, by helping individuals and companies find, share, and access content and interact and transact with each other. A study by Copenhagen Economics found that Internet intermediaries increased the European Union's GDP by €430 billion in 2012, or about 3.3 percent of its GDP; of this, €220 billion were gains from investment, private consumption, and exports, while €210 billion was the indirect effect of productivity increases in firms serviced by internet intermediaries.[40] An additional €640 billion gain stemmed from a range of sources—such as consumers' welfare gains from free online services and growth in online advertising.

Indeed, in a fascinating PhD dissertation, Min Jung Kim at the University of Minnesota argues that consumers score huge gains from the fact that many apps are free—they are like paid apps but with zero price.[41] Her finding is that smartphones created up to $271 in annual consumer surplus in 2011, with 90 percent of the welfare gain coming from free apps. And that was in 2011, by which time "only" 10 billion apps had been downloaded from the Apple App Store—a far cry from 140 billion in September 2016. Americans' time spent on apps has also grown, from eighty-one minutes per day in June 2011 to three hundred minutes at the end of 2016.

Such findings have fueled digi-optimists like Hal Varian, who argue that the measure of economic growth is too narrow to take into account consumer welfare gains from smartphones and apps. Meanwhile, digi-pessimists like Northwestern University's Robert Gordon believe that new technologies such as apps are not exactly transformative the way, say, steam engines were, and add very little to economic growth. Rubbish, trade economists would say.

Trade in YouTube

The Internet has already increased the role of trade in goods and services in economies. David Riker from the U.S. International Trade Commission shows that the growth in broadband use in 2000–2011 increased the world's trade-to-GDP ratio on average by over 4 percentage points, almost half of the overall growth in the world's trade-to-GDP ratio, which grew from 51 to 61 percent at the time.[42] Behind these numbers are millions of stories of sellers getting orders from people in other countries and growing their businesses. Because of ecommerce, you are able to search and compare products not only across your country's online sellers, but across sellers of the world. Like that good-looking shirt on eBay? Well, it is shipping from Italy and just made you into an importer.

As smartphones proliferate, the worldwide shopping mall opens up also to billions of shoppers in developing countries. Google's Consumer Barometer shows that most developed-country and Latin American online shoppers have already bought online at least once from a foreign country: 70 percent of Mexican smartphone users have bought from overseas, more than the 64 percent of Americans who have done so.[43] Less than a quarter of African smartphone users have bought products from a foreign country, but this too is changing as African online markets mature and address shoppers' two points of concern—price and logistics of overseas purchases. Already, Nigeria is the world's fastest-growing market for cross-border online purchases.[44]

People shop products across borders even when tariffs, taxes, and logistics costs double the cost of the shipment. In Brazil, well over half of shoppers have bought something from abroad online, despite the country's fabled maze of taxes and tariffs and 6 percent extra taxes on cross-border credit card payments. In Central America, wealthier parts of the population buy jackets, headphones, and gadgets from Amazon in the United States, often paying hefty premiums for logistics. In Mexico, 65 percent of men and 50 percent of women in the twenty-five to thirty-four age group buy from overseas at least once a year; in China it is Generation X and Y women who are the likeliest to fill their virtual shopping carts with foreign products, and buy from abroad at least once a year.[45]

The smartphone revolution propels not only trade in goods but exchange of content—videos, music, books, and advertisement. Download speeds have skyrocketed ten-fold in 2006–2015, propelling video, the biggest prize online yet: IT infrastructure giant Cisco expects video to account for 60 percent of mobile data traffic in 2020, with half coming from YouTube.[46] Already, over 50 percent of YouTube views in Canada, the United States, the United Kingdom, and Australia are of content uploaded overseas.[47] Plateauing in the United States, streaming company Netflix is on an aggressive global expansion drive to lock in smartphone-wielding viewers from Australia to Latin America and the Nordics, and next in China. At the end of 2015, it reported forty-two million U.S. and twenty-three million foreign users.[48] By 2019, Netflix's international user base had ballooned to almost 100 million, and to slightly over 60 million in the United States.[49]

Likely the most important development impact from smartphones will be in developing countries' access to educational, medical, and financial services that have traditionally been hard to ferry over and scale. Surveys show that massive open online courses from professors at universities such as Stanford and MIT, while still mostly viewed by people in advanced economies, have imparted the greatest gains in developing economies, where they have improved the career prospects of people with lower socioeconomic standing and less educational attainment.[50] These kinds of findings have inspired Bill Gates in the annual Bill & Melinda Gates Foundation letters to advocate smartphones as the next classroom. Imagine the potential gains to girls in Afghanistan, where female literacy is 12 percent and smartphone apps and simple text messaging have already helped women learn to read and write in private?[51]

These benefits can be stretched quickly to remote medical checkups, legal services, accounting, and so on, even carried out without humans. For example, Tala Mobile, based in Santa Monica, California, offers microloans to businesses in Kenya, Tanzania, and the Philippines through a smartphone app that draws credit information from the depths of the user's phone. The London-based Babylon, the online medical advisor powered by artificial intelligence, is diagnosing people who articulate their aches and pains on their phone apps in Rwanda and China. With a global pool of patients, Babylon's diagnoses too would get tighter: today the app gathers billions of data points collected from thousands of test consultations it completes every day, with 92 percent accuracy—a churn unmatched by human doctors doing about seven thousand consultations a year.[52] Even a simpler solution called Medic Mobile is transforming health care with African SMS users who might have to walk a hundred miles to get to a doctor.[53] Medic Mobile has equipped over a hundred community health workers with mobile devices that enable them to quickly diagnose and treat patients more effectively, for example in cases of tuberculosis in rural Malawi.

Smartphones enable people in developing countries to get access to a wider range of better products and services than ever available for the mankind. Indeed, the biggest gain from the smartphone may not be more trade, but a wider variety of products and services traded. Let's examine this next.

Choices, Choices, More Choices: How Ecommerce Fills Our Love for Variety and Makes Us Richer

When internationally traded products were first classified in 1922, countries traded 186 distinct products. By 1974, the number had ballooned to 1,214, and by 2011, it had surpassed 5,000. Each of these product categories can be broken into finer categories, such as "vegetables" could be broken into cucumbers and carrots, and further into fine categories such as "carrots, prepared or preserved otherwise than by vinegar or acetic acid, frozen." At such finer levels of distinction, there are 19,111 distinct products in U.S. import schedules.[54]

In the 1990s, as trade liberalization incentivized more companies to engage in trade, many countries began to export a wider variety of products. For example, the variety of U.S.-bound products from Mexico grew by 2.2 percent annually in 1990–2001, the first years of NAFTA's implementation.[55] Able to trade with the European Union post–Cold War, Southern and Eastern European economies doubled their export products. From 1984 to 2000, the number of Estonian exports grew from 388 to 2,670; Slovak from 2,681 to 5,471, Spanish from 6,260 to 13,652, and Greek from 4,225 to 8,037.[56] The stealth exporter, China, blanketed the global product space, doubling its export products in manufacturing and expanding its machinery exports nearly five-fold from 1972 to 2001.[57]

The growth of the online market works much like trade liberalization: it expands the feasible market for companies, now to the edges of the Internet. That the demand side grows enables a larger number of companies with similar but differentiated products to enter the market and thrive—so that ecommerce platforms and stores spread before consumers a giant smorgasbord of products and services that are different from what came before.

One differentiated product may be headphones. A search on Amazon brings up hundreds of different types of headphones made by an assortment of global brands and countless non-brand businesses in different countries. These are varieties of essentially the same product—such as noise-cancelling phones or lightweight phones, or black headphones and pink headphones. The point for trade is that some people in China may like brand headphones Made in USA, while some shoppers in the United States may like lower-end headphones that happen to be made in China. That consumers love variety is what makes ecommerce so vibrant—and that encourages intra-industry trade, trade in the same but somewhat different products, among nations.

Product variety in trade is also increasing due to the fact that ecommerce is enabling more small businesses to export—and small businesses collectively export a much wider variety of products than large companies do, typically precisely *in order to* differentiate themselves. For example, in a study my firm did for the Inter-American Development Bank, we found that in 2004–2008, small businesses in each of three Latin American economies—Argentina, Costa Rica, and Peru—exported some thousand products that were not exported by large firms, while large companies exported only two to three hundred products that small companies did not export.[58]

Adding to the mix of varieties are the new entrants on global online platforms, such as the Indian rural craftspeople empowered by Etsy and the so-called digitally native vertical brands such as mattress seller Caspar and eyewear seller Warby Parker that are fanatically focused on the customer experience and building a stand-out brand. In addition, consumers seeking "made by you and me" products by default create new stock-keeping units (SKU)s—such as new types of jeans on MakeYourOwnJeans.com, new sorts of running shoes at NikeiD.com, and an endless variety of consumer-designed toys at Hasbro's SuperFanArt. Next to mushroom are "Me2Me" products: clothes, toys, jewelry, tools, and so on that are conceptualized, designed, and 3D-printed by shoppers—or shoppers turned makers—themselves.

In early eras of globalization, gains from trade stemmed from inter-industry trade, the exchange of different products among different countries, such as Great Britain selling manufactured goods to colonies in exchange for commodities. Intra-industry trade grew in the past few decades as developing countries industrialized and exchanged cars and gadgets with advanced nations. As Korea industrialized and became more like America or Germany, it did not stop trading with these industrialized nations; rather, it grew its trade with them, selling to Americans and Germans the kinds of products that American and German companies also make—cars, industrial machinery, electronics, office equipment, and such. And many Americans went for it, preferring Hyundai and Samsung over Ford and Apple.

Since David Ricardo, trade economists had been able to explain why inter-industry trade happens, but intra-industry trade was more mysterious. Why would countries buy from other products they made at home? In the 1970s, Paul Krugman published the New Trade Theory, an explanation for why similar countries trade similar goods with one another, such as Japan and the United States exchanging Toshiba laptops for Apple laptops. Krugman's key insight was that consumers love variety: some Americans prefer Toshibas, others prefer Apples, and trade happens because not every American happens to prefer computers, cars, TVs, or gadgets made in the USA.[59] Trade makes us better off as it gives us access to our most preferred product—that is, the very same reason online bookstores make us better off.

Economists Christian Broda and David Weinstein built on Krugman's Nobel Prize–winning insights to show that the three-fold increase in available product varieties in the United States between 1972 and 2001 produced a large consumer welfare gain, captured as consumers' willingness to pay 2.6 percent of their income to access the wider set of varieties available in 2001 in lieu of the narrower set available in 1972.[60] As the smartphone proliferates, people around the world will be placed to realize gains from variety, revealing the brilliance of the New Trade Theory in ways that even Krugman probably did not anticipate. There is more to the story: since sellers of the world, once online, have to battle with sellers in the same category for the online shopper's wallet space, they also have to differentiate themselves more and increase their productivity, which too raises economic growth.

These effects are on display in China's countryside, where the Alibaba Group has been stoking ecommerce by investing in a "Rural Taobao" initiative that promotes trade between China's rural and urban regions by building rural ecommerce ecosystems. In a study, "The Alibaba Effect," a team of China- and U.S.-based scholars found that residents in small and remote cities purchase more intensively online than their big-city peers, mostly to access the wider varieties of products readily available in big cities.[61] This appears to be happening at scale: some seventy-seven million people in the countryside shopped online in 2015, 41 percent more than in 2014, vastly outpacing the growth of urban online shoppers.[62] As people in these small cities have improved their access to product varieties, they have also scored disproportionately greater consumer welfare gains from ecommerce than their peers in big cities—which suggests that ecommerce and smartphones can reduce income inequality *across* cities. Another rigorous study of Chinese rural households by Victor Couture,

Benjamin Faber, Yizhen Gu, and Lizhi Liu arrives at similar conclusions: ecommerce is enabling rural households, and especially younger and better off rural consumers, to access goods similar to those available to their urban peers, and thereby raising their welfare.[63] The gains were greatest in durable products such as appliances and electronics, stemming from product variety, as well as reduced cost and lowered travel time.

Their study also carries an important policy lesson: while smartphones and ecommerce terminals set up by Alibaba enabled rural Chinese to browse and order products online, it was the Chinese government's support of rural logistics that enabled the rural netizens to avoid paying an arm and a leg for shipping costs. After all, rural last-mile logistics are a huge cost center for ecommerce players, due to limited-scale economies involved with shipping to sparsely populated rural areas as opposed to shipping into a busy urban neighborhood with multiple high rises. The challenge is akin to that faced by major telecom companies that do not see a point in plugging a handful of households in remote villages in the Andes into a high-speed Internet. Governments interested in developing ecommerce across their countries may have to step in to subsidize last-mile delivery in rural areas, just as many of them have subsidized last-mile Internet connections. Several governments such as those in Egypt, India, and Vietnam have announced policies to invest in the use of ecommerce outside urban centers.

Conclusion

In the 1980s, if you wanted to know whether it was Sylvester Stallone or Arnold Schwarzenegger who starred in *The Terminator* or which universities would have particular strength in your chosen field of study, you might ask your friends or take a bus to your local library, browse its card catalogue, and then trek to find the book the card instructed you to consult. Today, you access these tidbits within a fraction of a second by Googling the giant worldwide card catalogue on the phone you carry in your back pocket, any time, almost anywhere. Not only do you have the data multiple times faster than in the 1980s, you also have more capabilities to compare and choose—you can today quickly see which movies are like *The Terminator*, see how thousands of people have rated *The Terminator*, join a Reddit conversation about violence in movies like *The Terminator*, or create a Snap video of yourself impersonating the Terminator and send it to your friends for laughs.

The smartphone gives us superpowers we could not even dream of even just twenty short years ago. But it is also transforming world trade in ways we are now starting to understand. It gives millions of sellers a storefront in a global shopping mall open 24/7 to sell their goods and services, and grow their businesses. It helps shoppers access the supply of the world, make better choices, and buy at lower prices. It also brings urban consumption possibilities to remote villages from western China to Northwestern Brazil and enables them to access financial services, free world-class diagnoses for chronic heartburn, and cheap astrophysics lessons from Harvard. It can accelerate trade and exchange of data across borders and increase consumers' well-being to the end of the Internet. And it is coming to workplaces worldwide, transforming also B2B transactions and work itself, with the smartphone becoming the work computer. And you can get these gains even without buying that new $999 phone; the one in your back pocket probably already delivers to you these twenty-first-century conveniences and gains from trade.

DRIVERLESS DELIVERY, DOOR-TO-DOOR

Despite slumping for five years after the financial crisis, world trade has been growing faster than the world economy in the past three decades—from $2 trillion in 1980 to $15 trillion in 2016, a nearly eight-fold gain, as opposed to the world economy, which grew four-fold from $18 to $75 trillion. Absent a sudden wave of protectionism or rapid proliferation of 3D printing across product categories, trade volumes will continue to rise at least in the medium run. Sea-bound merchandise trade is bound to soar by 4.3 times between 2015 and 2050; assuming that trade coming and going through major U.S. ports grows at a rather moderate 5 percent a year, container flows will double between 2015 and 2030.[1] The recent explosive growth in ecommerce has built a parcel mountain on top of the world's container-based trade, pressuring customs and border agencies, postal systems, and busy urban centers.

Burgeoning trade flows are a double-edged sword. Trade is a fabulous source of growth for economies, businesses, and trade intermediaries, such as shipping liners to express shippers, banks, freight forwarders, warehouses, and more. But trade growth needs to be matched by investments in new capacity in ports, shipping, freight-forwarding, last-mile delivery, and many other industries. In 2014, the U.S. Maritime Commission sounded alarms, writing that "congestion at ports and other points in the nation's intermodal system has become a serious risk factor to the relatively robust growth of the American economy and to its competitive position in the world economy."[2] Congestion in ships and ports could raise the costs of shipping, particularly for firms that ship commodities with high weight-to-value ratios over long distances, such as exporters in developing countries. High freight costs would also increase the minimum viable shipment, possibly freezing B2C and C2C ecommerce in low-value items.

To deal with the growing volumes of sea-bound trade, ports have pursued massive, multimillion-dollar expansion projects, liner services have made larger and larger ships, and truckers have added more wheels. Now, however, such supersizing is hitting diminishing returns. Fluid throughput in world trade is today less about brawn and mostly about brains: efficiency gains spurred by the Internet of Things, AI, and blockchain are accelerating world trade, while decreasing its costs and lightening its carbon footprint. Ships, trains, trucks, and ports are getting smarter and trade is becoming faster, cheaper, safer, and cleaner. How is this magic working?

When Bigger Was Better

Trade liberalization has been essential to trade growth in the postwar era. But there are two other unsung heroes driving world trade. One is economic growth, which is the main driver of trade for the simple reason that as economies grow, people and businesses in a country buy more, including from foreign markets. This is a key reason why America's trade deficits quite consistently track U.S. GDP growth rates. The other key driver of trade has been the interplay of expanded scale and technological progress in global shipping.

Early on in global shipping, big was also smart. Nineteenth-century American ship builders learned that longer ships could carry more sail and gain speed. In 1825, Black Ball Lines sailed from New York to Liverpool in twenty-three days, almost three times faster than the Mayflower's sixty-six-day voyage across the Atlantic in 1620.[3] Some twenty years later, ships would not be credited unless they made the trip in fourteen days.[4] In the nineteenth century, the rise of railroads and steam engines helped create the first modern wave of globalization. In 1819, the Savannah became the first ship to cross the Atlantic using steam power, which it accomplished in twenty-seven days. By 1937, the Normandie, running on turboelectric propelling machines, was able to hurry across the Atlantic in three days and twenty-two hours.

On the shore, things were still quite rudimentary: in the mid-nineteenth century, freight in the Port of Los Angeles was hauled by carts pulled by oxen and stagecoaches powered by horses. But the 1869 opening of both the American transcontinental railway system and the Suez Canal enabled around-the-world transport in record time.[5]

These breakthroughs helped double Western Europe's exports from 7 percent of GDP in 1850 to 18 percent in 1913.[6] They also boosted trade between colonizers and colonies—the Suez Canal increased British India's trade by 41 percent.[7] And they increased commerce within countries. MIT economist Dave Donaldson shows how the Indian colonial railway system, which grew dramatically in 1870–1930, increased intraregional and international trade, helped even out price differences among Indian states, and lifted Indian incomes.[8] For example, districts linked to the rail network scored a 16 percent gain in income from agriculture. In China, construction of new ports in 1880 increased the volume of goods imported and possibly was the key behind the six-fold rise of Chinese silk cocoon exports.[9]

Further infrastructure and technological breakthroughs followed in the twentieth century. The U.S. interstate highway system, which was finalized in 1992 with the opening of I-70 through Glenwood Canyon in Colorado, boosted trade in heavy goods, inherently sensitive to transport costs, in American cities such as Cincinnati, Birmingham, and Detroit.[10] The opening of the Panama Canal in 1914 reduced the maritime distance between U.S. East and West Coasts by eight thousand miles and expanded trade from Latin American countries—41 percent in El Salvador, 31 percent in Ecuador, 15 percent in Peru, and 11 percent in Chile.[11] Port expansions around the world fueled commerce flowing in global supply chains: in China, where exports grew over six-hundred-fold in fifty years, from $2.6 billion in 1960 to $1.6 *trillion* in 2010, the port of Shanghai was overhauled and expanded, by 2011 growing into the world's busiest port and handling three times the amount of commerce that passed through Los Angeles.[12]

With the internal combustion engine and gas turbine replacing steam engines during the century, maritime trade accelerated. By 2000, sea freight cost was 20 percent of its level in 1930. Containers were the next big disruption pushing world trade forward. Up until the mid-twentieth century, cargo came in all shapes and sizes and packages—crates, pallets, and small lots—which made unloading a ship a painstakingly slow process rife with theft and damage to cargo. This changed on April 26, 1956, when Ideal X, a World War II tanker converted by Malcolm McLean into a cargo ship, sailed from the Port of Newark to Houston carrying fifty-eight metal containers on a reinforced deck. By the time it docked in Houston, the company was already taking orders for containerized shipments.[13] Containers changed the game by standardizing shipments: they could be easily loaded, sealed, shipped, and moved from truck to ship to train, opening an era of global multimodal transport. Only five years later, in 1961, the International Organization for Standardization (ISO) had standardized container sizes, to ensure that containers were one-size-fits-all for ships, trains and trucks. McLean's business became Sea-Land Services, now a division of the Maersk Group.

Start of Smart

In 2011, the Triple E hit the market. This largest containership to date ran the length of four football fields, stretched 19 meters longer than the height of the Empire State Building, and could carry eighteen thousand containers (or 3,640,000,000,000,000 iPads). With thirty times the capacity of the early container ships of the 1950s, the Triple E delighted global traders by bringing unprecedented scale and efficiency into the shipping business, thereby helping to bring shipping prices to record lows.

When Triple E took her maiden voyage, the recipe of the ages to move more trade—increasing scale and improving technologies—was still working. Bigger was for a long time better: at the start of the twentieth century arrived the Panamax ship, able to hold 5,000 twenty-foot equivalent units (TEUs), then post-Panamax with about 12,000 TEU, and then Super Post-Panamax such as Maersk's Triple E, with 18,000 TEU. Ships were made bigger and bigger, to a point at which the Panama Canal, designed in the early twentieth century to fit U.S. navy vessels, had to be expanded. As the widened canal opened in 2005 to accommodate ships with up to 12,600 TEU, ships had outgrown it once again. Yet the continued quest for scale was compelling: increasing capacity from 8,500 to 15,000 TEU saved approximately $80 per container, and further increasing from 15,000 to 19,000 TEU saved another $40.[14] In addition, world trade was booming in the mid-2000s, supporting the notion that scale meant clients and big was beautiful.

But now the "bigger is better" formula that has served the shipping industry is hitting diminishing returns: every extra expansion in shipping volume is yielding less and less savings.

One reason is that there is only so much space to expand ports, airports, or highways to accommodate the cargo volumes in a giant ship. The race for bigger ships created problems downstream for the world's ports, which were having to expand their premises, dredge deeper harbors, raise bridges, and grow any which way to be able to welcome and turn around a giant ship quickly. For example, the transatlantic corridor is a third the distance of the corridor between China and Northern Europe—and would thus require a third of the time in port to realize projected savings from the new scale of the ship. Hastened further by the Panama Canal expansion, ports from New York and New Jersey to Savannah, Houston, and Long Beach and Los Angeles set out to raise funding to better service the era's megaships. However, this was going to work only to a point: the Organisation for Economic Co-operation and Development estimated that incremental increases in maximum container ship size could in fact increase the overall cost of transporting goods, due to disproportional increase in port and beyond-the-port hinterland costs.[15] Megaships also poised significant risks to supply chains—the damage from any one of them capsizing was gut-wrenching for insurance companies to contemplate.

Another reason why the formula based on size stopped working is liner services' collective obsession with size: with every line building more and bigger ships and world trade growth flatlining after the financial crisis, the shipping industry found itself in severe excess capacity. By 2017, total industry supply exceeded demand by 20 percent. Liner service executives marveled at the lost cost savings bigger ships were supposed to deliver; findings were made that size had not been the only driver of cost-savings anyway—over 60 percent of the savings stemmed from optimized engines.[16] Ships sailed half-filled for years and lines consolidated to fill or finance ships. The seventh largest shipping company, Korea's Hanjin, declared bankruptcy. Cost savings from added scale had peaked faster than the industry had anticipated.

Air cargo faced the same challenge of overcapacity, due to the aggregate expansion of belly capacity in the industry. In 2015, air freight rates dropped monthly by 9 percent. But the industry weathered better because of the even larger drop in jet fuel prices and the spectacular growth of ecommerce-related parcel shipments. The number of parcels traveling more than a thousand kilometers by air multiplied from thirty million in 2010 to almost four hundred million in 2015.[17] Air shipping also became more popular among ecommerce sellers and buyers. The total kilometers per ton of ecommerce traveling by air soared from 16 percent to 74 percent in 2015, and are poised to grow to 91 percent in 2025, meaning that air cargo will carry 950 million ecommerce items. Boeing expects the world will need 2,480 new freighter aircraft between 2018 and 2038.[18]

Low shipping costs have of course been a boon for exporters and importers, perhaps especially developing-country commodity exporters with high weight-to-value ratios, whose economics are very different from those of countries that ship iPhones or luxury watches. For example, in 2008 Latin America had 172 percent higher ocean freight costs than did the Netherlands in its U.S.-bound trade, mostly because Latin American countries shipped heavier items than the Dutch did.[19]

Another upside of extra space in ships is for SMEs doing ecommerce and ecommerce platforms. Dying to fill their ships, liner services have forged super-alliances with ecommerce platforms, as these can by virtue of their user base generate massive amounts of new business and help consolidate small shipments. For example, Evergreen Line, Maersk Line, and CMA CGM have partnered with Alibaba to enable SMEs selling on Alibaba to directly book cargo space from liner services when they need it through Alibaba's OneTouch shipping platform, which offers import-export services such as customs clearance and logistics capabilities, and also books air freight on behalf of Alibaba's customers.[20] As a result, a small business has to deal with just one entity instead of separate middlemen, and probably ends up with lower markups.

Alibaba too gains: with its logistics network of third-party logistics companies, Alibaba gets more control over logistics and lower costs, as liner services know Alibaba's switch costs from one line to another are very low and thus its bargaining power strong. On the shipping line side, Australia-based China Sea Rates is launching the world's first plug-and-play, door-to-door ocean-freight booking system for several ecommerce websites.[21]

In addition to looking for ecommerce customers, liner services have sought cost savings from technology. This is where cost savings are indeed found. The industry's most flamboyant concept is the driverless ship. Of course, crewless ships existed already: Rolls Royce piloted with a crewless ship in 2014, and Elon Musk's two Space X autonomous spaceport drone ships "Just Read the Instructions" and "Of Course I Still Love You" have long floated in the Atlantic and Pacific as receiving pads for recyclable rockets. But by now, the global shipping industry has caught on. Norway's crewless one-hundred-container, $25 million vessel Yara Birkeland is set to hit the oceans in 2019, and be fully self-driving by 2020, when regulations are expected to be in place for crewless ships to travel in international waters. Japanese shipping firm Nippon Yusen K.K. is building remote-controlled ships to carry containers across the Atlantic and Pacific oceans. The first ship is scheduled to sail in 2019; many more are planned by 2025. A Chinese alliance formed by HNA Group has set a goal of launching its first self-navigating cargo ship in 2021.[22]

Driverless ships have meaningful economics, promising cost savings to an industry with a decade of depressing annual reports—and can ultimately lower costs for exporters and importers, and markups for consumers buying foreign products.

In the first major wave of globalization at the end of the nineteenth century, ships required more than two hundred sailors; today, they require fewer than twenty. A ten-thousand-ton container ship can be manned by a crew of fourteen or fifteen. After that, scale economies truly kick in: a ship ten times the size can operate with five extra crew, or with nineteen or twenty seafarers in total. Yet even this minicrew has a cost, absorbing an estimated 44 percent of a ship's costs (think of a crew's salaries; plus their quarters, which take space from containers; the air conditioning they need; and so on).[23] The crewless ship, meanwhile, requires at most one person at the remote control. The impact on the industry's economics can be very significant—more than 1.5 million people globally operate the world's ninety thousand merchant ships. Automation should also help remove human error, the source of 96 percent of accidents on the high seas. Crewless ships save money also by optimizing their routes on the basis of the weather, maintenance schedules, and cargoes.[24]

They may also possibly displace other modes of transport. For example, the Yara Birkeland is specialized in short-range trips and can take on the various trips that are currently made along coasts by forty thousand truck trips each year. Since the Yara Birkeland is fully electric—it is nicknamed the "Tesla of the Seas"—it can shave off another 40-plus percent of ships' operating costs, and save on the gas going into trucks. Ships in general have far better energy economics than trucks: while a semi-truck moves one ton on one gallon for 59 miles, a freighter moves a ton on a gallon for 526 miles. Powered by electricity, Yara saves even more gas and has zero CO_2 emissions and almost no noise pollution.

That is, if the truck remains as it has been, a gas-guzzling eighteen-wheeler. In reality, trucks too are increasingly electric—in 2017, Tesla alone received orders for all-electric trucks from the likes of Anheuser-Busch, Walmart, and DHL. Trucks are also smarter. Using "platooning," trucks connected by sensors and other communication devices partner up with trucks heading in the same direction, following each other in a tight formation like competitive bikers, and reaping fuel efficiencies thereby. Sensors take care of speed and braking patterns through the convoy to allow for closer proximity than human reflexes and stomachs would allow. The new trucks also score high on self-awareness and self-improvement. To monitor their world, trucks carry dozens of sensors—four hundred of them in the industry front-runner Daimler's trucks—that stream weather, traffic, route, truck vitals, and other data into software with 130 million lines of code, a more elaborate system than a passenger jet. They can predict failures and self-diagnose problems, and order replacement parts to maintain themselves.

Liner services' supply-side cost savings do not per se turn the shipping industry's economics around—growth in seafaring cargo vis-à-vis growth of container space on ships will. This equation is still working for traders and against shipping lines, tempted as they are to add volume as trade recovers. Once in market, crewless ships may save liner services money after the initial investment has been recouped and lines have learned to manage the costs of ship maintenance in the middle of the ocean. Cost savings could also come from the merger-and-acquisition activity in the shipping liner market during its lean times—though experts are already heralding antitrust actions.

By consolidating, liner services have gained bargaining power vis-à-vis terminal operators, with which they negotiate long-term contracts. Liner services are also benefiting from explosive growth of ecommerce. But they may yet get disrupted by ecommerce giants with far better customer service, digital capabilities, and end-to-end data on shipments coveted by cargo owners and other players in the trade ecosystem, such as customs and banks that provide trade finance.[25] Amazon has been pursuing its top-secret Dragon Boat project, or "Global Supply Chain by Amazon," which is envisioned to control the supply chain end to end, from factories in China and India to customer doorsteps in Atlanta, New York, and London. To make the economics work, Amazon has leased twenty Boeing 767 jets for air-delivery service, registered as a freight forwarder to provide ocean freight services in China, and bought thousands of tractor trailers. The scale enables Amazon to offer small-volume sellers the same bulk discounts as large companies shipping in bulk. The tight end-to-end vertical integration brings together data across the supply chain for deeper insight into trade routes and customers.

Shipping and freight forwarding are primed for Amazon to enter: industries with manual, paper-based processes, high intermediation costs, and opaqueness. Startups too have been entering the space around the world. The San Francisco–based unicorn Flexport digitizes the opaque and paper-based freight-forwarding business with a platform on which importers and exporters can book shipping and track their products' journeys in real time and sleep at night; Flexport itself handles the intermediation with a network of ten thousand import and export experts and is possibly poised to Uberize ocean logistics. Founder Ryan Petersen set the company up after struggling with lack of transparency and efficiency in importing dirt bikes from China. In Uruguay, Gurucargo has a similar model serving as the freight forwarding world's Kayak, for Latin American firms to choose routes, freight forwarders, customs brokers, and freight insurance all from a single place.

Ghost Ports

In Qingdao in northeastern China, locals call the city's port "Ghost Port." Opened in March 2017 as Asia's first automated port, Qingdao has cranes that use laser scanning and positioning to locate the four corners of each container and decisively grab them and move them onto driverless electricity-powered trucks. It goes tirelessly through its motions day and night, running just as well in complete darkness as in broad daylight, with few human beings in sight. Instead of sixty workers to unload a cargo ship, the port requires only nine— mostly techies with remote controls, rather than workers operating cranes.[26] Labor costs have been reduced by 70 percent, while efficiency increased by 30 percent, meaning shorter port calls by megaships eager for their next assignment.[27] Accidents involving people are brought to zero. Its development turbocharged to fit in three years, the port now stands as a successful proof of concept for numerous other port automation projects in China, including the port of Shanghai.

Future crewless ships are increasingly likely to dock themselves to an automated port. Mother of all ports Rotterdam began automating years ago; the 445 million tons passing through each year are handled by software-run stacking cranes and vehicles and wind-powered operations. In the most highly automated container terminal in North America, Los Angeles's TraPac facility sorts cargo so that truckers can drop off an export container and pick up their import container in the very same stack and facility.[28] Robots are proving to be tough to beat: London's automated Gateway terminal has attracted two dozen *ad hoc* vessel calls in a two-month window from neighboring Felixstowe, the United Kingdom's top container port, which remains human-run.[29]

In the Port of Hamburg, the fourteenth-century Hanseatic League's crown jewel, Internet of Things applications choreograph the dutiful, slow-motion ballet of ships, trucks, and cranes to move twenty-five thousand containers and manage forty thousand truck trips every day.[30] All fat is cut: sensors optimize routes for containers coming in and going out by tracking the idle and excess capacity of trucks, cranes, carriers, roads, parking lots, and warehouses, and reallocating loads from the busy parts to less busy parts. The port is also using blockchain for the release orders from terminal and ports of particularly valuable cargo.[31] The new efficiencies are such that a truck driver can arrive at 6:30 a.m., leave with a container at 6:35 a.m., and have products on the shelves in Hamburg by that evening. The data collected over time are used to plan future traffic infrastructure investments.

The port is not only a grand choreographer, it is also a giant maintenance man. Its smart maintenance systems analyze the usage and wear-and-tear of fixed assets and engage machine-to-machine dialogues to prompt repairs as needed. Smart storage systems cater to the needs of cargo, assessing the storage facility's humidity, ventilation, cooling, barometric pressure, and so on, while heat detection sensors police unusual patterns in human presence. While this may seem futuristic, Hamburg barely had a choice: trade volumes through it are doubling from nine million to eighteen million containers between 2014 and 2025, and it has no room to expand, surrounded as it is by a busy city. So, the port authority thought, if you can't build wide, you need to play smart.

On the other side of the planet, the Port of Los Angeles and GE Transportation choreograph the movements of forty thousand trucks and ships each day through a portal where APM Terminals, Maersk Line, Mediterranean Shipping Co., and dozens of cargo owners and truckers share shipment information on a cloud-based system that uses artificial intelligence and machine learning to forecast shipment movements. This helps truckers to have a bird's-eye view of the shipments and plan their dispatch schedules, cargo owners to know how far their cargo is from being delivered, and terminals to maximize their labor and equipment.[32] The portal reportedly saves truck dispatchers an average of two to three hours per day. Other U.S. ports and the federal government fancy a similar portal for the entire United States. In turn, the smartest of trucks are connected to other players in the supply chain—the shipper, fleet, driver, law enforcement and municipalities, and border authorities can see where each truck is, how it is moving, and how its contents are faring in real time.

Ports can also create new revenue sources from the data their automated operations churn out. The port of Antwerp has created NxtPort, a platform sharing information among major companies such as BASF, MSC, DP World, and PSA, in a quest to ultimately commercialize the data from a wide variety of logistics players.[33] Other parties that can get on the platform include customs and other border agencies and app developers.

Port automation can be great for trade in developing countries: in the example of Latin America versus the Netherlands, differences in port efficiency (Latin American low, Dutch high) explained about a third of the difference in their respective shipping costs. For ports, spending in automation and other efficiency-boosting technologies such as drones that inspect the condition of warehouses and blockchain that enables all players in port ecosystems to access data on where a given consignment is and who is doing what can be easier to justify than the even more expensive dredging, paving, and building that steps on the toes of local residents and environmentalists. Granted, digitization gets push-back from port workers concerned about the impact of automation on their jobs. Smart port advocates need to address these concerns head-on by enabling workers to see how digitization can help them do their jobs better and faster and bring new business to the port, and retraining workers as needed.

Developing economies are today embracing port community system (PCS) platforms first pioneered in Europe in the 1990s that are not as sophisticated as blockchain but nonetheless enable data sharing and better coordination among the many port ecosystem players. At the verge of a collapse in 2007 with a surge in cargo, long wait times, contamination, and congestion in the city with six hundred thousand annual truck trips to and from the port, the port of Valparaiso in Chile created a PCS that enabled the many players in the port to better coordinate with each other. The port spent altogether $50 million in digital transformation. As a result, cargo handling times have plunged, enabling liners to turn around faster and trucks and terminals to locate information about customs clearance of a shipment within minutes, and emissions from waiting trucks and ships have been cut by 80 percent.[34]

Terminals in ports also are getting smarter. Leveraging a new terminal operating system (TOS) software, the Terminal of Manzanillo in Panama, one of the busiest in the world, could produce 360-degree data-driven reports on terminal operations with the press of a button and drill into such performance metrics as stacking crane turns per hour.[35] Some TOSs such as Navis are also helping terminal operators use their operating data to quickly generate more accurate invoices to shipping lines and charge for the full range of their services.

Granted, a great deal remains to be done in developing countries where digitization is still only beginning. Outside the better African ports of Durban and Mombasa, the average amount of time cargo dwells in sub-Saharan ports is close to twenty days, as opposed to three to four days in leading ports.[36] A World Bank team found that this sorry state results from a slew of perverse incentives. Importers use ports to store their goods. Customs brokers leave goods sitting because the cost of delays is borne by importers. And local companies that have a monopoly in an industry want to keep the cargo dwell times long as a way of deterring entry of other producers.[37] Technology could disrupt this setting, but the setting can only be disrupted if the players agree to adopt technology and disrupt. The number one solution is not new technology, but it is political—a crackdown on protectionism and collusion, so as to enable technologies to enter.

Last-Mile Economics

In 1962, management guru Peter Drucker wrote an article on "the economy's dark continent." Drucker referred to distribution logistics, then seen as the black box containing much poorly understood activity and possibly huge efficiency gains for businesses. Drucker's thesis was one of the catalysts of analytics in supply chain management and influential enough to induce retailers to think through their logistics.[38] In the 1970s, retail stores typically were replenished by direct deliveries from suppliers or wholesalers. A decade later in the 1980s, retailers wanted to gain more leverage over distribution, setting up distribution centers they controlled. In the 1990s, as global sourcing was in vogue, retailers set up import centers to receive and process containers. All along, they worked to lower inventory levels, accelerate product flow, and contemplate outsourcing of non-core activities to specialized vendors.

Then came ecommerce, and the journeys products take to arrive to their new owners changed drastically. No more does a product travel, as it has done for decades, in pallet loads and cases through retail import and distribution centers to local stores frequented by shoppers. It now travels solo through a giant sorting center to a parcel delivery company dropping it to the shopper's home. This may seem like a lonely ride for a parcel and a logistical nightmare for the shipper, especially in the heart of global-commerce, congested mega-cities. Yet deliveries are in the main getting faster and cheaper.

One reason is a revolution in warehousing. Amazon, Walmart, Home Depot, Target, and others have rushed to build massive fulfillment centers—in the United States, construction of mega-warehouses for ecommerce that are twenty-eight feet tall and as large as a million square feet in footprint increased six-fold in 2011–2015, led by Los Angeles, Inland Empire, Chicago, Dallas-Fort Worth, New Jersey, Philadelphia, and Atlanta.[39] These projects have been matched by supersized distribution centers in Shanghai, Hong Kong, and Taipei that measure fifty football fields in size, and by countless giant warehouses sprinkled across Europe. Those who cannot build wide are building tall: Australian developer Goodman has built a twenty-seven-story warehouse in Hong Kong with ramp access to the first thirteen floors and elevator access to floors 14 through 27.[40]

These are not big brainless boxes: they are the warehouse world's elites, complete with precise tracking systems drawing on sensors, and robot-driven pick-and-pack systems that minimize manual touches, space use, and returns. In comparison to drop-shipping—shipping from distribution centers or directly from factory to the buyer—the decades-old vendor-to-retailer-to-consumer supply chain model is, experts claim, very inefficient: it has higher inventory cost; involves extra "touches" of shipment that add to time, cost, and odds of damage; and has slower cash cycle times.[41] Drop-shipping saves freight, storage, and labor costs.

Further savings are generated by the various centers' specializing by time to market: those within the twenty-mile ring of a city handle the higher-cost, time-sensitive products such as smartphones and groceries, catering to the 80 percent of customers who want same- or next-day delivery, while their more distant and larger cousins specialize in less-time-sensitive products such as furniture and discount apparel.

The fiercest battleground in the warehouse world is city warehouse space. Amazon's "Prime Now" has penetrated city centers, with smaller, below-two-hundred-square-foot last-mile delivery centers and urban warehouses in London and several U.S. cities holding twenty-five thousand stock-keeping units that ship to the customer in an hour. The local edge is significant: when a typical store offers two-day delivery for a minimum order, Amazon delivers as fast as in two hours. And it is more competitive in both speed and price: despite high rents, urban warehouses can actually save Amazon money by reducing transport costs, delivery lead times, and inventory management costs, if the supply side anticipates demand well enough.[42]

The battle for urban warehouse space among Amazon; Alibaba; and delivery businesses such as Blue Apron, Hello Fresh, UPS, FedEx, and the U.S. Postal Service is pushing warehouse costs to record highs.[43] In the offline era, retailers planned on a 20 to 30 percent increase in seasonal peak traffic for pallets—but in the ecommerce era, peaks may be 100 percent or more, which makes long-term warehouse leases unattractive for retailers.[44] One super-peak occurred upon the day of a Harry Potter book launch, when tens of thousands of Amazon customers wanted the book on their doorsteps at the time of publication.

For smaller-scale operations with peaks, it makes sense to team up companies with different demand peaks and the same kind of handling equipment. It is like time share: one family occupies a home for the winter, another for the summer. One likes to ski, another to hike, but both like the same house and its sauna, washer and drier, and large kitchen island. An example, says logistics expert David Schwebel, could be an electronics company with demand peaks on Black Friday and Cyber Monday, a packaged candy company peaking by Valentine's Day, and a sports equipment company with peaks during back-to-school times.[45] Startups such as Seattle-based Flexe help retailers share warehouse space and find space, like travelers might on Airbnb, when demand spikes.[46] Sharing a 3PL facility, industry sources claim, can cut outbound freight costs by a third.[47]

Cities are happy about the rise of urban warehouses, as they produce point-of-sale taxes, create new jobs, and reduce truck traffic from traditional distribution centers. Owners of urban space such as old manufacturers and retailers are also winning, by flipping their warehouses to meet the needs of ecommerce players that require such amenities as modern technology and design, glass walls for natural light, LEED elements, and access to biking or walking paths for staff.[48] For example, in Minnesota, a redeveloper of warehouse space turned a former boiler room into a brew pub to entice companies to locate near the warehouse.[49]

In the rough and tumble of ecommerce real estate, old retailers have one edge—their stores that are close to urban and suburban shoppers. Companies such as Kohl's or J.C. Penney have found that after shutting down a store, they lose online sales on a ten-mile radius from the store—literally because they are "out of sight, out of mind"—and that physical stores enable them to lure in customers by providing a convenient way to make returns.[50] Nine out of ten J.C. Penney returns are made in-store. Yet this may be only buying retailers time—the growth of their ecommerce sales is not a match to the drop in in-store sales.[51] Within a five-minute drive for 70 percent of Americans, Walmart may be an exception: it has a special advantage in using its stores as ecommerce distribution facilities for the many shoppers that order online but want to save on delivery costs. Costco's shares have gone up after it relented and allowed customers to do similar click-and-collect.

Another key driver of new efficiencies in shipping is improvements in last-mile logistics. Before, the last mile was on the shopper who drove to Ikea, bought her items, and dragged them to her car and drove them home. Now with fast delivery and free returns, the shopper wants to outsource the last mile to whomever brings the product in quickly and cheaply. This desire, which according to surveys is even larger with people under thirty, has made the last mile into a dynamic business opportunity.

In the United States, many have rushed in to tap it. Uber, Postmates, Deliv, and Amazon Fresh provide spot-market deliveries by independent drivers. Roadie, the crowdshipping neighbor-to-neighbor service, puts anyone with a bike or a car in the delivery business. In the parts of Indian and Russian cities that still have poor local infrastructures, there is a boom of last-mile delivery men who ride on bikes through busy neighborhoods to bring the online order to the shopper's doorstep.

Aggregation technologies make the economics of the last mile work. For example, Roadrunnr, a hyperlocal Indian delivery business, uses data analytics to maximize the volumes handled in each trip as orders stream in. No fleet ever runs empty. Navigating busy neighborhoods, UPS trucks famously use a GPS system geared to averting left-hand turns, which saves shipping hours by the equivalent of $300 million in fuel. These technologies can now go farther in the addressless world that three-quarters of mankind live in. Many developing-country residences and businesses are locatable not by addresses but by directions such as "third house from the lake by the kiosk." Now startup What3words offers a geocoding system that assigns each of fifty-seven trillion three-by-three-meter areas of the planet an "address," a three-word code unique to that location. For example, the Statue of Liberty lives at "toned.melt.ship." The system can facilitate home delivery to four billion people in 135 countries who live without formal addresses and make it complicated to find the person who ordered pizza in a Rio favela of eleven million people. Indeed, Domino's Pizza uses the service to deliver pizzas in the Caribbean island of St. Maarten.

Last mile is an interesting puzzle in countries such as Mexico, where ecommerce is booming but delivery networks struggle to keep up. Amazon, Walmart, MercadoLibre, and other ecommerce giants are investing in creating their networks. The challenge, when shipping from the United States to Mexico or Latin America, is that there are only so many ports that also have customs. Parcels from abroad have to be flown to Mexico City, Monterrey, or Guadalajara, cleared there, and then shipped to the final destination in Mexico, creating a logjam in the three hubs and increasing delivery costs. Phoenix, Arizona, has built a different model: bring Mexican customs agents up to the United States to do pre-clearance and charge customs duties, and thus free the parcels to be flown from the U.S. closer to their final destination in Mexico—a smart move to also attract ecommerce players and warehouse and logistics providers to invest in Arizona.

Savvier postal systems have also caught on. Singapore's SingPost has invested hundreds of millions in a network of twenty-four warehouses in twelve countries, real-time stock inventory systems, and mobile phones by which mailmen track deliveries. If they so prefer, customers can pick up their parcels from SingPost's POPStations, open 24/7, whereby they can open parcel lockers with an app on their phones. SingPost also takes in shipments from outside the region and transships them to other Southeast Asian markets from Singapore. Deutsche Post's DHL is tasking a small cube van company, StreetScooter, to carry out last-mile deliveries.[52] Elon Musk's idea for a hyperloop going from Vienna to Budapest in ten minutes (as opposed to the two hours and thirty minutes it takes by train), could revolutionize postal and express delivery in Europe. Posts are breaking into new spaces—New Zealand Post has piloted Kentucky Fried Chicken delivery to compensate for the slump in mail delivery.

While a business opportunity, last mile is also a huge challenge. The cost of the last mile on average amounts to 28 percent of end-to-end delivery, and can run as high as 75 percent.[53] It can take a major bite out of the profit margins of businesses in competitive urban areas with plenty of substitutes right downstairs—such as meal delivery services in New York City. And the tighter the delivery window, the higher the costs have tended to run. In 2001, when ecommerce was starting to be big in the United Kingdom, Charles Nockold created a model for deliveries in London in which widening the delivery window from 180 to 225 minutes cut transport costs by 6 to 12 percent, and widening it further to 360 minutes cut costs 17 to 24 percent.[54] Eliminating the time constraint completely yielded cost savings of up to a third. Researchers in Helsinki arrived at similar conclusions in the early 2000s: expanding the delivery window to a working day from two hours cut costs by 40 to 60 percent; if the delivery was into shared delivery boxes that bunch together many people's deliveries and thus create new scale economies, the cost savings could be 55 to 66 percent from home-based personalized delivery within a two-hour window.[55]

The industry's cost per delivery rises further in sparse rural areas where "drop density" is lower: the rural customer is often at a distance and the sole customer there, which keeps scale economies in delivery low and delivery costs high. In my surveys, rural last-mile delivery is among the tallest hurdles for ecommerce sellers in developing nations; in Africa, for example, while urban delivery is among the least pressing problems, last-mile delivery costs defeat the purpose of selling to or buying from rural areas. Some solutions are emerging. In India, Inthree specialized in rural delivery and has succeeded at making money through partnering with microfinance organizations, agricultural boards, and India Post to form a distribution network and work with brands on a commission basis.[56] But for more people in rural areas to buy and access low-cost products previously only available to their urban peers may take more robust maneuvers by the public sector, as done in China, to subsidize rural last-mile delivery.

Game of Drones

Pedestrians in New York and Washington, D.C., concentrated cities with many offices and much paper changing hands, are long accustomed to look out for Red Bull–powered, ultra-fit couriers on the backs of bikes delivering this paper to be signed here and that document to be approved there. Though couriers on bikes still pose a considerable hazard for street crossers absorbed in texting on their phones, a new nuisance has emerged: ecommerce delivery trucks. In 2013, a Columbia University urban studies major, John Benjamin Woodard, set out to analyze the impact of ecommerce on New York City traffic.[57] Spying on Amazon deliveries and UPS and Fedex trucks, he found that on average, delivery trucks stayed parked for twenty-one minutes at a time, and two-thirds of them were double-parked—so that delivery trucks alone occupied road space for seven full hours.

Later on, another study of the forty-three zip codes of Manhattan found that in ten, the problem was way worse: the parking required by delivery trucks in these ten areas exceeded the full capacity of the streets.[58] And the number of delivery trucks has mushroomed: in Washington, D.C., for example, each day UPS delivers sixty-five hundred packages more than it did daily in 2010. Seattle, the home of Amazon, has set up a lab and is doing a study on urban goods delivery strategy.

There is not enough evidence to say that a substitution effect is at work, such that fewer trips by a family to the mall would be compensated by the increase in ecommerce deliveries. In fact, ecommerce may have made traffic much worse: a Saturday trip to the mall is in a New York area Regional Plan Association study comparable to ten separate home deliveries made at different times on different days.[59] Drop the mall day, add to the urban nightmare. The problem compounds if no one is at home to take the parcel. In the United Kingdom, twelve of every one hundred deliveries are delivered a second time, adding congestion to the roads and costs for the shippers that reach £850 million per year.[60]

Technology is overhauling the equation in which delivery costs are a function of labor cost, labor availability, and shifts. Robots are already delivering twenty-four hours a day in test runs in Hamburg and San Francisco for Yelp Eat24. In China, four-wheeled droids are already in full swing at Jingdong, China's second-largest ecommerce company. They can shoulder five packages at once and travel over twelve miles when fully charged, and find the shortest route from warehouse to destination, all at a fifth of the cost of a human courier.[61] Drones that reach places UPS brown does not, for example, flying sweets and medicine from land to offshore oil rigs and cargo ships. In Sri Lanka, ecommerce enabler company Grasshopper has launched drone delivery in the middle mile, for flights to and from the island of Sri Lanka. The use of drones in urban areas of America is ever closer thanks to President Trump's October 2017 executive order that gave local areas flexibility to test drones.[62] Granted, the handling also matters: a drone may or may not be the best vehicle for drugs, frozen foods, or spirits, whose condition, thanks to sensors, will be visible to sellers and buyers at all times during the delivery.

The question of which system—robots, driverless cars, UPS brown trucks, or postal services—will dominate going forward turns on both convenience and cost. The convenience part has largely been answered, at least in the advanced world. For example, a survey of forty-seven hundred respondents in China, Germany, and the United States found that 70 percent of consumers prefer the cheapest option of home delivery to anything less convenient such as lockers (and even if lockers came at a discount), and almost 25 percent of consumers and 30 percent of younger consumers are willing to pay significant premiums for the privilege of same-day or instant delivery.[63]

The cost question is more complex. A straightforward calculation might be, which is the cheapest home delivery? On cost, postal services do well though they are not fast. When the bracket is Fedex versus drone, Fedex may under certain circumstances lose to drones. Research firm Skylark Services has calculated on the basis of data from twenty-five commercial drone operators that if a large online retailer (read: Amazon) were to use a commercial unmanned aircraft system (UAS) for delivery to a customer's home and paid $2,000 for each platform, and the UAS could fly at least fifty hourly flights per week carrying the 91 percent of packages that are below five pounds, the cost would be $1.74 per trip—at least 76 cents below the $2.50 per last-mile trip they pay using traditional delivery methods. (A FedEx package that costs $8.50 tends to have ground costs of $2.72.)[64]

Skylark projects daily deliveries from a low of eight million to a high of eighty-six million by the end of 2030, meaning that for a midrange forecast of fifty million daily operations, the large retailer using drones would save $10 billion. This is assuming the UAS's costs are fixed—the wholesale cost of an individual commercial-grade battery with 250-hour life that can power a drone weighing up to five pounds and for at least ten miles is $100 when purchased in bulk; four motors each with a life of 750 hours that can lift a ten-pound drone that can travel at least six miles cost $60 each; and marginal electricity costs are approximately $.25 per trip.

Drones may be a particularly interesting solution in developing countries with poor roads, if and when their economics are better than those of couriers riding motorbikes. For example, in South Africa, the average wage is $2 per hour, during which a courier on a motorbike may deliver not the one package that can be airlifted by a drone, but perhaps five to ten packages, if going roughly in the same direction and unimpeded by traffic. It can of course be the case that drones are an outstanding solution in congested developing-country cities where even motorbikers wish for wings. It could be that price-sensitive shoppers will opt for either postal services or bikes—while experimental systems such as drones can service luxury shoppers who want the product pronto and in a tip-top shape.

Peering into the future of advanced markets, McKinsey bets on drones as the major future driver of ecommerce. The firm predicts that in all ecommerce, autonomous vehicles and drones will deliver 78 percent of all items, with traditional delivery accounting for only 20 percent and another 2 percent by bike couriers. In B2C and C2C ecommerce, autonomous vehicles including drones will deliver close to 100 percent.

The more interesting question is whether different delivery systems are substitutes or complements. Postal economics expert John Panzar of Northwestern University created a model with three players—express delivery services, postal service, and large retailer Congo (read: Amazon) with its own delivery system.[65] The battle of systems then becomes a battle over package volumes under the threat of self-delivery by Congo. Panzar argues that the likeliest outcome is "co-opetition" in which Congo uses its own delivery systems to carry the daily base load of parcels, but also has a daily peak load when it makes sense for it to contract with the post or express shippers to provide last-mile delivery of some or all of its morning and/or afternoon parcels.

The model seems to capture what is going on: Amazon has made the point of not saying it will seek to replace UPS and FedEx, but rather looks to ensure fluid delivery during peak delivery times. It may be that future delivery systems will be such amalgams of ecommerce platforms and express shippers moving product, with cheaper P2P shipments going through posts.

At the end of the day, winners in the last-mile business will be those with data to optimize delivery. Besides Congo that can predict what John will buy before John even knows he is going to buy it, legacy carriers that have amassed enormous datasets across practically the entire planet have an edge over up-start regional or local services, and they are now leveraging it. It may also be that those that combine shipping and warehousing into a "mobile warehouse" are the ones that will upsell and cross-sell most: they can load noncommitted inventory into delivery trucks, allowing drivers to upsell during the delivery process. Do you want fries with that?

Closing in On the Holy Grail of World Trade

In the 1990s, ecologist Suzanne Simard found that trees in the forest spoke with each other.[66] They communicate their needs and send each other nutrients through a network of latticed fungi. Now at the University of British Columbia, she has found that trees send warning signals about environmental change, search for their kin, and transfer nutrients to nearby plants that are wither-ing. In other words, the forest is not great because it has a set of great trees neighboring each other; trees are great and strong because they cohabit a for-est. Living in a symbiosis and running like neural networks in human brain, they make each other better.

IBM has argued that our world consists of eleven core systems, such as transportation system and health care system.[67] Each system or ecosystem has many public and private sector organizations that span multiple industries. For example, the health care "forest" includes doctors, hospitals, pharmacies, insurers, researchers, drug manufacturers, regulators, and so on. It also includes huge inefficiencies: think of medical records in health care—need to enter the same data over and over, tremendous amount of paper and duplication, and lack of effective sharing of data.

These inefficiencies are systemic—they weigh on all parts of the system, whether insurance companies, receptionists, or the consumer herself, and everyone contributes to them. Electronic medical records that enable efficient sharing of data and stop re-entry information have cut hospitals' costs by over 3 percent in three years—but only in hospitals ready to use them, such as those with robust IT capabilities.[68] Analyzing GDPs and surveying economists, IBM has found that the world's systems have inefficiencies. Not just some—a total of $15 trillion, or 28 percent of worldwide GDP.[69] The consulted economists agreed that global savings could readily be possible for $4 trillion, the size of the entire South Asian continent's economy and almost the economy of Japan.

World trade is a complex system of systems, with tremendous slack, such as duplication of entries in paper-based letters of credit, mismatched timings between ports and truckers in picking and dropping cargo, erroneous and delayed invoicing between terminals and ocean liners, and tiny errors and misunderstandings brewing into costly inefficiencies. For example, shipping and logistics companies process over forty documents for a single shipment, and up to 70 percent of their data are reentered at least once, which takes time and increases the odds of errors.[70] As of 2017, 41 percent of all airway bills used by major airlines are electronic.[71] Data are often imputed by hand, prone to errors and low quality. Different databases need to be reconciled against each other and sources of discrepancies hunted down, many still by hand. Digitizing and simplifying this process can shave 20 to 30 percent off the exporter's shipping costs, and reduce the many emails and documents that need to be sent to different parties to orchestrate a shipment.[72]

Now, however, the world trading system is becoming more symbiotic. Each transport mode such as trucks and ships is becoming faster, cleaner, and safer, and each node such as port, warehouse, and distribution center is more digitized, automated, and efficient. Increasingly, the various modes and nodes are learning to collaborate and make each other better; talking machine to machine, they collaborate by feeding each other the critical nutrient—data—that enables each of them to do its job better. While still nascent, the symphony of interoperable modes and nodes is poised to provide the greatest gains yet to global commerce.

The quest for interoperability in trade is not new. For example, to ensure that national railroads connect seamlessly, in the 1850s English railway pioneer George Stephenson pushed to get the width of railroad gauges standardized at 4 feet 8 inches, or 1,422 mm, around the world. This standard is now used across North America, most of Europe, Australia, China, and the Middle East.[73] Electronic ticketing standards have enabled airlines, travel agents, airports, and system providers to seamlessly choreograph another kind of trade—the movement of business leaders and tourists around the planet.

Today's opportunities to squeeze out waste and increase speed in trade are in two places—port-city integration, as is happening in Hamburg, and interoperability among the various players in a given supply chain, such as the various ports and terminals, multiple logistics operators, and fulfillment centers and warehouses.

In 2005, a team of researchers in Canada conceptualized this connected future of global shipping as a "Physical Internet," a system that connects all players in global logistics and transport ecosystems—realization centers, distribution centers, warehouses, transit centers—much like how the Internet connected computers in the 1970s.[74] Just in the United States there are 535,000 warehouses and distribution centers; if each of them was connected to a giant database or Internet, producers, distributors, and retailers could move their products from and to multiple similarly dispersed yet networked centers in a more efficient manner. The whole could be more than the sum of the parts. Now connect customs, ports, ships, and trucks to this and you have a global virtual logistics highway.

Such a decentralized and interconnected system would help particularly small businesses, often with one-off small shipments and relatively random demand patterns. Yet this setting is tough to attain in the logistics industry, in which players operate in their own data siloes. Experts agree that standardization of systems, data, and messaging formats is perhaps at 10 percent from the optimal. But such integration is now happening, in two ways.

The first way is inside the vertically integrated liner services. Maersk after all is not just a liner service—it also has its own trucks, warehouses, freight forwarders, and containers. Similarly, Chiquita has its own vertically integrated supply chain specialized to moving bananas from farm in Honduras to store in Sweden. Terminal giant DP World no longer just operates terminals, but also orchestrates an app for hinterland logistics to be matched to and move cargo faster in and out of terminals and to the customer. These players have a more end-to-end view into shipments and generating efficiencies.

The second and potentially seminal solution to enable players in trade to coordinate is blockchain. Invented by one or a group of anonymous and brilliant individuals who in 2014 published its seminal open source code, blockchain is a mechanism to operationalize the Physical Internet. It enables all players on the chain to have a bird's-eye view of the entire trade transaction, access all documents related to it, and share data and information; all entries are immutable and updated on everyone's screens in real time. A sophisticated database that codifies all transactions into successive tamper-proof blocks, it enables players to look back and see where glitches may have occurred.

Maersk has created an elegant blockchain-based TradeLens platform poised to bring the entire trade ecosystem—shipping lines, warehouses, freight forwarders, ports, customs, exporters, importers, and trade finance banks—to speak to and interoperate with each other. The platform has been piloted with flowers from Kenya, mandarins from California, and pineapples from Colombia, all sailing to Rotterdam. Maersk has calculated that an exporter of cut flowers from Kenya needs to carry out two hundred separate communications involving thirty players such as farmers, freight forwarders, land-based transporters, customs brokers, governments, ports, and carriers to move a shipment to the Netherlands.[75] The TradeLens platform undoes most of this work.

Just about every major company in global logistics has a blockchain pilot or lab. Alibaba's T-Mall has adopted blockchain-based technology for its cross-border supply chain with logistics company Cainiao, whereby the parties can record information on exports and imports onto a blockchain that keeps track of the products' countries of origin, shipping and arrival ports, shipment methods, and customs information.[76] Korea's Samsung is using blockchain to move 488,000 tons of air cargo and over a million twenty-foot shipping containers annually, cutting shipping costs by a fifth and lowering time between the launch of a product and its shipping, enabling Samsung to respond fast to rivals' product launches.[77] In Singapore, PSA International, Pacific International Lines Ltd., and IBM Singapore have successfully used blockchain to execute bookings of multimodal logistics and regulatory compliance, and to track cargo movement from Chongqing, China, to Singapore.[78] End-to-end digitized trade transactions are also coming to Southeast Asians' doorsteps: Thailand Post is working with Thai railways to use blockchain to track high-value parcel deliveries, such as packages carrying expensive and luxury items.[79]

Port communities have also embraced blockchain as a means to enable all parties in port ecosystems to have visibility into events and to use smart contracts to automate billing and payment events, such as among freight forwarders and terminals and importers and customs. For example, the Port of Veracruz in Mexico is piloting blockchain to enable Mexican customs, Hutchison terminal, and customs brokers to gain visibility into products and processes. Last mile is also blockchained, with the technology heralded as a means to help track and regulate drone deliveries. The main barrier to blockchain's adoption in the global trade ecosystem is making a compelling business case for all stakeholders, for them to share data and collaborate with each other. There are two dilemmas to overcome. One, everyone wants to access more data but hesitates to share their own. And two, everyone benefits from a common blockchain platform but no one wants to pay for it. A company that decides to invest on a platform for the ecosystem will have hard time getting its competitors to sign up, but getting a set of companies in an ecosystem to invest in a common platform is also challenging, given that everyone has incentives to free-ride. Joint venture structures and consortia, though challenging to build, are the key structures to diffused blockchain use across the trade ecosystem. As players are already building their own ledgers, also needed are standards that enable different blockchain ledgers to interoperate. A shortcut may be a solution like the IADB's ingenious LACChain, essentially a motherboard for different emerging blockchain ledgers in Latin America to plug into and interoperate, without the need for onerous one-by-one bilateral negotiations among the operators of the different ledgers.

Blockchain-powered end-to-end digitization is also happening in trade finance, subject of the next chapter, with efficiencies equally as impressive as in trade logistics. We are closing in on the Holy Grail of world trade: integration, interoperability, and automation of the physical, informational, and financial supply chains that undergird world trade transactions. The result: faster movement of goods, savings of time and money to exporters and importers, and a better shot for small firms to trade across borders.

Conclusion

When picturing world trade, most people probably still think of containers serenely sailing across the ocean. This image is still accurate—but when you next see an ocean liner making its way or parking in a port, you will see a quiet revolution in progress. Both ships and the backend of global shipping are changing. We are nearing an era of end-to-end automated physical supply chains, with automated trucks, driverless ships, data-driven automated terminals and ports, and seamless sharing of data among the many players that touch any one shipment, powered by blockchain. Fewer humans and less fuel will be needed to move a container or parcel door to door. Shipping will be faster, cleaner, better, and safer, while being carried by many more players, such as tech companies and ecommerce platforms, than traditional operators. Whether the cost savings are passed to users after costs of new technologies are recouped remains a question mark—but the possibility and promise are there.

Another major shift is the rise of parcel-based trade: trade of the future will be increasingly carried in the bellies of planes and by drones flying over rooftops, cutting back road traffic and increasing access to products in remote areas and places without formal addresses. All you will need is a drone helipad.

$$\boxed{6}$$

FINDING $1.7 TRILLION

Imagine sitting in your living room in the 1980s seeking to buy jewelry from a merchant in Mexico. First, you may have found the jewelry in a catalogue that came in the mail, as there was no Internet. Second, you probably would never have sent an order slip and a check—would it ever arrive, and could your seller ever even cash it? Or perhaps you'll send dollar bills? Third, if the seller was able to get paid, might she still send the product to you? Is the product like it was in the picture? Does she even have the product?

Today, the considerations are somewhat different. Now, you will find the product from eBay or the merchant's website. You may be able to pay her by credit card or by PayPal. Then you wait and, like your 1980s self, wonder "What if they won't ship?" You can at least retaliate, such as write a scathing review on the seller's eBay site if she does not deliver, and perhaps get your money back. If, however, you promise to pay only when you get the product, the seller will likely never send it because she won't believe you will pay.

These very same cross-border payment challenges also have an impact on large multimillion-dollar shipments of wheat, iron ore, textiles, medical equipment, and thousands of other products. For centuries buyers have asked about sellers, "Will he deliver what he promised?" while sellers have asked, "Will he pay once I ship"? and "Will he pay on time?" Sometimes someone ships but no one pays. In 2012, Indian rice exporters went out of business after their Iranian buyer failed to pay for two hundred thousand tons of rice worth $144 million.[1] On the other side of the planet, a Chinese buyer of a U.S. company's medical devices disappeared into thin air once the devices were delivered. The company is still hoping to get paid.

The trust gap between buyers and sellers can be bridged by multiple transactions in which the two sides consistently stand by their promises. But rather than waiting for trust to build through repeated interactions, buyers and sellers have delegated to banks the task of ensuring the seller gets paid when the buyer gets the product. Banks do this by preparing and issuing letters of credit. Another instrument, trade credit insurance, issued by insurance firms, has been used to cover the seller in situations where she has agreed to give the buyer several weeks to pay for the shipment. Banks have also orchestrated supply chain finance systems in which they provide the cash for a large corporate buyer to pay its small suppliers faster than it otherwise could, and then ask the buyer to pay the cash back over time.

Such trade finance transactions have been oxygen to global commerce since Babylonians used cuneiform tablets in 3,000 BC as promissory notes and letters of credit. It was refined in 1,500 BC when Phoenician traders invented "factoring"—the purchase of accounts receivable at a discount that is still a huge global business. Though banks and factors have since taken over, not much changed for centuries: cross-border trade finance transactions remain paper-based and manual—and thus highly inefficient, slow, and susceptible to fraud, and also time- and labor-intensive to manage. Increasingly complex financial regulations add to a bank's already high costs of preparing the documentation for any one transaction, and incentivize banks to deal with larger companies that offer bigger deals and are well known. In small transactions, banks' fixed fees for international wires and foreign exchange rate management quickly whittle away profits. Now new online cross-border payment technologies, AI, and blockchain are finally disrupting this setting, opening an era of fluid and transparent trade transactions digitized end to end.

The Famous Trade Finance Gap

In 1970, George Akerlof published a seminal paper "The Market for Lemons," which showed that when sellers (of, say, used cars) know more about products than buyers do, buyers may believe sellers cheat (intend to sell the buyer a lemon while claiming to sell a great used car).[2] Since buyers can never be sure about the quality of the car, they are not willing to pay sellers the full price that "peaches," cars in good condition, would merit, and thus sellers bring only lemons to market. As a result, the market may simply break down and transactions never happen.

In ecommerce, such informational asymmetry is in part removed by user reviews of sellers that signal to potential buyers things about the seller's trustworthiness and the quality of his products, and by online dispute-settlement mechanisms that enable buyers to seek damages when a seller reneges. But in cross-border shipments, informational asymmetries are legion, and are a boon for banks, which essentially get paid by harvesting information on the buyer, seller, product, and transaction, and structure the transaction so that that all pieces fall into place and the seller gets paid when the buyer gets his shipment. And here is where the challenge lies: these informational demands on banks are getting heavier. Since the global financial crisis, due diligence costs have soared. The main culprit is know-your-customer and anti-money-laundering (KYC and AML) rules, which were cemented after the 9/11 terrorist attacks. Needing to hire KYC and AML staff and gain more internal approvals for any one loan, banks' fixed costs per loan have been growing, making small loans less attractive.[3] Nine out of ten banks say KYC and AML rules are a significant or very significant barrier for them to offer trade finance, making them more biased to large borrowers and existing customers.[4] In a 2016 Thompson Reuters global survey of 822 banks, the average bank spent $60 million on KYC and customer due diligence, with the total amount of time to onboard a new client rising at 20 percent annually.[5]

Small businesses are worst hit. Estimates place the global trade finance gap at $1.7 trillion. Half of this pent-up demand is in developing Asia, especially India and China, and most of it has an impact on SMEs. Banks have rejected about half of all SME trade finance requests, as opposed to 21 percent of the requests from large corporations.[6] Survey after survey shows that financing is the number one challenge to small businesses and a top-three challenge to mid-size companies looking to grow their businesses and export. And one culprit stands out: KYC and AML rules.

The economic impact of the unmet demand for trade finance is less trade, less hiring, and less production, and thus less demand for trade. According to the Asian Development Bank, 60 percent of companies that failed to get trade finance from banks never executed the trade transaction—and thus forewent export revenue, production increases, and job creation that might have resulted. However, once small businesses are able to access trade finance, they increase hiring by 20 percent and production by 30 percent.[7] A vast body of academic work shows that SMEs that access credit are far likelier to export than companies that don't get funding.[8]

Banks also struggle with information about each other. Trade finance often takes two to tango—for example, for the importer's bank to release funds, and the exporter's bank to get paid. Since they do not know where business might next come from, the world's largest banks maintain correspondent banking relationships with local banks in large cities around the world. But the correspondent bank is not always as great as it is hoped to be: the rise of developing countries in trade has forced the world's most venerable trade financiers to deal with developing-country banks they have not worked with much in the past or whose standards may be laxer.[9]

In 2016, 40 percent of banks surveyed by the ICC Banking Commission terminated correspondent relationships, and in 2015, 44 percent did, due to compliance concerns.[10] Adding risk on top of risk is that the newer correspondent banks are in markets where macroeconomic and political risks are higher than in advanced economies, which to bankers heralds a deal gone bad. Alisa DiCaprio and Ying Yao's studies show that counterparty risk is with KYC and AML issues a leading cause of the trade finance gap.[11]

Two years ago, my company was approached by a small business in Singapore that was running a $500,000 transaction of steel from China to Russia. The company had gone to every bank it knew to create a letter of credit with the bank of the Russian buyer to ensure that it would be paid when the steel shipment arrived in Russia. But it had not been able to—and putting yourself into the shoes of a bank helps you see why: to make the transaction work, you would need to get data on the parties and on the Russian bank, and still seek to make some money on the relatively small, $500,000 deal. Even a 15 percent cut might not be worth the risk and opportunity cost: after all, why not instead analyze a $50 million shipment with buyer, seller, and correspondent bank you already know very well?

The challenge gets especially great when two developing countries with a shoddy track record of contract enforcement trade with each other. A Federal Reserve Bank senior economist, Tim Schmidt-Eisenlohr, found that countries' exports increase when probabilities for successful enforcement of trade finance contracts are high, and decrease when financing costs rise.[12] Waiting increases uncertainty, and hence financing costs rise the slower the return. This means that companies in countries with weak judicial systems and inefficiencies in supply chains will have lower odds to get trade finance, at least at decent rates.

Thus two developing countries with high financing costs trade less with each other than a carbon-copy developing country pair with low financing costs.[13]

Not helping matters for SMEs is that in the aftermath of the 2008–2009 financial crisis, regulators forged the Basel III capital requirements that increased the amount of cash buffers banks need to retain (as the buffers bolster their solvency) and liquidity requirements (that are to ensure banks have funding when deposits are withdrawn). As a result of Basel, banks have less money to lend than they did before the crisis to smaller companies that are riskier and thus require a higher capital allocation than low-risk corporates. Macroeconomic conditions have compounded the problem. Banks build up their buffers principally through retained earnings, but in the postcrisis era of slow growth and zero or negative interest rates in most developed countries, banks' profitability fell and it was harder to build retained earnings—which means banks were loath to make risky loans, such as to small businesses.[14]

Stuck on Manual

The informational costs in trade finance are on full display in banks' handiwork when issuing a letter of credit, often a forty-page stack of paper. Bigger transactions can involve a ten-inch-thick pile of documents, run by many parties. The preparation of a letter of credit for one trade, say of soybeans from Brazil to China, can take six weeks, as both the exporter's and importer's banks need to fill and double-check the same documents by hand. Bain & Company estimates that 56 percent of banks' cost for a letter of credit arises from manual document handling and checking.[15] In addition, banks need to access as much information as possible about buyer, seller, and the transacted goods so as to mitigate the risk of fraud, counterfeit products, human trafficking, and other ills. The exporter tends to get paid only three to four weeks after the shipment is delivered, and the mere settlement takes as many as five days, as monies make their way through banks that are involved. Brad Garlinghouse, FinTech company Ripple's CEO based in San Francisco, summarized the exasperation that drove FinTech companies to cross-border payments as, "Why is it that we can literally stream video from the [International] Space Station, yet I can't move my own money from here to London? The fastest way for you to get money from here to London today is to get on an airplane."[16]

The trade finance ecosystem as a whole is extremely inefficient. All players in the transaction—importer, exporter, shipper, banks, and so on—have to maintain their own databases with all documents related to a transaction, such as the letter of credit, bill of lading, warehouse receipts and invoices, and so on. Exporters have to rekey information from the paper letter of credit for an invoice, the packing list, and many other documents multiple times, dealing with the multiple players in the trade process. Still, things fall through the cracks and errors and fraud happen all too much. In 2008, J.P. Morgan Chase was defrauded of almost $700 million with fictitious purchase orders and fake invoices used to get loans for non-existent metal shipments.[17] In 2014, Standard Chartered lost $197 million to a fraud in China's Qingdao port, where a Chinese businessman used invoices for the same metals stockpiles several times to extract payments of hundreds of millions of dollars from banks.[18]

While physical supply chains such as warehousing, shipping, and port operations have been digitizing for years, the informational and financial supply chains in trade are as analog as in the 1970s. The health care sector was once in a similar situation. Then it came up with electronic medical records that would rid the sector of the endless paper and duplication of work that anyone who has visited more than one doctor has experienced. The banking community's response to its growing paper mountains has been the electronic letter of credit and its close cousin, bank payment obligation. J.P. Morgan has estimated that electronic letters of credit would cut the labor costs of banks' trade finance departments by 30 percent and fees by 50 percent.[19] Bank of America has found that digitized applications for trade finance have reduced times of sales outstanding by 75 percent and fully eliminated discrepancies in documents.[20] The trade community also set out to do trials of electronic bills of lading (eBLs), a document that specifies the contents shipped and that travels with the product.

But even these small breakthroughs did not get widely adopted. In 2015, only 7 percent of banks reported that their trade finance processes had been digitized "to a great extent," while 43 percent reported "very little" advancement.[21] The reasons for bank's sluggish digitization were many, such as sheer inertia and lack of urgency thanks to steady intermediation fees; the fact explained by a senior banker to your author that most senior bankers lording over the industry want a stress-free glide to retirement without having to deal with digitization experiments with an uncertain ROI; and lack of trust in the integrity of data included in digital documents and systems. EBLs were controversial especially because it was not clear that the electronic version was the legal equivalent to a paper bill of lading. Interoperability too was a problem: users were locked into their eBL provider's walled garden, unable to use eBLs with players that preferred paper or with users of other walled gardens. That no one really moved made everyone stay put: trade finance is a networked system in which all parties—banks and their counterparty banks, shippers, ports, customs, exporters, and importers—need to be digitized, for any one digitized node to be able to harvest its investment in digitization. Why change and digitize if all other players are stuck on paper? And why do so if you keep making money?

The Blockchain Revolution

In around 2015, the status quo of analog systems was finally ruptured.

One change was the application of AI to digitize trade finance documents. In the flashiest example, in 2017 HSBC and IBM partnered to digitize the hundred million pages of paper that HSBC's trade finance mavens review and process manually each year. IBM rams through the semistructured information in the papers to extract the sixty-five fields of most relevant data, delivering a structured database customized to HSBC's transaction-processing systems.[22] IBM's robots are accomplished linguists, able to read French, Chinese, and Spanish, and thus remove one of the problems in the inherently multilingual world of trade finance—things that get lost in translation. Not only will this speed processes; it paves the way for automatic improvements and regulatory compliance. The AI program can, like a human being, learn from experience, detect anomalies, and adapt on the fly—and do so faster and more accurately than a human can.

The other major driver of change is interest among banks to work together to experiment with blockchain, which brings multiple parties on the same system to operate and transact digitally and read from the same hymnbook, as it were.

Blockchain is quietly disrupting the cross-border payments by removing the problems of risk, trust, cost, and speed that vex twenty-first-century global companies as much as they preoccupied Phoenicians. Blockchain-based transactions are secure and carried out among private parties, but also visible from the bird's-eye view to all market participants such as shippers, customs, and banks. This ends duplication of effort and melts paper mountains: since the blockchain database is fully up to date and reflects the most recent transaction, there is no need for multiple copies of the same documents, stored on different databases across various entities. Transactions can accelerate dramatically: unlike wire transfers that can take a number of days to clear, chocking the exporter's cash flow, payments go through in seconds, just like emails. They can even be automated: a smart contract can trigger payments from buyer to seller based on the location of the good on its journey.[23] No one needs to make a call, press a button, or sign on the dotted line—all that's needed is an electronic signal, and the transaction is settled in seconds.

Blockchain has emerged as a solution in numerous areas, such as securing remittance payments, affirming property rights, and tracing products in the supply chain. But it can be especially transformative in trade finance, an industry with extremely high intermediation costs and constant worries about fraud. The pioneering blockchain applications included Singapore's DBS and Standard Chartered's 2015 proof of concept in trade finance invoicing, and the Commonwealth Bank of Australia and Wells Fargo's 2016 pilot to orchestrate a $35,000 payment for a shipment of cotton from Texas to Qingdao, China. In the latter case, the parties also experimented with smart contracts that automated the release of payments when goods hit their destination port.[24]

Since then, many have joined the fray. Bank of America Merrill Lynch, HSBC, and the Infocomm Development Authority of Singapore launched a blockchain prototype that mirrors a letter-of-credit transaction.[25] In Europe, Banco Santander, Deutsche Bank, HSBC, KBC, Natixis, Rabobank, Societe Generale, and UniCredit announced a blockchain system called "we.trade" to streamline trade finance transactions in Europe. In a push to help developing-country farmers get trade finance, IBM has partnered with BBVA and several Asian banks to test drive blockchain in twelve currency corridors across the Pacific Islands and Australia, New Zealand, and the United Kingdom. The consortium's litmus test is to enable a small farmer in Samoa to enter into a trade contract with a buyer in Indonesia that is written on a smart contract.[26]

Reflecting on the blockchain fervor, in 2017 IBM published a two-hundred-bank study that characterized banks as racehorses "hurtling toward blockchain."[27] The hurtling has been happening for a few reasons: blockchain helps banks deal with fraud, access real-time data on trade transactions, and gain visibility into SMEs in particular. Banks have opted to disrupt before they get disrupted.

As the shared ledger of transactions is immutable and maintained by computers, blockchain can also drastically reduce the time and documentation spent on KYC checks. At the moment, every financial institution in a transaction has to carry out its own KYC checks, meaning that the same customer could be diligenced five or six times in any one transaction. Granted, there do exist the SWIFT KYC Registry, formed in 2014 with more than two thousand bank members, and the large KYC registry KYC.Com, which banks can peruse to perform due diligence when a customer requests a new transaction. A blockchain-based registry would remove the need of KYC checks by multiple parties to a transaction, while creating an immutable audit trail of the activities of each user that can be shown to regulators demanding to see KYC analytics. In the blockchain hotbed of Southeast Asia, OCBC Bank, HSBC, IMDA, and Mitsubishi UFJ Financial Group have successfully completed a proof of concept for a KYC blockchain. The main benefit is the end of duplication: customers need to provide their information only once; all parties can access the same information in real time and digitally; and all information is secure and immutable, reducing concerns of errors and fraud and odds of actual criminal events.[28] Blockchain can be used similarly in AML checks and combatting the financing of terrorism.

The more intrepid developing countries have gotten on the chain. In Thailand, fourteen Thai banks, in cooperation with three state enterprises and four corporations, has created a common letter-of-credit platform to handle tens of billions of dollars of trade finance.[29] The system is tested in the Bank of Thailand's regulatory sandbox that enables new innovations to be brought to market faster than they would under a standards process. The banks expect that that platform will halve their operating costs. Digitizing the documents and shifting them to the blockchain can reduce the turnover time from days to a mere thirty minutes.[30] And by cutting out the middlemen and boosting efficiency, blockchain and smart contracts built on it could reduce Thai banks' overhead and infrastructure costs by $15 billion to $20 billion annually through 2022, and lower the odds of error and inconsistencies.[31]

Thailand's Electronic Transactions Development Agency says that it is now looking for ways to allow the use of blockchain-powered smart contracts, a fitting complement to blockchain-based trade finance platforms. A world in which informational and financial supply chains in trade (such as trade finance contracts) are married with physical supply chains (such as sensors emitting data on products' locations) is near. Exporters and importers are increasingly using sensors, the younger and more reliable brother of RFID, that stream information about the humidity, temperature, location, rough treatment, and tampering of their products sailing across an ocean. Weaving these movement data into the blockchain would not only give all parties the comfort of knowing where the goods are and how they are doing, but can also enable smart contracts to execute a payment to the seller or exporter when goods are in the importer's possession.

On their part, blockchain startups have been getting into trade finance, but while they have the technology, they lack the vast networks of users banks have, let alone multiple banks bunched together. Now the two are coming together. For example, Barclays and Israeli FinTech startup Wave partnered to use blockchain in a $100,000 shipment of cheese and butter from Irish cooperative Ornua to the Seychelles Trading Company.[32] Standard Chartered has tested Ripple's enterprise blockchain platform to run a pilot with an unnamed "major correspondent bank." The transaction was completed in less than ten seconds, or 17,280 times faster than the forty-eight hours needed by the bank's typical trade finance transaction.[33] Ripple claims its blockchain protocol lowers international payment infrastructure costs by 33 percent and its digital asset XRP by another 9 percent.[34]

Asian governments have been particularly active supporters of blockchain in trade finance. For example, People's Bank of China has expressed support for blockchain to help combat chronic fraud in trade finance deals. The Hong Kong Monetary Authority (HKMA) and the Monetary Authority of Singapore (MAS) have gone further to implement the Global Trade Connectivity Network, a platform that enables bilateral trade finance flows. Other countries that want to tag onto the network can do so by connecting their own blockchain system to the HKMA-MAS platform.[35]

Of course such experiments are only as useful as the data keyed into the blockchain—just like any database, blockchain has the garbage-in-garbage-out problem. Humans are the most typical contributors to the garbage—they make errors in entering numbers in databases, mishear the numbers floated by a French colleague on the phone, and are tempted to massage numbers for their own benefit. This problem however does have solutions. One is technology that spots garbage. For example, Singaporean FinTech Trade Finance Market has a new product called Invoice Check that uses artificial intelligence to spot a fraudulent trade invoiced on the blockchain. Another solution is what we might call peer monitoring: since blockchain provides real-time encrypted updates of client details to the banks in the system, any bank can also in real time alert others of suspicious activity.

Still another solution is to take the human being out of the equation and use machine-generated data as input into the blockchain. Machines after all are much more reliable and tenacious in recording events such as temperature in a warehouse or drawing the right numbers from a contract, doing an objective job, and losing little in translation when conversing with a fellow machine across the ocean.

Chaining the Supply Chain

Letters of credit are the ages-old way in which exporters got paid by importers. But they have been falling out of favor in recent years, as importers increasingly demand payment terms—that is, rather than paying when goods hit the port, they want to pay only in thirty, sixty, or even ninety days. Since exporters see the ability to offer payment terms as a competitive advantage they tend to seek to offer it, forcing other exporters to do the same. Up to 45 percent of trade transactions by value and 80 percent of transactions by volume are on open account terms.[36] Yet as the importer delays payment on a large order, the exporter's cash flow suffers, making it difficult for him to purchase the supplies and labor to fulfill new orders. In response, corporate importers and banks have devised a solution to help SME suppliers: supply chain finance.

Supply chain finance is reverse factoring, as opposed to the factoring invented by Phoenicians, in which the supplier would sell their receivables (unpaid invoices) at a discount to factors, to get paid faster than their client was prepared to do so. In the typical supply chain finance transaction, a corporate buyer helps the small business supplier access more affordable credit through a third-party financier. Demand for supply chain finance exploded during the financial crisis as governments and companies wanted to fuel SMEs amid the credit crunch. For example, in the United Kingdom in 2013, three dozen corporations such as Rolls-Royce, Vodafone, and General Dynamics created a supply chain program in which they notify a bank when an invoice to an SME supplier has been approved for payment; the bank is then able to offer a 100 percent immediate advance to the supplier at low interest rates, knowing the invoice will ultimately be paid by the large corporation with a strong credit rating.[37] Corporate clients like supply chain finance as a means to keep their suppliers stable and reliable.

Supply chain finance is especially valuable in developing countries, where small business suppliers have a harder time using their accounts receivables with the larger buyer as a base for lending money from a bank or selling the receivable to a factor. For example, Brazil's energy giant Petróleo Brasileiro, or Petrobras, has partnered with the six largest retail banks in Brazil to help its SME suppliers access credit based on the receivable from Petrobras, which has a triple A rating that banks then lean on. And realizing the power of supply chain finance to promote the hundreds of thousands of American SMEs that supply large American exporters, such as Boeing, Caterpillar, and Case

Holland, the U.S. Export-Import (EXIM) Bank enables SME suppliers to receive early payment of their accounts receivable in exchange for a small discount fee that is paid to the lender. The EXIM Bank provides a 90 percent guarantee of the invoices while the lender, such as Citibank for Boeing suppliers, bears 10 percent of the risk.

While it is every small business's dream to score a big contract with a large global buyer, the sale may choke a small business's cash flow if the large buyer does not process the payment promptly. The waiting period between shipping a large order and waiting for the payment to come can be like crossing the Sahara for a small company—which after all needs continuous free cash flow to pay staff, purchase new supplies to produce new orders, and cover ongoing business expenses such as rent and loan repayments. It can of course always borrow against its accounts receivable from the large buyer, but only if and when such a supply chain finance solution is available. The global unmet demand for supply chain finance is massive, estimated at $700 million, and contributing to the global trade finance gap. Where does it come from?

One gap is supply chain finance for second- or third-tier suppliers.[38] For now, the corporate supply chain finance programs focus on first-tier suppliers such as the maker of airplane seats, but do not travel to the second or third tier, such as to companies that make the handles, the faux leather, or the frames for the seats. First-tier suppliers get paid, but there are glitches and delays in payments to lower tiers, which is a risk boomeranging back to the corporate buyer in suppliers' inability to deliver. The bank has great visibility into the first-tier supplier, but not the supplier's suppliers—which are often smaller businesses with more fragilities than the first-tier supplier. Another challenge is cross-border supply chain finance: domestic supply chains in countries such as the United States or Brazil are massive, but in smaller countries, suppliers are often selling to a foreign company. The fact that these suppliers are abroad makes it harder to diligence them.

Still another challenge is banks' exodus from developing countries. In their efforts to assuage shareholders' concerns about their ability to make money, banks have announced they would be "derisking," a sanitized term for a great exit from developing countries as AML rules tightened in 2014, by way of breaking correspondent relationships. Countries such as Vietnam, Bangladesh, Cambodia, and Sri Lanka house an array of large corporations whose supplier base is fragile due to lack of liquidity.[39]

Now drop blockchain into this game. Imagine every tier of suppliers chained to the same blockchain, with every transaction carried out by a smart contract with clear triggering conditions, such as verified receipt of supplied goods. The first-tier supplier that gets, say, $10 million in payment automatically passes a fraction, say $2 million, to the second-tier suppliers, which in turn automatically pay third-tier suppliers their respective $200,000, for example.[40] Suddenly the entire financing food chain is automated, transparent, and a place for every player to build up their immutable history. Because the bank that expedites the payment can see both the original contract between the corporate client and its first-tier supplier, the order placed with the second-tier company by the first-tier company, the orders placed by second-tier companies with third-tier companies, et cetera, it can verify both the authenticity of the contracts and the provenance of the products. Meanwhile, the corporate client can be more certain that its supply chains are stable and run smoothly.

The idea of chained contracts and automated payments is not new. In 1999, Citigroup, British research business DCE, and Germany's SAP sought to address these problems by forming a joint venture, Orbian, an electronic payment system that would allow a buyer to pay a supplier with Orbian Credit, which could then be used by the supplier to pay its own suppliers in real time, and so on, without an actual currency. The idea was ahead of its time and has succeeded in part—by 2014, the company had three dozen supply chain finance programs, including with Fortune 1000 clients such as General Mills and Siemens, and four thousand other customers.[41] Blockchain has the potential to dramatically expand it, and make it more sophisticated. This is already happening. For example, Indian multinational conglomerate and lender Mahindra has partnered with IBM to run a blockchain pilot for supply chain finance among cash-strapped Indian suppliers.[42]

Are Smart Contracts Smart?
Challenges to Work Through

Blockchain is revolutionizing trade finance, but just like any technology, it still has growing pains.[43] For example, while blockchain can generate enormous efficiencies in executing trade finance contracts, smart contracts still need technical work to work optimally—one study found that some 3.4 percent, or thirty-four thousand out of one million, of Ethereum smart contracts are vulnerable to hacking.[44] Work also needs to be done to reconcile the assumptions contract writers make about the semantics associated with a contract execution, and the semantics of the smart contract system.[45] For example, a smart contract does not have the human intuition to judge the behavior or intentions of parties. One example that is used is whether parties to a merger agreement have made "reasonable efforts" to secure regulatory approvals.[46] A smart contract does not know the difference between reasonable and unreasonable. Writers of smart contracts thus need to be mindful that they are not writing contracts that other lawyers interpret, but those that a machine simply executes—and thus need to understand how the semantics they use can be interpreted by the smart contract. Meanwhile, creators of smart contract systems need to learn to think the way contract writers think.

Another major area that needs to be worked on is the security and access to blockchain systems. Think of a bank with a number of authorized users of the blockchain data: the blockchain can be damaged by just one person who has access to it. Who then should be able to access the data on the blockchain? Should they be able to access it in full or in part?

To answer these types of questions, the blockchain manager would need to balance many considerations. One is security and accessibility: for example, to control access, the bank might want to have passwords to a computer and data in an encrypted format, yet enable staff to easily access data.[47] Another major technical question is the interaction of a legacy database with a blockchain's database. Clearly it would be ideal to get all data on a blockchain fast if it is the case that blockchain provides superior business insight and connections—and it is increasingly possible to run the same queries and analytics in on-chain and off-chain data systems. But it could be that exporting on-chain data to an off-chain database renders the data vulnerable to alteration.

Technology firms and researchers recognize that data security and pooling, translating, and optimizing the sets of data on- and off-chain are challenges to work through.[48] Blockchain companies also have great incentives to solve these technical problems, to ensure the technology diffuses more widely.

Still another major challenge, and one that is particularly an issue in international trade finance, is interoperability of ledgers. Just like a social media network with individual users or an ecommerce platform of independent buyers and sellers, blockchain's value tends to grow as its user base scales. However, there will not be one global blockchain in any domain; rather, multiple blockchain systems are sprouting up around the world in all kinds of sectors. While this experimentation is very positive, it also implies that any one user, whether a business or a person, may end up being part of many blockchain systems, each with its own technology and governance. And it is likely that the data systems or "schema" of different networks will not always integrate and talk to each other well, preventing users of chain A from interacting with those of chain B.

Mishaps can also happen. For example, one blockchain records an entity or a user's data one way, while another records the same data referring to the same entity or user in another way. A fragmented system of multiple ledgers that are disconnected from each other would result in a world of operational silos, or "digital islands," in which users would need to sign up on many systems at once, to be able to transact with different parties for different purposes.

There are many realms with the same problem of "islands" or "walled gardens" that need to be interconnected, for all users of one garden to be able to interact with users of other gardens. How software talk to one another is through APIs. But this does not always work. A prominent problem in ecommerce in developing countries, where most people do not have credit cards and many do not have access to bank accounts or PayPal, is that a buyer and seller using different payment systems cannot easily transact with each other—both are only able to transact with buyers or sellers sharing the same network within their respective walled garden. This is clearly a suboptimal setting.

Connecting blockchains to build a larger ecosystem takes willingness by blockchain managers to integrate with each other and scale their user bases, as well as common data management and transfer rules and agreements on governance of the connected system. In other words, there is a need for interoperability standards for blockchains in trade finance. Several such interoperability standard processes are on the way or contemplated—your author is a cofounder of one of them called Digital Standards for Trade, in Singapore. Another possible solution is smart contracts that run across multiple blockchains.[49] While the International Organization for Standardization is working on blockchain standards across many realms, including trade supply chains and finance, the private sector needs to keep moving and setting voluntary interoperability standards. World trade is a giant network of traders that do not respect the boundaries of blockchain consortia; rather, it is the consortia that must come together to mimic and enable the network.

Conclusion

People and banks have for centuries monetized risk in trade, whether nonpayment by the buyer or a vessel's toppling in high seas. In ancient Greece, traders moving cargo took so-called maritime loans from wealthier Athenians to purchase their cargo. The interest rate was hefty, up to 30 percent, and the vessel was the collateral.[50] Nothing had to be repaid in case the ship did not make it to the destination. Today the rules of the game are somewhat different but the basic idea remains the same: there are information asymmetries between buyers and sellers and unforeseeable events that may impede goods from leaving or arriving as intended, and the instruments for dealing with these calamities are not too different from what they were in ancient Greece. Only now they can be delivered faster and more efficiently, on the back of technologies ancient Greeks may have envisioned but were hard-pressed to develop quickly.

Blockchain is a seminal, foundational technology that is transforming economic and social interactions, including trade. It can have its greatest gains in trade finance, where it can bridge the global trade finance gap and help SMEs engage in trade, by lowering companies' intermediation costs and fueling their cash flow. Proofs of concept on small trade transactions also appear very positive; in practice, much of the impact is still invisible, trapped in forthcoming use cases of the various blockchain experiments. For the technology to work requires two things—technology and network of users. Both exist; now they need to be assembled and pulled together—and then cyber risks need to be managed for adoption to accelerate.

7

THE BIG QUERY

In the movie *Hidden Figures*, based on a true story from the 1960s, three brilliant African American women pioneered in mathematics and computer science at NASA to help in putting a man in space and then others on the moon. The Apollo spaceship that landed on the moon in 1969 needed their intelligence: Apollo itself had only as much computing power as two Nintendo games.

Since that time, computing power has shot up dramatically. Not long before Neil Armstrong was bouncing on the moon, Intel co-founder Gordon Moore wrote his famous law that suggested the performance of computer hardware would double every eighteen months. And double it has: today many USB memory sticks are claimed to have more computing power than the computers that put man on the moon, and the Singularity, the moment when machine intelligence will be as supple as human intelligence, has become a real prospect. Especially impactful, computing power has become much more diffused. By the 1990s, cloud computing was enabling even small companies to access cloud-based pay-per-use services and data analytics previously available only to NASA and large companies. Then came smart everything: a mobile computer in the shape of a Tesla, a flying computer in the form of an Airbus, and a cleaning computer in the form of a smart washer.

Now we are verging on an era of mass diffusion of a technological feat: cognitive computing. Artificial intelligence (AI) makes companies better at optimizing, matching, and predicting, to a good extent without much human involvement. And it enables extracting information from data that are messy and unstructured, and recognizing patterns in it. It is powered by the stunning growth of the global datasphere, the qualitative and quantitative data inside and outside enterprises—33 times more than in 2008 by 2018, and 175 times more than in 2010 by 2025.[1] In 2019, global Internet traffic is equivalent to 142 million people streaming Internet HD video simultaneously, all day, every day.

Increase in data and computing power are rapidly disrupting world trade. The prior chapters have described Amazon's urban logistics and Alibaba's matching of buyers to products, both of which are powered by big data, AI, and predictive analytics. Companies are far better placed than just ten years ago to spot new markets and micromarkets, target and market to foreign customers, orchestrate their global operations, and manage their supply chains—including to forecast and avert the next tornado or tsunami. Trade flows and products traded are more visible and traceable in real time than ever before. It is still possible to get things very wrong in cross-border business. But it has also never been quite as difficult to be wrong.

Dark Arts of Global Marketing

In 1997, Reed Hastings and Marc Randolph started a DVD rent-by-mail website, Netflix, aimed at competing with the $3 billion behemoth Blockbuster. Netflix helped people who had been going to stores to rent videos first as VHS tapes and then as DVDs get their movies through the mail instead. The company soon hit the curse of the riches: demand was not matched by the number of DVDs of new releases in the inventory. To solve the problem without unnecessarily beefing up its inventory, Netflix developed an algorithm based on members' interests that helped predict items that would be in high demand and tailor marketing to user's preferences. Today, Netflix is primarily a streaming service, entertaining a 160 million users worldwide. Its success is based on the predictive analytics it created early in the DVD era.

The streaming service has also considerably beefed up Netflix's database: it generates a billion data points each year that it uses to tighten its algorithms and feed fully customized content to each registered user. It is playing especially in the long-tail of viewers, offering movies that may never become mainstream, but that algorithms suggest a user might enjoy. And by knowing what users want before they do, Netflix can develop its own content, which users then end up wanting. Netflix can do all this because it is digital. Or try serving a hundred million users with a rent-by-mail site.

Netflix was an early mover in a field of psychographics and microtargeting that has disrupted global marketing of goods, services, ideas, and politicians. Psychographics study consumers on the basis of their activities, interests, and opinions, "AIO" in marketing speak. While demographics would see only dramatic differences between a twenty-two-year-old college grad male in Paris getting his first job in an multinational advertisement agency and a seventy-nine-year-old female in northern Arizona who sits on four nonprofit boards combatting climate change, psychometrics might see a persona: both actually love ashtanga yoga and strawberry smoothies, donate to the World Wildlife Fund, friend Barack Obama on Facebook, and write Tweets aimed to appeal to logic (rather than emotion, say). Both might be the perfect target for a company selling yoga mats made of ocean plastics and susceptible to marketing that lays out logical reasons for purchasing the mat.

While psychographics was already discussed by American marketers in the 1980s, the difference between then and now is data provided by the Internet: companies can both find these personas (such as through sifting through their customer data, doing online surveys with their users, or even parsing their discussions with natural language processing) and target them (such as microtargeting them on Facebook) much faster. In the online era, serving a niche market can be big global business.

In contrast, in the past companies would size up in other countries the demographic groups that made up their customer base at home and then start marketing to them, using roughly the same approaches as in their home market. This had sorry results. Frank Lavin, former U.S. Undersecretary of Commerce and now the CEO of Export Now, which helps U.S. companies expand to China by ecommerce, recounts in his book stories of well-intentioned American businessmen who got a lead from Mexico, hopped onto a plane with a contract, and expected to fly back with a deal done—when the Mexican prospect was just getting started, wanting to build a relationship and converse on families and hobbies, and perhaps get to the transactional work in some months.[2] This "more of the same" syndrome has been perhaps the number one reason why American companies fail to globalize their offerings.

The Dollar Shave Club, the Los Angeles–based seller of subscription-based grooming devices, used the dark arts of psychographics to pave the way to its 2017 sale to Unilever for $1 billion. In its early days, the Dollar Shave Club ran a self-deprecating video, "Our Blades Are F***ing Great," to get online shoppers' attention—and attention it got: the video went viral so fast that it crashed the company's server in the first hour. When the company was further along, it used AI to uncover patterns that elude human analysts—such as which customers were worthy of marketing dollars and which were not serious about buying more, and which could use some extra love to stay on. To reduce abandonment and churn in the customer base, the Dollar Shave Club married customer exit survey data with transactional, behavioral, and demographic data to build a profile of users who canceled their subscriptions; this enabled it to identify users that were about to jump ship but that were worth holding onto.[3] It then built a new cadence and personalized messaging for each of these customers. This drive increased the resubscribe rate five-fold. It was not an outlier: McKinsey estimates that targeted, customized campaigns deliver five to eight times higher return investment and ten times more sales than one-size-fits-all campaigns.[4] Cambridge Analytica infamously used similar psychographics to place American voters in types defined by the Big 5 OCEAN personality traits—openness, conscientiousness, extraversion, agreeableness, and neuroticism—which enabled it to better target and tailor political propaganda by these psychological traits.

Taming Bullwhip

Ability to forecast and preempt customer whims is not just a boon for online marketers: it is nirvana for supply chain managers who want to minimize inventory costs (which can take up to 30 percent of the value of the inventory) but maximize responsiveness to customers. Most typically, the guesstimate of the amount of supply that would satisfy both objectives is off. As a result, companies have suffered from the "bullwhip effect," when the havoc caused by sudden changes in customer behaviors magnifies across the entire global supply chain all the way to raw material purchases from another side of the world.

When demand unexpectedly falls, bullwhip means that companies are left with obsolete inventories; when demand unexpectedly spikes, companies lack inventory and lose sales. In a study of 4,689 public U.S. companies between 1974 and 2008, two-thirds suffered from bullwhip, typically due to overoptimistic sales forecasts—that ended up costing $80 million each year in excess inventories.[5] The cause of bullwhip may not always even reside in intemperate shoppers. For example, the unusually mild temperatures that pervaded 2015 left Macy's with an 80 percent drop in its winter clothing sales and a huge excess inventory.

Granted, businesses have for decades used just-in-time techniques and lean manufacturing, Kanban, and other methods to coax profit out of their supply chains and inventories. And much like Netflix in the land of content, Amazon's anticipatory shipping technique has for years predicted customer demand for products in specific locations based on such factors as the customer's previous purchases and online searches—thereby helping Amazon build up inventory for products that will soon be in demand in a given location. But the explosive growth of data by and about the consumer enables also manufacturers to tame bullwhip. Manufacturers and retailers such as Siemens and Pirelli use point-of-sale data, unstructured data such as social media chatter to forecast consumer whims worldwide. Recent studies suggest demand forecasting is a much easier and effective way to deal with bullwhip, especially when using such cutting-edge methods as artificial neural network forecast accuracy (as opposed to traditional methods such as naive forecasting or moving average).[6] What seems to make a particular difference is the velocity of data, such as real-time access to point-of-sale data, as opposed to the volume and variety of data.[7]

Third-party data improve the possibilities for such demand sensing: for example, manufacturers and retailers can use weather data on how Mother Nature's moods shape shoppers' choice of clothing, price data on how price levels and shifts impact shoppers' future purchases, and AI-processed real-time images of inventory on store shelves to better react to demand spikes.

The Holy Grail for dealing with supply chain disturbances would be to break data silos—integrate data across all players in the supply chain from manufacturers, distributors, resellers, suppliers, and so on, to gain an end-to-end visibility. This has been a tough nut to crack: the various players have different incentives and are jealous of their data, and their datasets cannot easily be integrated. The advent of blockchain could change this—if blockchain champions can identify a business model in which there is something for everyone. Indeed, the biggest challenges facing blockchain's adoption in global supply chains is not the technology or its installation; rather, it is finding the formula in which every player has a meaningful value proposition to join the chain.

Datafying the Bottom of the Pyramid

In 2006, C. K. Prahalad published *Fortune at the Bottom of the Pyramid*, which opened Western companies' eyes to opportunities with hundreds of millions of poor people in the developing world, ready to purchase Western goods if only their unique constraints, such as annual incomes of $1,500, were met. Those types of consumers are unlikely to save large sums of money or be able to buy in bulk—so companies such as P&G, Colgate-Palmolive, and Unilever developed smaller packet sizes for their products to sell them for less than they would in the developed world.[8]

The book became a hit. But soon enough companies realized that knowing about a new market opportunity was one thing; devising a profit-making product offering for the price-conscious, logistically challenging developing market was completely another. The biggest hurdle of all was to understand the incentives and behaviors of the poor who seemed not to want things that common sense seemed to dictate were "good for them." For example, consumers in sub-Saharan Africa avoided using insecticide-treated bed nets created by such companies as Sumitomo Chemical, even if the nets are extremely simple to use and great at preventing malaria. Granted, the nets add heat—but they could not be easier to hang or take down. Similar challenges faced companies such as SC Johnson, which went to market in Nairobi slums with a "clean and healthy homes" slogan. It did not work, reportedly because consumers were so accustomed to their indecorous environments and ways of cleaning.[9]

Many a multinational went through such schools of hard knocks, bringing to market solutions from crop insurance to detergents that on paper made perfect sense but in practice never worked. Western companies frequently lost business to local rivals with a more intuitive feel for local markets, behaviors, and bottlenecks. Antoine van Agtmael's 2007 book *The Emerging Markets Century: How a New Breed of World-Class Companies Is Overtaking the World* argued that emerging market businesses such as Samsung of Korea, Haier of China, or Infosys in India would be better placed than Western companies to understand and operate in the rough and tumble of developing countries.[10]

Anecdotes seemed to confirm van Agtmael's hypothesis. For example, Huawei has excelled in Africa and Asia because it learned to play in frontier markets by starting out in the then-developing Chinese market. India's Tata motors has thrived in Africa, Latin America, and Asia. Sri Lanka–based ecommerce platform Kapruka has developed an app called Grasshopper for its sellers to navigate the complexities of South Asian cross-border logistics, a tool it is now scaling in East Africa, which has similar logistics challenges. The business model might never occur to entrepreneurs in Manhattan who are not exposed to low-income countries' ecommerce markets.

Now data are blunting the edge that locals have for intuiting the incentives and constraints of hard-to-reach developing country shoppers. The Colorado-based GeoPoll surveys two hundred million poor mobile phone users in Africa and Asia about their product preferences through SMS, voice, and mobile web, to bring companies such as Coca-Cola and Unilever up to speed on consumer fads and brand loyalty in South Africa, TV viewing habits in Kenya, and the behaviors and needs of maize farmers in Tanzania.[11] The rise of local digital businesses has created an army of boots-on-the-ground second-party data partners for Western businesses. For example, Coca-Cola has partnered with Rappi, a wildly popular Colombian meal delivery app that has evolved into an app of on-demand services, to understand where the likeliest Coca-Cola drinkers in Bogota and Medellin are and what they want and when.

Price data too are now available in real time, for companies to see their global competitors' prices even in distant markets and adjust on the fly. For example, the Chicago-based Dynamite Data recently acquired by Market Track crawls through a billion ecommerce buy pages in fifty-four countries at more than three thousand online retailers, generating real-time online and in-store price data for Fortune 1000 companies across countless verticals such as HD monitors in Ecuador or cars in Thailand.

Data pipes are also already in place to excavate offline price data—think of bananas and canned beans with prices on a sticker in developing-country supermarkets, or little posters of prices placed on the potato basket or peanut bowl in a Tanzanian open market. The San Francisco–based Premise, brimming with prestigious board members such as Larry Summers, keeps tabs on prices expressed in analog format. Using an army of part-time laborers to take pictures of the prices of thousands of food and other consumer products in the developing world's open air markets and supermarkets, Premise creates a giant stream of price data of interest to global businesses and to central banks that want to preempt approaching inflationary spikes and food crises.

Could sudden political crises in developing countries also be predicted better? In 2000, Zimbabwe seized 110,000 square kilometers of land from white farmers and redistributed it to black farmers. Never mind that the land mostly ended up in the hands of loyalists of president Mugabe's political party and that agricultural production fell by 3 percent—foreign investors were blindsided and spooked enough to stop investing completely. After all, who knew what Mugabe might precipitate tomorrow? Almost two decades later, investors were caught off guard by Brexit and the Trump presidency, and minor earthquakes such as Italy's 2018 political turbulence.

Political risk has long been the domain of pipe-smoking think tankers with thirty years of experience in a specific country and firms such as Eurasia Group that in many ways created the political risk industry by supplying Wall Street with forecasts of market-moving election results and tensions that could brew into the next Arab Spring. Now political risk is also quantified and "AI'd." For example, Eurasia spin-off Geocast uses artificial intelligence to plow through data on 250 variables based on online sources such as news and policy papers to forecast everything from coups and chaos to the more mundane, such as presidential race results in Chile. The Defense Department's DARPA is contracting experts for machine learning and other systems to predict geopolitical risks. While we may need to wait for results to come in, to compare the insight to that of political risk scholars such as Ian Bremmer and Condoleezza Rice, the field is ripe for disruption.

Walls Have Ears

In the world of Grubhub, Instacart, and Amazon, it is easy to forget that over 90 percent of our shopping is in physical retail, just like in the 1970s. What is also perhaps surprising is that digital natives are establishing storefronts, for consumers to touch and feel the products and, alas, to gather more data on the consumer. For example, Warby Parker, the business that disrupted the sleepy eyewear business with snazzy frames sold online, has built a set of physical stores. It initially used the stores for marketing, before realizing that shoppers used the off- and online channels the other way around: 75 percent of its in-store visitors had first toured its website. Warby's brick-and-mortarization started humbly enough: the company initially converted a yellow school bus into an august mobile shop complete with dark wood shelving and old books, and sent it on a class trip across America. It parked in random places in cities, to find where stores would thrive.[12] Today, Warby is considered the king of geolocational data—it uses 129 variables and foot traffic trails from more than 2.5 million Americans to determine where to place a store to maximize foot traffic and growth potential. Knowing who buys glasses where, when, and why is one reason why Warby Parker is now predicted to be among the top three Amazon acquisitions.[13]

Warby is not the first to use granular data that have revolutionized retailers' ability to choose a storefront. In 2014, Starbucks started to systematically use locational data to figure out the next locations for Starbucks, without cannibalizing its other locations in the same city. It has data on demographics, property markets, competition, purchasing power, and behaviors in neighborhoods, which it uses to identify patterns and drivers not readily discernable by human analysts to forecast demand for different offerings such as lattes and sodas. And it then uses data in stores to generate email campaigns and new offerings that appeal to its particular neighborhood.

Franchises can also use foot traffic forecasts to preempt customer disenchantment. Battling an E.coli outbreak in January 2016, Chipotle started to track supplier and supply data on the cloud, a good move. But Chipotle still struggled to use data to predict and preempt the fallout in consumer perceptions. Those that did cast dark clouds with great accuracy. In the spring of 2016, Foursquare CEO Jeff Glueck, armed with check-in and foot traffic data from Chipotle's and other restaurants, announced on CNBC that Chipotle's sales would fall by 29 percent in the first quarter.[14] Two weeks later, Chipotle reported sales had fallen 29.7 percent.

And this is the difference from the four walls of the 1970s and today: today walls have ears. In fact they are built to *be* ears. In Amazon's new experimental supermarket inside its Seattle headquarters, customers go in and shop for groceries and other goodies as they did as children—with the difference being that their moves are monitored by sensors and cameras that, with the help of computer vision, weight sensors, and artificial intelligence, can detect what they put in their baskets and charge them accordingly as they leave the store and get their digital receipt.[15] The store of the future has no cashiers, no petty theft, fully automated replenishment—and huge streams of data that enable Amazon to predict what kind of person will buy what and when and in which weather, for example from Whole Foods, which Amazon bought in 2017. The data should also enable Amazon to predict what a given shopper might order online from Amazon's online marketplace and online grocery, and, therefore, what should be stacked in an urban warehouse in a given part of town.

In the 1970s, a salesperson might be the aggregator of shoppers' sentiments; in the 1980s, point-of-sale technologies such as credit card readers supplied structured data to complement clerks' first-hand observations, and assist in inventory management that was growing more complex with the proliferation of product variety. As the Internet enabled crowdsourcing, companies could co-develop goods and services with customers—Fiat, for example, crowdsourced ten thousand people in 160 countries to design Fiat Mio, which received rave reviews at leading global auto shows. Today, the four walls do the job—by tapping into the massively rich data resulting from shoppers' facial expressions.

Empirically, wide smiles, enraged nostril flares, and micro-expressions such as flashes of contempt are found to be much more effective in determining a shopper's proclivity to buy than self-reporting in surveys or focus groups (no word yet how they compare to the salesperson of the 1970s).[16] We give the store away simply by looking at products and packaging in stores, often without realizing it. In 2018, the American Civil Liberties Union asked the twenty largest U.S. brick-and-mortar retailers whether the companies were using cameras in-store to gather facial recognition data. Only one, Ahold Delhaize, whose U.S. brands include the supermarkets Food Lion, Stop & Shop, Giant, and Hannaford, came forward to say no.[17] The rest refused to answer.

Granted, stores are just one place for harvesting data for facial analytics. The data are harvested from TV viewers and web surfers; a leading U.S. facial analysis business, Affectiva, is now tapping drivers' emotional data inside the next generation of cars, such as Porsches speeding away on the Autobahn.[18] Predicted to be a $15 billion market by 2025, facial analytics are poised to be the data-pipe that product and services businesses of many stripes have dreamt of for their global marketing: they can quickly test global consumers' uptake of movie scenes, video games, commercials, products, hotel lobby designs, players in sports teams, choreographs in concerts, new teaching methods and professors in class rooms, and so on. The technology can of course also help give early warnings about potential shoplifters, accelerate and improve the quality of passport checks as it already does in many advanced nations, enable families to detect how an ailing parent three thousand miles away who puts on a brave face is really feeling, or help psychiatrists to drill faster into their clients' emotional landscape—and foster emotional intelligence in humanoid robots.

At one level, this has a spooky feel of a Big Brother watching. However, the gains can be great for businesses of many sizes seeking to test and essentially crowdsource new products and solutions. They do not have to be Netflix to grasp what a customer around the planet might want, even before the customer realizes that herself, and then develop an offering to match the subconscious need. Rebecca Migirov of blockchain company ConsenSys suggests that today's supply chain has become a "supply circle," in which consumers co-create products and act as companies' R&D departments.[19] Now shoppers don't even have to do so consciously.

Fake Wine in Old Bottles

Have you ever ordered an expensive bottle of wine in a restaurant and not given any thought to the idea that the wine may be cheap wine in expensive wine's bottle? The global fake wine industry costs $3 billion annually and has given rise to such ventures as Wine Fraud, which stages wine authentication training classes. It has also created a long line of inmates who serve time for running spectacular fake wine schemes. But now a cure is in sight: the London-based company Everledger led by Leanne Kemp tracks bottles of fine wine using hidden codes added to them by vintners, enabling a dinner party to ascertain the origin of the $300 bottle they are about to order.

Everledger is even better known for a more expensive commodity with similar problems of authenticity verification and elaborate frauds: diamonds. The company has placed 1.6 million industrial diamonds on a blockchain, creating digital twins for each rock by cataloguing dozens of attributes for each diamond, including the color, carat, and certificate number inscribed by laser on the crown or girdle of the stone. These data prevent fraud, ease passage with border agents, and give assurance to the buyer of the stone's origin or "provenance" and its authenticity.[20] They also enable you to answer your to-be bride's surprising questions about whether the rock on her ring is a blood diamond that was used to finance tribal wars and other unsavory business in the developing world. Everledger is on its way to partnering with Tiffany's on consumer diamonds, enabling John looking for an engagement ring for Jill to explore the stone's origin on his iPhone. Museum curators and art collectors are similarly able to use Everledger to authenticate art, as long as the company works around the industry no-no of inscribing even small print on a painting.

Incidentally, lettuce has the same property as diamonds: it is hard to authenticate the source of any one item and track it. Like diamonds, heads of lettuce can get mixed up and be hard to trace to their origins. But now a head of lettuce also ceases to be anonymous. In 2017, the *New York Times* recounted how Walmart food safety manager Frank Yiannas sought for years to track lettuce, steaks, and cakes from farm and factory to Walmart's stores, to quickly track down the source of salmonella outbreaks.[21] Now this company, one of world's largest exporters and importers, is using blockchain to track the origin of pork in China and its transportation and warehousing in the United States. Walmart had cut the tracing time of mangos to two seconds from six days, eighteen hours, and twenty-six minutes, an astounding efficiency gain.

These are extremely valuable advances in the world of food supply chains, perhaps the most bedeviled of supply chains. Granted, blockchain has a harder time defeating bacteria—even with excellent tracing systems for each product destined for Chipotle kitchens, including data on the packing house that shipped the product and even which field grew it, Chipotle, like McDonald's, still fumbles and falls victim to food scares. But by enabling companies to trace ingredients to their respective suppliers and suppliers' suppliers and transport events on the way, blockchain offers the best chance yet to quickly trace food gone bad to its origin and target recalls to products from that origin.

Blockchain can also support efforts to address growing consumer interest in safe and sustainable supply chains. In Vietnam, the Trace Alliance is using blockchain to give consumers data on the origins of their fish, mangos, and pet foods—and who processed them, who shipped them, and when and from where.[22] The mechanics are simple. Fishers register their catches to the blockchain via a text message, and transport events are also recorded on the way. Perhaps soon Uber Eats will enable you to trace the fish in your fish tacos to the trawler that caught it and the cabbage to the field that grew it.

Manufacturers now have similar tools for dissecting the quality of products. As manufacturing digitizes and 3D-printable products start circulating more widely in global commerce, blockchain can help solve thorny questions industrial manufacturers have about the quality, origin, and intellectual property rights of those 3D-printed products. Using blockchain to codify and encrypt the data on the production process and products creates, much like the fish supply chain, a stream of secure data as to who made a given part where, when, and how (such as out of what materials). This in turn enables manufacturers to ensure and verify the quality of products and their producers, screen out pirated products, trace problems in parts to their source, and carry out recalls quickly if needed, and do all this using secure data. One of the pioneers is General Electric, which has patented a technology to use blockchain to validate and verify 3D files and the 3D-printing process and thus enable certification of 3D-printed parts.[23] The U.S. Department of the Navy brought blockchain to its additive manufacturing work, citing blockchain's security benefits.[24]

Technology is also improving the maintenance of parts and components. Case in point: in 2016, your author had a wild start for a flight from Washington's Reagan Airport, bound for Atlanta. The plane sped up on the runway and started to take off, only to suddenly pull its nose down and hit the brakes, in the process sending the planeload of people to a synchronized forward lean. The reason: the captain had discovered upon taking off that a critical part had gone defunct—its service light had come on. This brief episode that probably cost the airline a few angry notes and made me miss my connection in Atlanta might never happen five years from now. For example, Airbus is deep into using blockchain to analyze its suppliers and the origin of the parts, and share revenue with partners. The data also help the next node in the chain, airliners. The parts catalogued on blockchain can be read by, say, Lufthansa maintenance staff to determine how many flight hours the part has accomplished and whether to replace or repair the part.

Finding the Weakest Link

Blockchain and big data analytics are also helping manufacturers and retailers tame supplier risk. Every major company has thousands of potential weakest links in their suppliers—thirty thousand suppliers supply a Boeing Dreamliner and fifty thousand firms supply a global bank. In the mid-2000s, Barbie-maker Mattel's second-tier suppliers—subcontractors of Mattel's first-tier suppliers and largely invisible to Mattel—were discovered to be painting dolls with paints heavy in lead (which cost 60 percent less than lead-free paint) and producing parts that came loose and ended up being swallowed by little girls in America, leading to a death in 2005.[25] In 2007, Mattel announced the recall of 436,000 toys worldwide, of which 253,000 were in the United States—and ultimately ended up recalling 19 million toys sent from China due to lead paint and loose magnets.

That supplier risk became a giant nightmare for Mattel, a company known for its high standards, sent shivers down the spines of supply chain managers and OEMs across the world.[26] Companies were also blindsided by suppliers' business practices that turned Western shoppers off from their favorite brands, such as using child labor or pouring chemicals into rivers. In the 1990s, Nike became a lightning rod after its subcontractors in Vietnam were found to be violating humane labor practices in manufacturing Air Jordans. Retailers woke up to a reality in which the product was great, but its supplier was fundamentally flawed. As companies offshored production, human rights advocates and labor unions banded together to ensure that U.S. trade agreements, starting with NAFTA, demand that developing-country counterparts such as Mexico uphold labor protections. For labor lobbies, the extra motivation was of course to make production in Mexico less attractive to U.S. companies.

For years, companies and governments and their prime contractors spent enormous resources to find reliable, high-quality and low-cost overseas suppliers that adhered to rigorous six sigma processes and complied with labor laws, environmental standards, and transparent financial management and anti-corruption practices. Today, the search costs are lower, in part thanks to ecommerce platforms such as Alibaba and Tradekey that provide B2B buyers ways to identify and screen sellers and provide instant insight into thousands of suppliers. Though Alibaba is hardly free from scams, buyers can use many methods provided by them, from supplier assessments by third-party companies to satisfaction ratings by other buyers and on-site verifications by Alibaba teams to accelerate supplier screening.

Big data is the best separator of wheat from chaff. For example, Import Genius uses a hundred million ocean freight records, which previously sat idle in government databanks, to help U.S. manufacturers and retail chains see the suppliers used by such stalwarts as J.C. Penney and Boeing, and free-ride on the supplier screening these big firms have already done. Suddenly, everyone's global supply chain became visible to everyone. No company with sea cargo is immune to data's frank talk: Import Genius called out a large iPhone shipment by Apple from China to the United States before anyone knew when iPhone was going to hit the market. Tools are also more available to help defeat bad labor conditions. The U.S. Department of Labor lists on its website products from around the world that are used by some form of exploited labor; NGOs such as World Vision use the list to highlight violators and those that use them.[27] MasterCard has brought to market Track, a "know your supplier" software that covers 150 million businesses and plows through risk management alerts from 4,500 sanction, watch, and law enforcement lists and from 21,000 adverse media sources. The tool helps Fortune 500s to minimize legal, regulatory, and brand risk and prevent invoicing fraud in payments.

Telling You This, Machine to Machine

Machine-to-machine communications are skyrocketing in number and creating new value: the Industrial Internet of Things, whereby data flow among machines is often dispersed across continents and is expected to generate additional efficiency gains of up to $15 *trillion* between 2015 and 2035.[28] A review of the many applications tells us why there are such gains.

Take the Australian mining giant, Rio Tinto, which daily taps 30 gigabytes of data from its trucks, drill laboratories, process surveillance cameras, control systems, and maintenance system logs from its dozens of mines around the planet 100 milliseconds after the data are live.[29] Analyzing these data in Brisbane, Australia, the company is able to develop cut costs and readily improve the safety and environmental performance of its mines. A two-engine Boeing flying from New York to London produces 320 terabytes (that is, 320,000 gigabytes) of data that enables airlines to reduce costs and delays and to improve safety, literally on the fly. Unilever, the world's second largest consumer products company, pulls together data from 190 countries in real time to its U.K. data center of four thousand servers that help the company mitigate global supply chain risks, improve business performance, and lower the price of products. Brazilian energy giant Petrobras draws on 387 indicators to monitor its environmental performance and a platform to capture and process real-time operational data from the various drilling rigs.[30] In Malaysia, plantation conglomerate Sime Darby Berhad uses drones, soil sensors, and mobile devices carried by thousands of field workers in its businesses in Malaysia, Indonesia, and Liberia to capture production data, logistics, productivity, and field conditions; improve agronomic management; and ensure quality and worker safety and environmental compliance.[31] India's Tata Group has launched an entire analytics division to help its more than one hundred independent operating companies from software and tea to telecom analyze all the data they generate.[32]

Tech sector analyst Gartner forecasts that 40 percent of businesses' net investment will be on predictive and prescriptive analytics by 2020. The payoff can be massive: companies with first-rate business analytics could, according to McKinsey, increase their operating margins by up to 60 percent.[33] The economic gains come especially from moving traditional industries to the data era: 75 percent of the value-added created by data flows is in traditional industries, in part through increases in productivity.[34]

The biggest prize goes to those such as Sime Darby or Petrobras that successfully marry internal enterprise data with second- and third-party data, for example on consumers, prices in specific markets, supplier risk, and weather. John Deere, a midwestern farming machinery business founded in 1837, today uses data on soil conditions, crop features, weather, and many other factors to help farmers using phone app "Mobile Farm Manager" decide what crops to plant where and when, when and where to plough, where the best return will be made with the crops, and even which path to follow when ploughing. Using weather data, they can avert crop losses: most crop losses are due to weather events, and 25 percent of weather-related crop losses could be prevented by using predictive weather modeling.[35] In addition, sensors attached to tractors and other equipment give farmers data to reduce downtime and John Deere to predict the demand for replacement parts of its combines.

Even small companies can leverage data today by renting pay-per-use data services from companies such as Amazon or Salesforce, instead of having to buy expensive hardware and software systems and in-house data analysts. For example, by running its mid-Africa and Middle East online booking operations on Amazon Web Services, South African travel booking website Travelstart has realized operational cost savings of 43 percent and reduced downtime by 25 percent.[36] The Southeast Asian juggernaut ride-hailing company Grab uses real-time data streams of its 1.5 million bookings to predict future demand patterns and correct operational problems immediately.[37] This, the company claims, has translated into 30 to 40 percent savings in manpower and operations and improved customer service and lowered the cost to customers. Brazilian company WebMotors, which hosts two hundred thousand classified ads for new and used vehicles each month, has used Amazon CloudFront to transmit vast quantities of data that improved its performance by 45 percent and enabled it to scale up to support more than twenty million unique visitors per month from around the world.[38]

Conclusion

Data are an intermediate product that has suddenly become more available but also more valuable. The challenges for companies big and small is how to make sense of it all—in the words of Google's Hong Kong Managing Director Leonie Valentine, go from big data to big query. Even some of the largest and most renewed global consumer brands are still taking their first steps to systematize data, build data lakes that pool all data, and ensure that data are polished and made machine learning ready. "Data on data" is nascent as well: we are only now learning to know how data are improving companies' customer retention, supply chains, and operations.

Could predictive powers in a hundred years be so powerful as to enable us to engineer backward causation, or retrocausality, a mind-bender from physics and philosophy in which effects can precede causes?

Physicists have grappled with this question for decades, with many concluding that our perception of cause and effect and time is an illusion—and that the future can actually shape past outcomes. Imagine a normal course of events, in which event B is the effect of cause A. If reverse causation were real, it would be possible when B has occurred to intervene in the course of events and prohibit A from occurring. There are astounding experiments in physics and medicine, for example, that suggest that it is indeed possible to change the past outcome in the present.[39] The question that is easier to get one's head around is, Could big query give us so much power to forecast B that we could alter A? While most of us are not yet as evolved as to be able to go back in time and cancel bad quarterly earnings or havoc caused by a hurricane, the big query is leading us to a place where we are getting ahead of the future and able to manufacture a favorable outcome for businesses in the global economy.

PART II

The Challenges

8

OFFLINE

In 1994, the United Nations launched a global drive to bridge "digital divides" between developed and developing countries. Over twenty years later, digital divides are digital chasms. While 90 percent of Germans and Swiss are online, in sub-Saharan Africa, only twenty out of a hundred people were netizens in 2016; in developing Asia-Pacific, only 49 percent; and in Latin America 56 percent.[1] The less advanced parts of Africa, South Asia, Latin America, and Eastern Europe lag far behind their emerging market peers in digitization. As opposed to 44 people per 100 in Switzerland, barely over 10 out of 100 people in developing regions have fixed broadband; adoption rates are rock bottom 0.03 for every 100 people in Burundi (or 0.3 percent of the population), 0.28 in Kenya, 1.3 in India, and even only 12 in Mexico and Brazil. Of businesses, while 94 percent of developed-country companies use email with suppliers and 78 percent have a website, the share of companies with a website dips to 44 percent for all countries and 33 percent for companies in sub-Saharan Africa and 32 percent in South Asia.[2]

Granted, connectivity has improved drastically in the past twenty years. While most Americans and Europeans were connected to the Internet by 2000, only 0.5 percent of sub-Saharan Africans and 2 percent of people in Asia-Pacific were online.[3] Since then, mobile phones have proliferated and mobile broadband fees have come down in most countries to less than 5 percent or less of people's average monthly incomes, enabling hundreds of millions to join the online economy.[4] A cottage industry for connectivity has taken off. In the

Congo, one intrepid entrepreneur has built a sturdy ladder on which people from his village can climb up to a terrace he has set up at the top of a tall tree to get connectivity from the skies—of course paying him an entry fee at the bottom. But in the least-developing countries, many of them in sub-Saharan Africa, fixed mobile broadband penetration is still only 12 percent, keeping a large majority of businesses and potential shoppers from the online economy.

This reality is now changing fast, often due to commercial interests. For example, Google's Project Loon connects people in rural areas off-cable via solar-powered balloons.[5] Facebook has launched a high-altitude solar plane called Aquila to bring the Internet to remote parts of Africa and India.[6] Tech companies are also disrupting global submarine cables that carry transcontinental emails and data, including just about all online traffic sent from New York to California. The configuration of these cables has long mimicked that of the nineteenth-century cables that ran between North America and Western Europe and largely missed Africa and developing Asia.[7] Now, Google is laying fiber optic cables across Africa, gradually cracking open the online market for digital services, and connecting millions that to date have gotten online on high hills or tree tops.[8] Google is also building a cable between Los Angeles and Chile and between Hong Kong and Guam, connecting the company's data centers.[9] In the Pacific Islands, a region that has high costs of transporting products to and from just about anywhere, Huawei is planning to connect the region and enable it to grow through online services.

Getting connected is the first step toward crossing the digital divide. But many more digital divides need to be bridged for businesses and people to thrive in the global digital economy and engage in trade. Globally speaking, only a small slice of businesses are connected to 4G and 5G networks, selling online, and adopting new technologies such as AI; in another slice are businesses that are connected and perhaps here and there transacting online but that are not particularly technology-intensive; and still in another are Facebook merchants that lack capabilities to transact online and collect cash on delivery. In the final slice are firms that are still offline, as if toiling in the dark. The stakes for countries to grow the first slice are high. This chapter shows why, and what needs to change both in businesses and governments.

Wiring Up

The fact that over one-half of the planet is still offline can be hard to fathom. When you sit in a hotel lobby in Buenos Aires or Nairobi or Bangkok, you have a great WiFi connection, as do people around you fiercely typing and skyping on their smartphones. Go out to meetings and your taxi driver will likely have Waze and Google Maps. But get outside major cities and things change. There are gaping disparities in digitization between urban and rural areas, young and old people, and men and women. For example, while some 23 percent of people in urban areas in Africa used the Internet in 2016, only 10 percent of people in rural areas did; and while some 17 percent of African men had access to the Internet, only 12 percent of women did.[10]

Among companies, it is the larger, urban, productive, and export-driven businesses that tend to have digital capabilities and to transact online; many rural small businesses do not even have an Internet connection. Paradoxically, while the Internet opens an opportunity particularly for remote communities to shorten the distance to markets, it is also these communities that are least likely to be connected. Rural businesses pay a price for being rural.[11]

Connectivity and its quality are essential for companies to engage in ecommerce and trade. And as shown in Chapter 3, companies that sell online are likelier to export and grow than companies that are offline or companies that do not have online sales capabilities. In a survey my company ran in 2017, gaps in connectivity and IT infrastructures were shown to be a leading impediment for small businesses to engage in ecommerce in the least-developed countries.[12] In another study, I found that fixed broadband usage rates are a top predictor of the number of ecommerce sellers in countries around the world.[13] And just any connection won't do: companies are likelier to engage in ecommerce if their Internet connection speed is higher than 30 megabits per second (Mbps), when the global average is still less than 7 Mbps.[14]

These figures imply that the more economies digitize, the more digital divides shape companies' and countries' competitiveness—and a swath of humanity risks falling behind. One way to see the impact of the Internet on economic growth is to ask companies how much worse they would fare without the web. Specifically asked what the impact would be in their productivity (in this case, value of sales per employee) if their company ceased to have access to the Internet or other digital networks, 89 percent of Latin American businesses reported productivity losses of 5 percent or more, and 77 percent reported losses of 15 percent or more.[15] In other words, access to the Internet is a huge growth driver for companies in their internal and external operations. This is just as it is in the United States: most digitally intensive American businesses also say they would lose 15 percent or more of their productivity if they did not have access to the Internet.[16] Cut access online, and rob companies of 15 percent or more of their sales.

Connectivity has been a source of competitiveness for centuries, since the times when ancient Chinese and Native Americans sent smoke signals to warn their fellow tribesmen of imminent dangers. In the 1860s, the political news, commodity and bond prices, and other time-sensitive and profitable information journeyed in seconds between London and New York, giving those that could afford the $10-per-word fee an edge vis-à-vis their unconnected peers.[17] By the 1950s, more people could have their ear on valuable transcontinental information flows, thanks to the coaxial cable that could carry telephone conversations between Americans and their European cousins. By the 1990s, the fiber optic cable enabled the exchange of digital data in the form of light across the Atlantic, and the era of mass email was born. All governments understand the power of Internet connectivity and most have worked hard to connect their citizens and companies. Over 140 countries have developed national broadband plans in the past two decades, typically aimed at improving the quality of connections, such as upgrading from 2G to 3G and 4G networks and wiring remote regions. Success has in some cases been very rapid. For example, in Peru, the mobile broadband network expanded from 16.6 million people (of whom 600,000 were mobile broadband subscribers) in 2010 to 29.6 million (of which 6.1 million were subscribers) in 2015.[18] At 9 Mbps, speed for Peru's 3G and 4G connections was in 2016 among the top thirty in the world.

Such success took deft maneuvers. The Peruvian government enticed mobile operators to connect the vast jungle and mountain areas by giving operators access to the infrastructure it owned in remote areas, such as buildings and parks. The government also streamlined processes: as operators found that each Peruvian municipality had its own rules and restrictions for the deployment of the sixteen thousand extra antennas needed to meet the government's coverage and quality-of-service criteria, the government passed a law that standardized the requirements for an automatic approval to installation of mobile towers.[19] To connect the last mile, the government required operator Movistar to agree, in exchange for an operating license, to extend mobile broadband coverage to 1,842 remote villages by the end of 2015 and provide for ten years more than twelve thousand free mobile broadband connections in schools, health centers, and police stations, for the government to improve rural education, health care, and security services.[20]

In Africa, Rwanda has engineered a miraculous turnaround through digital transformation. A small landlocked country devoid of natural resources and emerging from the horrific civil war of 1994 when one million people were killed in a span of four months, Rwanda has since the year 2000 prioritized connectivity as its future, with a goal of becoming "Africa's India" with a booming business process outsourcing industry. In 2000, the government launched the National Information Communications Infrastructure policy and created a twenty-year plan to achieve full digitization, in four five-year phases. This was a tall order: in 2005, fixed-line penetration was at 0.3 percent of the population and mobile penetration 2.5 percent. But the government doggedly plowed forward, showing to people the power of connectivity. For example, in its e-Soko program, the government helped farmers access on their mobile devices real-time information about market prices for their agricultural produce.[21] The government also set up telecenters and "ICT Buses" equipped with twenty Internet-connected laptops, as well as projectors, TV monitors, and other equipment that toured rural areas to raise Rwandans' awareness of online services. This was not a "hi-bye" PR operation—the buses stayed in an area for a couple of months, delivering seminars and digital training to locals.

By the 2010s, the work had started to pay off. Thanks to aggressive public investment and competition among private telecommunications operators, by 2011, mobile phone networks covered 96 percent of the country.[22] By 2016, a third of Rwandans were online and connection speed was 8.7 Mbps, above the global average of 6.3 Mbps; some 70 percent of the people were connected to the mobile network. The costs of Internet connections dropped: the Alliance for Affordable Internet ranked Rwanda as having the twenty-first most affordable Internet among fifty-eight developing countries in 2017.[23] Co-working spaces started to sprout in Kigali; for example, the renowned kLab offers an open space for IT entrepreneurs to collaborate and turn ideas into viable business models under experienced mentors and tech workshops.

In Myanmar, it was still in 2010 illegal to own an email account, and journalists received years in jail by if they sent information via the Internet abroad. For example, twenty-five-year-old reporter Hla Win was sentenced to twenty years in jail for sending some of her content to the Burmese exile broadcaster Democratic Voice of Burma—a sentence that came to an end in 2012 as the country democratized. Since then, the Internet has roared—connections increased from 1 percent in 2011, when the military government started to ease restrictions, to 28 percent or fifteen million people in 2017.[24] Lives have transformed. U Ohn Maung, a tea and ginger farmer in a remote nine-hundred-person village, recounts how the 2014 appearance of the cell phone tower on a nearby mountain ridge led him to join Facebook and, with the help of a nonprofit, become aware of the Golden Paddy app with which he could get forecasts of the weather, market prices, and pesticides.[25] Realizing he had previously been badly cheated by middlemen to sell his ginger and avocados at rock-bottom prices, U Ohn set out to monitor his products' market prices in the city and avoided being shortchanged. His story is echoed by millions of rural people around the world.

Peru, Rwanda, and Myanmar all did the right things to wire up their countries: research shows that it is the combination of supply-side policies (such as long-term broadband development plans and public-private partnerships) and demand-side policies (such as provision of financial incentives for businesses to adopt broadband) that accelerate broadband diffusion when broadband penetration is low.[26] Demand-side policies such as tax breaks can also supplement supply-side policies when penetration rates are high and supply-side policies have been exhausted.[27]

One no-brainer of demand-side policy is tax and tariff cuts on devices. The Washington think tank Information Technology & Innovation Foundation calculates that participation in the eighty-two-country Information Technology Agreement, which removes tariffs on 97 percent of IT products, would bolster Argentina's economic growth by 1.5 percent and Pakistan and Kenya's by 1.3 percent.[28] In 2016 the reformist Argentine president Mauricio Macri realized the folly of the prior government's taxing laptops and computers at 35 percent, in the hopes that the tariff would help stimulate a local computer-making industry. Rather than helping Argentina build its own Samsung, the tariff punished Argentines eager to participate in the online economy: an iPad mini 4 went for $1,260 in Buenos Aires, while costing only $640 in the neighboring Chile.[29]

Better access to devices and the Internet is only the start for people and businesses to leverage the digital revolution for ecommerce, trade, and growth. A case in point is Anderson Ngbado Ndabahweje, a twenty-year-old student in Kisangani, Congo, who has learned English by watching YouTube videos of President Obama's speeches on his old Chinese smartphone.[30] Anderson can marvel over the products on eBay on his phone, but without a bank account and credit cards, he will not have any mechanism to pay for them (or buy bitcoins to pay for them). He also would not get products to his remote city without paying extraordinary shipping costs and dealing with customs and thieves along the way. He can browse the opulence of hotels in the Riviera and marvel the foods in Bangkok, but not be any closer to ever getting to them. He can watch the game, but not play in it.

Conversely, that South Korean companies enjoy the fastest Internet connection in the world explains only so much as to why Korea also has the third most vibrant online retail market in the world after China and the United States, why seven of the country's top-ten global beauty brands ranked by research firm L2 for their "Digital IQ" are South Korean, or why Korean executives most certainly have enjoyed a great meal in Bangkok that Anderson can only look at from thousands of miles away.[31] One of the first elements that has to go right, for people and businesses to translate connectivity into scalable transactions, commerce, and growth, is digital payments.

Instagram Sellers

Even in countries with solid Internet connectivity and with companies that have websites, most companies have yet to even transact online. In Europe, only 20 percent of SMEs sold online in 2015, the latest year for which data are available; the number is higher in the United Kingdom and Benelux and declines going eastward.[32] In the United States, only about 40 percent of digitally intensive firms sold goods online and 30 percent sold services online in 2014, and fewer than half of that set did so frequently.[33] Developing-countries' ecommerce usage rates are even lower, though estimates of how low vary widely. In 2016, the World Bank calculated that in mid-size companies in upper-middle-income countries such as Mexico or Turkey, only 35 percent sell online, while only 9 percent of small companies and 16 percent of mid-size companies in low-income, least-connected countries such as Ghana or Bangladesh sell online.[34] My company's surveys, carried out online with companies that inherently have some digital capabilities, show that a quarter of developing-country companies sell online, a third sell and buy online, while 14 percent only buy online and 27 percent neither buy nor sell online—meaning that about 40 percent of even the more connected developing-country companies have yet to exploit the web for their sales.[35]

The difference between my numbers and World Bank's is likely driven by different survey methods—but also by the fact that the definition of "online seller" is quite amorphous. There is a vast gray area of businesses that may or may not qualify: Facebook merchants that market online but do not use online payments to complete transactions online. Facebook merchants are very prevalent in the developing world—they make up the majority of small companies that may or may not deem themselves online sellers. A study by the Bangladeshi IT association suggests that 90 percent of online sellers are Facebook merchants.

In part the prevalence of Facebook merchants reflects a resource gap and learning process: the leap from Facebook merchant to ecommerce seller is often a stomach-wrenching, slow-motion journey in which the entrepreneur first gets on Facebook, Instagram, and Pinterest and then invests time and money to acquire the skills and knowledge to set up and run an online store complete with online payments and fulfillment capabilities. Take Janetssamoa.com, a Samoan crafts business started by Janet Sablan in 1989. Janetssamoa made its first export sales by shipping coconut earrings to Australian shoppers who had just visited the Pacific Islands. Janet realized that exports to tourists who knew the region would be the future, and in 1999, she set up a website and set out to advertise on Facebook, to showcase her products to Australian and Kiwi buyers.[36] To reach teens and people in their twenties, Janet also used Instagram, Twitter, and Pinterest. But one thing Janet, who by 2015 had a dozen employees, did not have was reliable online payments. She managed offline workarounds for years, before being able to accept bank deposits or use PayPal. She is hardly alone: a MasterCard study of German, Canadian, Brazilian, and Vietnamese companies found that while 90 percent of merchants had a website, only 20 percent were set up to accept payments online.[37]

In Cambodia, Chan, a young lady in her twenties, has developed a booming business by finding attractive products on Alibaba, posting these products on an Instagram account for sale to Cambodians, and then ordering products her followers want from Alibaba in bulk, followed by arranging local logistics—such as sending parcels in local and regional buses from Phnom Penh and getting cash back with the returning driver. She is a wayfarer to numerous young Cambodians who have turned to Instagram, Facebook, and local platforms, intermediating transactions between platforms and people.[38] But still, her ability to transact at scale is stunted by the rudimentary payment technology. After all, that she has to wait for the buyer to pay and the driver to return chokes her cash flow and complicates her planning of the next purchases to place with Alibaba.

Granted, where technology lags, workarounds emerge. In Sri Lanka, most Grasshopper sellers do not use ecommerce platforms—like most developing-country sellers, they sell their products on social commerce platforms such as Facebook or Instagram and get cash on delivery, as the buyer wants to inspect the product before paying. Yet Sri Lanka is developed enough for the buyers to often have debit or credit cards: 80 percent of citizens have either or both. In response to this setting, Grasshopper has mastered door-step payments as "card on delivery," in which the delivery rider has the mobile app with Square-type readers to take a card payment once the customer sees the product. This accelerates the flow of funds to the seller while giving courage to buyers still getting accustomed to online shopping to place orders.

This may not work everywhere, however: the prevalence of Facebook merchants also reflects gaps in financial inclusion. In developing countries, many people still do not have bank accounts, most people do not have credit cards, and online payment systems such as PayPal do not exist. In a 2017 survey, only 1 percent of people over twenty-five years of age in Cambodia had credit cards, only 6 percent in Ghana, and only 30 percent in Brazil.[39] Mobile payments are helping people exchange funds; 13 percent of Cambodians, 45 percent of Ghanians, and 49 percent of Brazilians over twenty-five made at least one transaction on mobile phones in 2017. Yet in some countries such as Ethiopia, the many national online payments platforms cannot as yet interoperate, due to prohibitive laws. Rather, users have to transact with others in the same providers' walled garden. Paying across borders is even more complex in many countries: small non-exporter firms in developing countries typically cite gaps in cross-border online payments as the foremost obstacle for them to start selling across borders.

The simplest way to get buyers and sellers to transact is to have them on one global payment platform, which today is PayPal. Just like card companies, PayPal has to work with banks—which in turn need to be able to credibly show it has screening mechanisms in place to identify and deny service to money launderers and other criminals. Finding and screening bank partners that are good to work with is hard work. PayPal also could surely benefit from the legal certainty provided by epayment laws that many developing countries still lack, and by relatively prompt and cost-effective processes to secure and maintain the regulatory approvals for operating a payment business.

Interoperability can be accomplished when different payment companies want it to happen and central banks bless it. For example, in 2015, bitter telecom rivals in Africa, Vodafone Group and MTN Group, decided to join forces to enable their respective customers to make mobile payments across their networks, including across borders between Vodafone subscribers in Kenya, the Democratic Republic of the Congo, and Tanzania and MTN users in Uganda, Rwanda, South Sudan, and Zambia.[40] The companies wanted to connect the makers and receivers of cross-border remittance payments in the region, who could not transact because they were on different systems. The maneuver cut fees on cross-border transfers from 20 to 3 percent, and earned the blessing of regional central banks.

B2B cross-border payments are particularly costly and complex, especially for small sellers. Annual cross-border payments are enormous, $150 trillion in 2015—twice the size of the world economy—and the payment industry grosses some $200 billion, 80 percent of which comes from B2B transactions.[41] But still, many companies struggle to get into this game. One problem with them is significant fees. A wire typically costs $50 to $75, meaning that for sellers and buyers making multiple small transactions, wires are unlikely to be attractive. In Brazil, companies that convert the payment into dollars from reals need to also obtain a document for currency exchange that costs $300, a prohibitive fee for small transactions.[42] In response to banks' fixed fees, companies have devised workarounds to avoid paying high fixed costs; for example, they bunch several small orders together in an invoice to reduce the costs of a wire.[43] But there are also variable costs to reckon with: a cross-border wire payment using SWIFT network can involve transaction fees of several percentages as each bank in the payment value chains takes its cut; usually these fees average 1 to 3 percent but can exceed 10 percent when the payment is small and travels through several banks.[44] In addition, banks' settlement process takes three to five days, an astonishing amount of time for those used to operating with the instantaneousness of emails. Companies could of course use cards—most cross-border credit card transactions cost 3.5 percent of the value of the shipment—but the economics lose their appeal for large payments.

Technology is alleviating some of the payment challenges that keep companies from globalizing. For example, in Brazil, FinTech company EBANX enables Brazilians who do not have international credit cards or even bank accounts to buy from international sellers: it is integrated to the national Boleto Bancario, a barcoded payment slip referring to a purchase, which can be settled at payment points such as lottery shops or supermarkets and does not require the users to have a bank account.[45] By now EBANX serves over five hundred international merchants such as Spotify and Airbnb; processes $1.2 billion in transactions; and has offices in Mexico City, Montevideo, New York, and London. On the

B2B side, Spanish bank Santander in Brazil has launched a service called One Pay FX to use blockchain in settling B2B cross-border payments. The value propositions are lower costs and shortened settlement: payments clear in less than two hours, as opposed to the forty-eight hours they currently take. In some cases, transfers can even be made instantly. To build the service, Santander used xCurrent, a software created by the U.S. FinTech company Ripple that instantly settles cross-border payments with end-to-end tracking. The service was piloted in Brazil in 2018, along with Spain, the United Kingdom, and Poland; starting in 2019, One Pay FX will enable wires in dollars to the United States and in reals to Brazil.

Getting online payment systems working brings many benefits. Online payments expand trade, SMEs' participation in trade, and cross-border supply chains.[46] They lower the many costs of cash: in an analysis of transitions of its developing-country grantees to online payments with their subcontractors, USAID found that both financial costs, such as transaction fees, expenditures for travel to a disbursement site, security, or insurance costs for transporting cash, and nonfinancial costs, such as staff time devoted to payment processing, payment leakages and inability to trace them, and risk of nonpayment in cash-on-delivery systems, declined significantly when online payments were adopted.[47] Online payments also help women business owners, who all too often in the developing world are bullied by friends and family into giving up part of their profits.

One simple regulatory fix to stimulate online payments is an epayments law that defines the requirements for nonbank providers, such as to obtain or maintain licenses. Such laws reduce payment providers' financial and operational risks. Non-banks are found to expand the competition in the payments market, such as has happened in India, Russia, Turkey, Uruguay, and the European Union.[48] Another rather simple fix is to adopt a risk-based approach (RBA) in KYC processing. Up until recently, KYC laws used to be highly prescriptive and thus resulted in box-checking exercises for financial institutions and payment providers vetting prospective customers; as a result, low-risk customers experienced unnecessary delays and high-risk customers were not screened as hard as they should have been. RBA makes the KYC process commensurate with customer risk.[49] In a study with USAID, I found that twenty-six countries have adopted some form of risk-based method, out of forty.[50]

Most developing countries by now appreciate the costs of cashlessness; the question today is not whether to get rid of cash, but how to do so. One way to get epayments started is demonetization shock therapy.[51] In many developed countries such as Sweden, where cash is used in only 0.5 percent of transactions, digital payments have diffused thanks to incentives provided by providers. However, in developing countries such as India, where 98 percent of consumer transactions have traditionally relied on cash, cash payments are not as easily digitized, and that is a problem. The costs of cash—the time spent to get cash and fees—to the Indian consumer are among the highest in the world, even controlling for a population size that tends to clog access to ATMs, for example.[52] The problems are graver in small cities with fewer financial services: one study found that residents of Delhi *collectively* spent six million hours and $1.5 million to obtain cash, while residents of the three times smaller Hyderabad spent twice as much on a per capita basis, or altogether 1.7 million hours and $500,000.[53] In India, it is government-driven digital cash programs that have helped to accelerate demonetization and the adoption of digital payments—while also pushing firms to the formal economy.[54]

In 2015, India went on a demonetization diet, becoming the first nation to seriously subsidize the use of digital cash such as eWallets and mobile banking. Users of online payments received 10 percent discounts for insurance policies, rail tickets, and highway toll charges.[55] The government also waived the service tax on online transactions below 2,000 rupees, created a 0.75 percent discount for digital payments at gas stations, and in November 2016 got rid of 500- and 1,000-rupee notes worth about $7 and $15, justifying its moves as a means to combat corruption and terrorism, and to end tax evasion by the 9 percent of Indians who do not pay their taxes.

Also, new infrastructure and tools were created, such as government-sponsored Bharat Interface for Money, which enables payment by anyone in India with a bank account and smartphone and saving Indians time and lowering transaction fees. The system clicks with India's biometrics-based ID program "Aadhar," which enables payments without any devices such as mobile phones that many Indians still cannot afford. All that is needed to pay for rice, for example, is for the merchant to connect the buyer's fingerprint to the Aadhar database, and then draw the payment.

It is said that the "demon" in demonetization is in the beginning. The Indian campaign was contentious and painful in the beginning as commonly used cash notes could not be used and consumers had to quickly adjust to other means of paying. A sentiment analysis of Twitter feeds around November 2016 shows a third of Indians protesting the government's execution of the drive and the sudden disappearance of cash, but also 45 percent in favor, seeing the drive as being in the "higher good."[56] But the cold turkey also worked. When the smaller notes were banned, cash in circulation fell by some 66 percent and digital transaction volumes grew in lockstep by 43 percent between November and December 2016.[57]

Why aren't all companies selling online if that generates more sales and exports to more markets? There is of course more to the puzzle than connections and online payments. Asked about why they have not started selling online, companies often report worrying about the up-front costs of starting an online store and uncertainties related to the return on that investment. But sellers' concerns, real or imagined, also differ from country to country. In Africa, where ecommerce markets are still nascent, companies mention the small size of their domestic ecommerce market as an obstacle to starting online sales, while South American companies cite poor or expensive logistics as an obstacle for them to start selling online. In Pakistan, the most-cited challenges are more elementary, including the high cost of broadband and lack of good Internet connections. In Turkey, shoppers' worries about the safety of online payments, though being much more secure than a shopper's handing a waiter her credit card, keep merchants from selling online.

In other words, there is an entire menu of needs to address, to get companies to digitize and to sell online and across borders. And not all companies that do sell online thrive similarly, both because they shoot themselves in the foot and because poor policies still stifle them. Who succeeds and who stagnates online, and why?

Killer Whales and Sailfish

In 1994, economist David Birch and co-author James Medoff published an influential study on why some businesses grow fast while others languish.[58] Birch was mesmerized by what he called gazelles, businesses that doubled their revenues every four years. These companies had an average of sixty-one workers, they represented 4 percent of all U.S. companies, and they generated 70 percent of all new jobs. For policymakers keen to create new jobs—and which policymakers would not want to?—gazelles were the ones to cheerlead and feed.

Subsequent studies sought to make gazelles easier to spot in the jungle of firms, which for Birch were elephants such as Walmart and mice such as mom-and-pop corner stores. In the 1990s, gazelles were found among tech companies;

in the 2000s, they were spotted in housing-related sectors. A 2012 analysis by the Kauffman Foundation broke ground in mapping Inc. 500 firms as proxies for gazelles, finding that the gazelles graze not only in the Silicon Valley, Austin, or Boston, but also in unexpected places such as Salt Lake City, Indianapolis, Buffalo, Baltimore, Nashville, Philadelphia, Louisville, and Washington, D.C., basking in the vibrant world of government contracting post–Great Recession.[59] Some of the Inc. gazelles were IT companies, but many were also in advertising and marketing, business services, health care, and government services.

Inspired by Birch, scholars have excitedly sought to analyze the features and determinants of gazelles, so as to predict which firms might grow into gazelles tomorrow that VCs and governments should back today. Some key factors shared by gazelles were access to human capital, networks to other firms, and finance; intellectual property; export-orientation; and certain managerial qualities such as high educational attainment and industry experience.[60] No scholar got the magic formula for high-growth firms down pat—if they did, more VC investments than one in a dozen might be a home run.

Today's jungle of businesses is virtual, and it has many species still unheard of in the 1990s, such as social media businesses, online dating apps, and online robo-advisor brokerages. The 2012 Kauffman study found a difference between Birch's gazelles and the gazelles of the Internet era of the 2000s—the digital era's gazelles are on steroids, with their year-on-year revenues growing a stunning seventeen-fold in 2008 and twenty-two-fold in 2010.[61] But it is also the case that while the online economy can help gazelles scale at an extraordinary pace, not nearly all firms in the online economy scale and grow.

Looking at survey data on developing-country firms, the aptest analogy that comes to mind is one of oceans. Online, big fish tend to be much healthier, stronger, and more successful than the little fish, which spend their days navigating traps and ocean currents big fish barely even notice, such as challenges to get a small working capital loan. Some big fish are like slow-moving manatees that are growing steadily, but many are killer whales—companies that have at one point truly gotten their act together. Killer whales sell online, export and import globally, and grow fast. They tend to be large, with five hundred or more employees; employ highly skilled workers and make use of technologies, so as to do more with less; and live in major cities and near ports. They also tend to be least hampered by the currents swirling around them. When they complain, they complain about macro issues none of them can change on its own, such as high taxes, poor transport infrastructures, and costly regulations.

The world looks very different from the vantage point of the little fish, especially the weaker types of little fish, herrings. They typically have a couple of dozen workers, tend to sell mostly offline and seldom export, grow slowly, and are found far outside capital cities. They wake up every day to struggle with the nuts and bolts of online business that are a breeze to big business—such as securing digital skills, locking in small loans, connecting to the Internet, and shipping goods. They are unhappy with the enabling environment for ecommerce. For example, some 60 percent of small developing-country companies I surveyed gave their countries' ecommerce enabling environment a score of 5 out of 10, and herrings give even lower ratings—when manatees and killer fish tend to rate enabling environments on average 8 out of 10. Because of lousy payments systems or fears about costs of selling online, many herrings are still Facebook merchants.

At the same time, there are small businesses that were merely *en route* to growing big at the time the researcher dipped into the stream of data. These are the online world's sailfish, the ocean's fastest swimmer. They are small and mid-size firms that tend to grow at 20 percent or more per year, use new technologies, sell mostly online, and export, as opposed to their meek herring peers that grow slowly and wring their hands about the up-front investments needed to set up proper online stores. Sailfish are globalists; they tend to have some foreign owners or shareholders, a familiar feature of companies that export. They uniformly see fewer barriers to doing ecommerce than herrings, and have better access to capabilities critical for thriving online: high-skilled human capital able to use technologies and adopt latest techniques in making, moving, and marketing products, broadband connections, and capital.

Sailfish just like killer whales outperform their peers before they start to sell online—simply selling online does not necessarily make them into what they are. But it seems that ecommerce helps these firms internationalize. While their life is not nearly as easy as that of killer whales, sailfish have entered the virtuous cycle of companies that sell online, engage in trade, grow, and thus have greater resources to acquire technologies and high-skilled people to sell and buy more online. They are on their way to becoming big and lethal.

How to make herrings and manatees into sailfish and killer whales? How to ensure that more companies starting today will get on the right path to become job-creating killer whales? One place to start is within companies themselves. A few months before finishing this book, I was jogging on the beach in Los Angeles (no less, on our "Silicon Beach" beach in the vicinity of numerous tech companies) and overheard a Millennial lady fume to her speed-walking companion, "Can you believe our boss does not want to set up a website for our company—and this is 2017! I mean, hello!!" The only more depressing thing than her boss who failed to listen to his Gen XYZ staff is how many bosses like that there still are around the United States and the planet.

In 2016, my firm Nextrade Group and the National Center for the Middle Market depressingly found that executives of U.S. companies with $10 million to $1 billion in sales—the backbone of the American economy—assessed their digital transformation as lagging and assigned themselves a "Digital Grade Point Average" of 2.8 on a scale of 0 to 4, the equivalent of a C+.[62] Only the fastest-growing firms that invested most in digital were happier with the progress of their digital transformation; the laggards cited scant management buy-in in digitization as the leading problem. In a similar survey of Latin American companies that I ran for the Inter-American Development Bank, 62 percent cited "getting senior management support" as an obstacle to increasing online revenue.[63] A more recent report indicates that only 11 percent of U.S. manufacturers and 1 percent of U.K. manufacturers can be considered "digital champions," or firms that are aggressively innovating.[64]

Management, in short, can be its own worst enemy, keeping their businesses on the wrong side of the global digital divide.

One way to think of management's tech savvy and overall managerial quality is that it is like any other technology in a company: improving it will raise productivity in firms and economies. In a survey-based study, World Bank and OECD economists Ana Paula Cusolito, Raed Safadi, and Daria Taglioni found that companies' overall management score based on such things as continuous improvements based on performance analysis, use of incentive structures, and goal-setting, is highest in advanced economies such as in the United States and Japan, and lags in China, Brazil, and India.[65] These economies could get a more than 15 percent overall productivity boost from rising to the U.S. managerial quality levels, which they could do by reducing redundancies and waste in businesses and improving the allocation of labor.

Firms can also take cues from their peers in other sectors. In advanced economies, the most productive firms, especially in such sectors as retail, media, and financial services, are well on their way in digital transformation, the diffusion of technologies across the long tail of firms and such sectors as manufacturing, health care, and construction will take work even in the most advanced economies.[66]

But not all is up to the hapless management team: policy certainly matters. For example, while sailfish have at some point done the work to adopt technologies and start selling online, they are also likeliest to be found in countries and cities with fundamentals conducive to success in the digital economy—where talent, connectivity, and capital are abundant, logistics work, and labor markets are flexible for labor to be allocated and used most efficiently. Governments that engineer this setting help firms engage in ecommerce and trade. The recipe is quite simple: it is no accident that countries that have globally speaking high ratios of technology-intensive firms and firms that sell goods and services on global platforms such as the United Kingdom and Germany also have world-class talent, excellent Internet connections, access to fast-disbursing loans, and world-class logistics.

Of course, policies need to be tailored to country and the type of firm, given that challenges to the adoption of technologies and use of ecommerce for trade vary significantly by country, firm size, and firms' export status. The kinds of hurdles that a mid-size company in, say, El Salvador faces are different from those that a mid-size company in Indonesia faces. Hurdles faced by small Indonesian firms are often different from those of large Indonesian firms, and hurdles faced by small Indonesian exporters, the local sailfish, are different from those faced by Indonesian non-exporters, the country's herrings. Policymakers almost by default make a choice: help sailfish swim and grow faster, or seek to make herrings into sailfish, or help killer whales roam freer.

The choice is what economists would call "endogenous"—in part determined by these different kinds of companies' respective lobbying prowess. But it is also one that involves philosophical questions about the role of the government, economic questions about which types of companies create the most jobs and raise productivity levels, and political questions as to what optics look best—supporting thriving mid-size manufacturers in the Midwest or cheerleading five-woman startups from Brooklyn. What is clear is that different types of companies need different types of policies—but also that there are basic policies that improve the enabling environment for all companies: none will realize their potential without great logistics; easy and fast access to capital; and smart digital, business, and labor market regulations.

Now put yourself in the shoes of a policymaker with multiple competing priorities. One response to calls to improve the enabling environment for digitization and ecommerce might be that digitization is already happening, and it is just a matter of time before companies adopt new technologies and engage in ecommerce. But there are three reasons why this argument would be foolish to make.

The first is that creating a right policy environment can have strong shorter-term payoffs, especially for exports and job creation. Asked to estimate the impact if the top three perceived challenges to ecommerce (such as lack of access to capital, poor logistics, or difficulties finding talent) were removed, developing-country businesses typically report 20 to 35 percent sales gains in both their domestic and export markets, and 15 to 25 percent job increases in their firms.[67] Second, inaction can exacerbate in-country disparities, such as between rural and urban areas that may be harder to bridge later, pushing people to the cities. Third, lags in firms' technology adoption today can have enormously negative impacts later on, on long-term economic development. Let's examine this further.

Convergence Machine

In 2014, Dartmouth professor Diego Comin wrote a paper that compellingly shows that developing economies' use of new technologies such as fertilizers, phones, heart surgeries, and PCs has been limited when these were introduced, not because they have not been available, but because developing-country companies adopted these technologies only after a lag.[68] Steam engines, for example, were adopted in developing countries some 120 years after they were introduced in Great Britain. Comin boldly argued that differences in the adoption rates of new technologies is a key explanation for the income divergence between advanced and developing countries, which has grown eight-fold in the past two hundred years.[69] Extrapolating the argument, today's widening digital divides between advanced nations and developing countries could only widen this income gap, leaving developing countries to forever play catch-up—including in the digitizing trading system.

Of course, Comin's study needs to be taken with a grain of salt. Economists have for years studied the sources of long-term economic growth, finding that three factors need to converge: labor (the sheer vast number of workers and hours worked), capital (machines, buildings, servers, routers, IT equipment and basic Internet software, and so on), and total factor productivity (TFP), the magic pixie dust of growth that is not only technological progress, but also includes human capital—educated workers—good institutions, rule of law, trade and economic openness, and other such variables that are harder to measure and track. TFP tends to become more important as countries develop, as at some point labor and capital hit diminishing returns—adding the tenth worker brings more bang for the buck than adding the ten millionth.

However, Comin's point is also provocative given the importance of digital technologies and the human capital to use them for economic growth, and the fact that some large emerging nations such as China are hitting the diminishing returns to labor and capital. In other words, it could be that technology adoption and diffusion across firms are even more important than in the past for separating the rich from the poor. Furthermore, some economists argue that digitization is the new "capital," including such intangible assets as designs that engage large numbers of users and improve their digital experiences, digital capture of user behaviors and profiles, big-data and analytics capabilities that can guide operations, and so on. Though standard measures of GDP have yet to account for any of these gains, the argument can be made that countries that do not effectively use the Internet, ecommerce, and other digital capabilities would be destined to fall behind those that do.

Positively, developing-country income levels have been converging with those of advanced nations in the past few decades—because the ratio of economic growth to population growth has been higher in developing countries than in advanced nations. India's per capita income increased nearly five-fold from $390 in 1980 to $1,862 in 2016, versus U.S. per capita income that less than doubled during the period, from $28,734 to $52,262. Also encouraging, Comin shows that the time it takes for a new technology to be adopted in developing nations has gone down. For example, PCs, once adopted in advanced nations, came to the developing world fourteen years later, while the Internet was adopted in the developing world only eight years after taking off in advanced nations.

However, it can also be argued that today's technological change is much faster than in the 1800s—such that lags in adoption can have equally far-reaching consequences as in the past two hundred years. When developing countries finally come online to transact, advanced economies have already run with 5G and built layers upon layers of innovations spawned by the Internet on top, such as online stores complete with AI-based matching of global shoppers to goods they never even knew they might love, and new medical techniques such as remote surgery and autonomous vehicles. These worries have not escaped business leaders. For example, in a 2017 survey of over three thousand industry leaders from around the world, 83 percent expect 5G to catalyze small business growth but also tighten global competition—and nearly 70 percent are concerned that without 5G, their country will become less competitive in the online economy.[70] It could also be argued that failure to catch up is more consequential than in the past: the Internet and technologies such as ecommerce, blockchain, and AI riding on it are not akin to a heart surgery affecting the lives of some thousands of people but rather cross-cutting technologies that affect just about every economic interaction and transaction in an economy and that shape economies' growth paths.

Will developing countries catch up with advanced nations in technology adoption, or will they lag behind?

At one level it is very tough to believe that developing countries would attain the technology adoption rates of advanced economies—or that their income growth would seriously accelerate enough for them to catch up quickly with advanced economies. Compare, for example, Korea to Nigeria. Already with the world's fastest Internet at 41 Mbps in 2016 and 93 percent Internet penetration rates, South Korea has become one of the first countries to formally announce the adoption of a 5G mobile network, targeting 90 percent of 5G penetration by 2026.[71] According to the Korean telecom operator SK Telecom, 5G has in demos been yielding speeds of up to 19.1 gigabits per second, nearly a thousand times faster than 4G LTE users enjoy. That speed would transform ecommerce by enabling augmented reality and entertainment by allowing a movie download in fractions of a second; accelerating the development of sectors where lags in data transmission can be life-threatening, such as when driving a car and depending on the network for navigation; and powering the machine-to-machine dialogue and transfer of large-scale data essential in the Internet of Things. In contrast, 5G seems distant in Nigeria, which started to embrace 4G connections in 2017, and where only a quarter of the population uses the Internet.

A more optimistic view is that developing countries and their companies can use advanced economies' technological advances to leapfrog, and forego the incrementalism and experimentation of first-mover advanced nations that pilot technologies. In the past few decades, developing economies have done a great deal of leapfrogging. For example, they leapfrogged to the telephone era by going straight for mobile phones and cell towers, rather than doing what advanced nations once did, laying cables and standing up telephone poles. Now some countries such as Thailand and Rwanda are leaping over various stages of digitization by going from paper-based processes to blockchain in such areas as banking, microfinance, customs, and voting.

So will Korea soar and Nigeria languish, or will Nigeria catch up? The answer to these questions will be of monumental importance and will shape incomes and the well-being of billions of people. It of course depends on many variables, such as growth in these countries' capital stock such as transport infrastructures, buildings, machines, and other "hardware," and the size of the labor pool (which is soaring in Nigeria and dropping in Korea and China, such that by around 2120, China and Nigeria will both have some nine hundred million people). While Nigeria's workforce may be growing, its businesses are certainly not keeping up with Korea's, which is swooshing to the era of 5G, AI, and blockchain by making new investments in technology, science, education, and managerial quality. In 2018, Paul Romer won the Nobel Prize in Economics for showing that technological progress is not coming from outside or exogenous to countries, but is inherently endogenous to policy, such as investment in human capital and innovation. Much for Nigeria and developing nations rides on policy: public investments in science and technology; improvements in human capital to apply technologies; and good governance, such as taming corruption that still scares private investors.

Will developing-country governments invest in bleeding-edge technologies, such as the expensive transport, radio, and core network components 5G connections require? Will allocation of 5G spectra be efficient and transparent in developing economies—when even in America, 5G deployment is also decelerated by red tape and regulatory processes, spectrum scarcity, and local government bureaucrats? Will they apply AI and blockchain to undo redundancies and weed out corruption? Will they ramp up education and leadership skills for business leaders to apply technologies like CEOs do in such tech nations as Korea, Israel, Singapore, and Finland? Will the younger generation of developing-country business leaders and policymakers, who just about invariably understand the importance of technology for development, be able to push through policies to accelerate technology adoption in their nations? Will the majorities, not just a handful of smart people in a handful of creative companies, be able to apply technologies and innovate?

Europe may offer a glimpse into the importance of answers to these questions. In no other region have poorer countries been catching up since the 1960s as quickly with the richer ones as in the European Union. Polish incomes, for example, converged from 52 percent of EU average in 2004 to 68 percent in 2017. The enablers were the single market that enables free trade and also some movement of labor across the continent, and the EU's structural funds in infrastructure and other investments in eastern and southern Europe.[72] But this "convergence machine" has slowed down in recent years, between northern and southern and eastern European countries and within economies, between productive and less productive firms, and between supercities and the rest. The explanation, according to World Bank economists and consistent with Comin, is technology that opens opportunities for skilled workers and tech-driven firms that are more abundant in the north and in cities, while low-skilled workers and less productive firms that are more prevalent in the south risk falling behind.[73]

Technology-driven economies are in a virtuous cycle: they have higher payoffs to schooling and work as both enable people to build their skills further, learning by doing: in Sweden, one additional year of work raises wages by 5.5 percent, while in Afghanistan, where workers are likely to toil in more manual labor with fewer technological changes, the payoff from working another year is only a 0.3 percent gain in wages (and perhaps a higher chance of being replaced by a machine).[74] Returns to work are low in developing nations because their people are not educated to have the skills to maximize the return on their labor. No matter how hard they run, they keep running in place.

One possible future outcome is a division of the world into four types of economies: today's advanced nations and China, who are doing well on technology adoption and whose firms habitually engage in digital trade; emerging markets such as Brazil and India that have made very smart moves and have extremely sophisticated pockets in their economies and produce a steady stream of globalized, tech-driven success story companies; countries such as Nigeria that have made progress but where firms still struggle to do business and digitize; and countries such as Afghanistan and Congo, where most people have even yet to come online, let alone acquire the human capital needed to successfully leverage technology. The outcome will have an impact on how these countries do in world trade and whether they converge with rich or poor nations: those with 5G connections, smart ports, blockchained banks, and digitized firms will race forward and increase their productivity and incomes.

Conclusion

As you next text your friend in Europe, you might tell her about the first transatlantic telegraph, a 509-letter message sent in 1858 from British Queen Victoria to U.S. President James Buchanan that took seventeen hours and forty minutes to cross the Atlantic. The positive fact is that just about the entire world is today far more like the connected world you inhabit than the Victorian world. The sad part is that much of the world still lives off the Internet's orbit. And even for those companies and countries that are online, the gains from digitization to trade and growth are far from automatic: they depend on management buy-in for the companies to adopt new technologies and business models that come with them, and on good policies that enable firms to access high-skilled workers, capital, fluid logistics, and online payments.

The following chapters discuss these different policy areas. How governments address them today can make a monumental difference in the lives of their citizens and the growth of their countries.

STUCK IN CUSTOMS

In their December 2013 ministerial meeting in Bali, WTO members reached the historic Trade Facilitation Agreement (TFA). Already flying back from Bali with an Australian colleague, we high-fived in Hong Kong upon landing for transit and learning about the last-minute deal. Many people felt the TFA gave the WTO, on a deathbed since the failed Doha Round, a new lease on life. The crown jewel of the organization's attainments, the TFA commits countries to expediting the movement, release, and clearance of goods at their borders. Economists have calculated that the resulting improved throughput of trade will unlock more than $1 trillion into the global economy.

Altogether, trade costs, the various costs of moving cargo from one part of the Earth to another, have dropped precipitously over the past two hundred years, contributing, with trade liberalization, trade agreements, and economic growth, to the 6 percent annual growth of world trade in the second half of the twentieth century. Policy has played a major role in lowering trade costs. Still exhausted from the decades of tariff reductions talks, in the 1990s and 2000s international agencies and governments turned their attention to trade facilitation, spending tens of billions of dollars to reform customs regulations, computerize border agencies, and upgrade countries' road and port infrastructures. This massive investment has delivered a return—for example, for the fifty-three poorest countries, every $1 million increase in aid money in trade facilitation is found to reduce by 6 percent the cost of packing goods, loading them into a container, transporting the consignment to the port of departure, and loading it on a vessel or truck.[1]

On the ground floor of commerce things are not as streamlined. Numerous countries continue having tremendous bottlenecks at their borders that delay shipments and cost companies time and money, undermining the gains from new technologies aimed to facilitate trade. Worse, hungry for customs duty revenue, hounded by protectionist lobbies, and worried about national security, governments are setting up a new obstacle course for the emerging traders, ecommerce sellers, to navigate—and one that TFA cannot touch.

Border Bottleneck

In 2015, Americas Market Intelligence (AMI) carried out a mystery shopping exercise for a leading logistics company, to assess door-to-door delivery times in different countries.[2] AMI sent packages to customers in all continents using several different logistics firms. In Asia, Europe, and North America, packages arrived to the customer as scheduled within two to five days, but in Latin America, delays were the norm. In Argentina, customs officials asked for bribes to expedite the clearing of the packages, while Colombian and Mexican customs did not clear the packages, arguing the receiver must become a registered importer. Consumers are not blind to the problems at the border. Though some 40 percent of Brazilian shoppers and over half of Mexicans buy online from abroad at least once a year, shoppers in these nations also report hesitations related to shipping costs and the ability to return items purchased.[3] The Argentine Chamber of Electronic Commerce found that even domestic ecommerce deliveries typically required at least a week to be delivered; a third took more than two weeks.[4]

Logistics challenges holding up Latin America's ecommerce are a big deal. For companies, delays in trade, such as due to arcane customs procedures or poor logistics, equal money down the drain: a day's delay in transit roughly equals a percentage point tariff—up to 2.1 percent in time-sensitive parts and components, according to the pioneering work by David Hummels and Georg Schaur.[5] And this is not counting the dents delays cause in a company's reputation and competitiveness, or the stranglehold a holdup places on its cash flow. Or, stress for company managers inquiring about the state of their cargo stuck in the bowels of a port. The repercussions on national economic growth can be significant: a one-day delay in goods reaching their destination is equivalent to a 1 percent decrease in the country's trade or to adding 70 kilometers of transport distance; a day's delay in time-sensitive goods results in a 6 percent reduction in trade for the country.[6]

At the same time, the challenges uncovered by AMI are also just old wine in new bottles. Trade in Latin America has for decades been held back by bureaucratic customs and inefficient transport and delivery systems. They are simply now affecting ecommerce. Customs procedures for ecommerce imports, market access to exports, total cost of delivery to foreign customers, and rural last-mile delivery are among Latin American firms' top constraints to doing ecommerce. On a scale of 1 (very poor) to 10 (excellent), small businesses in Mexico, Brazil, Argentina, and Chile alike rated these elements 5 out of 10.[7] These findings were echoed in another survey I ran with the Inter-American Development Bank: in it over 50 percent of Latin American companies find market access barriers to be a "very significant" obstacle, while over 40 percent find the same for poor logistics and a third of customs procedures.[8] In a 2014 survey of 3,466 American companies in digitally intensive industries, 48 percent of small and mid-size businesses viewed customs requirements as an obstacle to trade.[9]

To be sure, African merchants might be willing to trade their logistics challenges with those of their peers in the Americas. In one of my firms' surveys, Kenyan and Ghanian companies rated ecommerce-related cross-border logistics 4 out of 10. Problems in border clearance keep the entire ecommerce ecosystem from its potential. In a meeting in the outskirts of Nairobi with Africa's leading ecommerce platform Jumia, a managing director described tremendous hurdles for cross-border business, including delays and fees at customs and sheer lack of cross-border logistics operators. As a result, merchants lack incentives to use platforms or other formal channels for cross-border trade, opting for smuggling if they must.

In 1971, Uruguayan journalist Eduardo Galeano wrote the famous volume *Open Veins of Latin America*, which described the region's agonized eras of European colonization.[10] Almost forty years later, the Inter-American Development Bank published the cheekily titled volume *Unclogging the Arteries: The Impact of Transport Costs on Trade in Latin America and the Caribbean*, a set of policy ideas to unlock the region's trade arteries.[11] One bold solution to the border bottleneck has been to get rid of the border. The European Union has done the biggest feat of all—closed customs for trade within the EU. The gain from this audacious move, along with the overall trade integration, is as much as 20 percent extra per capita income for Europeans. Economists agree these gains outpace those from other integration groupings—even though they still pale before the gains the United States scores each year from being a customless and integrated, English-speaking country. But in most regions such as in Latin America, it is decidedly faster to improve customs than copy the EU, and in these regions technology has in three ways helped bypass inefficient border processes.

First, countries have modernized and digitized customs. The payoffs are very meaningful. The World Bank estimates that digitized customs clearance cuts border compliance time for imports on average from 110 hours to 37 hours; in the Philippines, after digitization to combat corruption, 70 percent of goods sail through in 2 hours.[12] Mongolia may have found another "technology": in 2015, it decided to end endemic corruption in customs by replacing all male customs agents with females. Express shippers hail the experiment a resounding success.

Second, governments have set up trade single windows to facilitate companies' regulatory compliance at the border, by enabling companies to submit the many documents required for export and import clearance to one single "window," often in electronic format. For example, Colombia's single window connects twenty-one public agencies such as customs, the food and drug administration, the agricultural institute, and others, and three private companies that provide electronic signature certificates and legal information with importers, exporters, and customs brokers to secure authorizations and certifications needed to import and export products.[13]

Ideated and piloted in Sweden and Singapore in the late 1980s, single windows have proliferated around the world in recent years; as of 2017, 27 countries out of 127 had a full electronic single window and 36 had a partial single window. All 164 signatories to the TFA are encouraged to adopt an electronic single window.

Studies suggest electronic single windows have helped halve document processing times in border agencies, cut trade compliance times to a third, increased adopting countries' exports and GDPs, and overall improved the transparency and user experience in border clearance.[14] In Colombia, partly thanks to the single window, the time to import a container fell from forty-eight to thirteen days and the time to export from thirty-four to fourteen days in 2006–2011.[15] After Costa Rica's adoption of an electronic single window in 2005–2010, exporters needed to only fill in a single form online once, which the single window then distributed automatically to the various agencies that needed to issue permits. Exports processed through this channel grew 1.4 percent faster than exports for which single window was not adopted. According to IADB estimates, without the single window, Costa Rican exports would have been on average 2 percent lower than they were between 2008 and 2013, or roughly 0.5 percent of GDP.[16] Costa Rica is estimated to have reaped a $16 economic gain from every $1 invested in the single window.

These benefits stem in part from the digitization of trade documents. Paperless trade practices are found to cut import compliance times into a third and export compliance times by almost a quarter from a fully paper-based setting.[17]

Reforms notwithstanding, border clearance processes hold hundreds of billions of dollars of slack. World Economic Forum research shows that if every country improved border administration and transport and communications infrastructure even halfway to the world's logistics superstar Singapore's level, world trade would increase by 15 percent and world GDP would increase by a mammoth 5 percent, or $3.75 trillion.[18] Four pain points are particularly pressing.

First, despite much talk about the importance of paperless trade, there is still a lot of paper at the border. *A lot of paper.*[19] By 2017, only 28 countries out of 119 had adopted electronic application issuance of export permits, 25 had adopted electronic application and issuance of preferential certificate of origin, 45 had adopted electronic submission of both sea cargo and air cargo manifests, and only 61 had adopted electronic submission of customs declarations. Low-income countries such as Afghanistan, Myanmar, Yemen, and Congo have yet to implement even the most basic paperless trade measures. Paper is drowning small businesses not staffed with trade compliance professionals. Sub-Saharan African importers spend on average 98 hours in handling paperwork for a single consignment, as opposed to only 4 hours in Thailand and an hour in Canada and Sweden, where traders use digital documents.[20] The time a company needs to set aside to complete just the paperwork for exports is breathtaking in some countries: 228 hours, or almost 10 days, in Afghanistan and 192 hours in the Congo.

According to Yann Duval, the chief of the trade facilitation unit at the UN Economic and Social Commission for Asia and the Pacific, the costs associated with trade documentation and cumbersome trade procedures are $350 billion per year for Asia and the Pacific, which is the equivalent of 15 percent of the region's trade.[21]

The persistence of paper in trade is caused by several factors: sheer inertia in trade agencies, lack of trust in electronic documents, perhaps in some countries' lack of electronic signatures laws, agencies' limited budgets, and concerns about job security among agency staff employed in processing paper documents.

Second, border clearance processes are still shamefully slow in countries such as Tanzania, where importing goods takes on average 402 hours, or Myanmar, where it takes 230 hours—a mind-blowing contrast to 1 hour in Switzerland and 2 in the United States, and one that inspires awe in firms that actually do cross-border business in those developing markets. One problem is that these countries do not have single windows. And in countries that do, single windows are not that efficient or digitized or even that single: border agencies operate in their respective data silos and can be reluctant to share data and collaborate with each other. Arcane customs duty payments processes also decelerate border clearance, as goods can move inland only after payment has been made and matched to a given shipment.

For example, even though their fees, taxes and duties are computed automatically via the UN-sponsored ASYCUDA World customs management platform, Sri Lankan traders still need to visit customs to submit paper documents and customs payments.[22] In the fifty-odd countries that have enabled electronic payments of customs duties, direct deposits and bank wires often have too little data for customs to quickly match them to a given shipment. Instead, customs operators have to manually intervene to match an electronic payment such as a direct deposit to a given shipment—which also lengthens clearance times.

Third, delays at the border also still have to do with graft. Customs officials are the key node between a buyer in their country and a foreign company eager to bring a product to the buyer, not unlike a DMV officer is a key node between you and the state government issuing your driver's license. In many developing countries and especially in Africa, they monetize delays and are incentivized to hold trade up. Frustrated by the wait and eager to get their cash from customers, companies eventually succumb. Corruption in customs is endemic and has been hard to weed out. It has been estimated to cost World Customs Organization members at least $2 billion in customs revenue each year.[23]

The fourth pain point at the border is the accentuated demands for customs security in the era of ecommerce: whereas before border agencies mostly dealt with a limited number of large companies doing regular, container-based transactions, today they have to contend with an avalanche of millions of parcel-based shipments and new small traders they do not know. Let's explore the consequences next.

The Four Horsemen of Trade

In his book *The Box*, Marc Levinson shows how the container, one of the simplest yet most important innovations in world trade, has become a curse for customs inspectors and security officials.[24] While each container has a manifest listing of its contents, no one knows what's really inside until taking all contents out. The problem is of course the time that would take. The largest ships, each with boxes floor to ceiling, can carry 19,100 containers (the cargo capacity of a thousand Boeing 747-400s). America's busiest of ports such as Los Angeles and Long Beach have throughput of millions of containers each year—4.8 million containers were imported via the Port of Los Angeles in 2017, or 13,150 on an average day. Assuming that x-raying each container would take four minutes, the total time spent x-raying per day would be eight hundred and seventy two hours, occupying the time of 109 workers working nonstop through an eight-hour day in one single port.

Now multiply that across the United States, whose sea port traffic alone is some six times that of Los Angeles. Much more comes in by truck, rail, and air. In 2015, 246 million tons of stuff was imported into the United States by sea, and altogether 1.1 billion tons (or over three times the total weight of the world's human population) came in by sea, truck, rail, air, or some combination thereof.[25] Not even a sizable army could inspect them all without jamming the trade lanes of the world's importer-in-chief, or inciting the ire of American tax payers.

The tug of war between businesses' needs for trade facilitation and customs' needs for border security has played out for decades, and intensified considerably in the wake of 9/11. Four solutions helped appease both those who wanted fluid flow of cargo and those who wanted to secure it.

First, in a stroke of brilliance, America's cargo security was moved offshore. In 2002, the U.S. Customs and Border Protection (CBP) launched the Container Security Initiative (CSI), under which U.S.-bound maritime cargo is screened in foreign ports before it departs for the United States. CSI became operational in fifty-eight ports in North America, Europe, Asia, Africa, the Middle East, and Latin America.

Second, cargo manifests became longer and more specific, and had to be submitted well before the ship would arrive in a U.S. port. The 2009 SAFE Port Act created the so-called "10+2" rule that made the U.S. importer or its freight-forwarder responsible for providing granular data and ten key data elements on the cargo at least twenty-four hours prior to its arrival at a U.S. port.

As importers complained that 10+2 added significant additional burden to trade compliance,[26] the United States and many other countries also set up so-called Trusted Trader or Authorized Economic Operator programs to fast-track verifiably low-risk companies' trade. Trusted traders would be businesses with compelling security measures on their premises such as fences, cameras, and locks protecting warehouses. In other words, if a trusted trader was a person boarding a flight for the United States, he could verifiably ascertain he packed his own bags at his home that morning and no one had put anything in his luggage between then and now.

Third, customs improved their data analytics to spot and inspect only suspicious containers before those arrive in U.S. ports, much like your bank may spot anomalous charges on your credit card. Roughly 5 percent of all seaborne containers are flagged as high risk and x-rayed; only a fraction of those are high risk from the national security vantage point.[27] This enables the 95 percent of legitimate, non-suspicious cargo to move through more quickly. In 2010, predictive analytics famously enabled U.S. authorities to identify a bomb that was contained inside a printer cartridge and shipped from Yemen to Chicago. The discovery was automatically made on the basis of trade data that showed that Yemen was an unusual provider of office supplies to the location destined in Chicago.[28]

Fourth, after the Yemen episode, CBP created the so-called Air Cargo Advanced Screening program with major shippers such as FedEx, DHL, and UPS, to help CBP access the names and addresses of the shipper and consignee, total package count and weight, and cargo description, as well as the air waybill well ahead of other data required for regular customs clearance, in order for the agency to perform risk-based targeting of incoming cargo.

Ecommerce has created new complexities for customs terrorized by the prospect of nuclearized containers. In the eyes of customs security officials, the millions of parcels sent by online sellers are just as efficient as containers for smuggling the feared four horsemen of trade—explosives, drugs, guns, and fakes—as they are for moving legitimate cargo. And not only do customs lack visibility into the content of these parcels, they worry about the lack of visibility into the small businesses shipping and receiving them. For customs, ecommerce makes risk in world trade increasingly fragmented, amorphous, and elusive.

Thus in parcels we have the new container: there are more and more and more of them, and we cannot for a fact know what's within them without opening them. Customs is spooked for a reason: in a five-day test at JFK airport

CBP and partner agencies found that of 3,000 packages, over 1,500 were not compliant with such agencies as the U.S. Department of Agriculture or the Consumer Product Safety Administration, or with U.S. intellectual property laws.[29] In 2016, there were thirty-two thousand seizures of packages, mostly originating from China, that violated U.S. intellectual property rules—and no one knows how many more got through.[30] Customs is also worried about growing shipments of the dangerous opioid Fentanyl.

A particular heartburn is caused by parcels shipped by post. While express shippers such as Fedex and DHL require their customers to fill out customs forms and comply with trade rules, postal systems are less demanding. In one of the trade world's open secrets, today millions of parcels move through postal systems with a limited amount of information on them—and often bypass customs altogether. A 2015 study showed that none of twenty-nine test buys from the United States from illegal online pharmacies from India and shipped by postal services was stopped by U.S. Customs.[31] Express shippers incensed about competition from cheap government-backed postal services highlight other troubles. A UPS-sponsored study on Canadian imports found that sales tax and import duty are significantly less likely to be collected when shipments are sent via postal services: import duty was collected on just 6 percent of postal shipment imports, compared to 98 percent in the case of express shippers.[32]

Yet the volume of parcels shipped through posts is bound to only mushroom as sellers and shoppers are unwilling to pay for the fees of express shippers. Businesses will as a result keep "going postal" when going global.

Inspecting each package and parcel by opening them is as unfeasible as it is foolish, and jams trade and wastes taxpayer money: most of the packages arriving on U.S. shores—457 million in 2016—carry T-shirts, running shoes, beauty products, or electronics, rather than one of the horsemen of trade. The optimal solution is also not saddling small businesses and consumers shopping and selling online with new and onerous trade compliance and filing requirements. After all, when shipments are small, the fixed costs involved with trade compliance can more easily usurp profits than when companies ship in bulk. The fixed trade compliance costs for a (typically smaller) business that ships one unit of an item worth, say, $1,000 are proportionally considerably higher than they are for a (typically larger) business that ships ten thousand units of the same item. One study of European companies, dated in the late 1980s but illustrative, found that businesses with fewer than 250 employees shoulder 30 to 45 percent higher transaction costs per consignment than those of larger firms.[33] Raising those costs further could freeze shipments of low-value items and small business trade. Yet in the damp world economy post–Great Recession, governments have hit importers and exporters with penalties and consent decrees, forcing small businesses to hire in-house trade compliance staff—or perhaps struggle or take chances. In a 2016 survey by the trade compliance firm Amber Road, 56 percent of U.S. companies stated they are not investing in trade compliance training, even though 28 percent had been fined or warned by the government for noncompliance.[34]

The most innovative customs agencies have passed the worries about the contents of parcels to computers. For example, Singapore Customs flags anomalies in shipments with a technology that risk-scores customs declarations on the basis of predefined criteria and historical datasets with such data as shipment clearance times and declaration-related information.[35] It has also put machine learning to work, to enable the analysis of hypotheses and associations in data much faster than is done in traditional econometric techniques. Machines have spotted such frauds as underpayment of duty for cigarettes through analytics that showed that the weight of goods declared in a declaration for cigarettes was lower than the historical norm. Singapore Customs is now teaching AI to read X-ray images of containers, in order to detect anomalies without humans and alert customs officials to open suspicious items manually.[36]

Blockchain is also helping to combat customs fraud and facilitate trade. It has for example been piloted in U.K. customs to enable the twenty-eight border agencies to coordinate risk management and interventions, a necessity for when the United Kingdom leaves the EU customs union and its customs declarations shoot up from 55 million to over 250 million (its non-EU trade plus its EU trade, when previously no customs documents were needed).[37] Blockchain seems like a saving grace for Britons anguished about these new demands. It enables the tracing of products to their origin, which can help customs determine the appropriate tariff, such as an EU tariff for a package destined for the EU. Blockchain entries can be shared in real time, securely, and transparently with multiple parties, for every border agency to have a bird's-eye view on any one shipment, and all paperwork and events associated with it. This helps coordinate inspections, reduce administrative costs and delays in trade transactions, and enable compliant companies and shipments to pass through customs faster.[38]

These solutions are promising means to balance governments' triple objectives of trade facilitation, customs security, and customs revenue. But most governments are only coming to understand them; broad-based adoption is still a distant prospect, and meanwhile parcel volumes in world trade mount. One simple method to accelerate border clearance is to let particularly the lower-value items to pass through duty- and tax-free and let machines catch fraudsters that undervalue their shipments—a net-positive for customs agencies whose revenue from small shipments does not cover the costs of border processes. But most lawmakers are pushing in the wrong direction.

Possibly the Worst Policy in the World

It was not too many decades ago that wars between major powers were *de rigueur*. The problem for all sides was how to pay for it all. Tariffs were a great solution: trade was happening, and it was rather easy to monitor and tax. Germany initially turned to tariffs to fund its World War I effort; America's independence may just have been built on tariffs, as the Founding Fathers used tariffs and excise taxes on alcohol and cigarettes to pay off the debts of the War of Independence.[39] Before the U.S. income tax was introduced in 1913 (those were the days!), U.S. government depended on tariffs to operate. Now that was also before agricultural subsidies or Social Security or Medicare. Since then, of course, the United States has become the most open economy of all advanced nations, with an average tariff of barely over 2 percent.

Quite a few developing countries, especially African economies with rampant tax evasion and vast informal economies of unregistered companies, to this date tax trade with the goal of filling the government kitty. In advanced economies, taxation is more effective and tariffs have become quite irrelevant as a source of revenue. Instead, along with their cousin non-tariff barriers, tariffs are in advanced nations a useful tool of patronage, deployed in selected sectors to protect (and thereby secure campaign contributions from) domestic business lobbies fearful of foreign competition. But even this use of tariffs has decreased as countries have traded tariff reductions to gain market access for their respective export industries—such as airplanes and computers for the United States or iron ore and soy beans for Brazil.

Or so we thought.

The rise of ecommerce has rekindled many governments' fancy for taxing trade. Start with the State of New York, which recently had an idea: why not charge state sales and income tax on small online retailers in Missouri (or any other state for that matter) selling to shoppers in New York? In the past, this taxation was possible if the Missouri company had a "nexus," or a physical presence, such as a store, in New York. However, as ecommerce has grown, many U.S. states like New York have gone out of their way to argue that nexus means any sales presence or online marketing.[40] Some states ride on the convenience of old definitions. In Alabama, for example, the creation of nexus hinges on the definition of "salesman"—the Amazon bot recommending you buy that pretty flower vase online may just qualify as an Alabama-based "salesman." The expansion of nexus has forced Amazon to pay sales tax in numerous states, though it has long argued it has a physical presence in only a few of them.

American states are not alone. For example, Brazilian states, each with their own taxes, have long made inter-state commerce in the South American giant much costlier and more complex than it should be. And in the era when just about all governments want to get small business to export, perhaps the most shockingly bad and counterproductive policies persisting in the books is low *de minimis*—the maximum value of an import that is exempt from customs duties, taxes, and complicated rules of origin. The idea behind *de minimis* has been to fast-track through customs low-value items not worth taxing—after all, the collection costs of duties and taxes on low-value items typically outweigh the revenue produced. Yet *de minimis* levels are still laughably low in major markets, for example $15 in Canada, $50 in Mexico, and $150 in the European Union.

The United States and the Philippines have been the only significant reformers. In 2016, both raised their *de minimis*, the U.S. from $200 to $800 and the Philippines from ridiculously arcane 48 cents to $210. Other governments keep this value-detracting system going, both to secure revenue and appease protectionist domestic retailers. Worse, many are going in the opposite direction from the United States, to tax the juicy stream of ecommerce.

For example, after vigorous lobbying by domestic retailers, in 2017 Australia instituted a 10 percent Goods and Services tax on imports below the country's $756 *de minimis* for sellers exceeding roughly $53,000 in annual sales into Australia (both in USD), thus in effect imposing a tax on offshore supplies bought by Australian consumers.[41] This was the handiwork of the country's retail lobby, which argued that if a foreign business is not charged a sales tax in Australia, it will gain an unfair competitive advantage vis-à-vis domestic retailers that are taxed. This despite that fact that the Australian Productivity Commission, which is a government-supported objective economics research entity, earlier found that Australian businesses, consumers, and the government would as a result of the removal of *de minimis* bear a collective cost of approximately $1.7 billion in exchange for about $520 million in new revenue, with a net loss of almost $1.2 billion.[42] Besides, removal of *de minimis* might just entice Amazon to come and set up giant warehouses in Australia, ship goods into the country in bulk at a discount, and take over the retail market from within, something Amazon set out to do in 2018.

Another crafty taxer, the European Union, has issued new measures to go after the little guy. The EU has a unique set-up—its customs *de minimis* is €150 but its value-added tax *de minimis* is only €22. With around 150 million parcels imported free of VAT into the EU each year, this system, EU businesses reason, discriminates against EU businesses that are liable to the application of VAT from the first eurocent sold, not from €22 up. And of course they have a point. Some imported high-value goods such as smartphones and tablets are purposely undervalued or incorrectly described in the import paperwork so as to benefit from the VAT exemption.

The latest idea that took hold was that online sellers selling up to €10,000 annually to the EU can treat their sales similar to their domestic sales and be exempt from VAT; the rest are not exempt.

Yet a recent study by a group of European economists found that it would have been much better for the European Union to *increase* the VAT *de minimis*: the total cost of duty and tax collection incurred by European customs administrations and the private sector currently vastly exceeds the revenues collected.[43] For a break-even, the study recommended keeping the customs *de minimis* at €150 but increasing VAT *de minimis* to €80. Under that scenario, cost-savings for EU economies would be some €32 million, while the net effect on VAT collected is insignificant.[44] What's more, the study covered only a fraction of trade, as shipments carried by postal services or non-express shippers, sea transport, rail, or truck transport were not included.

Similar studies have been carried out globally, with painfully similar results yet without much practical impact.

A 2016 study on Canada's *de minimis* finds that raising *de minimis* from $15 to $150 would imply foregone revenue of $117 million but save the government $278 million in collection costs.[45] Factoring in the costs and delays incurred by businesses and consumers, increasing *de minimis* to $200 would result in a $648 million net gain for Canada. In a study of twelve Asia-Pacific Economic Cooperation economies (Canada, Chile, the People's Republic of China, Indonesia, Japan, Malaysia, Mexico, Papua New Guinea, Peru, the Philippines, Thailand, and Vietnam), raising *de minimis* to just $200 would deliver an average net gain of $5.4 billion per economy.[46] A 2012 study of a *de minimis* hike in five ASEAN economies finds the ratio of benefits to costs is a resounding 5.6.[47]

In contrast, the United States and the Philippines are now harvesting the gains of their *de minimis* hikes. Imagine a Filipino small business owner importing input costing $209 to the Philippines, manufacturing his product, and then shipping the $799 product to the United States. His world changed in 2016 as he no longer needed to pay any duties or taxes on these transactions. Bet you his competitor in Thailand in the throes of the $28 Thai *de minimis* would like to have the discount on imported parts. They may also wish for a higher *de minimis* when their American customer returns the product she ordered from Thailand, as the returned item, even if never opened, worn, or used overseas, may have to pay import tariff upon reentering Thailand. Canadian importers stuck with the $15 *de minimis* are surely wishing to have the $800 *de minimis* their American competitors enjoy.

In 2011, Gary Hufbauer and Yee Wong at the Peterson Institute of International Economics analyzed the impact of an $800 *de minimis* in the United States, still then a pie-in-the-sky concept.[48] Shipments in the $200 to $800 range were then "Informal Entries" that required the filling out of CBP Form 7501, a document with instructions of thirty-two pages and one that called for numerous details about the merchandise. It probably also required new file cabinets: Form 7501 must be stored for five years. For express shippers such as Fedex, the paperwork required about 9.2 minutes per entry, or 0.15 hours. Assuming all-in labor costs at $21 per hour, express shippers and USPS paid about $24 million filling out the required forms and $1 million in storing them each year. Assuming customs spent 2 minutes per entry, its paperwork costs in the $200 to $800 bracket were $8 million a year. This meant that prior to the U.S. reform, the paperwork alone in the $200 to $800 bracket cost $32 million, almost the same as customs revenue from these low-value items ($37 million).

When savings for American importers and shoppers from duty-free imports are factored in, the gains vastly exceed the losses. After all, in a conservative estimate, the time burden on the seller, express shipper or postal systems, customs, and the ultimate buyer of the product for goods above the $200 threshold is four to eight hours. Much of this is time spent on investigating the relevant customs schedule, understanding rules of origin, filling out paperwork, dealing with a customs broker, and collecting the goods and paying customs duty upon delivery.

These hassle factors incurred costs especially for small businesses with limited staff and higher per-shipment fixed costs due to smaller shipments.

Therefore, America's *de minimis* increase was pure free trade for small business exporters worldwide, and for all American importers, big and small.

Taxation Without Representation

Low *de minimis* levels have not stayed in governments' books by ignorance or accident. They reflect political economy dynamics—customs and finance ministries' imperatives to find sources of revenue in the insipid global economy, and entrenched interests of traditional domestic retailers fearful of foreign online competitors. Yet the low *de minimis* levels clash with at least two types of arguments against forcing small remote retailers to pay taxes in a market where they have no meaningful local presence.[49]

First, consumption taxes on sales made by small foreign online retailers can be seen as discriminatory. The rise of the omnichannel model to replace pure-play online or brick-and-mortar models and Amazon's construction of massive warehouses in markets it serves attests to the value of market presence in retail—time to market and responsiveness. In industries such as fashion, companies with in-market presence can have four-wall showrooms where consumers can touch and feel the products; such companies also do not have to deal with cross-border returns. Retailers with facilities in-country impose burdens on the local infrastructure that remote retailers do not: a large store or a distribution center needs water, sewer, run-off, roads, power, police, schools, and other parts of infrastructure. Small, remote online retailers do not enjoy the edge that in-country presence brings, nor do they impose any such costs. There is thus a strong argument that imposing sales or other taxes on retailers without in-country presence where they sell is discriminatory.

Second, compliance costs with foreign taxes are excessive and onerous on small business and possibly unenforceable. Large companies have lawyers and tax professionals to comply with taxes in different markets; small businesses don't. Ironically, the success of small businesses in growing into multimarket sellers, something ecommerce enables them to do, is also their curse, as it entails burdens of regulatory and tax compliance in multiple markets, each with different rules. If taxes are applied without any real connection to local presence, as many propose, small businesses selling online become subject to every government's tax enforcement. Meanwhile, major government resources may end up being spent on enforcing taxation on far-flung foreign online sellers for what are likely modest sums in per-company taxes.

Even the brightest star of international trade and digital economy, Singapore, has opened a debate on making foreign companies pay the 7 percent sales tax, by requiring them to register for GST if they were to provide to end-consumers in Singapore. In addition, there have been proposals that Internet platforms collect sales taxes from small sales. For example, in one proposal, firms selling more than about $750,000 in goods and services into Singapore in the B2C markets start paying sales tax, and companies selling less than that will be registered by online platforms that collect the sales tax on behalf of these companies. This is clearly a new fee for sellers, and a challenge for platforms to execute.

Where governments get it very wrong is thinking they are merely taxing *foreign* companies and goods. After all, most of the gain from ecommerce is for their own countries' companies and consumers able to access a wider variety of products at world prices. A low *de minimis* is simply a tax on domestic importers and consumers. And taxing foreign companies gives license to other countries to tax too. Or what does a little Australian online retailer selling to European shoppers think of Europe's VAT *de minimis*?

Conclusion

The proliferation of parcels and packages in trade is giving rise to new security concerns, protectionist kneejerk reactions, and creative taxes. For customs agencies expressing legitimate concerns about illicit trade, there are tools such as blockchain and machine learning to separate illicit and licit trade. For protectionist retailers, there is little hope: while small foreign e-tailers unlikely pose a huge competitive challenge, giant online retailers will disrupt. The proliferation of parcels and packages in trade is giving rise to new security concerns, protectionist kneejerk reactions, and creative taxes. These obstacles hamper the players most enabled by ecommerce to trade across borders—small businesses, which are already struggling with red tape, paper, and corruption at borders. Technologies such as blockchain, machine learning, and artificial intelligence can be powerful solutions for border agencies to manage the parcel tsunami and meet their triple objective, to secure and facilitate trade and collect customs revenue. For protectionist retailers, there is little hope: online retailers, embraced by consumers worldwide, are disrupting brick-and-mortars. Protectionism by way of new taxes, tariffs, *de minimis* cuts, and limits to foreign direct investment in the country's ecommerce sector only make domestic consumers and small businesses worse off, and do not obviate the reality: retailers must digitize or die.

10

SPLINTERNET

It was only a quarter century ago that larger developing countries had 50 percent average tariffs, foreign investors in developing countries had few protections against expropriation, and governments even outside the Soviet orbit, such as Argentina or Thailand, ran many sectors of their economies. The handmaiden to help bring about a more open and integrated world economy in which business leaders ran businesses and investors were protected was good policy. During the 1980s, developing countries and the post-communist economies emerging from communism drastically cut their tariffs and removed restrictions on foreign investment. Countries around the world came to the table to negotiate the Uruguay Round, the most encompassing multilateral trade agreements yet, and formed the World Trade Organization, poised to drive liberalization and manage trade disputes.

Unrivalled after the fall of the Berlin Wall, free market ideology forced a wave of privatizations around the world, transforming governments from managers of economies into regulators of markets. In his book *The End of History*, Francis Fukuyama famously declared victory to the twin forces of capitalism and democracy.[1]

This grand policy experiment has paid off. Backward developing nations have leveraged trade and foreign investment to become booming emerging markets. Millions around the world have gained employment through trade—in the United States alone, seventy-two million people derive their livelihoods from companies that export. Study after study shows how trade openness has made consumers around the world better off, sharpened countries' comparative advantages, and lifted people from poverty. If the world economy was a TV show, the episodes of the past thirty years featuring liberalizing economies, freer enterprise, and rise in cross-border flows of goods, services, capital, and people would get the best ratings yet.

Yet trouble looms. Today's global digital economy has no unifying ideology or policy framework like the one that made countries march in the same direction in the 1990s. It has no common, enforceable rules that would give certainty to businesses operating across borders. It does not even have a common set of norms everyone would want to adhere to. Instead, countries around the world are fashioning and implementing their own digital regulations in such areas as data privacy and transfer, Internet intermediary liability rules, and taxes on digital sales. What many have called "digital protectionism" seems to be on the rise. Exiting from the Trans-Pacific Partnership, an agreement with first-rate digital trade regulations, and mentally stuck in protecting jobs of a bygone era, America is failing to lead. China, the other trade power that in the 1980s was still a rather powerless developing nation, firewalls its own citizens from using such basic global digital services as Google search and Wikipedia.

The Splinternet—national policies that territorialize the web—is undermining the promise of the Internet as a tool especially for small companies to scale and globalize, and for people around the world to access digital services to better their lives. This chapter analyzes the various models of national digital regulations in privacy, rules affecting the liability of Internet service providers for the content posted by their users, and taxation and regulation of Internet services such as old-school telecoms, and seeks to put a price tag on the costs of Splinternet.

What's Your Data Worth?

In the movie *The Circle*, a young woman, Mae, played by Emma Watson, lands a job in a Silicon Valley startup that is making everything private public. The Circle's tiny cameras on deserted beaches, busy city centers, and a person's living room stream information 24/7 to customers ranging from surfers to intelligence agencies and friends curious about each other's lives. After the cameras help Mae to be rescued from a raging storm during a canoeing trip, she decides to become the Circle's poster girl and advocates a world of complete openness, including opening each minute of her own life to the Circle's billion viewers around the world.

Many good things come from this end of privacy. The Circle's cameras help capture an outlaw in ten minutes, and the company helps drive its community to vote, producing a massive turnout in fifty states. But as private events at her parents' home get broadcast too, Mae faces a hard choice between complete visibility and privacy. Torn, she makes a plea for the company's founders to open their own lives to 24/7 viewing—which the two champions of "no secrets" end up declining.

Though earning a lousy 17 percent score on the movie review site Rotten Tomatoes, *The Circle* encapsulates the challenges surrounding privacy. All of us want to keep ours, but we also want data that help law enforcement capture bad guys and rescue services to find missing family members. The success of reality TV suggests many of us are also like Mae's fans, endlessly curious about other people's day-to-day lives. Yet we do share quite liberally on Facebook and Snapchat, and most of us at least in America do remain rather unconcerned about the use of our personal data. Without much thought, we regularly trade our search, contact, credit, and consumption data to free online searches, videos, white papers, and customized shopping experiences. Algorithms drawing on our data simplify our lives: according to a poll by Intelliverse, 45 percent of American online shoppers are more likely to shop on a site that offers personalized recommendations, and 56 percent are more likely to return to a site that offers product recommendations.[2]

However, as questions about how that data are being used have burgeoned, trading of our data for convenient online services and information has become less appealing. The Snowden revelations about the NSA's use of personal data made especially Europeans anxious about their data being retailed by businesses or ending up in the hands of opaque intelligence agencies. Concerns have been compounded by the 2013 exposure of Prism, the U.S.-U.K. intelligence services' project to harvest data from major tech companies, and by the barrage of data breaches, such as the hacking of the U.K. pub company JD Wetherspoon in 2015 and the breach of the U.S. credit score company Equifax in September 2017 that resulted in the exposure of four hundred million social security numbers. In a 2017 survey, 75 percent of American consumers expressed concern about identity theft resulting from breaches.[3]

Growing concern about privacy has a direct bearing on globalization in the twenty-first century. Many governments limit companies' access to citizens' personal data and its transfer across borders—when those data are tremendously useful for companies and organizations that serve those citizens. The issue is as intense at it is old between Europe and the United States.

Data Policy's Four-Letter Word

October 2013 was when Angela Merkel finally lost her cool. Calling U.S. President Barack Obama, the normally collected Merkel was reportedly livid, comparing the American NSA's spying on her private calls to the practices of Stasi, the feared secret police of the communist East Germany where she grew up in the 1970s. Obama could not give assurances to Merkel that no spying would ever take place, and Merkel's frustration took months to subside. But the episode scarred Germans, with a deep-seated need for privacy, resulting in calls for stringent protections for personal data.

This is nothing new. Germans and Americans have historically had a very different view of privacy, to the point that even their respective scholars disagree on use of data. In his book *Privacy and Power: A Transatlantic Dialogue in the Shadow of the NSA-Affair,* Russel A. Miller shows that German privacy scholars have been deeply influenced by such experiences as the 1938 census that enabled Nazis to develop demographic profiles and tend to see technology as a threat.[4] American academics meanwhile have had a more balanced approach, and found value in such practices as identification—connecting a certain piece of information to an individual.[5]

These differences were stark even before the Internet was a word. In 1978, *Science* journal commentator John Walsh wrote an article that could well have been written in 2018, stating, "The integration of computers with modern communication systems has made it possible to transmit massive amounts of data worldwide relatively cheaply.... The United States has been the major begetter of the new technology and maintains a dominant position in utilizing it. The economic and social implications of this dominance are a source of increasing tension between the United States and other countries, particularly those in Western Europe."[6] Germans and the French were branded as data hawks, Americans as data doves.

The difference between Walsh's world and today is that there is unimaginably more data. The Internet and businesses are brimming with structured and unstructured data, ranging from millions of social media posts and tweets from Hollywood celebrities, White House occupants, and Joe Blows to reams of operational data transmitted by one machine to another. The global datasphere is poised to grow from 2 zettabytes in 2010 to 160 zettabytes in 2025.[7] In 2016, the world's Internet traffic hit a zettabyte. (Zettabyte is a serious number: one equals 152 million years of high-definition video.) When machines get connected, data-drive interactions will surge from 85 per person per day in 2010 to 4,785 in 2025.[8]

Walsh might never have envisioned Twitter, interactive refrigerators, or a full zettabyte, but his insight that data flows were becoming a source of turmoil in international trade policymaking was prescient. German and French worries about privacy find an expression in the globally most far-reaching privacy regulation yet, the EU's General Data Protection Regulation (GDPR), which entered into force in May 2018. The GDPR protects the data of all individuals within the European Union and regulates the transfer of personal data outside Europe. All companies with 250 employees or more need to adhere; companies with fewer than 250 employees whose data processing is not occasional, or includes certain types of sensitive personal data, also need to comply. Companies can store and process personal data only when the individual consents, and they must have a "data protection officer" when they process large amounts of data. Any data breaches need to be reported to authorities and individuals affected by it within seventy-two hours.

The GDPR's application is extraterritorial: a U.S. company in Kansas with data on EU citizens is subject to the GDPR even if it has no "nexus," or any physical presence, in the EU. What's more, for the Kansas company to easily move Europeans' data to Kansas for the company to analyze, the United States needs from Europe a stamp of "adequacy" with the EU's data regime, as data on EU citizens can be transferred to countries deemed "adequate." Tougher rules apply for countries with protections deemed inadequate. Adding complexity, the GDPR's implementation will vary across the EU. For example, a foreign company that wishes to transfer data from Germany needs to contend with state and federal data protection laws, review the data in Germany, and ask their own country's court or government entity to request the documents from Germany, for example citing a mutual legal assistance treaty.[9]

Privacy is important, and the GDPR is excellent news to European Internet users incensed by the Snowden revelations. But its costs make it a "GDP Robber." For one, the GDPR's implementation costs are very high for European and foreign companies. Two-thirds of American businesses spent between $1 and $10 million just to implement the GDPR.[10] For companies that fail to get up to speed, penalties run as high as €20 million or 4 percent of a company's global revenues. Many lag: GDPR fines are expected to cost European banks $5.2 billion in hard cash in the first three years.[11] The hundred companies listed on the London Stock Exchange could face fines of up to £5 billion for GDPR

breaches.[12] While stricter fines conceivably benefit the consumer by pressuring global businesses to take action or else risk a hefty fee, those fees may be
so exorbitant as to have a lasting financial impact. A recent survey conducted
by Veritas of nine hundred companies across eight countries showed that 21
percent feared that fines for noncompliance with the GDPR could lead to layoffs
and almost as many thought the fines could be a death knell to their companies.

Companies that do comply with GDPR are also poised for losses. Given its
limits to access to data that curb efficiencies, the GDPR is estimated to result in
an immediate loss of $66 billion in sales for EU companies.[13] The more profound
implications, such as the curtailment of credit information on consumers and
ability for web analytics firms to function, are expected to result in losses of $173
billion and 2.8 million European jobs.[14] Losses incurred by companies snowball
into economic losses. According to simulations by the European Centre for
International Political Economy (ECIPE), the EU's data privacy and localization laws, depending on their final outcome, will lower EU GDP by 0.4 to 1.1
percent, domestic investments by 3.9 to 5.1 percent, and welfare by $334 to $806
per worker per year.[15] The ECIPE's data suggest data rules also bite into the EU's
exports, lowering them by 0.4 percent.

Worse, the European Union is proselytizing GDPR in emerging markets—
and many countries are flirting with the idea of adopting the regime, often
because they have not considered its various costs, and at times because they
themselves may have a history of concerns about data security like Germany
does. In a world of great complexity and policymakers distracted by emails and
travel and worn out by bureaucratic battles, the GDPR is also a neat regulation-
in-a-box solution to mounting questions about data and privacy. The problems
are its high costs—and likely inconsistency with trade agreements such as the
WTO's General Agreement of Trade in Services.[16]

The EU is not the only data hawk. For example, Russia is building a strict
data protection regime that prohibits companies from moving Russians' personal data outside the country. The Chinese government has introduced policies
to keep financial and personal data, such as credit history and health records,
in China. Vietnam has decreed that providers of certain Internet-based services
must locate at least one server in the country as a precondition for market access. Nigeria mandates that all subscriber, government, and consumer data be
stored locally.

Globally, the Information Technology & Innovation Foundation calculates that such national data localization measures have surged from ten in

1995 to eighty-three in 2015.[17] Countries have legitimized these measures in various ways, such as on the vague grounds of "national security" and "public safety." For example, Vietnam and Indonesia mandate that companies have servers in-country, for law enforcement agencies to better access data. Many developing-country governments position forced server localization rules as a means of job creation—even if server farms employ only a handful of people. China and Russia quite explicitly advocate the idea that each country has its "Internet space" that is to be controllable by the government for reasons of national security and the need to control their citizens.[18]

Such policies have a price. For example, they may force local companies to use more expensive domestic cloud services in lieu of cheaper, centralized data storage and processing that has great economies of scale. A Google-sponsored paper finds that countries that require data to be cordoned off increase costs for their own firms that have to turn to costlier domestic services, paying up to 60 percent more for their computing needs.[19] It is estimated that European businesses could save some 36 percent on their server costs if they moved their servers outside the EU.[20] In its simulations, the ECIPE finds that data privacy and localization would limit domestic investment by 1.4 percent in India, 3.1 percent in Vietnam, 4.2 percent in Brazil, and 1.8 percent in China. The macro-economic impacts of data localization are significant. Data localization in India imposes a welfare loss of 11 percent of the average worker's monthly salary; in China, almost 13 percent; in Korea and Brazil, 20 percent.[21]

True, some empirical work on the economic impact of limits on data flows is sponsored by major digital companies with a vested stake in free flow of data. But there is nothing odd about their findings: taxing or limiting data is akin to forcing manufacturers to pay a tariff on intermediate products or making them use local raw materials or components as a condition for market access, policies that raise costs on end-consumers.

What's more, business surveys in the United States and developing countries show that small businesses complain about limits to data transfer just as much as the giant tech companies do. In the U.S. International Trade Commission's 2014 report, over three-quarters of large and over one-half of small and mid-size American companies in the digital communications sector felt that data privacy and protection requirements presented an obstacle to their cross-border trade.[22] These are not just advanced-country or big business challenges: in surveys my company has run, small developing-country companies notably worry about data privacy and localization practices both in their home and in export markets.

Is the future one in which companies are constantly dodging lawsuits for using consumers' data and paying extraordinary legal fees to comply with privacy regulations? Or are there alternatives that balance the needs for data privacy and use of data for the development of better operations and new products and services?

Perhaps the best alternative and one that is philosophically very different from the GDPR is the U.S.-championed Asia-Pacific Economic Cooperation (APEC) Cross-Border Privacy Rules (CBPR), endorsed by APEC ministers in 2011. Businesses and organizations that opt in to the CBPR system must submit their privacy practices and policies for evaluation by an APEC-recognized "Accountability Agent"; in the United States this organization is called TRUSTe; in Japan, JIPDEC. They study such aspects as a company's online properties (websites, mobile apps, cloud platforms) and customer and employee data-management practices. Upon certification, the practices and policies will become binding on that organization and enforceable by a privacy enforcement authority (such as the Federal Trade Commission in the United States). Participating businesses are required to develop and implement data privacy policies consistent with the APEC Privacy Framework.

While the EU's GDPR has a prescriptive approach to regulating data transfers, the CBPR is based on self-assessment with third-party verification underpinned by national enforcement authorities. And unlike the GDPR, which is a law applying uniformly to EU economies, the CBPR system does not displace or change a country's domestic laws and regulations, nor does it determine whether a country's privacy protections are "adequate." Furthermore, while the GDPR has a centralized enforcement mechanism, CBPR relies on enforcement by countries. The CBPR is a more flexible framework than the GDPR.

The CBPR's main challenges have been business leaders' lack of awareness about it and the fact that many APEC countries do not yet have the domestic laws in place that would enable the CBPR to work in their economies. However, that the businesses that do participate in CBPR have agreed to uphold certain data standards means that they also provide privacy protection in economies where there is no data protection law.[23] The CBPR is also expected to fuel FDI flows into developing nations. For example, Japanese stakeholders interviewed for an APEC study said Japan would invest more in economies where there is no data protection law if those economies and their businesses participated in the CBPR System.[24]

Another way to treat data flows is through free trade agreements. Ironically, it was the United States that led the crafting of the Trans-Pacific Partnership's sophisticated digital trade standards. Now that TPP minus America is the Comprehensive and Progressive Agreement for Trans-Pacific Partnership that entered into force in December 2018, the United States gets its standards, while not being part of the deal. The TPP's digital chapter also lives on in other trade deals, such as in an agreement between Chile and Uruguay, which is 99 percent word for word the TPP's chapter on electronic commerce. The revised NAFTA, the September 2018 U.S.-Mexico-Canada Agreement (USMCA), includes the most advanced rules to date in any FTA to fuel digital trade among the three countries. The agreement among other things ensures data transfer among the parties and refers to APEC's CBPR as the means to ensure data privacy and transfer.

In the short run, the peacekeepers in the battle for data privacy and transfer may be the so-called D9+ group of by now twenty northern and Eastern European economies that dislike German and French data hawkishness. D9+ and the United States, which has called for a deal on digital trade with the United Kingdom as it leaves the EU, could work together on middle ground free data policies.

Subverting the GDPR

To the extent that the GDPR raises operating costs for companies in Europe, the tough call for companies is whether to invest more in Europe or look for easier markets. The call is especially tough for U.K. companies that will not be governed by the GDPR post-Brexit, but that will in practice need to adhere to it given that 75 percent of their data flows are with the EU and many have extensive operations in Europe. If the GDPR undermines the EU's attractiveness as a place to do business, global companies may bit by bit disinvest and focus on locations where they enjoy easier access to data. This will likely happen gradually, without much notice, like sand flowing from a small hole in a bag, until enough is lost for the costs of the regime to be self-evident.

However, before that happens, the GDPR may get subverted from within. Powerful German companies are mostly in B2B business, and not like Google or Facebook in B2C markets collecting personal data. But what happens when

German manufacturing wunderkinds start to access Europeans' personal data? For example, the mapping company HERE that is part-owned by BMW, Daimler, and Audi aggregates data from consumers' cars worldwide, so as to provide traffic updates, hazard warnings, and parking updates.[25] It is only a matter of time before data collected on driving patterns touch on privacy—and when they do, are the beacons of German industry ready to bow to the GDPR, or will they want a softer, 2.0 version? Chancellor Merkel has been prodding German manufacturing superstars such as BMW to expand their big data projects as a pillar of the Germany Industry 4.0 strategy—what happens if the GDPR undermines it?

This would not be a first: governments are coming face to face with the economic costs of their tough data rules. For example, in 2017, Colombia finalized a rule that added the United States to the list of safe nations for data transfer purposes.[26] The measure was crucial for Colombia to enable small Colombian companies to use American cloud services, and to retain U.S. companies in the country. Consider, for example a major industry in Colombia, call centers that serve U.S. companies needing client service in Spanish: without clear rules that specify data can be transferred across borders, U.S. companies might want to find another location for their call centers.[27] Similar issues pertain to ecommerce platforms. The U.S.-based PriceSmart Inc., the largest operator of online membership warehouse clubs in Central America and the Caribbean, has a new presence in Colombia, something made possible by the fact that it can access user data and transfer it San Diego, California, for analysis and improve its services in Latin America.

In the extreme, if governments territorialize data, consumers will push back. Imagine a world in which no personal data could ever cross borders. Traveling overseas, you could not use your phone or credit cards, or access, in case of an accident, your medical records.[28] You might sit at immigration in a foreign country as your airline was not able to send information on you to your destination ahead of you. At home, you could not ask Daimler or Volvo to remotely upgrade the software in your car. If you were a farmer, you could not forecast the weather, as those data also need to cross borders. If you ran a small ecommerce business in Miami, you could not access information on your customers in Latin America, let alone use artificial intelligence to predict their future shopping patterns. If you were a social impact enterprise in Berlin making online loans to entrepreneurs in developing countries, you could not do credit scoring on the tentative borrowers. If you were a researcher at a university, you could not access a global dataset that might have helped you, say, create cures for malaria, or analyze impacts of different tax policies.

The interests each of us have in the privacy of our data on the one hand and access to others' data on the other will negotiate themselves for a long time, with the GDPR being a major catalyst of debate.

New Speech Police: Who Is Liable for Content Online?

In Manila, far from Mountain View, California, sit hundreds of young people shifting through harrowing pictures and videos posted on Facebook of violent crimes, child porn, terrorist propaganda, and other disturbing images posted on the social networking site, and making split-second judgments of what to remove. In March 2017, after a spout of live streaming that featured a murder in Ohio, rapes in Sweden and Chicago, and torture of a teenager with special needs, among others, Facebook increased its web sanitizer staff by 80 percent. The company reported closing each day one million accounts opened by fraudsters and spammers.[29] The young workers cleaning up the web are traumatized by the daily bombardment of mankind's worst, and seldom last in their jobs.

Is the Internet sick? A medium that started out as a fun, liberating tool for connections, information, match-making, and smiley faces has also magnified the ills of mankind, enabling online recruitment by ISIS, networking among white supremacists, and misogynist hate speech by Russian trolls. Most Internet users want their web free from terrorists, fraudsters, and haters. But the question of where to draw the line and who polices it is a complex one. That countries have widely different answers to that question threatens to balkanize the global Internet economy and complicate international trade.

So far, countries have protected intermediaries with "safe harbor" laws. For example, in its renowned Marco Civil Internet law of 2014, which defines Internet users' rights, Brazil has a "safe harbor" that limits the responsibility for hosting or transferring third-party content. In 1998, Bill Clinton signed into law the Digital Millennium Copyright Act (DMCA), which included a safe harbor provision credited to be the leading reason why the Internet user base grew twenty-seven times larger between 1998 and 2018. The DMCA and the so-called Section 230 of the American Communications Decency Act of 1996 rest on the notion that Facebook is no more liable for posts with hate speech its digital garden sprinkler fans to the world than the postal service is for delivering a package without knowing it contains anthrax.

In turn, it can be quite safely assumed that had Internet services since their start been liable for what users published or did with the content online, far fewer music, social media, ecommerce, and other companies would have ever been started—resources would likely have flowed to the handful of firms staffed and resourced to screen what users posted. Anupam Chander of the University of California, Davis who in 2005 wrote a pioneering book *The Electronic Silk Road* argues that one of the key reasons behind Silicon Valley's success is freedom of speech undergirding the American Internet laws.[30] In contrast, Chander argues, Europe and Asia imposed strict intermediary liability regimes, inflexible intellectual property rules, and strong privacy rules that have stifled innovation.

The exponential uptick in problematic online content has made many countries look to Internet companies to police illegal and other problematic content, and hold them accountable for the legality of user-generated content on their sites. For example, Germany requires social media companies to remove "manifestly unlawful" content within twenty-four hours of receiving a complaint from a user, and all other unlawful content within seven days—which in Germany can mean things as mundane as calling someone du instead of Sie—to avert a fine of up to €50 million. Wanting to play in this major digital market, Facebook has obliged, removing fifteen thousand posts per month of hate speech in Germany.[31] But how much legal content is censored in those streams of decisions by Facebook sweepers of what is legal and what is not?

Worse, will the frustrated efforts to "speak" on Facebook drive the anger elsewhere, resulting in violence or illegal activity offline, where it is harder for law enforcement to follow? After all, having bad stuff in the open, online, may not be that bad. In the United States, online prostitution ads have numerous times helped lead law enforcement to criminals and to prosecute them.[32] Even human rights lobbies may prefer seeing bad things in the 24/7 light of day of the Internet. In 2016, seventy nonprofits wrote to Mark Zuckerberg that Facebook's deleting of posts with human rights violations was unduly sweeping injustices from sight. A 2018 U.S. law, Stop Enabling Sex Traffickers Act, was in that sense feared to weaken Section 230, exposing platforms to criminal liability and thus forcing them to censor and move this content, as unsavory it is, offline, where it is harder to track. However, the U.S. Congress has been clear that the DMCA and Section 230 protections remain paramount, and the United States has stressed the importance of these laws also in international forums, such as the World Trade Organization.[33]

The European Union has its own safe harbor in its 2000 Electronic Commerce Directive, which exempts Internet intermediaries from liability when they are a "mere conduit" for the content, or if they are caching or hosting it. However, safe harbor protections are now eroding in Europe. In September 2018, the European Parliament passed a copyright law that makes website operators liable for copyright infringements of content their users upload. The law demands these operators use "upload filters" to prevent users from uploading copyrighted content, and compensate copyright holders (such as journalists or musicians) for the use of very small portions of their content.[34] Positively, small and micro firms that operate websites are exempted, as the law could place onerous implementation costs on them. The EU's 2018 Audiovisual Media Services Directive places video-sharing platforms under a limited liability regime where they must remove illegal content (such as hate speech and public provocation to commit terrorism) when they have knowledge of it.[35]

Essentially, Europe is making intermediaries patrol around user-generated content with algorithms they will pay for. But should it really be YouTube's fault if a person posts a video singing a song they wrote and someone on the other side of the world copies it and sells it to a record company?

There are also concerns that rolling liability on Internet services may undermine freedom of speech, as platforms err on the side of caution and remove legitimate speech. The Parliament's law seeks to enable freedom of expression by exempting hyperlinks to articles and individual words that describe them—but critics argue that legitimate content such as parodies and memes can easily be censored.[36]

The issue of course runs the other way around as well—when there is copyrighted online content that an individual or business wishes taken down when they have been infringed upon by the users of a platform. In 2014, Argentine supermodel Belén Rodríguez sued Google and Yahoo for linking her online images to websites of escort services and pornographic sites that had appropriated her image, even though she is neither an escort nor a porn star.[37] The case was ultimately fought over in the Argentine Supreme Court, and set a precedent for legal liability of Internet intermediaries. The Court sided with Google, arguing that Google's liability is only triggered when it can be proven that the company has actual knowledge of infringing third-party content and have not acted to correct the situation.

This landmark decision set a precedent for similar rulings in other Latin American countries. However, the Court also held that intermediaries can be held subjectively liable for content generated by third parties when they have "actual knowledge" of the illicit content. But when intermediaries have "actual knowledge" varies widely across countries. Under the DMCA, contents are to be eliminated upon notice by an individual arguing that there has been copyright infringement. In the Brazilian Civil Rights Framework for the Internet, judicial notice is the trigger. But here is another area in which the regulatory leash may be getting shorter.

In 2016, a U.S. federal judge ordered Internet provider Cox Communications to pay $25 million in damages to BMG Rights Management, which controls the rights to the music of some of the world's most popular artists. Cox was found liable for copyright infringement by its customers of the music produced by the artists in the BMG Rights Management network.[38] The case was more complex than that—it revolved around Cox's refusal to pass on to its infringing users notifications from a BMG vendor tasked to identify those users. Cox had argued that the accusers had never proven in court that those users had broken the law so that the infringement claimed by BMG did not merit further action.

Of course, companies push back against onerous liability regimes that can be costly and complex to implement. U.S. tech giants did secure liability protections into a renegotiated North American Free Trade Agreement, the U.S.-Mexico-Canada Agreement. Much more is at stake than large companies' quarterly profits, for two reasons.

First, liability rules hit hardest small companies that can neither pay millions for digital rights management software to monitor users nor wage the legal battles against claims of copyright violations. The real risk is that only big players who are able to monitor their users are able to play—and even they need to be lawyered against disappointed users whose speech is violated or players whose copyright is infringed by their users. The additional costs carried by online platforms, and resulting from the erosion of competition, will be passed to users. And if entry costs for small players are too high, competition is limited, again to users' detriment. These costs come on top of a high pile of regulations already in place. The U.S. National Federation of Independent Business, which represents 325,000 small U.S. companies, has found that its members think of "unreasonable government regulations" as the second-biggest threat to their businesses, after rising health care costs.[39]

Second, tough legal liability rules can curb startup funding. A

PricewaterhouseCoopers survey of early-stage investors in digital companies finds that nine out of ten investors would prefer to invest in companies operating under U.S. rather than European copyright laws.[40] Regulations holding websites liable for user-uploaded content without a license would reduce the pool of interested investors by 81 percent. In the presence of strict regulatory regimes, investors gravitate to companies promising a very high return multiplier—which likely means that investors would only focus on a handful of promising digital businesses, rather than place bets on a range of potentially transformative moonshots. Meanwhile, clarifying copyright regulations to allow websites to resolve legal disputes quickly was found to expand the pool of interested investors by 111 percent and limiting penalties for websites acting in good faith would expand the pool of interested investors by 115 percent.

Of course, many companies get started with their owners' capital and subsequently are astounded by the cost of complying with various regulations. A study supported by Google found that a liability regime that defines clear and cost-efficient requirements for Internet intermediaries would bolster success rates for Internet startups by 4 percent in Chile, 8 percent in Germany, 22 percent in India, and 24 percent in Thailand.[41]

Cord-Cutting and Tax Loving

On July 21, 2002, the telecommunications industry began imploding. The collapse of WorldCom that day was followed by the bankruptcy of twenty-three telecom companies, and the loss of five hundred thousand American telecom jobs. The market cap of the $7 trillion industry shrank by 30 percent. Cataloguing the industry's undoing in the *American Prospect*, Paul Starr wrote, "While Internet telephony still has its drawbacks, services based on 'voice over IP' (Internet protocol) are improving.... For the old telephone industry—and for the hundreds of thousands of people who work for it—voice over IP is the ultimate gale of creative destruction."[42]

Since then, telecoms and cable companies have had few reasons to celebrate. Consumers have been on a cord-cutting spree thanks to Netflix, Hulu, and other streaming services that provide audio, video, and other media over the Internet without subscriptions as required by traditional cable companies. Messaging services, such as services provided by WhatsApp, Skype, Viber, and Facebook, require no telephone lines, and make a dent: Facebook has two billion monthly users, WeChat a billion. Consumers' cord-cutting has been intensifying since the 2008–2009 financial crisis; by 2013 pay TV subscriber growth rates had turned negative, a trend that only intensified in 2015. By 2016, over a fifth of Americans were cordless.

The impact of these Internet services, also referred to as "over the top" (OTT) services on telecoms has been dramatic: Skype, launched in 2003, by 2013 had fifteen billion minutes more of international phone traffic than telecoms.[43] SMS disappeared almost overnight, from over 95 percent of all messaging globally in 2011 to less than half by 2013 and less than 10 percent in 2016.[44] Now OTTs are also delving into B2B markets, such as Amazon positioning itself as a B2B sales platform. IBM and Microsoft are also vying for their place on the B2B totem pole.

Telecoms such as Telefonica that did not die in the telco massacre of the 2000s have put up a fight, pressing for regulations that would force digital companies to apply costly over-the-top rules regulating online and audiovisual productions. For example, in 2017, there were proposals in India that would place online services under a licensing framework applied to telecoms, while the Brazilian National Cinema Agency was pushing for regulations on audiovisual platforms to levy taxes regardless of their geographical origin, create a minimum quota of 20 percent of Brazilian content on TV and audiovisual companies' catalogues, and require investments in co-production of original content equivalent to 4 percent of gross income.[45] Latin American countries are working to figure out how to impose "Netflix taxes," or value-added taxes on online services—how else can they tax these digital stars located in Silicon Valley or Luxembourg? Colombia launched a 19 percent value-added tax on digital services in 2017, followed by Uruguay with a 22 percent tax and Argentina with 21 percent in 2018.

Internet services push back by arguing that they do not share the same technical and market characteristics as telecommunications services. Empirically, they are right. For one, proposals that would force Internet services to get a license or register with the government before they can make their services available in a country can also limit free expression and innovation: in 2011, the United Nations Special Rapporteur on the Freedom of Expression wrote that "unlike the broadcasting sector, for which registration or licensing has been necessary to allow States to distribute limited frequencies, such requirements cannot be justified in the case of the Internet, as it can accommodate an unlimited number of points of entry and an essentially unlimited number of users."[46]

Rigid OTT rules and taxes on digital services also hurt companies and consumers' bottom line by forcing them to pay a premium for the digital content, such as via apps.[47] As discussed in Chapter 4, consumers score major gains from the fact that many apps are free.[48] What if you and your friends had to pay a fee, imposed by regulations, to access Facebook, Twitter, Whatsapp, or Uber, and pay a premium every time you use Netflix? What if poorer developing-country consumers had to? How well would online services diffuse across societies that would gain from them?

EU member states are discussing an interim 3 percent digital sales tax (DST) on Internet services' online advertising, digital subscription fees, and the sale of users' activity data, preempting the decision by the Organisation for Economic Co-operation and Development (OECD), which is developing a global taxation framework model. EU members appear to be exhibiting caution as Northern European EU members oppose the tax and France and other nations seek immediate action. There are also disagreements about the tax level, which some member states believe is too low and has led to concerns of a patchwork of national tax regimes. EU member states also disagree on the coverage of data sales, and the size of companies that would be included.[49] Late 2018 proposals would extend the law to only about two hundred firms, many of them American, with global annual revenue of at least €750 million ($876 million), and annual EU revenue of more than €50 million.

The EU has also suggested taxing digital companies' corporate profits and assessing the tax on the basis of a company's gross revenues, rather than on its net profit. This practice could force a company with large revenues but with limited or negative profits—a description of a typical fast-growing tech company in the first few years in its life cycle—into bankruptcy. DST proposals face opposition from EU states such as Ireland, the Netherlands, Malta, and Sweden that host the headquarters of U.S. and European digital giants. Germany is reportedly cool to the idea as it is concerned about the broader trade relationship with the United States. The U.S. could formally raise concerns at the WTO for the EU's use of DST to discriminate against U.S. multinational companies.

It is important to note that digital companies in the EU have lower taxes than some traditional companies—but it is also the case that many multinationals beyond tech have low effective tax rates and that the new digital taxes likely would unfairly discriminate against *U.S. companies* as it is U.S. companies that would be their primary target. These taxes would also undermine the European public policy objective of encouraging the use of digital services and data, especially among poorer segments of the population that are the most price-sensitive.[50]

If the policy objective is to maximize access to a service or technology across consumers and businesses, the tax rate on the service should be low or zero. Empirically, tax cuts and exemptions generate more economic growth and, ultimately, more government revenue than high taxes that raise the technology's cost of ownership.[51] After all, as companies use digital goods and services and cloud computing services as a critical input in their operations and production, excessive taxes on them are akin to a tariff or tax on intermediate products. Similarly, consumers of digital goods and services will be dissuaded from using them when taxes raise the total cost of ownership of digital goods and services. Taxes can also stunt the network effects that make a technology useful and valuable, by penalizing network users. For example, 3G penetration rates decline with a tax burden on 3G services.[52] The result of taxing key services is lower adoption of digital goods and services, particularly among the poor, the most price-sensitive consumers, who could realize particularly significant welfare gains from digitization and free apps.

Since digital goods and services affect practically all industries, much like any critical infrastructure or financial services or energy do, taxes on them have economy-wide spillovers in productivity, new business creation, and investment. For example, when North Dakota ended its 6 percent sales tax on wireless and wireline services, investment per capita in these services more than doubled in a year.[53] Not only are the effects positive on investment: lowering taxes on digital goods and services generates more growth and revenue over time, as these services boost economic growth and the use of services across population. Access to digital devices and services should be a particularly high policy priority in countries with limited technology adoption.

Smart telcos have survived the death of voice traffic by realizing, "If you can't beat them, join them." For example, Malaysian mobile service provider DiGi telecommunications has entered into a partnership with WhatsApp that enables DiGi customers to get unlimited access to WhatsApp for a fixed fee.[54] In India, Bharti Airtel attributed its over 30 percent increase in net profits in the first quarter of 2015 to increases in mobile data revenue.[55] Swedish telco profits have *grown* annually since 2002, with data services making up an increasingly sizable share of total revenues.[56] Innovative telecoms may also be boosted by machine-to-machine dialogues in the Internet of Things, which they could monetize by storing, processing, managing, and helping to share data.

More collaboration between telecoms and their bitter Internet rivals may be in the books. For example, Facebook, which has had a complicated relationship with telcos after twisting the knife in their stomachs with the 2014 acquisition of WhatsApp, is lending some of its artificial intelligence experts to telecoms through its Telecom Infra Project, which is an umbrella for Facebook and other companies to collaborate on telecommunications technologies, such as open-source long-distance antennas to spread connectivity in remote regions, or small cellular stations that can be planted on street lamps or other infrastructure to accelerate the deployment of wireless service.[57]

How Much Does the Splinternet Cost?

In world trade policy, liberalization at the border has not been paralleled by regulatory harmonization behind the border. Countries that have cut tariffs have largely retained their unique food regulations, product standards, and certification of service providers. Private standards driven by the likes of Walmart and Whole Foods added to the mix.

Divergent national product standards complicated life, especially for small companies that are seeking to export to many markets at once. For example, a Mexican avocado company will upon seeking German and Nordic supermarket space have to comply with the private GLOBALG.A.P. "good agricultural practice" certificate, besides other food standards. In the United States, it will need to meet America's phytosanitary rules and at least the "U.S. No. 2" grade as defined in the U.S. standards for Florida avocados (specifically, "mature but not overripe, fairly well formed, clean, fairly well colored, well trimmed and which are free from decay and freezing injury and are free from serious damage caused by anthracnose, bruises, cuts or other skin breaks, pulled stems, russeting or similar discoloration, scars or scab, sunburn, sunscald or sprayburn, cercospora spot, other disease, insects, or mechanical or other mean").[58]

While aimed at fueling trade among partner countries, bilateral trade deals have often only complicated rules further. For example, each of Mexico's free trade agreements has its own rules, and in many cases those rules differ significantly—so that a Mexican company seeking to enter the U.S. market under NAFTA will need to comply with a different rulebook than if it were to enter Korea or the European Union under the Korea-Mexico and EU-Mexico free trade agreements (FTAs). Columbia University's Jagdish Bhagwati called the setting of the overlapping and different FTAs crisscrossing the world a "spaghetti bowl" and described the many FTAs as "termites" chomping on the multilateral trading system.[59]

The spaghetti bowl is especially entangled in the area of rules of origin: differences among origin requirements across FTAs might mean that a company would have to change its sourcing patterns or production processes to qualify for the market access each different FTA promises.

The spaghetti bowl problem is also real: it costs businesses money and market opportunities. In 2009, my colleagues and I surveyed it in Latin America, finding that over 20 percent of Chilean companies, one-half of Mexican and Colombian companies, and three-quarters of Panamanian companies view savings from harmonizing rules of origin across their countries' respective FTAs as "high" or "very high."[60] The results also suggested that the spaghetti bowl problem impedes SMEs from taking advantage of most of the market opportunities their countries' FTAs would offer: SMEs export only to markets where they can meet the rules, rather than to all markets that could use their products and with which the SME's country has a trade deal.

Similar splintering of trade by national rules is now occurring in the digital economy. Imagine for a moment what might have happened to the growth of Facebook, Twitter, Google, eBay, or Netflix if every state in the United States had widely different interpretations of such issues as electronic signatures, freedom of speech, data transfer, or intermediary liability. Would these companies have attained the scale they did in the early stages of their growth, had they had to deal with different state regulations? Granted, there has been and is a constant negotiation between federal and state laws surrounding the digital economy as technologies, consumer concerns, and case law evolve—but federal laws and the Constitution have provided a very useful national plank for digital businesses to operate across states.

In Europe, the setting is messier. It is a region with diverse national digital regimes now seeking to back into a common Single Digital Market, it is estimated that common consumer protection and other Internet laws could save EU consumers €11.7 billion each year in online shopping, with the gains stemming from access to the variety of goods and services sold online across the EU region.[61] Companies, in turn, would expand sales: 57 percent of European companies would either start or increase their online sales to other EU economies of ecommerce-related regulations that were more similar across EU markets.[62] Altogether, the European Commission estimates that a digital market with common rules would increase Europe's economic pie by €415 billion a year. An industry-sponsored study on Southeast Asian countries suggests that a regional digital agenda and strategy, including harmonization of cybersecurity, data security, and privacy laws across the region and creation of a single digital payment platform, could add $1 trillion to the regional GDP over the next ten years, providing a 40 percent boost to the region's output.[63]

Interoperability of rules is not only important to big business; it matters especially to small companies that by virtue of the online economy are more scalable than ever, but which because of their limited resources are less able to deal with different rules in each new market than are large companies. In surveys I have run, small businesses in such countries as Brazil, Bangladesh, and Colombia all highlight interoperability of digital regulations with their trading partners as their top regulatory challenge in cross-border ecommerce.

Mismatches in national standards is an ages-old problem in world trade. In the 1800s, settlers in different parts of South America feverishly built railroads, only to discover that their respective railroads had different gauges—so that goods had to be offloaded and onloaded manually where one track ended and another began, often at national borders and sometimes even within the same country. Today's railroad may be the Internet, but same problem persists: for example, the global mobile phone association GSMA estimates that the Asia-Pacific region, where countries have different mobile spectra, could unlock up to $1 trillion in GDP growth by 2020 through the harmonized adoption of the 700 MHz spectrum band for mobile services.[64]

The online economy has its own tariffs in the form of censorship and limits on data transfer, and its own spaghetti bowl in the many national digital regulations in such areas as data privacy, Internet intermediary liability, licensing, taxes, and consumer protection. It is possible even if not easy or fun to meet the different rules when a company has the time and money to pour into legal services needed to secure licenses and regulatory approvals to operate in any given market. For smaller companies, the choice is probably incremental growth in large markets with rules that are quite similar to their own.

Who can make the Splinternet whole? The WTO should, but there is as yet no global deal on digital economy and trade. At the WTO's eleventh biennial ministerial meeting in December 2017 in Buenos Aires, Kai Mykkänen, the exasperated trade minister from Finland, home to Nokia and such gaming apps as Angry Birds developed by Rovio and Clash of Clans made by Supercell, fumed, "It's ridiculous that we don't have global rules for ecommerce in 2017. It would be quite problematic and quite hard to make it work if Clash of Clans had to pay duties in some countries and not in other countries. It would mean much more bureaucracy."[65]

A thick silver lining for Mykkänen was an agreement in Buenos Aires among 71 of the WTO's 164 members, including the United States, the European Union, Australia, and several Latin American countries, to start a plurilateral agreement outside the WTO negotiations on such issues as digital signatures and taxes on digital services. The talks got another boost at the World Economic Forum meetings in Davos in January 2019, when countries pledged to kickstart the talks after a year of working on the agenda. This is very positive news. But the deal will not be a global deal. Much of the WTO membership is stubbornly uninterested in addressing digital trade issues. Astoundingly, global agreements for goods and services were last negotiated in 1994, the year Amazon was established and five years before the cloud company Salesforce.com came to life. To be sure, many of the disciplines in these old agreements still apply even to the digital economy. But the only real success WTO has had on digital issues has been the 1998 moratorium on levying duties on electronic transmissions, essentially stopping each other from imposing new tariffs on any downloads of digital services such as games, movies, or streamed music crossing their borders. Mykkänen's bid for broad-based agreement for the membership to launch discussions on digital trade has ground to a halt. India and South Africa have led the lobby of the difficult and the disgruntled, with India initially blocking in Buenos Aires what should have been a routine renewal of the moratorium.

The world remains split on the Internet: as half of WTO members establish rules conducive to digital trade, developing economies that of their own volition have opted not to join the talks to craft global digital trade standards will risk falling behind. And countries that are part of the talks—the United States, the European Union, and China—have rather different views on how the digital economy ought to be governed. Also falling behind is the WTO: as members go their separate ways and work in their respective cliques, the multilateral trading system as we have known it for eighty years is over. Plurilaterals and bilateral trade deals will remain as the primary, and perhaps only, way for countries to make digital trade policy together.

Conclusion

As the world digitizes, trade policy problems that have not been dealt with are surfacing like rocks from a receding tide. Consensuses in areas such as cross-border data transfer, liability of platforms of user-generated content, taxes on digital services, and customs duties on digital goods are distant. The Internet is a superhighway of world trade, but it has too many security checks and stop signs, such as limits on transfer of data across borders and demands for legal liability and licensing regimes. Restrictions and differing national regulations will impede companies that otherwise could service many markets. Without policy leadership, the world economy will remain a global marketplace splintered by national regulations that small companies cannot meet, tech investors are repelled by, and consumers pay for.

CREDIT CRUNCH

As the face of world trade changes, so change the constraints to trade. Small businesses are better placed to engage in trade than ever before –but few obstacles are as thorny for small businesses wishing to scale in world markets as lack of finance. Survey after survey shows that capital is the number one challenge to small businesses and a top-three challenge to mid-size companies looking to grow their businesses and export; the challenges are particularly acute in Africa and developing Asia. There are financing gaps for every occasion—for an Italian micro business that urgently needs $100,000 working capital to fulfill an order; for an Indian tech startup that sees a market opportunity for its software and needs $2 million to beef up its sales team and after-sale service to seize it; for an American mid-size company selling clean tech equipment that needs $10 million for its African customer, who will have no credit available in its own country, to buy the equipment.

In Chapter 6, we saw that estimates place the global trade finance gap alone at $1.7 trillion. This mostly measures the availability of instruments that ensure exporters will ultimately get paid by their foreign customer, such as supply chain finance and letters of credit. But there is an even vaster gap of old-fashioned loan products, such as working capital loans, that research shows are essential for businesses to do business and engage in trade. The World Bank has estimated the small business credit gap at $8.9 trillion—twice the size of the Japanese economy.[1] As for equity finance, only a quarter of companies seeking angel funding and 2 percent of companies seeking venture capital get funded. In my surveys, access to finance is the number one constraint for SMEs in practically all developing countries to engage in trade and ecommerce, out of forty other major challenges.[2]

How is it possible that financing gaps keep devouring companies even today, an era of unprecedented financial innovation and a wide array of financing windows—twenty-five thousand banks, tens of thousands of angel investors, over ten thousand annual VC rounds, over five thousand FinTech companies, seminal technologies such as blockchain, and new government funds aimed to invest in innovative firms? Why do these gaps persist? And is that altogether a bad thing for trade and economic growth?

Beautiful Marriage

The best way to see the interplay of credit and trade is to ask, what would happen if there suddenly was no credit?

Sadly, there is a natural experiment to answer that: the global financial crisis of 2007–2009. SME lending during 2007–2009 fell like a sun setting in the ocean. In the United States, small business loans of less than $100,000 dropped from a total of $146 billion in 2007 to $57 billion in 2010, and the number of these small loans fell from 13 million loans to 3.9 million.[3] The drying up of credit caused companies to cancel their plans to export; by 2009, the financing dry spell had helped make a 12 percent dent in the $20 trillion yearly flow of world trade—almost the equivalent of China's and Germany's combined exports suddenly stopping. Of course, credit froze partly because of the demand shock in the world economy—fewer companies sought financing as their customers ceased placing orders. But for the most part causality ran the other way. For example, a study of Peruvian firms showed that credit shortages explained 15 percent of the decline in Peruvian exports during the crisis.[4] An analysis of French exporters in the crisis reveals similar deterioration, especially in reduction of exporters' export volumes rather than outright death of exporters.[5]

SMEs are particularly vulnerable to crises. When a crisis strikes, lenders go for the safer assets, larger companies. Upon crises, financing challenges can be particularly acute for exporters in sectors that are structurally more dependent on external finance (such as cars and other durable goods) or that have few collateralizable assets (such as information technology or professional services firms).[6] Though many companies stopped borrowing in the crisis—why borrow to make anything when the world is in a recession and no one is buying anything?—companies that wanted credit to grow their global business found getting it to be a challenge. In a 2008 OECD survey of SMEs in advanced economies, access to working capital was ranked as the greatest out of forty-seven hurdles to trade.[7] A 2009 U.S. International Trade Commission survey found that American SME manufacturers rated access to financing as the steepest out of nineteen hurdles to trade.[8] A 2010 European Commission study found that 54 percent of European SMEs viewed lack of capital as the biggest obstacle for doing business in extra-EU markets.[9] No other barrier, such as paperwork, laws and regulations, lack of information on overseas markets, and so on, was considered as important to going global.

The global financial crisis was a dramatic show of what economists have long known: there is a virtuous cycle between credit and trade, and riding this cycle is especially important for small businesses to export. Small businesses that have fewer financial constraints tend to start exporting earlier than other firms. And once companies have credit and export, availability of credit increases their export volumes and product mix, which helps them diversify their risk. These impacts ore especially strong for small companies. One study found that every 10 percent increase in availability of short- and long-term loans increases small Colombian firms' exports by 1.2 percent, a mid-size firms' exports by 0.7 percent.[10]

Most typically, the financing that companies need to export is working capital to buy the supplies and labor to produce a large export order. Of course, there are those that, when struggling to raise external funds cover the costs of export entry, decide to tap internal cash—something small and new firms seldom have stashed away—or credit cards, the trusted tool for small business finance.[11]

Those companies that do have the capital to export have a chance to ride the virtuous cycle in which access to capital fuels exports and successful exporting eventually fuels access to capital. The early part of the ride is however a roller-coaster: SMEs that start exporting and *are* able to access credit are also found to have higher leverage ratios than those of comparable non-exporters, which suggests that entering foreign markets is not cheap, and forces companies to either draw down liquidity or increase leverage.[12] This can be Russian Roulette: if facing high interest rates, the company may have to cover its borrowing costs by raising its prices, which in price-sensitive market segments can bite into its competitiveness, which can reduce its ability to repay its loans... and so on. When a crisis hits, these firms' debt servicing costs surge—to the point of forcing them to end exporting and even end their businesses.[13]

However, things get better at some point. Exporters with some years of export activity typically have more liquidity than non-exporters, and lower credit constraints.[14] One reason is that exporters' cash flows are more stable than those of non-exporters, possibly because they are diversified across markets and products and thus not as exposed to domestic business cycles or customers' whims as non-exporters. Exporters, in short, are more resilient, able to withstand negative shocks in any one market or product line—something any lender would like to see. For example, a study of British firms found that exporters with a decade of exporting are significantly healthier financially than non-exporters or exporter entrants—which struggle with the high leverage to cover sunk costs of export entry.[15]

Why is it then so hard for SMEs to get loans? For the same reasons listed in Chapter 5 as hampering trade finance—KYC and AML requirements that make small loans less interesting to banks, capital adequacy ratios that rise with risk and similarly disincentivize lending to small businesses, and so on. In developing countries, conditions on loans are often onerous. In Latin America, for example, the collateral is nearly 203 percent of the loan's value; 238 percent in many sub-Saharan African countries; and outlandish at 456 percent of mid-size companies in Myanmar.[16] Such exorbitant collateral forces companies to self-censor and not even try—in Myanmar, 88 percent of investments made by mid-size companies are financed by the companies themselves, and 8 percent by banks.

Though in part a product of inadequate competition in a banking sector, collateral is not an evil design by greedy bankers. Rather, it is a mechanism by perfectly rational banks to compensate for the cost and risk of lending to small businesses, such as time and money for banks to efficiently examine borrower risk, especially given that many SMEs operate in the informal sector.[17] Though over 90 percent of Latin American banks consider the SME sector to be part of their strategy, over 50 percent of them have trouble assessing SMEs' creditworthiness, and over 40 percent report high administrative costs to processing SME loans.[18]

Interest rates may not be the problem—studies in India and Mexico have found that entrepreneurs can deliver returns that are much higher than even the three-digit interest rate they are charged.[19] This suggests that at least for some types of entrepreneurs, high interest offered by off- or online lenders is not necessarily the problem—they would take the loan if it were available. The problem facing small businesses seems to be ineffective intermediation in which borrowers and lenders do not find each other. This is where technology can go a long way in helping to streamline credit analysis and intermediation, if regulators play along. Is it working?

The New Gap: Microloans for Microtraders

In 2015, an enterprising woman named Shamim set out to sell gorgeous handmade quilts on Bagdoom, a Bangladeshi ecommerce platform. The quilts gained in popularity and soon sold out. To fulfill the many incoming orders, Shamim needed $3,000 in working capital, which she planned to use to buy supplies and pay workers. Going from bank to bank, she never managed to get the capital—her loan request was too small for a bank to make money on, and banks questioned her ability to pay back, as that hinged on her customers' paying when they actually received the quilt. Precisely the kind of person policymakers want to encourage to be an entrepreneur and to use ecommerce, Shamim lost her customers because of a credit gap of a mere $3,000.

Shamim's situation is emblematic of developing-country entrepreneurs whose products have gained in popularity online, but who cannot secure minor working capital to meet the demand. In business surveys I ran in thirty countries, no other challenge vexes small ecommerce sellers in Africa or less developed parts of Asia as much as lack of finance. Lack of access to working capital loans is the number one of forty conceivable problems a developing-country small online seller may face.

Innovations do exist. For example, Tala Mobile, based in Santa Monica, California, offers microloans to businesses in Kenya, Tanzania, and the Philippines through a smartphone app that accesses basic biographical information on the loan applicant and the number of people he connects with daily, a proxy for the applicant's network and support system. Further data points include where the applicant goes during the day, whether he is consistent rather than erratic (for example, does he call his aging mother every day?), whether he pays his bills on time, and so on.[20]

In advanced economies, online lenders have filled financing needs. By curtailing credit to smaller businesses, the bank regulations and consolidation that followed the 2008–2009 financial crisis produced in the United States a financing gap and, to fill it, an army of non-bank online lenders for small businesses. Most of these providers, such as Fundation, Funding Circle, Dealstruck, OnDeck, and Lending Club provide loans of $16,000 to $130,000, using fast and creative credit scoring methods and algorithm-driven automated underwriting. The borrower can get a loan with even a low credit score, with minimal paperwork, and within a day or two, compared to the one to two months it takes him to negotiate with banks. In exchange, he pays a higher interest.[21] Some platforms are matchmakers for peer-to-peer lending; others have their own capital provided by major banks or Wall Street investment banks that diversify their portfolios to include these higher-interest small business loans.[22]

These companies have bridged major gaps. OnDeck found that 90 percent of its borrowers, who by 2017 had borrowed $3 billion, had "some type of borrowing constraint that precluded them from pursuing loans from other financing sources, whether due to time, credit, or budget constraints."[23] PayPal's working capital loan product, underwritten with PayPal's own data on transactions the borrower has conducted, has enabled companies in remote areas of America to access credit. As the Dodd-Frank regulations induced banks to consolidate, and local and community banks, the primary providers of SME debt financing, shut down in places such as rural Idaho, Nebraska, or Montana, PayPal and other online lenders have filled the gap.[24] A quarter of PayPal loans were disbursed in the 3 percent of counties that had lost ten or more banks since the financial crisis. Online payments and lending have flattened access to credit to entrepreneurs in rural America. An objective observer, the Federal Reserve Bank of Cleveland, ran through online lending data to find similarly that online borrowers are likely businesses that were denied credit in banks, and that the impact of the small loans on the businesses seemed positive.[25]

Why are these innovations then not solving the SME credit gap?

First, the adoption rate by SMEs is gradual. Businesses are often still unaware of online lenders. To be sure, in the United States, the peer-to-peer business-lending market is growing at over 150 percent annually, as opposed to bank loans to small businesses that are growing at 10 to 15 percent.[26] Some fears do persist: for example, small businesses tend to worry about some online lenders' opaque loan terms and pricing, and about their business and personal data getting into the wrong hands. Customer satisfaction is highest for businesses that got a bank loan, also higher for borrowers who got an online loan than for those that got no loan at all.[27]

But bit by bit these fears subside—and more of a symbiosis between banks and FinTech companies emerges. In 2015, Lending Club partnered with BancAlliance, a nationwide network of some 200 American community banks.[28] In the arrangement, banks direct their customers who need small loans to

Lending Club, and in exchange get an opportunity to purchase the loans made to their customers. Banks can also purchase loans from the wider Lending Club portfolio, allowing them to add loans outside their area to their portfolio. Lending Club's competitor Prosper has formed a similar arrangement with Western Independent Bankers, a consortium of 160 small community banks.

The second reason credit gaps persist is friction in information flows in the market. Credit providers live off great data on borrowers, but those data also need to travel to them. Often a bank looks at an application, then rejects it, and then nothing happens; the bank does not refer the applicant elsewhere, and the applicant does not ask about alternatives or look for them. A pioneer in alternative finance regulations, the United Kingdom has gone a step further to *mandate* that banks that cannot service small businesses pass those businesses to online lenders. The motivation was that in the wake of the financial crisis, U.K.-based banks, just like banks around the world, were mandated to perform more extensive due diligence on borrowers, which raised their fixed costs per loan and incentivized them to work with larger, well-known borrowers. Yet still most U.K. SMEs approached only their main bank for finance, and over a third gave up completely if they were turned down. Only 28 percent approached different providers. The law was to encourage more SMEs to look elsewhere.

In 2018, the United Kingdom went even further to mandate "open banking" practices, whereby U.K. banks that hold data on their SME customers' financials and other business vitals share that information, upon permission from the SME, with non-bank lenders.[29] As a result, the non-bank lender can amplify its database on a borrower and better assess its creditworthiness. However, banks also gain. Per the European Union's Payments Services Directive 2 (PSD2), any U.K. or European consumer's data will be portable—for example, a borrower can ask an ecommerce platform to store data on its transactions on the platform and pass that data to a bank, as another data point for the bank's credit analysis. Thanks to PSD2, SMEs get in charge of their data, which should encourage new lenders, faster credit decisions, and fewer defaults. Open banking is now spreading around the world, both by government fiat and often by enlightened banks who see a point in growing the pie and the fluidity of data.

The third reason why gaps persist is a regulators' fear that the lending market will become too big to fail. Are online lenders Trojan horses that carry the next financial crisis?

At one level, online lending to small businesses is still a small share of economies and overall lending—so even a deluge of defaults on small business loans would be unlikely to have much impact on the economy beyond the lender, except that such an event could precipitate a regulatory tightening to ensure a higher bar for borrowers and more transparency by the platform. And so far, regulators in the United States have sought to induce transparency to borrowers while appearing to appreciate online lenders' expanding access to financial services for underserved businesses.

At another level, online lending to small businesses is booming, and it has been taking place in rather good economic times—during rock-bottom interest rates, increasing employment, and strong overall credit conditions—which means it has yet to be tested when the market bottoms and defaults are likelier. And if one considers online lending to individuals and across segments such as real estate, health care, an and so on, the stakes rise quickly, as a calamity in one area of online lending may precipitate a crackdown on all areas. A 2016 U.S. Treasury review, however, also suggested that "[h]igher charge off and delinquency rates for recent vintage consumer loans may augur increased concern if and when credit conditions deteriorate."[30]

Of course, the stakes are still quite modest: the American consumer lending market is a $3.5 trillion business, but the twenty-two largest online marketplace platforms originated only $5 billion worth of unsecured consumer credit in 2014 and some $10 billion in 2015.[31] Things are different for Chinese regulators, facing a booming online loan market. In 2017, the online lending market reached $224 billion, and adding to it were $19 trillion in unregulated loans issued by smaller regional banks.[32] In November 2017, China took forceful steps to screen out vicious loan sharks charging 1,000 percent interest from the online loan market and harassing people to pay.

Former head of the Small Business Administration Karen Mills has been leading the charge in thinking about regulations related to online lending.[33] She calls for the industry to offer small businesses the kind of loan information as by regulation needs to be available for consumers, including broadening companies' participation in "Borrower's Bill of Rights," the industry's self-enforcement tool. Mills also advocates analytics on the effectiveness and impact of online lenders and data to help regulators understand the benefits and vagaries of the online market. The regulatory pressure may compel online lenders to remodel themselves into those they disrupt, such as by becoming, buying, selling to, or partnering with banks. OnDeck, for example, has partnered with J.P. Morgan to now offer online loans to its existing small business customers using OnDeck's platform.

The fourth reason why the SME financing gap is gaping is that lending to a small business can be hard work and difficult for a bank. Take Alipay's financial services, including loans provided by MYbank (formally known as Zhejiang E-commerce Bank Co. Ltd.), which is majority-owned by Alipay's FinTech arm Ant Financial. The bank reports issuing ¥100 million in loans to small business owners daily, with typical loan sizes from ¥10,000 to ¥20,000 ($1,500 to $3,000) at about 14 percent interest.[34] Default rates are at 1 percent, lower than the national average of 1.74 percent, thanks to algorithms tirelessly culling through data. To be sure, getting into the riskier small business loans forced the bank to almost double its capital adequacy ratio from 11 to 18.5 percent.[35] In other words, small loans are possible, but they come at a cost—and many banks, unless affiliated with an ecommerce platform or armed with particular expertise in screening small businesses, will never want to originate or underwrite small business loans. The upfront costs are significant; the upside is uncertain, especially as regulatory compliance bites into profit margins.

That's not to say banks could not lend to small businesses—only that they cannot do it at the same scale. Investment bank UBS puts China's Bank of Taizhou to the top of 237 banks in profitability and asset quality—and it happens to be Bank of Taizhou that uses the so-called IPC lending model, named after a German consulting firm that ideated it and recognized by the World Bank as a means to unlock financing for small businesses that do not have great records or credit histories.[36] The model lies not on algorithms but on old-fashioned screening of signs in applicants of inconsistencies and nervousness, albeit via a systematic approach to measure repayment capacity—account executives might ask for the same information in various ways to detect inconsistencies, such as asking, "What's your monthly income?" and after ten other questions, "What is your annual income?" The companies that are risking default on any payment will receive a barrage of phone calls and be visited by the bank's "Risk-Fighting Unit," aimed at shaming them into repaying—and be taken to court if nothing else works. But most banks are not interested in running these types of business models.

Fifth, financial innovations are hard to scale. Compare social media platforms such as Facebook, that scaled to a billion users across just about every country in eight years, to OnDeck, the most prominent U.S. online business lender, which after eight years had managed to expand only across the United States and to Canada and Australia. One reason is that bringing FinTech innovations to market is costly; internationalizing them even costlier, due to the myriad regulations surrounding financial services that give innovative entrepreneurs cold feet about getting into the sector.

Of course, nowadays the social media industry also is under much more scrutiny, and national laws regulating platforms are becoming more idiosyncratic and stringent. And certainly financial regulations are in the books for a good reason—such as to prevent fraudulent or predatory lending practices, or scams in crowdfunding campaigns. And governments are coming up with policies to help FinTechs scale. The United Kingdom helpfully has lowered FinTech companies' time and money to market with the sandbox approach, whereby companies can bring to market a new financial product or service without the entire gamut of regulatory approvals, and regulators can watch the market develop and regulate undesirable behaviors out. Various countries such as Australia, Singapore, and Thailand have copied the sandbox in order to energize their FinTech ecosystems. With nearly a dozen federal and a range of state agencies regulating online lenders, the United States has its own sandbox proposal—in a bill calling for a "Financial Services Innovation Office" to support the development of financial innovations.

Yet even with sandboxes, a critical problem remains: each country (and in the United States, each state) has its own financial services regulations that do not interoperate well. This forces FinTechs scaling across borders to adopt rules and apply for licenses specific to each new market. For example, a British (or for that matter, an American) online lender seeking to service all U.S. states will have to meet each state's regulations. The feat is just about impossible but for those with deep pockets. On average, it takes $2 million and two years to make a U.S. FinTech company to scale and get it into the black. Granted, venture capital for FinTech companies is more amply available in the United States than in the United Kingdom, but it is probably tougher to build a FinTech company in the U.S. without it. European lenders, typically more obsessed with cross-border lending than Americans, have to secure licenses in each EU market—though the EU's Capital Markets Union seeks to change that. And not all markets are ripe for loans. Lendico, for example, has pulled back from Spain, Poland, and South Africa, citing a lack of quality loan requests.[37]

The obvious solution is better interoperability among national regulations; something the United Kingdom and Canada have made headway on. In February 2017, the U.K.'s Financial Conduct Authority (FCA) and the Ontario Securities Commission of Canada signed an agreement to refer to one another innovative businesses seeking to enter the other's market and help them navigate regulations and lower time to market. The deal is hailed as a template for the first cross-border regulatory collaboration in the FinTech market. And so it probably was intended: just a month earlier, the FCA's new chief executive, Andrew Bailey, gave a speech stressing the need for global regulatory standards as the basis to govern market access for financial services firms. For its part, the Ontario Securities Commission of Canada had earlier concluded a similar deal with the Australian Securities and Investments Commission. Meanwhile, U.S. states and the federal bank regulator Office of the Comptroller of the Currency are on their respective fronts (and encouraged by each other) working on more uniform rules for online lenders across states. Thirteen countries, including the United Kingdom and the United States, have also joined a multinational sandbox to better enable FinTech companies to try their wings across various markets and regulators to learn from each other. More needs to happen, for online lending to work globally.

Growth Capital Gap

In 2015, David, the CEO of a nascent U.S. tech company that helps broadband users keep a good connection when usage surges, such as at 5 p.m. in hotels or 8 a.m. on college campuses, asked for help with his fundraise. He had by that time raised a good million dollars in successive seed and bridge rounds from angel investors. His product was in demand in the United States, and his eyes had been opened to its international market potential after Marriott in the Middle East placed an order. Emerging markets and developing countries with shoddy broadband connections and strong broadband demand surges at hotels and universities would all benefit from his technology. Development agencies might also like it, to accelerate connectivity in the developing world. But to fund his developer team to create a cloud-based version of his product, develop after-sale service capability, and hire a salesperson to travel around the planet to lock in contracts with international clients, David needed more firepower— about $5 million, to be raised from a venture capital fund. Nothing other than lack of growth capital kept him from internationalizing, possibly big time.

David's case is emblematic of the changes in the types of financing needs globalizing companies have today, versus ten to twenty years ago. When a nascent tech company observes strong global demand for its products or services and wants to seize it, it needs much more financial firepower than a bank or a lender would ever offer for a company of its size. Post-export supply chain finance will not do. A company like David's needs financing *in order to export*—to identify, lock in, and deliver to the international customer. This means that a company like David's typically needs equity: an investor who puts cash into the business in exchange for a piece of the business. Such a need is nothing new—countless companies regardless of their target market are out there as you read this sentence, perfecting their pitch decks and emailing angel investors and venture capital funds. What is new is that in the twenty-first century, access to equity financing is for the first time a critical determinant of companies' international competitiveness.

The fact that a company does not get angel or venture capital does not mean it cannot exist—much depends on its business model, technology, and burn rate. But it does appear to be the case that those that do are likelier to globalize. Data show that companies that have international shareholders (such as foreign VCs) are much likelier to export than companies that have only foreign shareholders, and that companies that have secured equity investments are likelier to export. The main reason, studies suggest, is that the investor itself is foreign and helps the investee expand to the investor's market, thanks to its contacts and help in legitimizing the unknown foreign players in that market.[38] For example, the VC landscape has improved enormously in Latin America in the past five years, and its "Tecnolatinas," or regional tech startups, are often helped by Silicon Valley investors' cash and contacts to service new markets.[39] Some VCs and private equity funds are geared to taking companies global—for example, Chicago-based Blue Point Capital invests in lower- middle-market U.S. companies and then helps them deploy in Chinese markets.[40]

Of course, an investor does not necessarily *cause* the company to export— the causal relationship may be the reverse, namely that a company may simply go for investors in the foreign market it targets or sells in already. And it could be that investors are drawn to such companies—globalizing, export-driven companies are, as discussed in Chapter 3, an asset class that outperforms the broader market by key metrics: productivity, revenue growth, skill levels, wages, and financial stability, all metrics that should herald a return on investment.

Equity finance has become central because of the "shrinking exporter": even the smallest businesses, once they have a website and an attractive product or service, can get interest from global customers. Today's companies are often "born global," poised to internationalize since their inception, because they are "born digital." Only a quick glance at the news shows it often costs to be born global, and much more to lock in a market: Berlin-based property portal Lamudi raised $18 million to expand in Asia and Latin America; China's Airbnb-copy Tujia raised $300 million to expand overseas; Uber poured billions into expanding in sixty Chinese cities. Being digital, today's companies can scale faster than your 1970s manufacturing business would ever have dreamt of—but they seldom scale without serious cash. They may get a $100,000 loan from OnDeck, but that does not take them too far, especially if they want to grow fast. Most of them do, because they want to grab market share before competitors do, and because they are entrepreneurs—people who perennially feel the world revolves infuriatingly slowly. They need growth capital.

So what then is the problem? Don't companies move to San Francisco and meet some VCs and get funded and become Ubers, for all intents and purposes blanketing the world with their services?

For each Uber, there are ten thousand non-Ubers. Even in the United States, the deepest capital market in the world, only a small number, perhaps 2 to 5 percent, of companies that are like David's and seek venture capital get it, and they are typically the survivors, perhaps four to five years old at the time. And most that get their Series A Round done don't raise again—that is, do not amass the capital that tends to make companies grow fast to unicorn valuations. Of a recent study of 1,098 U.S. tech companies that had received seed capital, only 46 percent were able to raise the next round (typically A Round) from a VC, 28 percent raised C round, and 14 percent raised D round—while 40 percent failed to raise even a B round (and 14 percent had an exit such as a sale to a larger rival rather than doing another raise). By contrast, Uber, founded in 2009, and Airbnb, founded in 2008, both raised their E Rounds in 2015.

When peering into funding by company characteristics, what stands out is that companies in the "flyover territory" outside major cities and women-led companies are underfunded—women founders get just a quarter of the funding they ask for, while male founders get 50 percent.[41]

One key reason why women are not getting funded is the fact that angels and VC partners are some ten times likelier to be men than women, and male investors are less likely than female investors to believe women can make them money, or they harbor some other type of gender bias, and/or they are less likely to feel connected to the products or business models of those women whose target market is other women.[42] The first VCs met by Jennifer Wyman, creator of the women's high-end clothing-share business Rent the Runway, now valued at over $1 billion, told her, "You are just too cute. You get this big closet and get to play with all these dresses and can wear whatever you want. This must be so much fun!"[43] By now Rent the Runway has raised nine rounds, seven years after its founding in 2009.

Internationally, Seed and VC raise numbers are even lower. According to an OECD survey, Israel has the highest percentage of VC investments to GDP in the world. Israel's born digital companies typically are born global—there is only so far to scale in a market of five million. But also in Israel, only a small share of businesses get funded. In regions where a serious startup scene is more nascent, such as Latin America or Africa, there is an upsurge of Google- and Microsoft-backed accelerators, but angels and VCs are still few in number.

Why can't more companies get funded? One simple answer is that too many do as is. Investors do not make money on most deals. Of VC bets, over 70 percent of companies either failed or perhaps hung on but never raised again and over 99 percent did not become a unicorn, a company with a $1-billion-plus valuation.[44] For many startups, burn rate goes unmatched by revenue growth or add-on investments. In the VC market, a sliver of investees makes up for the failures, which means that companies in that sliver must go big for an investor to make money on her portfolio.

There are two main reasons why companies don't get funded: moral hazard (when the entrepreneur playing with OPM, or "other people's money," acts recklessly when spending the investment proceeds) and asymmetric information (when the entrepreneur may be the classic car salesman selling the investors a lemon that does not merit the valuation he has given it, but the investor has no perfect way to verify whether it is a lemon or a Lexus). Of course, an investor almost always thinks, and has an incentive to think, that the prospect is overvalued and wants to drive the valuation down; that is why intermediaries such as brokers and crowdfunding platforms that make money on consummated deals also persuade companies to lower their valuations, to make their raises more sellable to investors. In principle, VCs are experts at solving these two problems—that is why they get funded by pension funds, sovereign wealth funds, and others.[45] But their work is still hard and more art than science.

The work is even harder at angel stages—investors have very little else to go by other than the company's management team and its track record. It's no surprise then that angels tend to be particularly heavily involved in the company to limit moral hazard and supply value-adding advice. Angel is a co-builder that schools the founder, VC a monitor that mitigates principal-agent problems.[46] Both like to go for founders that they know, that have succeeded in the past, or that are referred to them by a trusted person whose judgment they trust.

For a new company on the fundraising trail, these informational issues tend to mean that fundraising is a very time-consuming endeavor. Even for a founder who is a known quantity, it takes several dialogues with investors before funds are transferred. One of the most typical constraints for a busy founder to get funded is thus time: a typical startup has only three to four key people and typically only one who can compellingly speak with investors, and typically that person is working to get clients in the door and dealing with day-to-day issues. That $5 million fundraise is all too easily usurped by other burning priorities of the day, day after day—so that the raise may in data appear as "tried and failed," but the "try" is actually very weak. The fact is that founders have a finite number of investor contacts and time is what has given rise to an entire industry of brokers and, later, funding portals that vet companies on behalf of investors—that is, take it on themselves to reduce the information asymmetries—and help match right companies to right investors. But even then, the growth capital gaps persist.

Policy challenges complicate fundraises. For example, rigid labor market regulations have long made Europe and developing countries rather unattractive to investors when compared to the United States, where securities rules and digital regulations tend to encourage investors to invest in Internet companies, lead to faster deal screening, and help attract board members.[47] Cross-country studies show that cross-border investments tend to be made in proximate countries and countries with which the investor's country shares a language and colonial ties, and in countries with top-notch human capital, business environment, and deep financial markets.[48] And investors tend to invest in places they grow to know.

This was also the reason why before the 1990s, venture capital was mostly an American industry—and in many ways still is. The main difference now is that U.S. VCs have ventured into the world, investing in startups in Europe, Israel, and, more recently, Latin America, which has experienced a VC boom, with FinTech deals leading the way. In a sample of one hundred countries, cross-border deals increased from 15 percent in the early 1990s to over 40 percent in 2007, with the United States as the leading exporter of venture capital.[49]

Governments have long recognized the need for growth capital—whether venture capital, private equity, and long-term debt—for fueling small businesses. The European Union, for example, is seeking to incentivize venture capital in "scale-ups," companies beyond the riskier startup phase.

Many governments have started their own VCs to invest in tech companies, either directly or with private investors, or as limited partners that invest in privately managed general partners. Some governments have internalized the need to fuel funding to women. For example, Business Development Canada's Women in Technology Fund places bets in early-stage Canadian-women-led technology companies across sectors, in Series A and B rounds alongside accelerator partners, investors, and other corporate venture partners. Mexico's new women's SME program lends to micro, small, and medium-sized enterprises with at least a 51 percent female ownership Mex$50,000 to Mex$5 million (or up to about $500,000) with 12 to 13 percent interest for five years.[50]

The idea that government should "pick winners" among private companies is rightly controversial, and evidence of the performance of companies backed by government VCs is mixed. Some research finds that some level of engagement may be positive: a modest amount of government venture funding seems to improve the performance of businesses relative to those supported purely by private venture capitalists.[51] High levels of government support—especially when governments become involved in the venture's business decisions—are associated with weaker performance. Other studies suggest that government-backed funds do not yield particularly resounding outcomes, but that syndicates involving governments and private investors do outperform purely private funds, and that governments may best act as limited partners (or as funds of funds).[52]

Governments could also be more proactive in enacting equity crowdfunding laws. Equity crowdfunding, in which companies can sell securities online to investors, has expanded dramatically in recent years—and is empirically found to expand investments in a wider set of geographies and to help open financing to companies that may not have extensive investor networks.[53] However, except for Canada, where one criteria for investments by government-backed vehicles is that the company show global growth potential, most governments have yet to connect the dots between the growth capital and competitiveness in international trade, and some may worry that backing exporters is a subsidy barred by WTO rules. Therefore, the trade policy community has neither pushed hard for regulatory changes needed to unlock early-stage funding for companies nor systematically addressed if and how export credit agencies could help early-stage companies secure the funding they need to grow in international markets. Smart tactics could be used. For example, tiny Malta has had an innovative royalties-based financing program for young Maltese companies, including for internationalization purposes.

SMEs Are a Big Part of the Problem

An unknown number of data points do not enter the number of declined loans or VC raises, as many SMEs never even try—knowing how stacked odds are against them and how long it takes to underwrite a loan, among a myriad reasons. A recent study of Tanzanian women entrepreneurs shows that collateral requirements, high personal guarantees, high interest rates, *and* perceived bias by lenders against women turn these women off from formal lenders.[54] And of course, SMEs do not ask for funding when business is bad—why do so? In the wake of the financial crisis, American small business borrowing hit rock bottom mostly because weak earnings and economic uncertainty gave SMEs no reason to borrow.[55] In addition, collateral such as real estate dropped in value, curtailing the amount that a small business owner could borrow.

But it is also the case that many factors conspire against creditworthy small businesses' getting funded or even seeking funding: high search costs to identify the right lender, long, paper-heavy underwriting processes, high loan decline rates, and tough loan conditionalities. SMEs often do not work hard enough to understand the needs and requirements of different investors and lenders—just as banks are told to "know your customer," SMEs should "know your bank." Founders are seldom as savvy as believed from accounts of storied Silicon Valley superstars. Many fail to put themselves in an investor's shoes or do the homework to understand which specific types of deals an investor likes, or pitch their businesses in a way meaningful to bankers and investors. Startup decks often discuss the company's technology rather than what interests the investor—market potential for the technology, the team running the business, and a plan to use proceeds to get to the multiplier investor covets as a reward for taking a chance on a new team and the many unknowns lurking around it.

The Trillion Dollar Question

Let's take a step back. Is it beneficial for long-run economic growth to support emerging new firms and microbusinesses run by solo entrepreneurs or small teams? Or would it be better for governments to support larger firms that create jobs for the people who might otherwise lead small firms? Perhaps another way to articulate the question is, are small loans for microenterprises at the end of the day good for the microentrepreneur? To answer yes, we must believe the microentrepreneur will still have a margin after paying back the loan with interest and ideally be able to improve her standard of living, rather than ending up in a cycle of debt. We must believe she loves her work and would much rather do that than work in a nearby factory. If mounting a public policy intervention to support loans in her segment, we must believe we are making people better off, catalyzing innovation, propelling job creators, and so on. In other words, we must believe from a policy perspective that the return for investment (against a public policy aim) would be superior if the government were to support a thousand loans of $3,000 rather than to back a $3 million investment in a manufacturer that could employ the thousand microentrepreneurs.[56]

All of us running our own companies have a visceral reaction to these types of musings. But of course we should have better access to capital—we after all work much harder than people in steady jobs, risk our own capital, constantly think about "next big thing," and innovate more than most large firms! This knee-jerk reaction is also empirically valid. Though data are limited still, a broad conclusion across studies is that young firms are more innovative than larger ones with more than twenty employees, and that they create more jobs (even if they also destroy jobs as young firms fail). Startups, it is found, are disproportionately important in terms of growth and productivity.[57] As startup creation has slowed in the United States in recent years, so has job creation and churn. Young firms are also important for multinationals to access new innovations, such as for old, stodgy banks from dynamic FinTechs— just in 2018 some three hundred FinTech startups were acquired by retail banks.[58] In other words, there is a compelling public policy case for governments to buttress startups and their scaling across markets.

But it is also the case that there has been a dark side to microloans in developing economies. The renowned MIT economist Esther Duflo and co-author Abhijit V. Banerjee argue in their book *Poor Economics: A Radical Rethinking of the Way to Fight Global Poverty* that "there are more than a billion people who run their own farm or business, but most of them do this because they have no other options. Microcredit and other ways to help tiny businesses have an important role to play in the lives of the poor, because these tiny businesses will remain, perhaps for the foreseeable future, the only way many of the poor can manage to survive. But we are kidding ourselves if we think that these businesses can pave the way for a mass exit from poverty."[59] A better way, they propose, would be such things as macroeconomic policies that propel growth.

Such questions about the impact of small capital injections on borrowers were first raised systematically with the microfinance revolution of the 1980s and 1990s. In 1974, the legend goes, Mohammed Yunus made a $27 loan to a Bangladeshi woman who manufactured furniture but did not have access to credit, except at an exorbitant interest rate. The woman paid back the $27 with interest, and eventually born was the microlender Grameen Foundation that would earn Yunus a Nobel Peace Prize. Grameen loans were made to individuals but through small groups who thus had joint liability; the loans were for business, not consumption; and collection was frequent, usually weekly—but interest was low, about 20 percent. Grameen, of course, was one of dozens of experiments to provide small loans to developing-country entrepreneurs by Acción International, SEWA Bank, Women's World Banking, FINCA, and Podem/Banco Sol in Bolivia, and countless others.

The industry brewed to some fifty million microfinance loan accounts by 2004, and ideological fights broke out.[60] Critics claimed microcredit was "all hat but no cowboy," a glorified but patronizing product that at best supported people that stayed micro, never hired staff, and had few assets or chances to scale, and at its worst fed entrepreneurs to loan sharks and kept poor people in poverty, forced to grind away to make the next loan payment and slowly drown in the cycle of borrowing and repaying. A smart critic, Aneel Karnani, observed that China, Vietnam, and South Korea significantly reduced poverty with little microfinance activity, while the hubs of microfinance such as Bangladesh, Bolivia, and Indonesia had not.[61] A plausible explanation was that microfinance was perpetuating companies destined to stay small, not power the kind of new manufacturing and export businesses that propelled Korea from a rice-farming rural nation to the ranks of advanced nations.

The industry countered with the success stories, such as of a woman beat up regularly by her husband until the day he sold the roof of their house to pay off gambling debts, the rain came, and she had enough, moving with her children to live with her brother. Initially borrowing $30 to buy a goat and sell the milk, she secured more loans to produce scarves, and went on to employ twenty-five women.[62] These success stories were, however, a small fraction of all borrowers, and overall questions remained as to whether entrepreneurs were entrepreneurs by choice or out of necessity.

However, research has also found caveats. In an experiment in India, Duflo found that companies that had been established before the microfinance entity they now used was available did much better than those that had their entrepreneurial birth afterward and likely used the microfinance entity to set their business up.[63] This finding, if holding across markets, is seminal, as it means that prior studies that lump old and new borrowers together underestimate the impact of small loans on small businesses.

In 2015, six studies on the impact of microcredit on thirty-seven thousand individuals in Bosnia and Herzegovina, Ethiopia, India, Mexico, Mongolia, and Morocco also illustrated the benefits of time and staying power: modest improvements in the lives and financial well-being of individuals one to four years after they accessed microloans.[64] All of the studies found some evidence of expanded business activity, but these investments did not often result in significant increases in profit. Other studies refined this, arguing that credit is most transformative when the entrepreneurs are also trained to run a business.[65] An experiment with women entrepreneurs in a Peruvian village revealed that those that received thirty- to sixty-minute coaching sessions alongside their normal weekly or monthly banking meeting over a period of one to two years improved their business practices and revenues much above those that did not receive such add-on support.

Microloans made in the microfinance boom are smaller than those needed by Internet entrepreneurs—typically less than $1,000 in developing countries, and averaging $9,000 or so in the United States. But they are one way to gauge the impact of loans to small businesses—and to strive to answer whether the small loans by players such as Alipay to small entrepreneurs will have a transformative impact on entrepreneurship, poverty reduction, and job creation. Duflo likes to say that while microcredit may not improve everything, that does not mean it improves nothing.

An unexplored hypothesis is whether economic and social gains from small microloans might be different in the ecommerce era, precisely because ecommerce and other technologies enable companies to scale, very unlike in the 1990s. It could well be that the Internet can enable companies armed with small injections of credit to quickly sell more product, turn a profit, invest in marketing, and get more customers, and again get more credit. In other words, the Internet and technologies such as ecommerce and online payments may be the road to scalability that the offline era's microentrepreneurs did not have, unless they somehow battled their way through FDA and U.S. customs regulations to sell organic peas from Guatemalan highlands or coffee from Peruvian jungles. This hypothesis is extremely important and has yet to be systematically explored.

Conclusion

Does a chapter on small business finance belong in a book on trade? Trade economists might argue it does not—that small business finance is not unique to trade, but cuts across many topics, such as burning questions about ways to catalyze entrepreneurship, accelerate economic growth, and respond to recessions. At the same time, the trade finance gap stunts the potential of technologies such as ecommerce to enable small firms to trade. If we are serious about enabling technology-powered trade in the twenty-first century and helping small firms take advantage of technology to scale their sales, the trade finance gap is a gap to address. This goes to the bigger point of this book discussed in Chapter 13, namely that we have to stop thinking about what is "trade-related" and what is "finance-related" and what is "infrastructure-related," and so on—stop working in silos and start working across departments, sectors, and disciplines because that also is how trade works, and that is the only way to make trade work.

Granted, the small business finance gap is probably never going to close. Few if any small businesses ever feel that they have enough capital: just about every entrepreneur has ideas she could readily invest millions in. Surveys on the financing gaps will thus probably always find gaps. Human foibles may never be perfectly screened out by AI-driven credit scoring—fraudsters intent on using their new business loan to buy a TV, arrogant business owners who take foolish risks and eventually default, or honest entrepreneurs running into roadblocks they cannot recover from. But technology is making such risks easier to forecast and manage, thus enabling funding for companies that make money for their lenders and investors. If, that is, technology can roam freer and financial regulations interoperate.

12

TECHLASH AND TRADE WARS

Technological change is changing the economics of making, moving, and marketing goods and services, and quietly revolutionizing world trade. The last few chapters have discussed several challenges to the twenty-first-century's technology-powered trade, such as digital divides, arcane customs procedures, and stringent data transfer rules. But no challenge is as difficult to solve as fears about the impacts of trade and technology on jobs, incomes, and equality. These fears have power—they helped produce Brexit and the election of Donald Trump. In a September 2016 poll in the eve of the U.S. presidential election, an astounding 47 percent of Republicans, traditionally staunch free traders, said that trade deals had hurt American communities over the preceding decade, while only 18 percent though trade deals had helped.[1]

Paradoxically, while unlocking new opportunities and value creation in countries around the world, the twin forces of technology and trade are more often feared to cause unemployment and inequality than celebrated as sources of opportunity. Developing countries interested in building their own ecommerce ecosystems have additional concerns about the dominant role of U.S. and Chinese tech companies. And where there is fear, there is political opposition, accompanied by counterproductive policy proposals to raise tariffs, tax robots and the rich, block foreign companies, and protect factories of a bygone era.

Are there grounds for these fears? What is the empirical record on the impact of trade and technology on jobs and incomes? And how useful, or perhaps counterproductive, are the proposed remedies?

Crazy, Stupid Tariff Policy

On March 2, 2018, the world woke to President Trump's announcement of a 25 percent tariff on steel. This baffling move was one of the most counterproductive trade policies since the Smoot-Hawley tariff of the 1930s. It raised costs of many American products and businesses that use steel and hurt exporters in America's largest export sectors—aircraft, computers, medical equipment, and vehicles—that use steel as input. It seemed to only undermine the Trump administration's own objective to reduce the U.S. trade deficit.

Targeted at China, the policy also seemed to be toothless, in that Chinese steel makes up only 3 percent of America's steel imports. It wasn't even that useful politically. Over 40 percent of Americans thought the policy would hurt America; only about a quarter, perhaps those who anyway agree with the president no matter what, thought it would be useful. It risked retaliation by American allies and unraveling the good will American trade policymakers have built internationally. Soon, the policy was modified to exempt allies and new ways to rib China were found.

Companies, economists, and seasoned trade policymakers have condemned the tariff and its many successors in hundreds of blogs and op-eds. While necessary, the debate on the impact of the Trump tariffs also deviates us from the bigger points: no amount of trade protection will bring the twentieth-century jobs back from the dead, and trade will not be what it has been in the past decades. Granted, trade will still be voluntary exchange of goods and services for some instrument of monetary value between buyer and seller located in different countries. But what is traded, how, and by whom is changing. Trade will be much more about trade in digital services than goods, digital products and designs rather than physical parts and components, and millions of small parcels traveling by air rather than containers sailing on the ocean. World trade will be increasingly generated by individuals who order goods and services on ecommerce platforms; businesses that find suppliers on Amazon or Alibaba; and small and large firms buying specialized IT and data services from freelancers, boutique businesses, and cloud computing giants in other nations. Globalization of 2025 will be different from that of 2000. Digitization is defying decades-old trade models taught across universities and reshaping the outcomes of trade agreements negotiated around the planet.

But let's nonetheless look at trade as it has been—what is the real empirical record on its impacts?

Mutually Consenting Traders

Answers start from two hundred years ago. In 1817, David Ricardo established a theory of comparative advantage that explained why trade happens.[2] His conclusion was that trade enabled countries to focus on what they did best and where their opportunity cost was lowest. Thus France would specialize in making wine and Britain in making cloth, and each would sell a portion of its output to the other. Both would as a result be better off: Brits would get wine they did not grow, and the French would get cloth they did not make. And that is exactly what trade is: voluntary exchange between mutually consenting parties that expands the consumption possibilities of a country's consumers.

Trade since the times of Phoenicians and Mayans has been nothing different than your exchanging money for getting a haircut from a hairdresser you like: a trade in which you get something when your opportunity cost of doing it yourself (cutting your own hair) would be higher than your paying the hairdresser to cut your hair (whose opportunity cost of cutting your hair is low as he excels at it and does it better than he would do other jobs, including yours). You have a lifelong trade deficit with your hairdresser—just as you have with Starbucks and the grocery store, and just like your clients have with you.

Ricardo's insight was that everyone is better when everyone specializes in doing what he is best at and then trades a part of his output with others. In his stylized world, Spain was best at making olive oil, Poland in potatoes, France in wine, and Britain in cloth. Why should a Spaniard living amid olive trees grow potatoes and make cloth if he could buy those from Poles and Brits, the experts in potatoes and cloth? By growing olive oil, Ricardo reasoned, the Spaniard could essentially make Poles and Brits work for him to grow potatoes and make cloth. And that is the brilliance of trade: it enables us to hire the capabilities best suited to create the product or service we want.

In developing countries, trade still happens in part because of Ricardian reasons: consumers and companies import simply because they do not have certain products or parts made in their own countries—and often not made because foreign businesses have a comparative advantage in them and foreign parts and components are cheaper and of higher quality. Trade enables developing nations to play to their comparative advantage and forego producing things they are not best at. As Paul Krugman showed in the 1970, people and businesses in advanced economies (and increasingly in emerging and developing ones) buy imports of product their countries make because those imported products suit their preferences better than domestic products—whether they prefer the quality, price, color, shape, brand, and so on. In large advanced economies, a consumer or company can find a domestic version of an imported product—it is possible to get Spanish TVs in Spain or American cars in America, but still Spaniards import Samsung TVs and Americans buy Hyundais *because they choose to do so.* Just as American companies that buy cheap foreign steel or textiles choose to do so.

In the 1930s, two Swedish economists, Eli Heckscher and Bertil Ohlin, finetuned Ricardo's ideas. They showed why countries had the comparative advantages they did. For example, the United States would export computers because it had an abundance of high-skilled labor needed to make them, Vietnam would focus on making apparel because it had an abundance of low-skilled labor, and Brazil would focus on soybeans because of its abundance in arable land. When countries traded, the sectors that used their "abundant endowments" would expand, while others would shrink: the United States would export and make more computers but fewer apparel than it did before trade was allowed.

A few years later, two economists, Wolfgang Stolper at Swathmore College and future Nobel Prize winner Paul Samuelson of MIT, used the Heckscher-Ohlin model of trade to understand the distributional impacts of trade. They theorized that workers in sectors that expanded upon trade liberalization would see their wages rise relative to the wages of other sectors. In other words, if America were to liberalize trade with Mexico, the wages of American tech companies (which use the high-skill labor America has in abundance) would expand relative to the wages American workers had in such sectors as textiles and vehicles that used lots of cheaper labor (that Mexico had in abundance). Meanwhile, all workers in all countries would gain as consumers: as trade is liberalized, Mexicans would see high-tech products become relatively cheaper, Americans would see shirts and cars become cheaper, and everyone's consumption possibilities just shot up.

What about workers in America's textile sector? Their fate would depend on how quickly they could get employment in sectors that were expanding, or how successful they might be at persuading lawmakers to block trade with Mexico, or perhaps how easily they could be bribed to take free trade in exchange for alimony payments. One such payment is Trade Adjustment Assistance, launched by the Kennedy Administration; it has in recent years spent roughly $800 million annually in assisting and retraining workers hurt from trade and been the key bargaining chip for Republicans to get Democrats to vote for contentious trade deals like CAFTA.[3]

Tariffs would be a bad deal for American consumers and apparel companies and Mexican textile workers. Tariffs would also be a bad deal for Mexican consumers and the America tech sector, if Mexico were to decide to keep its trade barriers on America's tech products in exchange for America's reluctance to remove its barriers on Mexican textiles. In turn, alimony payments would be another cost borne by American taxpayers, but possibly an opportunity for the textile workers to get retrained and learn to code, say.

These staple theories of trade probably sound very familiar—because empirical findings roughly correspond to those theoretical postulates, in two ways.

First, studies by a range of economists show that every American is roughly $3,000 richer *each year* because of America's postwar trade liberalization carried out unilaterally, in the context of the multilaterally, and in bilateral or regional trade agreements.[4] We are better off for two main reasons. The first is that trade enables us to buy a wider variety of products at lower cost—this book has shown that the Internet and ecommerce dramatically expand those possibilities by giving us visibility into the offerings of businesses and peers around the world. Another reason we are better off because of trade is the dynamic effects that start to unfold in the economy after trade is liberalized. Trade liberalization induces companies in export-oriented sectors to expand, hire more and better workers, get more capital, and become better. Companies that are not competitive go out of business unless they raise their game, become more efficient, and help with the export-driven companies to raise the economy's overall productivity and growth. Through this rough and tumble of what economists call "sifting and sorting," bad companies die and other companies get better, raising the batting average of the economy.

Second, trade does hurt some workers. The real-life distributional impacts of trade have been quite textbook, working out as Stolper and Samuelson thought—though they are rather small in the scheme of things and far smaller than typically assumed. In the best analysis yet, pro-trade economists Daren Acemoglu, David Autor, David Dorn, Gordon Hanson, and Brendan Price looked at the rise of imports from China in different American districts in 1999–2011, finding that those that had experienced the most import surges tended to see a drop in manufacturing jobs and wages of manufacturing workers. American manufacturing job losses due to the rise in import competition from China in 1999–2011 were as high as 2.4 million.[5] That is not insignificant considering that net manufacturing job losses during the time totaled 5.7 million.[6] A loss of 2.4 million jobs also does sound like an awful lot. But it came during a period of thirteen years—and it is still a small share of the annual labor market churn, which in 2016 alone involved 16 million hires and 13.3 million separations.

Quickly lost in this debate about trade and jobs is that imports have benefited many American *workers*. Trade is not simple import and export. Made in China is not really only "made in China," and most products made in China are even more made in America. When you read "made in China," you may just as well read "made in China and the United States and Korea, Germany, Poland, and Australia." The Apple iPhone famously comes together from U.S. R&D and design, audiochips, cameras, glass screen, and touchscreen controllers; Korean LCD screen, processor, and battery; and Japanese LCD screen and camera. What's more, just about all these parts makers have several facilities around the world.[7] At the end of the day, the value-add of China's assembly is less than 5 percentage points of the price of the iPhone, Made in the World as it is. Moreover, imports create new jobs right in America, in transport, logistics, warehousing, retail, and so on—an impact that has so far been very poorly accounted for.

If free trade is good for the majority, why don't all policymakers then embrace it? One way to look at it is that they have done so—the past fifty years has been an era of dramatic trade liberalization globally, enabled by enlightened policymakers who chose to educate their constituents rather than give in to what Berkeley economic historian Barry Eichengreen terms a "populist temptation," saying what keeps constituents happy.[8] Another, formidable force behind trade liberalization was the presence of a counterfactual—the socialist Soviet Union, whose collapse provided free marketers with an enviable teaching moment about the perils of protectionism. Still another and perhaps the main force behind liberalization and openness has been the rise of multinationals and exporters that have grown into an influential, deep-pocketed global pro-trade lobby.

Yet the populist temptation has not vanished; examining waves of populism through the ages, Eichengreen argues that populists thrive in the wake of economic downturns, when masses can be coaxed to believe the elites have failed us, and foreigners colluding with elites can be blamed for the rest of the ills.

And then come tariffs, which are risky and counterproductive instruments, even if their end goal was to squeeze other countries to play fair. At the time of writing, President Trump had imposed tariffs on 12 percent of U.S. imports. Tariffs aimed at China were hurting American consumers and the many U.S. companies that use Chinese imports, while China's retaliatory tariffs undercut the American exporters Trump has pledged to help, such as farmers. Tariffs benefit a few U.S. steel firms but do little to prod blue collar jobs—after all, if the Chinese don't make products, robots will. And they hurt the U.S. companies that manufacture products in China and export them from there to the United States: few U.S. manufacturers have had any interest in lobbying for tariffs on goods made in China.[9] And to the extent that tariffs end up significantly hurting China's growth, U.S. companies exporting to China will see lower demand, and Americans with investments in Chinese stocks will see lower returns.

Tariffs can also sorely miss their target. In a November 2018 analysis, Trump's steel tariffs had actually hurt small and poor economies—Bangladesh, Guatemala, and Peru—worst.[10]

Tariffs are also a blunt tool to accomplish the Trump administration's obsession with reducing the U.S. trade deficit, first because they just about force other countries to retaliate against U.S. exports, and second because they ultimately have an impact on the value of the dollar, the leading driver of U.S. trade balance. Joseph Gagnon calculates that a 10 percent tariff hike would certainly reduce the imports of foreign goods, but it would also reduce the demand of foreign currency, appreciate the dollar, and undermine American exports, offsetting the impact of the tariff on the trade balance.[11] To balance trade with a tariff is like taking one step forward and one step back.

The China Problem

The flaws in U.S. tariff policy do not mean China should not be targeted. Arguments for free trade tend to assume that countries play fair and their companies compete on a level playing field. But what if companies and countries cheat? For example, foreign companies can gain an unfair edge vis-a-vis domestic companies by dumping their products at less than they would sell their products for at home, getting government subsidies, faking their ingredients, and stealing American companies' intellectual property (IP) and technology. Chinese businesses have checked all four boxes. What brings a particular edge to China trade policy discussions is the Chinese government's support (and state's ownership) of Chinese companies, which is extraordinary both by historical and comparative standards and rightly irks other countries and their businesses. China's 2018 WTO trade policy review, a peer review process of a WTO member by other members, starts off with many polite statements about China's "recent reform initiatives aimed at broadening market access and investment opportunities," but it also tersely states, "Members expressed serious concerns about the preponderant role of the State in general, and of state-owned enterprises in particular . . . several Members also noted continuous issues in China's IPR regime and encouraged continued IPR protection and enforcement."[12]

In their 2017 review of China, the U.S. government's trade experts minced no words. "Today, almost two decades after it pledged to support the multilateral trading system of the WTO, the Chinese government pursues a wide array of continually evolving interventionist policies and practices aimed at limiting market access for imported goods and services and foreign manufacturers and service suppliers," the U.S. Trade Representative (USTR) wrote.[13] "Many of the policy tools being used by the Chinese government... are largely unprecedented, as other WTO members do not use them, and include a wide array of state intervention and support designed to promote the development of Chinese industry in large part by restricting, taking advantage of, discriminating against or otherwise creating disadvantages for foreign enterprises and their technologies, products and services." Another country that received strong condemnation was Russia. "So far, Russia's actions strongly indicate that it has no intention of complying with many of the promises it made to the United States and other WTO Members. This trend is very troubling," the USTR concluded.

Indeed, the problem does not stop in China. Countries around the world have devised various restrictive trade measures, such as anti-dumping, IP violations, mandatory use of domestic content in production, import licensing, restrictions in government procurement (such as favoritism of local products and services), a variety of technical barriers to trade, agricultural subsidies, and at least fifteen other tools of trade policy malfeasance. Just about all countries use some of them. These are not tariffs, but some of them, such as local sourcing or production mandates or import licenses, can have the same effect as tariffs—and, studies show, they are often used by governments that have agreed to tariff reductions as a substitute for tariffs that blunts the competitive pressure brought by liberalization on local businesses. According to the policy tracker Global Trade Alert, countries have imposed 9,614 such harmful measures in 2009–2018 while effecting only 3,601 liberalizing measures.[14] Large traders like India and the United States had a bit of both.

Yet as the world's largest trader, China's unfair practices have particularly far-reaching implications. And there is no question its practices are unfair. There are certainly trade rules that limit the extent to which an exporter country can manipulate prices and products to gain more market share, and there are remedies against those who violate these rules. The United States has a domestic Countervailing Duty Law that has already been applied liberally on imports from China. The United States has also employed the WTO to battle against Chinese dumping—during the Obama years, the U.S. filed sixteen anti-dumping cases against China. Also, other countries have been pushing China, initiating ninety-one anti-dumping cases in 2016 alone. Chad Bown shows that G20 economies have since 2005 imposed anti-dumping, countervailing duties, or safeguards especially on intermediate imports such as steel and steel products from China.[15] Have these then hit China where it hurts?

Two Chinese scholars, Guobing Shen and Xiaolan Fu, conclude they have. They find that when countries gang up against China, China is hit hard while the petitioners all get relief from Chinese imports. In other words, anti-dumping can work, if done in concert.[16] A U.S.-only anti-dumping petition does limit U.S. imports of the filed products from China—but it also makes the balloon expand elsewhere, diverting Chinese dumped goods to other countries. The exact same has happened with Trump tariffs: cargo from China to the United States has dropped—but then found its way to third countries, such as Japan, South Korea, Taiwan, Germany, and Italy.[17]

Small Fish in a Big Pond

Perhaps the most important and least discussed empirical fact in the often emotional debates about the impacts of trade is that trade is a "small fish in a big pond." It is only one and typically a very small factor among the great many factors that shape economic growth, job churn, employment patterns, employment levels and wages, income inequality, and poverty in a country. The drivers of job losses include such major factors as technological changes, lack of economic growth, imposition of rigid labor market regulations that disincentivize firms to hire workers, and so on. The main determinant of wage levels in a country is productivity, a key driver of economic growth that is made up of such things as accumulation of human capital through great education systems, new technologies, utilization of technology with smart workers, good governance and institutions, free markets, and so on.

Revered trade economist Gary Hufbauer provides a great example of how trade is easily blamed when it has little to do with an outcome. Consider that U.S. auto workers' salaries dropped by 40 percent during the first decade of NAFTA implementation. It would be tempting to argue that NAFTA *caused* the salary drop. Yet the wage drop had very little to do with NAFTA; it owed to the shift of U.S. auto industry from northern states to the southern states that had lower union membership in auto manufacturing and thus less power in wage bargaining with auto manufacturers.[18]

Trade is only one component that determines the fate of national economies. When I teach MBA students at UCLA, my students often ask if trade keeps poor countries poor. The thought is that if a country just keeps buying foreign imports, it will never build its own industry. What can be said as an empirical fact is the opposite: no country with a closed economy with high tariffs or other limits to imports has ever gotten rich. Import substitution experiments to cultivate domestic industries behind tariff walls have mostly not worked, and closed economies are wretchedly poor—they do not attract investors, access new technologies, or have a chance to export quality products, and their consumers and companies pay high markups to local monopolies. How would you like to live and seek to build a business in North Korea, or Cuba before the lifting of the embargo, or in Vietnam in the communist times? Or even in Argentina in the late 1950s, when government drastically hiked tariffs or barred imports of various industrial products and their parts and components, in order to cultivate local industries?

True, some open economies are also very poor. If we were to compare North Korea (a very closed economy with $583 in per capita income) and South Korea (a very open one, except in agricultural products, and with per capita income of $27,539 in 2016), we might hypothesize that openness to trade makes a country rich. But if we take South Korea and Mexico, which has somewhat lower average tariff than South Korea but only $8,201 in per capita income, we might reject that hypothesis. We might decide on a completely different hypothesis by comparing Haiti, a very open economy with GDP per capita of $740, with the United States, a similarly very open economy with GDP per capita income of $57,467. That hypothesis may be what macroeconomics has told us for decades: trade is only one of a great many factors shaping major national economic outcomes such as poverty or inequality.

Empirical evidence says that trade typically helps: Haiti would be even poorer without trade—without the chance to export garments and citrus that a simple calculation shows it has a huge comparative advantage in, and to import machines and computers. The United States would be poorer without trade too. Especially the poor would be poorer without trade: they are hit hardest by tariffs, partly because tariffs tend to concentrate on products that the poor buy, partly because the poor buy more imports, and partly because they cut a proportionally bigger hole in thinner wallets. A recent study of twenty-seven industrial and thirteen developing countries finds that turning trade off would deprive the richest 10 percent in these economies of 28 percent of their purchasing power, but the poorest 10 percent would lose 63 percent because they buy relatively more imported goods.[19]

Trade is also a small fish in a big pond when it comes to inequality. It has been argued over and over that while U.S. productivity and median wages rose together in the twenty-five years after World War II, starting in the late 1970s the two diverged and productivity grew faster than median wages. For left-leaning analysts, this has been taken to mean the rise of bourgeoisie and proletariat—that people who own capital (companies, infrastructures, and technologies) are gaining while people who work for them are where they were in the early 1990s. In 2015, *New York Times* columnist Eduardo Porter claimed automation that displaces middle-skilled jobs and "a harsh new global economy" were responsible for "stagnant wages" and a "vast, expanding income gap."[20] But as shown by Acemoglu, Autor, Dorn, Hanson, and Price, this statement vastly overstates the impact of trade on equality. It also overstates the level of inequality.

In 2016, labor economist James Sherk of the conservative Heritage Foundation, who was subsequently tapped as labor advisor to the Trump White House, wrote a paper titled "Workers' Compensation: Growing Along with Productivity," which points out three errors in the analyses painting a growing productivity gap between the top and the median workers.[21] First, the pay of only *some* workers was included in those studies, while productivity of *all* employees was included, making the wage line flatter—a methodological choice that is 45 percent of the supposed gap. Second, the productivity growth of self-employed 1099 workers was included, but their pay growth was excluded, again making the wage line flatter—a methodological choice that is another 12 percent of the supposed gap. Third, inflation was measured differently to calculate pay growth and productivity growth—still another methodological choice that explains a whopping 39 percent of the supposed gap. In other words, the gap was a quirk of methodological choices, all of them questionable.[22] It does exist, but it is tiny. The median worker's productivity has increased by 81 percent, while the median worker's compensation has increased by 78 percent. America employee compensation has not stagnated, but rather risen in lockstep with productivity since 1973, both on average and across industries.

Sherk was not alone in making these points. Harvard trade economist Robert Lawrence, who served on Bill Clinton's Council of Economic Advisers, reaches similar conclusions, with somewhat different methods.[23] He looks at growth and wages and benefits that have grown faster than wages; makes apples-to-apples comparisons between price indexes for wage and output growth in constant dollars; and measures output as net of depreciation rather than the gross measure of output that fails to account for wear and tear of machinery, infrastructure, and technology—in other words, that measures the consumption of capital. With these corrections, the gap between productivity and wages disappears, leading Lawrence to conclude that "from 1970 to 2000, and perhaps to as late as 2008, the growth in overall worker compensation was precisely as rapid as the growth in average labor productivity would imply."[24]

Another Harvard professor, Martin Feldstein, the former president of pre-eminent economic research group the National Bureau of Economic Research, and staff at the Federal Reserve Bank of St. Louis, also found that productivity and pay have been rising together.[25] In other words, while the overall economy has been getting richer, so have workers—all during the heyday of trade liberalization and globalization.

One of the most spectacular findings about inequality is that people generally believe it is deeper than it really is, and that it is widening. In an eye-opening paper, Vladimir Gimpelson of the Higher School of Economics in Moscow and Daniel Treisman of UCLA find that when shown five possible income distribution graphs for their countries, respondents picked the right income distribution only 29 percent of the time, slightly more often than they would have by chance. Those that were wrong typically overestimated inequality.[26] The study covered forty countries from around the world, but only in five small countries where it is easier to see what's going on nationwide—Norway, Denmark, Cyprus, Israel, and Iceland—did most people choose the right chart to characterize their countries' inequality. The worst part is that even if widely off the mark, these perceptions of inequality correlate strongly with demand for redistribution and reported conflict between rich and poor. In other words, people around the world are wanting to bridge gaps that do not exist.

Only in the post-financial crisis years has there been a stagnation in middle income wages. Its sources are keenly studied. A share of evidence points to automation, though research shows even this causal arc is not as clear as it previously seemed. Let's take a look at that next.

Are Humans Redundant?

"The bogeyman of automation consumes worrying capacity that should be saved for real problems." So argued Carnegie Mellon University professor Herbert Simon—in 1966.[27] A scholar of scholars who studied and taught economics, computer science, political science, and sociology, Simon went on to win the Nobel Prize in Economics in 1978. While his science was new, the fears he pointed at about machines taking our jobs are as old as machines themselves. In 1961, *Time* magazine announced, "The number of jobs lost to more efficient machines is only part of the problem. What worries many job experts more is that automation may prevent the economy from creating enough new jobs."[28] Even the father of comparative advantage, David Ricardo, sourly argued in 1821 that the "substitution of machinery for human labour is often very injurious to the interests of the class of labourers. . . . [It] may render the population redundant and deteriorate the condition of the labourer."[29]

If technology replaces workers, then why are there still any jobs? How is it possible that over the past century, the most vigorous time of technological innovation in human history, there has not been a clear, long-run increase in unemployment? In the booming postwar economy American unemployment in 1947 stood at 3.9 percent, and 57 percent of Americans (over sixteen years of age who were not in the military or incarcerated) were in the workforce. In 2017, unemployment was 4.4 percent and 63 percent of Americans were in the workforce.[30] What's more, the share of people outside the labor force has decreased from 43 to 37 percent during those seventy years, reflecting women's entry into labor markets. In short, more people are working than are at home, and just about the same share of people are unemployed as were seventy years ago. The difference is negligible even if counting people who may not show up in unemployment data today because they have stopped looking for work for a myriad of reasons like going to grad school or being part of the FIRE (Financial Independence, Retire Early) community, or perhaps being white blue collar males that stopped looking for work (and assuming the 1947 data accounted for all these people).

The worst rise in unemployment was in 1982 when U.S. unemployment hit 9.7 percent. If technology replaces people (or globalization causes unemployment), then the U.S. unemployment rate should not have come down to 4.4 percent during the past thirty-five years, a time of astounding technological change and a tsunami wave of globalization. If technology permanently devours jobs as many already feared two hundred years ago, you should by now observe swaths of your American friends being unemployed. Are they?

There are jobs today because workers and businesses constantly adjust, often in response to technological change. In a story the Internet seems to love, in the 1980s, banks started to replace tellers with ATMs.[31] Did this kill tellers' jobs? No—it changed them. While the number of ATMs rose from 100,000 to 400,000 in 1995–2010, U.S. bank teller employment *increased* from 500,000 to 550,000 in 1980–2010. ATMs did not end tellers—they indirectly increased the demand for tellers. While the number of tellers per branch fell by over 33 percent in 1988–2004, the number of urban bank branches rose over 40 percent. As ATMs and IT systems handled routine cash-handling tasks, bank personnel could be deployed in relationship banking—helping customers with such things as their mortgages, car payments, and purchases of CDs.

Another example is accounting. In the 1990s, Quickbooks emerged as the software of choice for small businesses to track revenues and expenses, and TurboTax enabled them to do their own taxes. These types of innovations seem menacing to bookkeepers and CPAs—and Quickbooks did destroy many accounting jobs that used to be done by hand. For example, before, one CPA would handle the accounts of a product line in a major company, and dozens of accountants would be needed overall—plus a head accountant who would bring all these individual books together into a consolidated account. Quickbooks and sophisticated versions such as provided by Oracle enabled rapid combining of all these accounts, displacing many corporate accounting jobs (and saving trees). But these technologies have also improved individual CPAs' lives: online access to a client's books and new tax software enable CPAs to do taxes and other tasks required by the client faster and more accurately, handle many more clients at once, and free their time to do what humans do best—provide advice to clients on complex business and tax issues. Clients benefit from these scale economies in the form of lower fees and more advice. CPAs are in growing demand—the number of accountant and auditor jobs is expected to grow by 10 percent in 2016–2026, faster than the U.S. average expected job growth rate of 7 percent.[32]

Such realignments are occurring across industries. In 1900, 41 percent of the U.S. workforce was employed in agriculture; by 1947, it was 8 percent, and by 2017 it was only 1 percent. Those 40 percent of Americans who no longer work in agriculture were substituted for by more efficient means of production—agricultural productivity grew by about 155 percent in 1948–2011—and went to work elsewhere. Similarly, in manufacturing there were 5.6 million net job losses in America's manufacturing sector in 1991–2011 and manufacturing employment dropped by 31 percent, a period when nonmanufacturing employment grew by 40 percent.[33]

If overall employment has held largely steady for decades amid technological changes and labor market makeovers, and if technology such as ecommerce is creating an array of new jobs, then why are so many people, including leading technologists, so concerned today about the advent of mass consumption of artificial intelligence? For example, Tesla and SpaceX founder Elon Musk believes AI can make machines into humans' overlords that will learn to do everything better than us, replace us, and ultimately destroy mankind.[34]

Given the messenger, this message is very hard to ignore. But at the same time, there are as many views as techpreneurs. Mark Zuckerberg is highly optimistic about AI, and Microsoft founder Bill Gates thinks AI is good at first for workers, and then it can turn against them.[35] Economists too disagree on the impact of new technologies on jobs. The World Economic Forum forecasts that more than five million jobs will be lost between 2016 and 2020 as a result of developments in genetics, artificial intelligence, robotics, and other technologies. Five million is a big number, but that is no more than 0.01 percent of global employment. The World Bank, however, forecasts a disastrous future in which automation threatens 77 percent of jobs in China and 69 percent in India.[36]

Which forecast to believe? Is this time then different—one in which few workers will be spared as robots storm offices and force us off our chairs and unemployment soars?

One reason to argue that this time is indeed different is the acceleration of technological change—that when even knowledge workers become unemployed, they will have a hard time to get back in as their skills become obsolete quickly, with each passing day. This is probably true. But another reason why people fear may have nothing to do with actual outcomes. Technological changes such as the dot.com boom are known to create "hype cycles," when a technology produces a "peak of inflated expectations," followed by a "trough of disillusionment," and stabilizes into some plateau of productivity, a time when hype has died and people have moved on with their lives, often to enjoy the technology they initially hyped up, such as the Internet.[37]

There are three fallacies in the AI and man-versus-machine hype cycles. The first fallacy is thinking that technology only substitutes for labor, when it often complements labor. This is because most jobs, and especially middle income jobs, are each bundles of several tasks across the skill spectrum. Bankers may provide rather mechanical teller services at one moment and turn to advising the client on his mortgages and investments in the next. David Autor and David Dorn provide examples of the many jobs in which workers are still much less likely to get outsmarted by AI than to use AI to do some of their discrete tasks involving computations and quick analytical reasoning, such as radiology technicians, nurse technicians, plumbers, builders, electricians, and heating/ventilating/air-conditioning installers.[38]

To date, much of AI is used to solve discrete, well-defined problems. AI is not that good yet at general tasks—this is also one of the reasons why there have been "AI winters," troughs in interest and funding in AI that have occurred a number of times since the 1980s. Machines in general are not yet good at jobs that require human ingenuity, flexibility, judgment, interpersonal skills, dexterity, intuition, or eureka moments. Some human tasks can and will be automated, others will not, at least not yet. For now, it is likelier that automation of some tasks makes a nurse or plumber more productive in what they as humans are good at.[39] Where change is happening faster is in fields in which a human being spends most of his or her time on tasks that machines can do well—for example, high-frequency trading or portfolio allocation.

The second fallacy in the man-versus-machine debate is ignoring the speed and cost of the switch from man to machine. In reality, once a technology such as a robot is available, a business owner will not immediately go and hire one and fire her workers. She may, but this will take her some time. At one level all she needs to do is calculate whether a worker or machine costs more—but in real life she needs to learn about and be convinced about the cost-benefit, such as considering the up-front fixed costs—in smaller firms, those are larger, while the gains from using AI may be less than they are in very large companies with bigger costs, revenue, and gains from automation. She will also need to factor in such unknowns as maintenance costs, tax deductions, and severance payments for the workers replaced with the machines.

There will be lags due to uncertainties, risk aversion, knowledge gaps, and the simple fact that a small business owner gets quickly wrapped up in the urgent tasks of the day and seldom has a great deal of time to consider and test new technologies. It is much easier if a neighboring company goes for a technology first and demonstrates a gain. Once a few businesses dare to make the leap and reap gains, more will pay attention and mass adoption starts to occur. But even if large multinationals and financial services were to eliminate thousands of jobs to automate wealth management, trading, investment banking, media, and business analysis, the turn to robots may be far slower among small businesses that employ 46 percent of American private sector labor; in such industries as education, construction, professional services, and health care; and in the federal, state, and local governments that employ about 17 percent of Americans. AI will have an impact on labor markets, but it won't be fast and furious, except in certain industries.

Besides, AI may be a force of great good in labor markets: it can accelerate the matching of workers to jobs. For example, AI can help break down more finely the attributes of two workers who look similar on paper, including by their ever-important soft skills and motivations. This means that workers can be matched to right-fit jobs faster, labor markets can become much more efficient and differentiated, and everyone can play to his strengths and workers to jobs much faster globally. These benefits are all the greater in markets with several labor market mismatches, such as in Africa, where nepotist practices and informational gaps result in wrong people getting hired. Swiss company Roam has built a sophisticated platform to take stock of Africa workers' skills and match them to the right jobs, while also doing skills development. In Ethiopia, AI company iCog Labs has a similar portal, only for workers at the lower rungs of the skills spectrum such as clearers and gardeners. The platform enables people in these categories to automatically generate a CV and identify work near their homes, thus undoing their transport costs that otherwise can obliterate a day's paycheck.

The impacts of using technology to optimize labor markets can be very significant. Just by enabling better searches for workers and workers for jobs, the Internet has already reduced joblessness. In a U.S. International Trade Commission study, the U.S. unemployment rate was 0.3 percentage points lower in 2012 than it would have been at 2006 Internet usage level. Where the web is newer, it has squashed unemployment even more—in Russia, by 2 percentage points; in China, by 2.5 points; in Brazil, by 1 point.[40] AI can also help iron out inequities among workers. Microsoft has developed a tool for a blind person to "see" her work environment and help a disabled person to write text with his moving eyes.

The third fallacy in the man-versus-machine debate is ignoring that not only do robots and their cost evolve—so do workers. Rather than being like a deer in headlights, caught off guard by the onslaught of machines, workers are adjusting in direct reaction to the rumors about the vast skillsets of their robot competitors, with Wall Street traders, pre-med students, and accountants alike taking data science and coding classes.[41] Just as in the early twenty century when seamstresses learned to work with the sewing machines feared to take their jobs, people are adjusting today, to work with today's machines. Of course, whether they then get hired and see wage gains depends on their supply. If they are abundantly available, their wages will unlikely increase. Real estate brokers' wages did not increase as much as expected during the housing boom of the 2000s because of the rise in the number of real estate brokers in response to the rise in housing prices.[42] What will likely happen is that wage premiums in the future will go to those who have adaptable, transferable skills and who *continually* keep improving their skills.

This will augur changes even for the most technologically advanced countries. Germany's brilliant vocational training for technology fields helped the country become the most automated country in Europe and the world's star exporter of technology products. Take Siemens, which picks people fresh out of secondary school at age sixteen and transforms them into trainees who receive a small salary to learn skills for their job at Siemens. But assuming technological change keeps accelerating, the premium on such vocational training erodes fast.[43] Economists Dirk Krueger and Krishna Kumar show that in the 1960s and 1970s per capita GDP growth rose faster in Germany than in the United States but technological changes were relatively gradual; however, in the 1980s, as U.S. companies started to adopt new technologies more quickly than their German peers, U.S. income growth also sped by Germany's.[44] Their argument is that Americans trained to solve complex problems did better with new technologies than Germans trained to do a specific technical job. As an exclamation point to their story: in Germany, unemployment goes up and lifetime earnings fall when workers get into their mid-forties—that is, when workers' skills learned in their twenties and thirties are obsolete, thanks to technology. This is especially the case with those trained in vocational schools; university graduates, who tend to be armed with analytical and problem-solving skills, do better.

These findings suggest that at a time of rapid technological progress, people educated in critical thinking, problem solving, application of various technologies, teamwork, and outside-the-box creative thinking enjoy a premium. And as discussed in Chapter 8, it is these types of people who also increase their value each day they work.

Middle Class to Leisure Class

What would happen if the supposedly apocalyptic scenario actually did happen—robots took over, unemployment soared, and hours worked dropped radically?

In 1870, people in industrializing Western countries worked for 2,950 hours per year, when in 1998 they worked 1,500 hours per year, and meanwhile mankind became, depending on whose GDP calculation you go by, roughly thirty-six to forty-six times wealthier, while the number of people on the planet grew four-fold.[45] This massive wealth creation and fattening of paychecks amid halving our work commitments owed to many factors—but economics reduced those into three buckets: labor; capital (such as infrastructures and machines); and total factor productivity, which contains such hard-to-quantify value drivers as human capital, technologies that enabled us to create scale economies and make much more with the same, and good governance and institutions, as well as openness to trade and foreign direct investment.

As we got better, we did less. The eighteenth- and nineteenth-century hand-wringing about the impacts of machines on labor turned out to be unfounded; rather, the outcome of mechanization was to end the concerns of the Brits and others about factory workers' social alienation as they put in their twelve- to fourteen-hour days as cogs in the wheel, often in dangerous and depressing conditions.

Not only do we have more leisure today, we are also more able to enjoy it than people two hundred years ago. Today there are countless shows on amazing TVs, books available within seconds on Amazon, endless places to eat exotic meals at rock-bottom prices, Uber and Lyft to whisk us for a baseball game or to a friend's house, Facebook posts by our globetrotting pals and YouTube videos that teach us to cook or make us laugh at pets' antics, endless numbers of blogs where we find counsel for our questions and online communities where we can share our heartaches, and virtual reality for us to trek across the Himalayas and Mayan trails on our living room couches. As much as we work and complain about burnout, in historical terms we are a vast leisure class.

It is likelier that we have more of that fun coming up, rather than poverty and joblessness. We'll have more fun jobs—less rote learning and repetitive tasks, more imagination and capabilities to actualize what is in our minds at low cost. AI's huge positive is that it enables us to do what humans are specialized in: imagining, ideating, creating, fashioning. We are not at our best as the mechanical men portrayed in Charlie Chaplin's *Modern Times*, though conditioned over time to that role. We are born to create and build, and technologies are freeing us to do so. Paradoxically, while human beings have been able to imagine and build a succession of innovations in industry, science, and the arts, they have failed to imagine mankind's own innovativeness and ability to adapt.

The repeated adjustments made by human beings in response to new technologies have far exceeded scholars and pundits' forecasts of human's ability to adjust—let alone build on new innovations and technologies. The products and services some of us and our children consume in 2060 will surely be vastly different from those we watch, get lights and music from, and live, sleep, and go to work in today. The way we live, die, and are born will be different. Yes, we humans will work on these new products and services and the next big thing in 2060, just as we do today—but we may work less if we so choose to, and our work and workplaces too will be different, as will be our commutes. And instead of flying to meet our clients and vendors across the oceans, we may show up as holographic avatars.

Tenuous World Domination

Nowadays in trade conferences trade economists are trapped in the unhappy situation of being asked about winner-take-all dynamics. I often get asked whether Amazon will ultimately be the only player running the world's ecommerce. Even more often I get asked whether it would not be great if every country, especially small developing countries, could have their own platforms. The thinking goes that platforms have power: they earn profits, they pay taxes, and they have data, so shouldn't every country have its own?

One reason questions about market structures keep coming up in trade events is because of trade policy concerns—namely whether a small developing country, once welcoming Amazon or Alibaba, will forfeit its chances to build its own local ecommerce industry and production base. This discussion is nothing new—it has swirled for decades in different industries, such as in shoes, cars, and airplanes. Policies to prod local infant industries with "import substitution industrialization," or a range of tariffs, non-tariff barriers, and subsidies, have mostly had sorry results. Yet developing countries in particular raise the idea of building their own platforms, often due to fears that Amazon may enter and "take over" their countries by bringing in products and services that local businesses cannot possibly compete with. The thinking goes, as it went at a time of import substitution industrialization, that developing countries need more time to build their companies' capacity to compete. Partly the argument is of course motivated by interest by developing nations to secure advanced country aid dollars for such capacity-building.

Another reason why questions about market structure are posed to trade economists is simply because they are economists in front of people to whom these market dynamics and dominance of an industry by a handful of large companies are top of mind. After all, we have by now been told over and over how technology companies' low variable costs enable them to increase output extremely quickly to create a winner-take-all dynamic in which one superstar company dominates an entire industry and possibly somehow ends up exploiting its dominant position to the detriment of us all—and thanks to its networks has moats so deep that only the most foolish of entrepreneurs would ever wish to challenge it. Or would you like to take on Google in search, LinkedIn in professional networking, or Twitter in tweeting?

Yet these fears are overblown, for five reasons.

First, we're far from a one-platform world. Just about every country has many ecommerce platforms and all regions have their powerful platform—Asia has Alibaba, Latin America has MercadoLibre, Africa has Jumia, which IPOed in 2019. While Alibaba appears to be on a rapid growth spurt in Asia, it is not the only game in town—Rakuten of Japan and Flipkart in India are formidable, Amazon is expanding to Vietnam and other Asian markets, and Etsy and eBay's presence are also growing in the region. And just like in the United States, in various countries there are differentiated niche platforms, such as Red Wheels Trading in Malaysia, which provides rain- and safety-wear solutions to Malaysia's corporations, and Zilzar.com, which supplies halal food products to catering businesses in Malaysia and Indonesia.[46]

Second, a big player's entry into a market does not mean others go out of business, or that local platforms would not have a fighting chance to set up and operate. For example, after entering in Mexico, Amazon has not taken over—it continues as one significant player in Mexico's ecommerce ecosystem, coexisting with eBay, Alibaba, MercadoLibre, Walmart, and others. Instead, eBay and Alibaba have worked with the Mexican government to help Mexican companies export, including to the United States and China, and Mexican companies and consumers get more products at better prices.[47]

Third, large platforms such as MercadoLibre, Lazada, Jumia, Alibaba, eBay, or Amazon open an unbeatably powerful channel for local companies in a small developing country to instantly reach millions of foreign customers. They are already doing so, undercutting the idea that local firms in developing countries will not have much to sell online and will be outcompeted by foreign products brought in by Amazon. Would it really be better for small businesses and consumers around the world if every country had its own little platform that was working from scratch to increase its user base, or for small businesses in all countries to get access to a handful of global platforms that have built a base of hundreds of millions of buyers and sellers from around the world?

Fourth, aggressive inorganic growth by these major firms could of course produce different outcomes. But they might not be all pernicious. If one large platform were to acquire Jumia and MercadoLibre, just as Alibaba acquired the leading Southeast Asian platform Lazada, the network that makes a platform valuable would naturally expand—suddenly Jumia's sellers could sell directly to Amazon's buyers, making Jumia more valuable to firms in Africa and encouraging them to join.

But, you ask, are we then in for a world in which one or two companies squeeze the rest out, as happened with personal computer operating systems, and leverage data to service also our logistics, financing, and payments needs? And if so, would the two giants exploit their pricing power and data to forever lock us into their universe? Or, as is likelier, would they rather drive sellers to provide buyers better deals and better prices, just like Walmart did with its suppliers some decades ago, or to provide consumers more products and services at lower prices and a globally interoperable system, as Microsoft Office does? And would they not catch the eye of antitrust officials if they did exploit their market power?

And fifth—would they be able to stay on top? To believe in winner take all and its applicability to platforms, one needs to believe in the durability of networks built on platform users and their data, and the idea that bigger and bigger is better and better. So far, we know little about the staying power of networks. In a baseball analogy, the platform game is somewhere between the first and the second inning. The platform industry is very new, only twenty years old. The audience seems to expect the game to keep unfolding exactly as it has so far, with the team that scored in the first inning to keep scoring more and more in each new inning, by, in this case, garnering more users and more data points with which to garner more users and thus revenue.

The bigger point is that the winner-take-all concept does not offer a particularly useful analytical lens to the platform economy—because platforms and networks have much less staying power than industries that gave rise to the "winner take all" concept.

The first reason is that platform users are promiscuous. In many sectors from ecommerce to social media and crowdfunding there is no compelling need for the users to be on just one network: they are on many—which as a result battle over advertiser dollars and users' attention spans. Advertisers can reach 65 percent of Snapchat users on Facebook and 54 percent on Instagram the very same day—something seen as Snapchat's feat of garnering unique users.[48] Some Facebook executives have been concerned about being cannibalized by Instagram, which Facebook acquired in 2012.[49] In short, companies' netizen users overlap. Users are on many platforms because each provides a very different experience; perhaps in small part to reach different communities.

Second, platforms are differentiated—most sectors have room for many different players, rather than steep entry costs that discourage new startups. There are many differentiated platforms in just about any category, and new ones keep being born. For example, in 2015–2016, more than a thousand venture capitalists participated in at least one of 774 deals for U.S.-based ecommerce startups.[50] And even if a platform dominated its niche, its situation can be fragile due to users' low switch costs. Let's take ecommerce again—granted, there are network benefits from being on eBay, but that does not mean that companies on eBay use only eBay. They also each have their online store, and many are probably also on Etsy and maybe Amazon. This suggests that entry costs in platforms are not as steep as often assumed. In a world in which online retail is still often less than a fifth of all retail, there is room for many. Industries such as ecommerce and social media break down into finer and finer differentiated industries, they capture slices of the market, rather than winning it all. Amazon will not build a niche in everything—why should it, if someone can do it on its behalf, prove a market out, and Amazon can simply buy that someone?

Third, bigger is not necessarily better. The believed currency of online dominance, data, has diminishing returns in many sectors. For example, for searches of addresses on mapping software, there comes a point after which more data are rather irrelevant. Venture capitalist Ben Evans provides a neat example. If a driver "can drive in Naples for a year without ever getting confused, how much more is there to improve? At some point you're effectively finished. So, a network effect means that your product gets better if you have more users, but how many users do you need before the product stops getting significantly better? How many cars do you need to sell before your autonomy is as good as the best on the market? How many companies might be able to reach that? And meanwhile, machine learning itself is changing quickly—one cannot rule out the possibility that the amount of data you need to get autonomy working might shrink dramatically."[51]

Fourth, for Google-style general purpose searches, having more data appears to be better and better—the more input, the tighter and more relevant the output, and the better the search engine does in getting advertisers. But even more search data may not be as valuable as it first seems. In a fresh look, Lesley Chiou of Occidental College and Catherine Tucker of MIT (some of whose other work has been funded by Google) suggest that cutting the amount of historical data companies such as Yahoo! can retain on Internet searches does not drastically affect the quality of search results.[52] In other words, data are not as critical as believed. One implication then is that limiting companies' access to historical data and enforcing an individual's "right to be forgotten" may pose fewer costs to large tech companies than typically believed. Another implication is that if access to troves of historical data does not provide a major competitive advantage for search, then it ought to be the case that smaller companies are poised to access sufficient data and compete or coexist with giants like Google in areas such as artificial intelligence that turn on big data.

Fifth, data are also not as proprietary as often assumed. Many companies monetize the data large companies generate—the March 2018 expose of Cambridge Analytica's using and analyzing fifty million Facebook users to support the Trump campaign being an infamous case in point. Courts have so far sided with data sharing rather than data hoarding. HiQ, a Silicon Valley company that sells predictive analytics to employers on the likely moves of their star employees, for example to help an employer sweeten the deal for the star employee to stay, gets the bulk of its data by scraping it off LinkedIn.[53] If you ran LinkedIn or were its shareholder, you would probably be furious: after all, you invested to grow the network and monetize the data it generates. But in 2017, LinkedIn lost its lawsuit against HiQ for the practice, with the court pointing out that LinkedIn's data were public for all to see—it was not hidden in a vault. HiQ's lawyer, Harvard's constitutional law luminary Lawrence Tribe, argued successfully that "[i]f LinkedIn has this power [to ban others from making use of publicly available information], so does Facebook, and the entire universe of cyberspace can be gobbled up by a small number of private owners.... That can't be what the law of an open, democratic society with the First Amendment means."[54] In Tribe's view, LinkedIn's effort to prevent use of its publicly available data was tantamount to the government controlling who has access to a library book.

In most online sectors, winner take all is not as real or lasting as often assumed. And zealous regulators and ambitious populist policymakers keep going after platforms. In 2017, the European Union slapped a handsome fine, over $2.5 billion, against Google for what the EU deemed as anticompetitive practices promoting its online shopping service, and at the time of writing is working for another against Google's AdSense. Lacking its own online giants in part due to policies that discourage scalability, the EU has decided to go after U.S. online giants. Former Missouri state attorney general and junior U.S. senator Josh Hawley is crusading against big tech companies and igniting fellow senators and state attorneys general to examine the web giants too.[55] Such inquiries, even if more politically motivated than based on empirical evidence of monopolistic behavior, will unlikely be the last of their kind.

These points certainly undermine the increasingly popular arguments that Google, Facebook, Amazon, and others are "data barons" who ride on the "free work" we, their users, provide, and that it is time for these giants of the Internet to give their data "back" to us all, for us to use. Oxford University's Viktor Mayer-Schönberger has proposed what he calls a "progressive data-sharing mandate" that would apply to all businesses. This would require a company that has passed a certain level of market share such as 10 percent to share some data with other firms in its industry that ask for it.[56]

These proposals are highly impractical. Data are something these firms have invested in obtaining and are an asset—so why would these companies' shareholders want to hand an asset over? Why would anyone in Silicon Valley or Shanghai or Nairobi or Buenos Aires ever want to start or invest in an Internet company it thinks could be the next Uber if that company's core data might at some point be expropriated "by the public" as a thank you note for these users' "hard work" in using the digital service they chose to use? And if the Internet giants did in fact turn over their data to the public, who would ensure the data were not used for malicious purposes? Would data be in better hands if given to the public or the government, or apportioned to many small companies? Tech companies already often lend their data to academics and researchers for use in exploring interesting questions, for example about economic development. We are for the foreseeable future in a setting in which we willingly trade our data for better matches, new offers, and free services—a world in which we are readily compensated for our work in providing for our "work" in providing data.

Digital Trade War?

Will the trade wars of the future be about digital trade, when countries block foreign tech companies, service providers, and digitized products' access to their markets and foreign companies' ability to ship data out, perhaps out of concerns about foreign firms' access to domestic strategic assets or their predominance as a service provider, or that foreign firms with sophisticated technologies such as AI could wreak havoc in domestic labor markets?

The sad news is that a digital trade war is already on. The missile shield in it is China's Great Firewall, which bars Western companies from the Chinese market by blocking Chinese consumers' and companies' access to Western content and online services. China relentlessly firewalls U.S. online companies from catering to Chinese citizens and businesses—at least a hundred of the top thousand websites such as YouTube, Google, Facebook, Flickr, SoundCloud, and WordPress are blocked in China—while copycatting U.S. businesses like Uber and Google. The handiwork is that of Xi Jinping, who upon becoming president in 2012 started to limit the nascent Chinese Internet freedoms. Chinese citizens migrated to using virtual private networks (VPNs) to access blocked websites.[57] In January 2015, the government blocked many VPNs, revealing its preferences for territorializing the Internet and controlling online traffic over the many benefits VPNs and Internet freedoms provide for multinationals, banks, retailers, researchers, and so on.[58]

China subsequently launched the Great Cannon, the smart cousin of the Great Firewall, that is able to adjust and replace content as it travels on the Internet. One of the first cannon balls hit the U.S. coding and software development site GitHub, which was trashed on Baidu. This is but the tip of the iceberg in the Chinese government's monitoring and controlling of the Internet. In 2016, Harvard scholars estimated that the Chinese government fabricates and posts 448 million comments on social media annually.[59] That same year, the Office of the United States Trade Representative (USTR) declared China's Great Firewall to be a trade barrier to American suppliers, stating that "China's filtering of cross-border internet traffic has posed a significant burden to foreign suppliers."[60] When first launched in 2009, the Trans-Pacific Partnership (TPP) was created to coax China into adopting good digital trade practices if it were to join the club; with Xi (and without the United States in the TPP), it is highly unlikely China would ever join a club with such rules.

Various other countries make USTR lists of imposers of digital trade barriers: Indonesia (barriers to Internet services), Vietnam (restriction to online advertising), Turkey and Russia (forced localization, meaning no cross-border transfer of data on Turks or Russian), and Korea (limits on exporting location-based data overseas).[61] Worse, there are other leaders with Xi's penchant for thinking about the Internet as national territory rather than a global medium, such as Vladimir Putin of Russia and Tayyip Erdogan of Turkey. Xi Jinping reportedly sees the Internet like he sees the offline China—a society to be coaxed to adopt homogeneous political values and ideals. China does have astoundingly successful Internet companies, and a wealth of technical talent and work ethic and drive unmatched by Western nations. Its AI firms, robotics, and online marketplaces are first rate. But its digital trade practices are among the greatest challenges of our times. They run counter to the aspiration of an open and fair global trading system. They limit American companies' potential in world markets. They blatantly undercut political freedoms. And it is not clear how they can be dealt with under current international trade law—whether WTO rules that apply to trade in services and to IP apply to them, for example.

China is of course hurting itself in the process. Since it's hard to run an online survey with Chinese executives about what they honestly think about the impact of China's cybercensorship, one might ask Europeans and Americans. In a 2018 survey run by the European Union Chamber of Commerce of 532 European executives with operations in China, 64 percent stated that "unstable connections, slow internet speeds and restricted access have seriously impacted their business" in China; 58 percent reported difficulties in exchanging data and documents with their headquarters, partners, and customers; 50 percent saw lower productivity in the office; 49 percent pointed to an inability to search for information; and 16 percent saw lower productivity in R&D and manufacturing.[62] According to the American Chamber of Commerce's 2018 survey of 411 U.S. executives, 47 percent stated that slow cross-border Internet speeds have had an "extremely negative" impact on their company's competitiveness and operations in China. Issues with Internet access via VPN as well as Internet censorship top the list of IT-related concerns for American companies. Such difficulties spiked during political events, such as the 19th National Party Congress, when Internet controls were tightened even further. Given that China permits only expensive state-sanctioned VPN services for business use, concerns about data security deter foreign investors and certainly SMEs that are less resourced to deal with such hassles.

Digital trade war is not just about barriers to trade; it is also about barriers to investment. On this front countries' weapon of choice is a claim of national security. It is hard to blame the United States for invoking national security concerns when Chinese companies bid for American tech companies in strategic sectors. Connections between the Chinese government and its tech companies range from opaque to extremely explicit—Robin Li, CEO of Baidu, China's knockoff of Google, is a member of the Chinese People's Political Consultative Conference, an advisory legislature, and Lei Jun, who spearheads mobile phone giant Xiaomi, sits on the National People's Congress.[63]

In 2017, the Committee on Foreign Investment in the United States (CFIUS), a bipartisan committee under the Treasury Department charged with evaluating the national security implications of foreign investments in the U.S., blocked the bid by Alibaba's Ant Financial to buy U.S. company MoneyGram in part out of concerns that the deal would have given Chinese company access to airplane Wi-Fi networks. In March 2018, the administration issued a presidential order prohibiting Chinese Broadcom's proposed takeover of U.S. 5G leader Qualcomm, as CFIUS had recommended. In July 2018, China retaliated by blocking Qualcomm's proposed takeover of a rival chip maker, NXP.[64]

Every president since Gerald Ford, who established CFIUS, has wielded the body to block foreign bids on U.S. companies. In the Reagan administration, the main concern was economic rival Japan; in the post-9/11 Bush 43 and Obama administrations, the main worry was terrorism. Now the focus is on Chinese companies' bids for U.S. companies with major intellectual property assets and a direct role in America's digital infrastructure. After a surge of Chinese inbound investment in the past five years, members of Congress have been worried enough to pass a law that expands CFIUS's powers. While openness to investment is most definitely good for economic growth, while the United States may invite retaliation from China and others when U.S. companies seek to acquire foreign firms, and while many countries use "national security" as a catch-all excuse to block foreign companies from their markets, there is no question that China is a serious national security challenge for America that needs to be assessed carefully. At the same time, there need to be reforms in such areas as America's at times antiquated export controls, to help American tech companies export.

Standard-setting is another weapon in digital trade wars. Given the tremendous potential gains from 5G, it is critical for the United States to accelerate the adoption of 5G, but it also is absolutely vital that 5G systems be secured once in place, lest they make America's critical infrastructure vulnerable to hostile powers and bad actors—and give rise to capricious policies that may not in the longer run be in America's interest. The Trump Administration has been extremely concerned about Chinese technology players' access to U.S. critical infrastructure and technology companies. For example, a leaked proposal revealed that the administration had considered a "moonshot" federal government effort like the construction of the interstate highway system to accelerate 5G deployment—a project akin to nationalizing the country's 5G telecommunications network.

American-made 4G standards allowed U.S. companies such as Apple to benefit greatly from a world market ready to buy and use its devices; now, the United States worries about the specter of dominance of Chinese standards. The makeup of standards, fought in part at the International Telecommunication Union in Geneva, will shape the fortunes of such companies as Huawei, Qualcomm, and Verizon—as standards affect who reaps billions of dollars in royalties from patents adopted globally.

Of course digital trade battles are waged on many other fronts as well. As discussed in Chapter 10, the United States and the European Union are tussling over digital taxes that tend to hit U.S. companies hardest; the EU's data privacy and transfer rules and copyright law, which annoy U.S. tech executives; and the supposedly predatory practices of U.S. tech companies in Europe. The EU has time and again imposed fines on U.S. tech companies for various claimed violations. In July 2018, it fined Google $5 billion for unfair practices—making Android smartphones come equipped with Google products as the default software. This is the largest fine ever levied by the EU—never mind that European app developers benefit from the one-stop system Android provides to reach 75 percent of cell phones that use the software. A year earlier, the European Commission fined Google $2.8 billion for giving priority to its price comparison service, Google Shopping, over rival services in search results. In 2016, the Commission argued that Apple had received tax treatment amounting to "illegal state aid" by EU member Ireland. Lacking its own digital superstars, the European Commission has been trigger-happy with America's.

Conclusion

In 1927, U.S. Secretary of Labor James J. Davis noted, "Every day sees the perfection of some new mechanical miracle that enables one man to do better and more quickly what many men used to do. . . . For a long time it was thought impossible to turn out machines capable of replacing human skill in the making of glass. Now practically all forms of glassware are being made by machinery, some of the machines being extraordinarily efficient."[65] However, Davis also observed, "In the end, every device that lightens human toil and increases production is a boon to humanity. It is only the period of adjustment, when machines turn workers out of their old jobs into new ones, that we must learn to handle them so as to reduce distress to the minimum."

The real challenge today is what the challenge has been in the past, before and through James Davis's time: the adaptability of labor—how workers affected by technological change can be retooled and rehired. As in the past, people themselves will find a way to learn new skills and use emerging technologies. But public policy will need to play a role—and education systems in particular need to be radically rethought. Finding policies to help those who can't leverage new technologies is one of the defining challenges for governments in our time. It is also essential for an open world economy: broad segments of the electorate quickly if unfairly relate unemployment and inequality, when rising, to international trade. But if we do it right, we may be in for more leisure, more prosperity, and more creativity.

13

BETTER TRADE BY MORE PEOPLE

Productivity growth that drives income growth has been sagging around the world over the past decade. No one knows exactly what is causing this. One hypothesis is that workers have been squeezed to the max—that technological advances and lean manufacturing, six sigma, and other management techniques that before boosted growth have now hit diminishing returns, a problem compounded by a decelerating private sector investment in new technologies after the 2008–2009 financial crisis. A starker version advanced by Robert Gordon is that new technologies and innovations coming to market are not transformative enough to shift the needle in growth statistics—such that real innovation is decelerating. The tech industry laments small businesses' trend-hopping. "What failed attempts to jump on trends have in common is a lack of self-awareness that translates into tone deafness. They end up feeling like parodies rather than adding anything of value," warns Kevin Allocca, head of culture and trends at YouTube.[1]

Another idea, advocated by Andy Haldane, chief economist at the Bank of England, is that while there are many robust companies that are driving growth, their contributions are dragged down by a "long-tail of laggards" that have failed to keep up amid the great recession and global competition—but, some would argue, have been kept afloat by bailouts and loose monetary policy. In 2015, the OECD found that this is happening within industries—that the difference in productivity between the top one hundred companies and the rest in various industries was rising.[2] Another study shows that while the dispersion of wages within U.S. firms has not changed much, the dispersion of wages between U.S. firms has soared—providing further backing to the idea that there are zombie companies dragging economic growth down.[3] Jason Furman and Peter Orszag, who served in the Obama White House, offer a variant to this genre—namely that concentration of industries after the crisis has reduced competition and the need to invest in getting better, faster, and leaner.[4] Many blame concentration of the banking sector as having undermined credit and other financial intermediation that fuels growth.

All in all, companies are unable or unwilling to make productivity-related improvements: either they lack the financial or human capital to deploy technologies, or they lack confidence that the investment generates a return.

This is where public policy comes in. The past few chapters have discussed a number of problems impeding firms from taking fuller advantage of technologies for growth and trade—restrictive regulations and regulatory uncertainty, digital divides, costs and complexities of cross-border payments and logistics, arcane customs procedures, uncertainties about the costs of new technologies, and so on. Policy and institutions have to be revised to enable a digital revolution in the world trading system. Granted, many countries have been making strides in the right direction—the United Kingdom's work to expand open banking and build a vibrant and seamless small business finance ecosystem; India's drive to create digital, interoperable payments among its 1.3 billion people; advanced countries' adoption of 5G technologies that will generate new efficiencies across sectors; U.K., Peruvian, Mexican, Korean, and U.S. work to bring blockchain and AI to customs; China's enabling its society and rural regions to engage in ecommerce.

This chapter lays out a policy roadmap for countries to make emerging technologies work for their trade and revive their productivity.

New Rules for the New Era

Create a Coalition to Set Rules of the Game

The priority for trade negotiators in the past twenty years has been to accommodate corporate supply chains by freeing trade and protecting foreign investors around the world. This has largely been accomplished via bilateral and plurilateral free trade agreements (FTAs) whose provisions tend to be "WTO+" or go beyond multilateral rules. Now rules are needed to govern digital trade. Again, FTAs need to drive. The WTO has upheld the multilateral trading sys-

tem for decades, but in recent years has become much too calcified and contentious to deliver on new topics. At times your author has considered the WTO's
fine location by Lake Geneva to be more productively used as a luxury hotel. Though a critical mass of countries have joined to negotiate a plurilateral
ecommerce agreement at the WTO, the era of genuinely multilateral trade talks
is over. Fastest progress and deepest commitments will be made in FTAs. Progress is happening, on four fronts.

First, the revised NAFTA, the September 2018 U.S.-Mexico-Canada
Agreement (USMCA), includes the most advanced rules to date in any FTA
to fuel digital trade among the three countries. The agreement among other
things ensures data transfer among the parties and refers to APEC's Cross-
Border Privacy Rules (CBPR) as the means to ensure data privacy; cements
safe harbor protections for Internet intermediaries; prevents customs duties on
digital products; and ensures that government open data need to be in machine-
readable format, to be easily used and applied. The deal stands in stark contrast
to Chinese Internet firewalls and Russian troll propaganda. USMCA partners
share a combined market of nearly four hundred million people and economic
output well above $20 trillion, a formidable market for free digital trade.

Second, the Trans-Pacific Partnership retained the U.S.-inspired ecommerce
chapter even after the United States left the agreement, and some countries in
Latin America are now including similar digital trade rules in their own free
trade agreements.

Third, Washington and London have been quietly discussing a U.S.-U.K.
free trade agreement for when the United Kingdom leaves the EU. The ongoing
dialogue among these two likeminded technology heavyweights and massive
users of ecommerce, data, and digital services can help cement a new transatlantic coalition for free and fair digital trade.

Fourth, the plurilateral ecommerce talks at the WTO are making progress.
Australia, Japan, and Singapore are leading this effort, and many others, such
as Costa Rica, Chile, and Argentina, are constructive and enthusiastic. Their
leadership is positive also for engaging other emerging markets and developing
countries in the process.

This progress can now be built upon in four ways.

First, the United States and the United Kingdom have a huge stake in free
and fair bilateral and global digital trade. As the U.K. leaves the European
Union, it should work with America to ink a bilateral trade deal with a digital
trade chapter that at a minimum matches the USMCA's digital trade com-

mitments, such as to prevent data localization; prohibit web blocking; uphold basic immunities for Internet intermediaries from liability for user-generated content; uphold duty-free treatment for digital products; bar restrictions on encryption technologies such as via country-specific standards; commit to a bilateral *de minimis*; and collaborate on the use of blockchain in customs to facilitate trade in parcels and packages.[5] And while at it, they should also commit to long-term public-private dialogue in such areas as collaboration on consumer protection online, cooperation on cybersecurity standards and solutions, and voluntary blockchain standards aimed at fueling the interoperability among digitizing banks, shipping companies, border agencies, and exporters and importers through digital technologies.

Second, the United Kingdom could join the USMCA as an observer, creating a North Atlantic digital free trade block. U.S. FTA partners Colombia, Chile, and Peru are together with Mexico pursuing common digital trade policies and programs and negotiating new digital trade chapters with various partners such as Australia and Canada, and should also be invited.

Third, the United States and the United Kingdom could work with Northern Europe's "Digital 9+" digital leaders (a block consisting of Sweden, Denmark, Finland, Estonia, Belgium, the Netherlands, Luxembourg, Ireland, and the United Kingdom) came together in 2016 to shape the agenda of the EU's Digital Single Market and share best practices on global competitiveness. The U.S. and the U.K. should work closely with the D9 in addressing contentious transatlantic digital issues, set common technology standards and sandboxes, and seek to engage Germany, where businesses are concerned about their future access to data. These players could also gradually consider a "third way" approach to the protection and movement of data instead of the EU's General Data Protection Regulation (GDPR)—perhaps finding a common approach between the GDPR and APEC's CBPR.

Fourth, all countries will benefit from measuring the impacts of digital regulations and FTAs' digital rules on trade, consumers, and firms in different sectors, geographies, and size categories, with the idea that what you don't measure you cannot change. Readjusting trade rules as needed is nothing new: for example, the United States, Canada, and Mexico relaxed their rules of origin after realizing that the initial set negotiated in the early 1990s was too straitjacketing for manufacturers to meet. Measuring the impact of regulations will also help obviate ideologically driven digital dialogue and dealmaking.

Create Washington Consensus II

The longer game of digital trade policymaking will need to be different. As the pace of technological change accelerates, the "technology" of trade negotiations will need to change. Future commitments may more appropriately be common codes of conduct that can be attained quickly and adjusted as needed. In the 1990s, the Washington Consensus helped set off a wave of deep trade and investment liberalization across the developing and post-communist world. The Consensus referred to ten economic policy prescriptions—privatization, trade liberalization, deregulation, and so on. Now a new Washington Consensus could serve as a north star for countries to address digital trade issues. This "Washington Consensus II" could be called the Seoul Consensus to celebrate Korea's rapid ascent to becoming one of the most technologically advanced and digitized economies in the world.[6] The Consensus could be forged among stakeholders and thought-leaders—independent think tanks and academics and seasoned "wise women and men"—to guide nations' behavior. Such guidelines would focus minds around the world, guide the work of think tanks and international organizations, and enable watchdogs to keep governments' feet to the fire.

In their book *Digital DNA: Disruption and the Challenges for Global Governance*, Peter Cowhey and Jonathan Aronson make excellent proposals to deal with the contentious issues in the digital era through such soft laws and flexible policymaking approaches.[7] These types of flexible approaches that can become *de facto* standards ideas should form the basis of the agenda of the Seoul Consensus–type effort. Using soft laws is a hardnosed practice: for example, if North America, the United Kingdom, and the European Union could agree on at least the basics, they could preempt the opportunity for China and Russia to set rules of the game in the global digital economy.

Such soft laws and principles could be implemented through pilots among small groups of reform-minded countries, which can be offered access to foreign aid and other incentives in exchange—a bit like what is happening at the WTO and in FTAs but that could be applied across a broader range of topics. For example, a group of countries could adopt good Internet intermediary liability rules and epayments regulations and in exchange access funding to do what just about every government on earth wants to do—help their small businesses use ecommerce to trade. The most successful of such experiments can then be scaled. Though this type of commitment for "aid for trade" did not get the Doha Round done, future digital trade deals with developing countries will be less impactful without it.

Use Standards and Sandboxes

Many technologies covered in this book such as blockchain and AI are still nascent, and their power and applications have yet to come fully into view. There is no particular urgency to regulate these applications; what is urgent is for governments to support the ongoing experimentation with these applications, development of uses cases for them, and scaling of the successful ones. Governments can take three measures.

First, they can help further the creation of common digital and blockchain standards that enable companies in general, and companies in different countries in particular, to interoperate. One obvious place to step on the gas is in ports and logistics supply chains, where players such as terminals, customs, shipping lines, trade finance banks, and single windows are still stuck in their data siloes and struggle to exchange data and information, but are also adopting blockchain. Such standards-setting is ongoing but too slow and frustrating; it is said the participants age three decades in one decade of work.

Standards could provide several specific benefits for the development of blockchain, such as creating commonly agreed-upon blockchain terminology and governance of data among blockchain users and on- and off-chain databases. There is no need to start from scratch: governments can follow the lead of private sector consortia that are drafting voluntary industry standards in such areas as the Internet of Things or blockchain in transportation or trade finance. The International Standards Organization is developing blockchain standards.

There is also a vibrant private sector activity around the world to develop standards in such sectors as autonomous vehicles, drone delivery, 3D printing, MedTech, and FinTech, and in the seminal cross-cutting technologies that companies in these sectors leverage, such as artificial intelligence and the Internet of Things.

It is important for the United States to play an active leadership role in such standards-setting work, for two reasons.[8] First, China is active in driving its preferred blockchain and technology standards. And second, there exists the potential that the ongoing standards frenzy will result in a complex mix of national standards that are not compatible with each other—so that a company seeking to scale across markets would have to apply different national standards in each new market, a costly endeavor that might deter companies from trying. Many such companies might be American. Just as has been the case for national product standards under the WTO Agreement on Technical Barriers to Trade, there needs to be mutual recognition of national digital and technology standards as long as those standards are non-discriminatory vis-à-vis trading partners.

The second way governments can further the application and scalability of new technologies is through regulatory sandboxes. Bringing technology solutions to market can be very costly, due to myriad national and subnational safety and other regulations. In a brilliant move, the United Kingdom has lowered FinTech companies' time and money to market with the sandbox approach, whereby companies can bring to market a new financial product or service without the entire gamut of financial regulatory approvals it might have to otherwise meet, and regulators can watch the market develop and regulate undesirable behaviors out. Australia, Singapore, and Thailand have recently copied the sandbox in order to energize their FinTech ecosystems, and some have also applied it to blockchain.

In August 2018 the United States and the United Kingdom formed with nine other governments the pioneering global FinTech Sandbox.[9] It is time to adopt these multicountry sandboxes more widely, for example for firms to experiment with blockchain applications. They should promote good dialogue among regulators and implicitly build the capacity of regulators from less developed countries. And they could result in a setting in which regulators end up by default adopting common, and thus interoperable, standards—which would obviate rounds of dialogue and time-consuming technical and policy work for countries to back into a common standard.

Third, governments can consider a safe harbor for blockchain similar to that created in the 1990s in the United States for Internet intermediaries via Section 230 of the Communications Decency Act. Blockchains should be governed by the same principle: it is the users not the blockchain manager that are liable for the data entries.[10] In the United States, a federal safe harbor could also be executed as "partial preemption": all states could have the safe harbor, but the federal law would provide exemptions for state policymakers to be able to override the safe harbor in cases of malign uses of blockchain.[11]

Nimbler Logistics

Digitize Customs, Borders, and Ports

Customs is a major bottleneck for world trade and for developing-country companies engaging in trade and cross-border ecommerce. Companies see challenges both with importing products into their countries and with exporting through other countries' customs. Delays and unexpected costs add to another top concern shared by SMEs seeking to do ecommerce: the total cost of delivery to the end customer. Meanwhile customs too struggle: in just about all countries they are facing significant surges of inbound shipments, particularly of parcels with products that businesses and consumers have ordered online from other countries. Most countries have refused to increase their *de minimis* levels to facilitate this parcel-based trade, out of (typically misplaced) concerns for foregone tax revenue, and out of worries that raising *de minimis* would open the floodgates for cheap foreign products that might compete both with politically influential retailers and with mom-and-pops that in many countries employ significant numbers of people. Yet cross-border ecommerce volumes are rising: solutions must be found to facilitate and secure this parcel-based trade.

Emerging technologies—such as machine learning, predictive analytics, and blockchain—offer what appears to be a seminal solution to these challenges. Experiences and pilots in several countries such as Korea, Mexico, the United Kingdom, and Singapore suggest that these technologies can dramatically accelerate customs clearance, while also enabling customs to much more easily spot illicit goods and fraudulent declarations. In other words, these technologies seem to meet the key desirables of developing-country governments: facilitate and secure cross-border ecommerce, defeat customs fraud, and enhance revenue collection. The World Customs Organization is also advocating these technologies' adoption. In Latin America, blockchain has also been used among countries to share data on the certifications for authorized economic operators. Indeed, the next step is to use these technologies for interoperability of national single windows and customs, for them to efficiently share information on shipments with importing or exporting nations. The demand for such interoperability among single windows is very high and technologies now enable it, but it also requires a great deal of work, including to ensure that the participant countries' laws and regulations also interoperate.

Blockchain and new technologies would have a particularly great payoff in developing countries in light of the inefficiencies and corruption in their customs. But developing countries are still not well aware of these solutions or the capabilities needed to leverage them, such as a pool of data scientists and cybersecurity protections. The dollars aimed at implementing the global Trade Facilitation Agreement need to help bolster the adoption of blockchain, AI, and predictive analytics in developing-country customs. One key vehicle for doing this is the Global Alliance for Trade Facilitation, a $50 million facility supported by the United States, Canada, the United Kingdom, Australia, and Germany aimed at building developing countries' trade sectors and accelerating customs clearance.

Customs also need to become cashless. Developing-country importers and custom brokers still all too often stand in lines to pay duties and fees by cash or check, a time-consuming task with opportunities for error and graft. Similarly, freight forwarders and their agents have to make a maze of cash and check payments to liner services, express shippers, ports, and terminals—a practice that constrains their cash flow, as they have to give up funds today whereas their customers get around to reimbursing them often only ninety days later, if then. The customs and ports ecosystems need to be forced to embrace electronic payments and the acceptance of credit cards that would give customs brokers and freight forwarders thirty to forty-five days breathing room before they have to pay their credit card bill.

Transform the Political Economy of De Minimis

Low *de minimis* weighs on economic growth in the country using it: it imposes a net cost on customs, tax authorities, shippers, importers, and consumers. The silver bullet to undoing these concerns and fueling SME trade is for governments to raise *de minimis* levels. Despite overwhelmingly compelling empirical evidence on the benefits of higher *de minimis*, governments have kept *de minimis* levels low and remarkably unchanged. Where economists see more fluid trade, governments see loss of tax revenue and political backlash from domestic retailers—without any tangible, immediate upside.

It is time to turn this lousy equation around, through a vehicle that enables governments to secure new economic as well as political gains from raising their *de minimis* rates: a plurilateral agreement on *de minimis*. The deal could be negotiated among a coalition of countries that want to free their SME exporters from frictions in their key export markets. Each member government commits to ratcheting up its *de minimis* level over a period of five to seven years to

$1,000, in exchange for a similar commitment from the other members. In other words, each member government gives a little market access at the lower rungs of trade in order to gain a lot more foreign market access for its own country's SMEs in return. The mechanics are exactly the same as those governing tariff reduction in a trade agreement: a plurilateral *de minimis* is a free trade agreement for low-value items, free trade for small businesses.

This approach turns the endless debates on *de minimis* on their head: rather than seeing raising *de minimis* as a way to lose revenue, governments could now cast a higher *de minimis* as an instrument for expanding market access for their own countries' SMEs. While still incurring the wrath of protectionist retailers, governments would by raising *de minimis* gain the support of thousands of small business online exporters and the services ecosystem that supports them, and business lobbies that favor trade. They might even gain the support of players that have resisted change in the past: many traditional retailers are today exploring omnichannel sales that are now seeking to reach foreign shoppers. Perhaps the most impactful way to drive the concept is through the WTO ecommerce talks.

Bridge the eTrade Last Mile

This book has shown that by enabling businesses and consumers to access the global pool of quality parts, components, and services they might not have available in their smaller domestic markets, ecommerce can foster companies' competitiveness and improve consumer welfare.

Yet the cost of last-mile delivery holds ecommerce back, particularly in rural areas: the delivery cost is high relative to the value of the item shipped. One key reason is that shipments to and from rural areas tend to lack the economies of scale of shipping in busy urban neighborhoods. Businesses such as Amazon and Walmart that tend to invest heavily in logistics are unlikely to be interested in serving remote rural communities that present limited revenue potential and whose limited scale economies make the last mile too expensive for the shoppers to begin with. The setting is akin to major telecom companies not seeing a point in bringing high-speed Internet connections to remote areas, as demand was not there for suppliers' price points. This suggests that in the digital era, rural consumers and businesses are penalized simply for being rural—and that there is a market failure that governments need to bridge, in order to enable rural companies and consumers to sell and buy goods and services from global and national markets and gain from trade.

Indeed, the success of rural ecommerce in China was primarily due to the Chinese government's support for rural logistics: it was the removal of the logistical barrier that enabled Chinese consumers in remote areas to score welfare gains. Such logistics support, if offered also in other markets, could have similar social and economic gains and help reduce in-country disparities. A global "Last Mile Bridge" fund to bring ecommerce markets to remote areas would have two additional benefits. First, it would enable ecommerce platforms and logistics companies to do more business in developing regions. And second, it would help stimulate and increase the volume of shipments to and from local regions and thereby improve economies of scale in rural last-mile delivery. This, in turn, would lower the costs and improve the incentives for the private sector to offer last-mile delivery solutions—and enable the government sponsor to withdraw. The concept has been applied to bridge the last mile in Internet connectivity and in medical supply delivery. So why not in ecommerce?

Smarter Financing

Guarantee FinTech Loans to SMEs

Online, even small businesses can acquire a sizable global clientele. Yet fulfilling international orders is not simple: companies need capital on hand to pay for raw materials, supplies, technologies, and labor needed to make the products and services needed to fulfill the order. These micro-multinationals typically do not need large bank loans; they need fast-disbursing microloans. Luckily, as shown in this volume, an army of online lenders have surfaced to provide capital to small businesses, using innovative credit-scoring methods and algorithm-driven automated underwriting. Products such as PayPal's working capital loan have opened significant new opportunities for low-income businesses and companies in remote areas devoid of brick-and-mortar financial services.

While small businesses are often still unaware of online lenders, this is changing fast: the peer-to-peer business lending market is growing at over 150 percent annually, as opposed to bank loans to small businesses that are growing at 10 to 15 percent. Data show that once small businesses are able to access trade finance, they increase hiring by 20 percent and production by 30 percent.

The rise of online sellers and online lenders opens up a fantastic opportunity for export credit agencies (ECAs), which traditionally have helped finance exporters with such means as by guaranteeing the bank-issued export working capital loans an exporter uses to pay for raw materials, labor, and inputs that go to fulfilling the export order. Riding the online lending revolution, ECAs such as the U.S. Export-Import (EXIM) Bank could also guarantee small export working capital loans issued by online lenders, thereby incentivizing lenders to lower their loan interest rates and expand loan coverage.

By automating credit scoring and loan guarantee underwriting, ECAs would overcome their own lack of underwriting bandwidth. And by testing various credit-scoring methods from, say, three to four online lenders with the lowest default rates and diversifying their exposure across borrowers from different sectors, sizes, geographies, and risk levels, ECAs would also protect their backer: the taxpayer. Working with online lenders could thus also help the EXIM Bank hit its goal to place 25 percent of its funding behind small businesses and improve its standing with the many lawmakers that chastise it for being biased toward larger businesses.

The benefits of such microloan guarantees on online loans could be great in the United States, and immense in the developing world, with shallower capital markets. What's more, easier access to credit for developing-country buyers could remove another chokepoint for U.S. sellers: small importers' limited access to affordable loans in their home markets.

Offer Equity for Exporters

Policymakers and development practitioners concerned with export promotion also need to pay as much attention to growth capital for globalizing companies. If the company observes strong demand for its products or services and wants to seize it—either speed up the generation of new international sales or add capacity to meet a surge in international demand quickly, such as by hiring more operations people or buying new equipment—it needs financial firepower. This typically means it needs access to growth capital.

Few in the policy world have made the connection between growth capital and competitiveness in international trade—call it equity for exporters. Yet it is essential in an era when companies are able to internationalize early in their life cycles but also need sizable capital injections to build their technologies and scale their solutions fast. Left unserved, these companies are forced to leave money on the table in the form of foregone international sales.

Meanwhile, targeting globalizing companies makes great sense for investors. They are time and again shown to be an asset class that outperforms the broader market by key metrics: productivity, revenue growth, skill levels, wages, and financial stability. Globalizing companies are, in short, a proxy for high performance and return on investment. Investors can bolster globalizing companies' outperformance, through capital, contacts, and advice.

This is where public policy could make a difference. Without subsidizing exporters outright, governments and multilateral development banks can measure globalizing companies' access to growth capital, analyze the impact of growth capital on international trade, help lower investors' per-deal search-and-transactions costs for promising globalizing companies, and provide co-financing or risk-mitigation instruments to incentivize investments in these companies. For example, the U.S. SBA's small business investment company (SBIC) program, which offers low-cost debt for venture capital, growth capital, and mezzanine fund managers to invest in small businesses, could incentivize to target export-driven companies.

Set Up a Digital Transformation Fund

Ecommerce is opening new opportunities for SMEs to trade across borders, but surveys and anecdotal evidence suggest that developing-country companies see lack of financing as the main constraint to starting to sell online and growing ecommerce sales, including cross-border. After all, succeeding at ecommerce takes sustained focus and investment—in expert staff capabilities and technologies in such areas as mobile and online marketing, reverse logistics, and ecommerce fulfillment. In light of this universal, pressing challenge for small businesses to engage in ecommerce, it is time to set up a "Global Digital Transformation Fund," a financing facility whereby governments co-invest with other funders (such as social impact funds, developing-country government funds, and developing-country investors and banks) and with SMEs themselves in SMEs' transformation into ecommerce sellers and traders. The selection criteria for firms to enter the program would need to be highly rigorous, and each company would have to have goals and milestones to meet and be required to invest substantially, so as to have skin in the game. There could also be a prescreened list of first-rate providers of digital transformation and logistics services that the chosen companies can use.

The beauty of a facility like this is that it can be self-sustainable. If the early funders play it smart and tap multiple data points on each applicant and each investee, they can create a data pipe that enables increasingly accurate forecasting as to which types of companies in which conditions deliver financial, economic, and social returns and are worth the investment risk. These analytics, along with a few success stories, are essential for attracting private investors and making the facility into a self-sustaining fund in small businesses' digital transformation.

This facility could also operate as on a social impact bond model, in which private investors invest first, and upon the company hitting metrics of interest to the public sector (such as some percentage point expansion of online export sales or number of online sellers), public sector funders "buy" successful projects and compensate the private investor for generating social impact.

Promote Funding for Women-Led Tech Firms

As discussed in Chapter 2, early data suggest that women-led firms are in no particular way disadvantaged vis-à-vis men-led firms as online sellers—women-led firms that sell online are just as likely to trade across borders, grow at certain rates, and face certain barriers to trade as men-led firms. In other words, it seems that getting women to set up formal firms and into ecommerce is critical—once they are in business and selling online, the outcomes depend less on the entrepreneurs' environment or gender than on their ability to hustle and work hard.

One area in which advanced economies can support women is in startup funding. Data and anecdotes still tell a story about gender discrimination and biases among male investors who invest more in men, proportionate to fundraising by men and by women. This picture is changing with the rise of women as investors, both as angels and as VCs; with organizations such as Astia that bring investors together to invest in women-owned tech firms; and with VCs such as the $36 million fund that invests exclusively in companies led by women of color, the group that has hardest time breaking through. Yet the world of angels and VCs is still a world of men. Large pension funds often on paper have programs for women- and minority-led venture capital funds, but the criteria are often broad enough to enable traditional teams with men to apply. Governments can induce changes. The U.K. and Canadian governments have funds squarely dedicated to investing in women-led tech companies; the U.S. SBAs' SBIC program, which enables VCs, mezzanine funds, and other types of early-stage and growth capital funds to secure leverage from the government for equity capital raised from pension funds, family offices, and so on, could adopt a special branch focused on women and collaborate with funds exclusively focused on women-led firms.

Smarter Systems

Bust Silos

The world of trade is a complex system of systems, with tremendous slack and duplication. Digitization, the Internet of Things, and blockchain promise enormous efficiencies in the global trading system and are bringing us closer to the Holy Grail of trade—integration of the financial, information, and physical supply chains. But fueling trade will also take changes in the paradigm human beings have in their heads and the way we are used to working—in silos rather than in systems. And thinking and acting in systems means busting silos.

Silo-busting is essential also in trade promotion and international development. Governments and development agencies are famous for operating in sectoral silos, where one sector covers technology development, another trade facilitation, and still another SME finance. People populating these sectors are the world's leading experts in their own disciplines—and cannot possibly have a deep, comprehensive knowledge of all parts of a problem. Yet often people even within the same sector or department do not know what the person next to them is doing, and they know very little about what the people in the next sector or department are doing. The problem is widely recognized and often a source of both jokes and some desperation among staff in government agencies and international organizations.

Helpfully, most experts are aware of their limitations and the problems caused by organizational stovepipes. They know they have to work with other experts to solve multidimensional, systemic problems. For example, building ecommerce markets in developing countries requires IT infrastructures, trade facilitation and logistics, online payments, digital regulations, ecommerce skills development, and access to finance—and thus requires many government agencies to work together. Yet collaboration is complicated by turf wars, sheer inertia and the need to get work done, some hubris and fear of looking silly, and managers worried about coming across as bullies among their peers. These challenges are not just inconvenient—they are outright detrimental to an organization's responsiveness and client service, whether the client is a leading exporter or a small developing-country government.

Silo-busting is also needed between governments and the private sector. For example, making mobile payments work and interoperate in developing countries requires collaboration among central banks, finance ministries, banks, payment companies, and telecom operators. Similarly, as the world urbanizes, the international trade community needs to start partnering up with urban economists to decongest cities for world commerce, and work on intelligent traffic systems that direct flows, emerging driverless delivery systems, and companies that generate big data on urban traffic.

Helping trade flow in the twenty-first century means breaking silos and leveraging every expert and institution's comparative advantages—creating multisectoral teams of experts, cross-sectoral programs, and public-private partnerships. This takes leadership right at the top of organizations, and intrepid, humble managers who are excited about multidisciplinary work. It may take Millennials: unlike older generations, Millennials are bent on working, and trained to work, in cross-functional teams on a specific problem.

There are silo-busters also in Generation X and among boomers—I have personally had a chance to work with several in leading international organizations, government agencies, and businesses. One such silo-busting venture was launching with the United Nations in 2016 a multistakeholder "eTrade for All" initiative, which by now brings together thirty-five leading development agencies and donor governments to develop common, incisive diagnostics and offer support to ecommerce development. By virtue of this effort, any developing country has a single door on which to knock when seeking to develop ecommerce, and is able to access a comprehensive, custom solution from a group of leading experts and institutions.

Use Public-Private Partnerships and Social Impact Bonds

Another silo that needs to be broken is the one separating the public and private sectors. The private sector is closest to the opportunities, challenges, and solutions in trade and ecommerce development issues, and as such is critical for informing and guiding policymaking on trade issues around the world. As the world digitizes and innovation accelerates, governments and agencies are falling behind in grasping the patterns and problems the private sector sees every day, let alone thinking of creative solutions to these challenges. The private sector also has far better and real-time data on market gaps and solutions. Governments have to work with companies in order to best prioritize investments in digitization and ecommerce, and can readily build on the private sector's ongoing work to boost connectivity, fuel logistics, and, indeed, create entirely new markets.

Progress has already been made. In numerous countries there are concerted efforts by public and private sectors to cultivate ecommerce in their economies. For example, in Turkey, the public and private sectors have come together in a specialized ecommerce council that is roadmapping policies and solutions for such issues as ecommerce regulations and SMEs' participation in ecommerce. In Mexico, the export promotion agency Proméxico and the Ministry of the Economy are researching with ecommerce players the needs and opportunities for Mexican firms in ecommerce. In Guatemala, several government agencies that work on trade (such as ministries of economy and agriculture and tax and bank oversight agencies) have come together with various industry associations to create a roadmap to unlock ecommerce in the country and develop position for foreign trade negotiations on digital trade. In Bangladesh, the IT and ecommerce industry associations have fashioned regulatory solutions working closely together with the government. These efforts are instructive for countries that have yet to adopt them—and are a very simple but effective solution for governments and development agencies to support and systematize across developing economies.

I have had a chance to work on enterprise-led development with USAID and several businesses in the Alliance for eTrade Development, in which we pool the private sectors' data and expertise with USAID funding to establish best practices for developing countries to help SMEs sell and export on ecommerce platforms. I have also had a chance to work on launching an entity, Digital Standards for Trade, with a set of banks, companies, the government of Singapore, and the Asian Development Bank, to digitize trade transactions end-to-end. These efforts, as I have observed, have an excellent side benefit: they help the public sector learn from the private sector about challenges and opportunities in a given area of development, and give the private sector a sense of the full range of activities pursued by the public sector, for example in markets where business is looking to expand next.

This type of work is not easy—public and private sectors speak different languages, and their timelines and success metrics can be different. It takes tenacity and ability for at least one person to translate between life-long public servants and private sector leaders who have never stepped into the public sector.

Yet there are many opportunities for joint gains. For example, companies in the global ecommerce ecosystem are leading a stunning array of projects to bring women, rural populations, and SMEs into the stream of ecommerce—precisely the projects that aid agencies want to see. Large players such as Alibaba and eBay have multiple initiatives around the world in these areas, but so do a wide range of local players such as Grasshopper from Sri Lanka, which is solving cross-border shipping and payments, and TCS Holdings, a courier enterprise based in Pakistan, which has been rolling out gender diversity initiatives aimed at increasing the participation of women in the workforce in Pakistan, currently at only 25 percent of the total. TCS has been working on increasing gender parity within its ranks through a series of women's initiatives—such as to hire women as ecommerce couriers or to teach other women in far-flung villages how to use ecommerce on mobile phones or tablets. It's a win-win situation: it empowers women and builds TCS's ecommerce business capacity and the Pakistani ecommerce market.

The private sector makes these types of efforts with a long-term profit motive in mind—and that is the very point for public and private sectors to partner on. These efforts create markets that last, rather than dying after the initial investment is spent. They therefore present a great opportunity for governments and development agencies: the private sector has already designed them and covered the costs of piloting them, and has quantifiable results on them.

A low-hanging fruit for the public sector is to take the best of the projects seeded by the private sector and use public sector funds to scale or replicate them. This model also leverages the partners' comparative advantages: the private sector spots problems and creates and seeds solutions; the public sector provides growth capital in proven projects—and saves costs in designing and managing high-performing projects. This is low-risk, high-yield development for the public sector: all it does is fund what the private sector has already made work. A more sophisticated version is to craft entire portfolios of private-sector-led projects aimed to drive digitization and ecommerce, complete with performance metrics and forecasts, and enable the public sector to invest in these portfolios—and diversify their risk thereby.

An even more systematic and novel approach would be for governments and companies to co-finance projects through "social impact bonds." In this model, private foundations, social impact investors, and/or ecommerce platforms make the initial investment in ecommerce projects, such as an SME training program, and get compensated at a premium by the government and public development agencies if the program meets certain preestablished performance indicators, such as a target number of ecommerce-related jobs created or an amount of new online exports.[12] The social impact bond instrument is superb at incentivizing investors and project implementers to deliver results desired by the public sector.

Social impact bonds (also known as development impact bonds) have been successfully used to cure malaria and save rhinos. They lend themselves very well to the development of trade and ecommerce markets, given the considerable interest by the private sector to accelerate the rise of new online sellers and to break bottlenecks in ecommerce. They are also risk-free, performance-based development for the public sector: upon success and metrics hit, governments secure both trade gains and economic and social returns. Resting on rigorous measurement of results, this model would by default create transparency in project evaluation.

Make Development Banks into "Banks-as-a-Service"

Multilateral development banks and aid agencies invest tens of billions in trade-related development each year. Often this work is bilateral, with a certain country and often with its government that wishes to take a loan for a development project. In the digital era, the delivery model can be different: a platform-based "Bank-as-a-Service," when a development bank delivers the same service to multiple countries at once. For example, it in principle makes no sense to develop a blockchain-based customs clearance system for just one country, when other countries could readily use a copy of it. Development policy needs to evolve from country-specific assistance and development bank staff being rewarded for generating loans to regionally and globally scalable interventions enabled by common technology. Perhaps one model to finance such interventions is to reward the first-mover country and borrower for taking a chance on an intervention that others then also would like to acquire, by lowering the first-mover governments' interest and principal payments proportionately.

Stop Protecting Jobs and Empower Workers

In 1950, a person stayed in a job for his life. In the 1980s, people held three to four different jobs, within the same occupation. Now, the average person has ten jobs by age forty. If she has great skills to start and works in technologically advanced firm and society, she will add value in herself with each passing year—at the order of nearly 6 percent annually in the Netherlands and Sweden versus less than half a percent in Afghanistan, as discussed in Chapter 8. Jobs are changing faster, and workers have an easier time switching jobs, at least in certain cities. Hiring in turn increasingly is for discrete tasks rather than occupations. In this task-based labor market, terminal degrees weigh less than retooling in real time—continued education powered by massive online courses and digital on-the-job learning. Career moves can be less daunting than going from the factory floor to a computerized office—for example, coding, programming, and web design are increasingly accessible even to lower-skilled workers. And learning new skills takes a fraction of the time it used to, thanks to an endless supply of excellent online courses on even the most complex matters.

Policymakers accordingly should empower workers—rather than raising tariffs and protecting jobs whose time has passed. Singapore gets the point. SkillsFuture Singapore, a statutory board under the Ministry of Education, offers various life-long learning and workforce development programs for people of all ages, including students, early-to-mid-career professionals, and even seniors. Its SkillsFuture Credit offers direct subsidies of about $400 to all Singapore citizens over the age of twenty-five for a preapproved list of courses (and even higher subsidies for mid-career professionals). This is popular: in 2016, the program offered over eighteen thousand courses and is used by over 126,000 Singaporeans.

Businesses are also filling the void—including Codecademy and General Assembly, which help people to quickly learn a new skill such as computer programming while they work and apply it immediately in their jobs. Your author is learning machine learning this way. Retooling is not just about workers themselves—it is critical for the competitiveness of the companies where those workers work, both to retain workers and to cultivate their skills. In the United States, Capitol One is exceptionally good at the "last mile" programs that instill in new hires the right attitudes and attributes to do their jobs. For example, a college graduate in business or math might be put through a boot camp to learn to code. Supporting businesses in retraining their labor force is perhaps the best education policy—firms know what they need and can readily start training, avoiding the months and probably a year that a local university would take to recraft its curriculum to meet businesses' needs. Businesses that think of their employees as perennially new collar workers and train them to do new tasks should get a tax deduction for their investment. AI and machine learning can be harnessed more systematically to accelerate matching of the right people to the right jobs.

But transferable skills are not enough: what is truly needed are workers with visions—an ability to envision new futures and ideate new products, services, and business models. It's one thing to have the skills to edit words on a page; it's quite another to ideate and put concepts on a blank page. The latter requires an employee to get deep into her field and exposed to up-and-coming technologies, trends, business models, and applications in other fields she can then quickly apply in her field. In his books, self-improvement expert Dr. Joe Dispenza emphasizes that human beings' brains are malleable—they make new synaptic connections and neural patterns when we learn something new or have a new experience.[13] The more input and new lessons that come in, the more connections we have, and the more creative we get, if we intentionally work on creating. Dispenza is hardly alone—the very profession of energy healers, hypnotists, and neuroplasticity experts is based on our brains' endless coachability.

Hard and soft skills enable a person to do a variety of tasks and jobs and move into emerging jobs; carving time to systematically gain new information and think of ways to apply new technologies and business models enables a person to architect entirely new categories and new jobs. Virgin founder Richard Branson has highlighted the importance for CEOs to help their staff nurture innovation, quipping that "CEO" should stand for "Chief Enabler Officer."[14] CEOs can fuel creativity systematically by enabling employees to have "dabble time" and dabblers to have a real path to have an avenue to grow in a business, offering prizes for best new innovations that are substantial enough to appetize workers and overcome fears of failure, and staging Hackatons and innovation tournaments. They can reward employees for best new questions, the alpha and omega of creativity; employ people in the jobs they are intrinsically motivated to do, a creativity accelerator; and give employees equity, for them to co-own the fruits of their creative endeavors.

Obsess About Growth

In his epic contribution *Capital in the 21st Century,* Thomas Piketty showed that inequality is rising because capital makes capital holders richer.[15] He then proposed that those making $500,000 or more a year should pay an 80 percent tax, plus there should be a "global tax on capital" topping at 10 percent on the largest fortunes. The book was on the *New York Times* best-seller list for six weeks, a feat for a book published by an academic press, let alone a door stopper of seven hundred pages. Interest in Piketty's work reflected the worries about the impacts of income inequality.

Those who vouch for policies aimed at equality at times justify their quest by arguing that equality keeps social harmony and trust that undergird growth, and claiming that unequal societies have less growth. Others argue that equality results in economic growth because supposedly median voters will push for redistributive policies that fuel growth, such as investments in public education or infrastructures.

In his book *The Populist Temptation,* Barry Eichengreen sees President Trump's rise as resulting from a lack of an adequate floor for people who feel victim to technological change, perhaps to trade liberalization, and to the superblow of the global financial crisis.[16] He is not alone in this view—in 2012, World Bank veterans now at Carnegie Endowment for International Peace, Uri Dadush and Kemal Derviş, along with Sarah Milsom and Bennett Stancil, argued that America's response to the distributional impacts of trade surges and technological changes in the 1990s and 2000s would lead to political storms and merit a rethink of U.S. education, tax, and international policies.[17]

Should an American welfare state then be reformed and made to resemble, say, that of Denmark, which has by global standards very successfully balanced openness to trade, flexible labor regulations, and an enviable level of income security when a person gets laid off? The Danish employment rate is higher than the EU average; its structural unemployment rate is lower than the EU average; and its Gini index, which measures inequality, is among OECD nations' lowest.[18] The United States already by and large has checked the boxes for open trade and flexible labor markets. But the collective bargaining process Denmark and many European countries use between labor unions and employers to set minimum wages, or the high taxes Danes pay for the "curity" in Denmark's world famous flexicurity model, would have a harder time being adopted in the U.S.

There is also as yet scant evidence of an association between equality and economic growth that after all is needed to boost income growth. Hypotheses abound as to why. Some argue that inequality makes the median voter vote for high tax rates, which in turn reduce incentives for investment and undermine growth. This is true—tax hikes just about always dampen economic growth and can be recessionary, while tax cuts tend to increase growth and thereby increase tax revenue.[19] Taxes just about always undermine investment and the human quest to create value and acquire wealth.

So how do inequality and growth relate? The relationship is more complex than typically thought. In a 2017 paper, Gustavo Marrero, Juan Gabriel Rodríguez, and Roy Van der Weide find that overall inequality is negatively correlated with the future income growth of the poor and positively correlated with the income growth of the rich.[20] Most notably, their finding is almost completely driven by a subcomponent of inequality, namely inequality of opportunity. It is not the rich-poor income gap but the lack of opportunity to get top schooling or move past glass ceilings of race or gender that keeps holding the poor back.

Studies suggest that such measures as reducing high school dropout rates and lowering long-term unemployment (also done when companies invest and economies grow) can increase equality of opportunity and alter the path traveled by a person on the low end of the opportunity spectrum. We can, in short, raise the income growth rates of the poor with smart, targeted remedies that open new opportunities, rather than single-mindedly focusing on taxing the rich. Growth and opportunity lift spirits and fatten bank accounts. We need to get obsessed by growth—making it, measuring it better from different angles at every level, each person, gender, group, business, city, sector, neighborhood, and nation.

What would happen if technology adoption accelerated so quickly that most people actually did lose their jobs to a bot? Would the old paradigms break down and radical solutions like Piketty's be needed?

In 1987, economist Paul Romer wrote a paper titled "Crazy Explanations for the Productivity Slowdown," which hypothesized that women and baby boomers' entry into the American workforce might decrease productivity by increasing the supply of labor and lowering the cost of labor, and thus discouraging investments in labor-saving technologies (that propel productivity).[21] Simply put, employers might be loath to adopt machines because workers are cheaper. The dip in productivity was real, some studies show, but its driver was somewhat less straightforward: as then-inexperienced baby boomers went to work, firms hired low-quality "left-over" staff from the previous generation to manage them, which lowered productivity, until baby boomers got some experience and claimed these management jobs for themselves.[22]

Economist editor Ryan Avent offers a modern-day version, a fantastic future in which adoption of technologies that substitute for labor raises aggregate productivity growth but pushes more people to look for new jobs, which means more people compete for low-skilled jobs, which in turn places downward pressure on wages, making workers cheaper.[23] This labor glut then ultimately might do what happened in Romer's paper: reduce employers' incentives to invest in new labor-saving technologies. Then if people get back behind the wheel, productivity growth will slow down—unless there is a very fast increase in educational attainment that increases workers' productivity. Would there be a way to avert this cycle—keep the economy's productivity rising without the labor glut and lowering wages?

One solution is to relentlessly retrain workers along the lines of IBM CEO Ginni Rometty's concept of making employees perennially "new collar"—so that labor's productivity would keep rising, perhaps at the same cost of labor.[24] Another might be the old trick of shorter workweeks that reduce the supply of labor. Still another solution might be a creative approach to vacuum up labor supply by radical income distribution. After all, if machines keep productivity increasing, mankind's perennial problem of scarcity comes to an end. Then the "problem" becomes, how to distribute the incredible abundance produced by productivity hikes? Perhaps Piketty's ultra-progressive taxation would do it, or schemes such as universal basic income (UBI) supercharged to give everyone a strong living "wage" for doing nothing.

These musings are of course hypothetical, underpinned by the idea that technology (capital) will be cheap compared to people (labor)—and the idea that when employers replace labor with capital, labor will merely wander around in daze. Even with UBI, most people would not sit around browsing Facebook. Human beings are hardwired to grow, create, build, and improve their lot—just pause and look at the buildings, cars, metros, planes, stores, and products around yourself and you will realize that probably none of them were around a short hundred years ago. Someone put pen on paper and pooled the capabilities that made them all happen. Many someone elses put pen on paper and came up with those capabilities—trained workers, new financing instruments, new materials, and new techniques and technologies, new laws and public policies. Most people, if sitting idle and offered free money, would use it to improve themselves and their families, create their own businesses, and invest. One way to see these incentives at work is to look at the spending of remittances and of unconditional and conditional cash transfer programs provided to the poor in numerous developing countries. In the main, these various "free money" programs have enhanced recipients' spending in education, health care, housing, and better nutrition and improved development outcomes, rather than resulting in vice spending, such as in pizza, beer, and TVs.

Unleash Watson on World Trade

In five to ten years, there will be dozens of studies about the trade effects of blockchain, the impacts of additive manufacturing and robotics on locational choices of firms, the distributional impacts of cross-border ecommerce, and the geospatial impacts of digitization. There will be works of this kind because technologies will have advanced from pilots to use, because data will be more available, and because even finer patterns will be more discernible. Today we have forecasts and projections and early evidence based on survey data produced by pioneers; tomorrow we will have large-scale flow data and robust evidence, contested among scholars. Today we have new initiatives and partnerships; in a few years, we will have discovered their strengths and impacts just as we will have seen the flaws in some of the assumptions they are based on, and we will adjust, for our action to be more sophisticated.

What should be in the policy research agenda on trade and technology? We still know very little about the impact of online payments and ecommerce on poverty, jobs, and firm growth. Do companies that sell online ultimately grow, scale, and create jobs? Or are they like the many companies that at the height of the microfinance euphoria got funded but then kept doing what they were doing year after year, with no particular leap in productivity or new hires?

We don't know much about distributional impacts. What are the longer-term impacts of digital trade on in-country disparities—does it empower firms in remote and rural areas, or does it widen the gaps between them and their urban peers? Does it reduce or widen social disparities and gender disparities, and disparities between large and small firms? How to best create digital oases in the rural digital deserts? What are the optimal methods and technologies to help optimize labor markets—to match right people to right jobs?

We also know very little to date on the impact of existing policy and aid interventions aimed at accelerating the adoption of technologies to expand and fuel trade in development nations. What have been the trade effects of the many investments in ICT and SME capacity-building to use ecommerce?

We know almost nothing about the trade effects of the proliferating digital regulations—rules of data privacy and transfer, Internet intermediary liability, OTT rules, taxes on digital services, online payment regulations, and so on—let alone the trade effects of the Splinternet, the divergence of such rules across markets.

And we have barely scratched the surface to understand the extent and costs of lack of interoperability among players in trade transactions. What are they and where exactly do they stem from? Are they worst in certain developing-country trade corridors, or just bad everywhere? Are they dropping in the trade of countries such as Singapore, a champion of interoperability?

While we know quite a lot about trade costs—the cost of moving a container from factory to port, across the ocean, and through customs—we know precious little about the combined costs of poor interoperability and inefficiencies in the global trade ecosystem. We also know quite little about the frictions and cost centers in moving a parcel from a firm in one country to a customer in another, especially through postal systems. Is the logjam in trade really at the port and border, or is it rather in a congested urban center and inefficient back offices of posts?

To answer these questions really well, we will need much better diagnostics and data, and predictive power. Granted, data on the obstacles to trade and growth have sharpened over time. For example, there exist cross-country data on the time and money it takes to export or import a container, logistics quality, and very granular data on customs clearance times. Data on trade policy barriers have also become better and more real time—for example, the Global Trade Alert collects quarterly data on how countries restrict or liberalize trade in such targeted areas as local content regulations or food standards. Such data are very useful for industry to keep government's feet to the fire and for governments to self-diagnose problems and engage in races to the top. For example, after seeing that Georgia sat in place 100 out of 155 countries in the World Bank's Ease of Doing Business Index in 2005, its government pursued forty-seven reforms that raised the country's ranking to ninth in 2018. Data drive action. However, the traditional methods keep interventions general and reaction times poor.

As economies and trade change and diversify, old methods—annual stock-taking, perceptions-based surveys done by phone, coding of qualitative data into quantitative formats by humans by hand—need to yield to pipes of granular data open 24/7 that enable real-time troubleshooting and forecasting. We need both better measures and, to produce the fresher and sharper questions, data at a higher resolution. The private sector, particularly tech companies and platforms, is driving and will drive the development of such granular, real-time data. The best insights into development solutions are locked up in proprietary datasets that make public-private partnerships even more compelling. The public sector will also need to set aside bigger budgets to purchase data and analytics solutions from the outside. And the public sector needs to learn to partner with business to share data, for mutually desirable ends.

Data also have to be rethought. If we started today from scratch to think of how to harvest economic data, we would think of data from mobile phones, social media, platforms, and satellites rather than from time-consuming telephone surveys and censuses; create data pipes to see patterns in real time rather than do annual stock-takings that are old by the time they're processed; and report findings by neighborhoods not countries. The possibilities are there: it has become possible to understand poverty and digitization from satellite imagery, see flows and gaps in global ecommerce by posts' data, and take the pulse of thousands of businesses with mobile surveys that stream in within hours. Institutions need to take risks to pilot new analytics using these and other 24/7 data sprinklers.

Similarly, instead of working to do research with a handful of research assistants plowing through and coding data, poring over literature, and developing econometric modeling, economists need to start using AI-based tools that are able to quickly digest mountains of economic research and project evaluation reports into actionable insights, identification of best practices, and assessment of emerging needs for interventions and impacts of new policies and projects. IBM's Watson could gobble together more data in minutes than ten thousand research assistants could within days. In short, technology diffusion is needed also among trade and development practitioners.

Are New Politics Possible?

Students of the political economy of trade typically study two main schools of thought. The first is that trade policy is shaped by battles among interest groups—unionized labor and uncompetitive industries that want tariffs against export-driven companies that want free global trade. The weapon of these interests in the political arena is campaign contributions doled to policymakers. So far, pro-trade forces have largely prevailed. The other school turns on the ballot box. In the so-called median voter theorem, trade policy is determined by the vote of the most typical voter. To ride with this school, one needs to assume that voters primarily vote on trade rather than social issues or taxes or health care, and so forth, and that they are passionate enough to show up to vote to begin with.

Today's concerns about the rise of protectionism turn on the median voter model: that voters anguished about globalization will take on the ballot box and cause tariffs to go up, and industries such as textiles, washing machines, and vehicles will lobby for protection. While the median voter theorem may seem like a depiction of the dynamics that propelled Trump to the White House, it discounts the fact that American and other countries' trade policy has been mostly shaped by export-driven industries warring with the AFL-CIO in the corridors of Congress—and that the content of trade and traders themselves will be radically different ten to twenty years from now.

What happens to trade politics when trade is no longer about planes and cars on a ship, but perhaps 3D-printable designs crossing borders, or architectural, IT, or legal services performed online? Is it really plausible that trade policy will remain as it has been, a battle of unionized workers and large multinationals? Or might union politics evolve in a bad direction, if goods are increasingly made by 3D printers and robots where they are sold, rather than traded across borders? For example, might the future of lobbying be much more about taxing robots than trade?

The biggest shift in trade politics may yet be that trade is becoming more important for a wider set of people. In a DHL study, 90 percent of companies said they would sell to international markets by 2025. Main Street businesses scoring gains from trade are a new free trade lobby—first and foremost wanting to keep other markets open for their exports, but also calling on American policymakers to keep trade barriers low at home, to ensure other countries are not tempted to raise their barriers too, following America's example.

Two decades ago, NAFTA negotiations consolidated American big business into an export lobby to drive trade deals through; today, small businesses and ecommerce merchants need to be brought together into a new force for free trade. The wave has already started: Etsy and eBay regularly fly their sellers to Washington to champion new trade agreements and lower trade costs; newer lobbies such as the Global Innovation Forum bring entrepreneurs to influence policymakers in major capitals. Protectionism will not go unpunished, not by large multinationals or the small businesses that depend on the global marketplace, and likely ultimately by consumers angered by the costs.

Export-driven services industries will likely also grow louder in American trade policy. The United States is by far the largest services exporter in the world; services exports are growing fast when most manufacturing exports are shrinking. Over one half of all services jobs are digital services, and over one half of jobs supported by exports are services jobs—for example, legal services by a law firm in Dallas to a client in Germany, IT services from a freelancer in Maine to a company in Canada, or tourism services by a five-star resort in Hawaii catering to wealthy Chinese tourists. Will these people not push for more open markets and reduction of the still steep barriers to trade in services and discrimination in government contracting for services? Wouldn't a U.S. data scientist not want to be able to bid for a contract with a Brazilian state government seeking to identify faster ways to fatten cattle or regrow Amazon forests?

Even if the median voter theorem was the right lens though which to understand trade policy outcomes, it might augur well for free trade. In surveys, most Americas say the Trump tariffs will hurt the economy and also their families in the long run—but most also do not pay attention to the tariffs and unlikely trace the cost of the washing machine to them.[25] So far, American consumers have been supine on trade issues. The famous example is sugar—the fact that America's sugar market is protected with quotas means that all of us spend $8 each year more than we would if the sugar market was liberalized, not an outlay that most of us ever know about or, in the era of social media, would mount a Facebook campaign to abolish. However, to the sugar industry it is extremely relevant—their annual "subsidy" is $2 billion, a nice payday for intense lobbying. If the quota was ended and any country could export sugar to America, the price of sugar would go down, and any candy bar and soda and loaf of bread that has sugar would also be cheaper. America's sugar companies would either go out of business or have to deal with less income and fewer workers. But what about going forward? Will consumers remain indifferent to trade policy at the ballot box and refrain from putting pressure on their Congressional representatives now that tariffs hit prices on store shelves and showrooms?

America Must Lead

America must lead. We can be helped by many good countries—Sweden, Chile, and Costa Rica are among the many small ones that have stepped up to further global collaboration on trade in the digital era. But there is no substitute for the United States. In the past few years, Americans have been spookmeistered to fear this time of openness and opportunity. According to pollster Frank Lutz, we are less hopeful about the future than almost ever. Most Americans today believe their children will be worse off. Our image has plunged around the planet and our credibility sunk. Our children have to wage their war against the NRA and, still in 2019, young women have to continue the battles against sexual harassment and for equal pay. And astoundingly, we still have to resurrect arguments for free trade.

We are better than this and must do better than this—stand up for openness, innovation, growth, and opportunity for all. Japan will be there, Europe has no choice but to be there, the United Kingdom will be there, most of Latin

America will be there, as will most of Southeast Asia. Hillary Clinton was right that America is great because America is good. We are still the beacon, only dimmer for the moment. Many Republicans say, "I have not changed, the party has," or "not my party anymore." Today, the party, a party that was mine too and that espoused free trade, free markets, economic freedom, and the small business and private sectors as drivers of growth risks looking like a party of isolationists, chauvinists, fans of strongmen who can't bear dialogue and disagreement, and people finding an excuse in the Second Amendment for failures to keep children safe in school. Leading one of the greatest feats of mankind, the American democracy, our president coddled a foreign leader who attacked our elections, praised another leader with a chilling record of human rights violations, and applauded a leader—China's, to boot—for getting rid of term limits.

This is not what America is or stands for. We need to get back to the business of leading by example and continuing the greatest democratic experiment on the planet. And we need to keep driving for free trade and for the discovery and diffusion of the technologies that fuel trade and open opportunities for all. It's an era of great opportunity in world economy. We must get it right.

Conclusion

In 1944, Friedrich Hayek wrote *The Road to Serfdom*, an anti-socialist thesis that defended economic freedom as a pillar of political freedom. These ideas inspired twentieth-century economists such as John Maynard Keynes and Milton Friedman. In the 1980s, as the Soviet empire crumbled and capitalism and democracy spread and flourished, the meaning of "economic freedom" was less about the battle against socialism and more about perfecting private ownership and enterprise through deregulation, privatization of state-owned entities, and free trade. Heritage Foundation, Freedom House, and other think tanks developed rankings and indices of economic freedom. Literature on welfare economics entered into the concept of "economic freedom" the concept of "freedom of choice."

In the twenty-first century, the concept of economic freedom needs to expand still more. Economic freedom today needs to mean every human being's opportunity to connect to the Internet and transact freely in the global virtual marketplace, as far as the web reaches and unfettered by arcane tariffs, Internet firewalls, and old and new red tape at the border. Every individual, regardless of where she or he is based or what her or his state of life, needs to be free and able to do what the Internet enables her or him to do—buy from and sell to just about anybody, anywhere, any time, and almost anything. This, after all, is how a human being in the twenty-first century can realize his or her full economic potential. Economic freedom is not only free trade, but freedom to trade.

People are hardwired to create, build, communicate, and exchange. Technologies are increasingly enabling us to do so, at a global scale. We need to free ourselves from old ways of doing business, from siloed divisions of the world into disciplines and public and private sectors, of rules that take years to write. Governments and companies need a new modus operandi to maximize the technology-powered opportunities in world trade. The aspiration for twenty-first-century economic freedom may sound lofty, but the solutions are infinitely practical. Fortunately, many are already on the way. Let's push for more.

NOTES

CHAPTER 1

1. Nelson D. Schwarz, "Can Trump Save Their Jobs? They're Counting on It," *New York Times*, November 12, 2016, https://www.nytimes.com/2016/11/13/business/economy/can-trump-save-their-jobs-theyre-counting-on-it.html.

2. "Travis Baird," eBay Main Street blog, https://www.ebaymainstreet.com/fr/node/130011.

3. See, for example, World Development Indicators, World Bank, https://datacatalog.worldbank.org/dataset/world-development-indicators; and "World Investment Report: Annex Tables," United Nations Conference on Trade and Development, 2017, https://unctad.org/en/Pages/DIAE/World%20Investment%20Report/Annex-Tables.aspx.

4. Scott C. Bradford, Paul L. E. Grieco, and Gary Clyde Hufbauer, "The Payoff to America from Global Integration," Peterson Institute for International Economics, https://piie.com/sites/default/files/publications/papers/2iie3802.pdf (accessed March 18, 2019).

5. José De Gregorio, "Productivity in Emerging Market Economies: Slowdown or Stagnation?" Policy paper, Institute for International Economics, November 2017, https://piie.com/system/files/documents/2-2de-gregorio20171109paper.pdf. Other growth calculations include human capital (such as years of schooling) in TFP; De Gregorio includes it outside TFP.

6. "Global Trade Growth Loses Momentum as Trade Tensions Persist," WTO Press Release 837, April 2, 2019, https://www.wto.org/english/news_e/pres19_e/pr837_e.htm.

7. Data extrapolated from "Pitney Bowes Parcel Shipping Index Reveals 48 Percent Growth in Parcel Volume Since 2014," *BusinessWire*, August 30, 2017, https://www.businesswire.com/news/home/20170830005628/en/Pitney-Bowes-Parcel-Shipping-Index-Reveals-48; World Development Indicators, World Bank; "Number of Smartphone Users Worldwide from 2014 to 2020 (in Billions)," *Statista*, https://www.statista.com/statistics/330695/number-of-smartphone-users-worldwide/; "Number of Annual Active Consumers Across Alibaba's Online Shopping Properties from 4th Quarter 2013 to 4th Quarter 2018 (in millions)" *Statista*, 2019, https://www.statista.com/statistics/226927/alibaba-cumulative-active-online-buyers-taobao-tmall; eBay, "eBay Inc. Reports Fourth Quarter and Full Year 2016 Results," Press Release, January 25, 2017, https://www.

ebayinc.com/stories/news/ebay-inc-reports-fourth-quarter-and-full-year-2016-results; Thomas Franck, "Amazon's US Sales to Match Walmart's Within Three Years, JP Morgan Predicts," CNBC, May 15, 2018, https://www.cnbc.com/2018/05/15/amazons-us-sales-to-match-walmarts-within-three-years-jp-morgan-predicts.html.

8. See Adam Ostrow, "How Many People Actually Use Twitter?", Mashable, April 28, 2009, https://mashable.com/2009/04/28/twitter-active-users/; "Number of Monthly Active Twitter Users Worldwide from 1st Quarter 2010 to 4th Quarter 2018 (in Millions)," *Statista*, 2019, https://www.statista.com/statistics/282087/number-of-monthly-active-twitter-users; and "Number of Monthly Active Facebook Users Worldwide as of 1st Quarter 2019 (in Millions)," *Statista*, 2019, https://www.statista.com/statistics/264810/number-of-monthly-active-facebook-users-worldwide.

9. "Number of Annual Active Consumers Across Alibaba's Online Shopping Properties from 4th Quarter 2013 to 4th Quarter 2018 (in Millions)" *Statista*, 2019, https://www.statista.com/statistics/226927/alibaba-cumulative-active-online-buyers-taobao-tmall.

10. Global Apple iPhone Sales from 3rd Quarter 2007 to 4th Quarter 2018 (in Million Units)," *Statista*, 2019, https://www.statista.com/statistics/263401/global-apple-iphone-sales-since-3rd-quarter-2007.

CHAPTER 2

1. Thomas Friedman, *The World Is Flat: A Brief History of the Twenty-First Century* (New York: Farrar, Straus and Giroux, 2005).

2. Atev Lohr, "Stress Test for the Global Supply Chain," *New York Times*, March 19, 2011.

3. Richard Baldwin, "Trade and Industrialisation After Globalisation's 2nd Unbundling: How Building and Joining a Supply Chain Are Different and Why It Matters," NBER Working Paper No. 17716, issued December 2011, revised January 2013, http://www.nber.org/papers/w17716. See also Richard Baldwin, *The Great Convergence: Information Technology and the New Globalization* (Cambridge, MA: Harvard University Press, 2016).

4. See Bureau of Labor Statistics, "Manufacturing in China," https://www.bls.gov/fls/china.htm#tables and https://www.bls.gov/cew/ewo2sect3133.pdf (accessed March 3, 2018).

5. See for example, Kaname Akamatsu, "A Historical Pattern of Economic Growth in Developing Countries," *The Developing Economies* 1, no. 3-2, 1962, https://onlinelibrary.wiley.com/doi/abs/10.1111/j.1746-1049.1962.tb01020.x.

6. Kaname Akamatsu, "A Historical Pattern of Economic Growth in Developing Countries," *The Development Economies* 1, Tokyo, Preliminary Version (1962): 3–25.

7. See Richard Baldwin, "Trade and Industrialisation after Globalisation's 2nd Unbundling: How Building and Joining a Supply Chain Are Different and Why It Matters," NBER Working Paper No. 17716, December 2011, http://www.nber.org/papers/w17716.

8. See "Reshoring: Total Cost of Ownership Estimator," Reshoring Initiative, http://reshorenow.org/tco-estimator (accessed April 21, 2019).

9. Matthew Ponsford and Nick Glass, "The Night I Invented 3D printing," *CNN Business*, February 14, 2014, http://www.cnn.com/2014/02/13/tech/innovation/the-night-i-invented-3d-printing-chuck-hall.

10. Lyndsey Gilpin, "10 Industries 3D Printing Will Disrupt or Decimate," TechRepublic, February 12, 2014, https://www.techrepublic.com/article/10-industries-3d-printing-will-disrupt-or-decimate.

11. Michael Molitch-Hou, "3D Printers Now a 'Good Thing' Declares Martha Stewart," 3DPrinting Industry, January 13, 2014, https://3dprintingindustry.com/news/3d-printers-now-good-thing-declares-martha-stewart-22238.

12. John Patrick Pullen, "What 3-D Printing Could Mean for Small Businesses," *Entrepreneur*, March 14, 2013, https://www.entrepreneur.com/article/225446.

13. Laura Griffiths, "Volvo Trucks Cuts Production Times by 94% with Stratasys 3D Printing," *tct Mag*, March 20, 2015, https://www.tctmagazine.com/3d-printing-news/volvo-trucks-cuts-production-times-by-94-percent-stratasys-3d-printing.

14. Tomas Kellner, "An Epiphany of Disruption: GE Additive Chief Explains How 3D Printing Will Upend Manufacturing," *GE Reports*, November 13, 2017, https://www.ge.com/reports/epiphany-disruption-ge-additive-chief-explains-3d-printing-will-upend-manufacturing.

15. Max Gicklhorn, "Lace Up! 3D Printed Shoes: An Overview," All3DP, August 3, 2017, https://all3dp.com/3d-printed-shoes.

16. Clare Scott, "Is Egypt Ready for 3D Printed Fashion? Designer Sara Hegazy Hopes So," 3DPRINT.COM, August 5, 2016, https://3dprint.com/145046/egypt-3d-printed-fashion.

17. Sneha Jha, "Hero Moto Corp Powers Ahead with 3D Printing," ETCIO.com, February 18, 2015, https://cio.economictimes.indiatimes.com/news/case-studies/hero-motocorp-powers-ahead-with-3d-printing/45599691.

18. Nick Statt, "iPhone Manufacturer Foxconn Plans to Replace Almost Every Human Worker with Robots," *The Verge*, December 30, 2016, https://www.theverge.com/2016/12/30/14128870/foxconn-robots-automation-apple-iphone-china-manufacturing.

19. PricewaterhouseCoopers, "3D Printing Comes of Age in US Industrial Manufacturing," https://www.pwc.com/us/en/industries/industrial-products/library/3d-printing-comes-of-age.html, accessed March 14, 2019.

20. Jörg Bomberger and Richard Kelly, "Additive Manufacturing: A Long-Term Game Changer for Manufacturers," McKinsey.com, September 2017, https://www.mckinsey.com/business-functions/operations/our-insights/additive-manufacturing-a-long-term-game-changer-for-manufacturers.

21. Sam Jones, "When Disaster Strikes, It's Time to Fly in the 3D printers, *The Guardian*, December 30, 2015, https://www.theguardian.com/global-development/2015/dec/30/disaster-emergency-3d-printing-humanitarian-relief-nepal-earthquake.

22. AFP, "Myanmar Farmers Reap Rewards from 3D Printing," December 25, 2015, http://guardian.ng/technology/myanmar-farmers-reap-rewards-from-3d-printing.

23. Leah Bell, "Aftermarket Spare Parts and 3d Printing: Is the Technology Worth

the Investment?," *Syncron*, March 8, 2018, https://www.syncron.com/aftermarket-spare-parts-and-3d-printing-is-the-technology-worth-the-investment.

24. Kellner, "Epiphany of Disruption."

25. Lance Ulanoff, "World's First 3D Printed Car Took Years to Design, But Only 44 Hours to Print," *Mashable*, September 16, 2014, https://mashable.com/2014/09/16/first-3d-printed-car.

26. "Why Aviation Companies Are Finding Promise in 3D Printing," *The Atlantic*, October 2, 2014, https://www.theatlantic.com/live/articles/2014/10/3d-printing/380573.

27. Cristina Constantinescu, Aaditya Mattoo, and Michele Ruta, "The Global Trade Slowdown: Cyclical or Structural?" IMF Working Paper 15/6, 2015, https://www.imf.org/external/pubs/ft/wp/2015/wp1506.pdf.

28. See Paolo Del Nibletto, "Nike Teams Up with HP to 3D Print Shoes for the NFL," *itbusiness.ca*, November 22, 2017, https://www.itbusiness.ca/news/nike-teams-up-with-hp-to-3d-print-shoes-for-the-nfl/96745; and Andra Cheng, "Foot Locker Gets Back to Center of Sneaker Culture by Focusing on More Than Shoe," *Forbes*, March 29, 2019, https://www.forbes.com/sites/andriacheng/2019/03/29/how-foot-locker-plans-to-stay-at-the-center-of-sneaker-culture/#5289e28f283d.

29. Pricewaterhouse Coopers, "2015 Commercial Transportation Trends."

30. ING, "3D Printing: A Threat to Global Trade," September 2017, https://www.ingwb.com/media/2088633/3d-printing-report-031017.pdf.

31. See, for example, Michael Kassner, "3D Printing Security Risks Threaten the Public's Health and Safety," *TechRepublic*, August 25, 2017, https://www.techrepublic.com/article/3d-printing-security-risks-threaten-the-publics-health-and-safety.

32. Bridget Butler O'Neal, "Partially 3D Printed Adidas Futurecraft 4D Shoes Launch Commercially This Week in NYC," 3Dprint.com, January 15, 2018, https://3dprint.com/200338/adidas-futurecraft-4d-launch. See also Andria Chen, "How Adidas Plans to Bring 3D Printing to the Masses," *Forbes*, May 22, 2018, https://www.forbes.com/sites/andriacheng/2018/05/22/with-adidas-3d-printing-may-finally-see-its-mass-retail-potential.

33. Marc Bain, "Nike Has 3D-Printed a Stretchy, Water-Expelling, Customizable Sneaker," *New Dimensions*, April 16, 2018, https://qz.com/quartzy/1254503/nike-just-debuted-flyprint-a-3d-printed-stretchy-customizable-sneaker-upper.

34. Eric Lai, "Chanel Announces Plan to Mass-Produce a 3D Printed Mascara Brush," 3DPrinting Industry, March 20, 2018, https://3dprintingindustry.com/news/chanel-announces-plan-mass-produce-3d-printed-mascara-brush-130715.

35. David Rotman, "The 3-D Printer That Could Finally Change Manufacturing," *MIT Technology Review*, April 25, 2017, https://www.technologyreview.com/s/604088/the-3-d-printer-that-could-finally-change-manufacturing.

36. Ivana Kottasová, "Volkswagen Will Use 3D Printers to Mass Produce Parts," *CNN Business*, September 28, 2018, https://www.cnn.com/2018/09/28/tech/volkswagen-3d-printing-parts/index.html.

37. Aarian Marshall, "GM's 3-D-Printed Seat Bracket Heralds a Future of Cheaper,

Better Cars," *Wired*, August 22, 2018, https://www.wired.com/story/general-motors-auto-industry-3d-printing-additive-manufacturing.

38. Daniel Ren, "Can You 3D-Print a Car? This Company Will Mass Print Cars by 2019 for US$10,000 Each," *South China Morning Post*, March 19, 2018, https://www.scmp.com/business/companies/article/2137737/worlds-first-mass-produced-3d-printed-electric-car-be-sold-china.

39. Trefor Moss, "China's Giant Market for Really Tiny Cars," *Wall Street Journal*, September 21, 2018, https://www.wsj.com/articles/chinas-giant-market-for-tiny-cars-1537538585.

40. Maximilian Holland, "China EV Forecast: 50% EV Market Share by 2025," *Clean Technica*, February 24, 2019, https://cleantechnica.com/2019/02/24/china-ev-forecast-50-ev-market-share-by-2025-part-1.

41. See, for example, Beth McKenna, "4 Facts You Probably Didn't Know About Stratasys (or Its Stock)," *The Motley Fool*, June 13, 2017, https://www.fool.com/investing/2017/06/13/4-facts-you-probably-didnt-know-about-stratasys-or.aspx.

42. Panos Mourdoukoutas, "The U.S.-China Trade War Could Give 3D Printing a Second Chance," *Forbes*, September 9, 2018, https://www.forbes.com/sites/panosmourdoukoutas/2018/09/09/the-us-china-trade-war-could-give-3d-printing-a-second-chance.

43. Bromberger and Kelly, "Additive Manufacturing."

44. Marshall, "GM's 3-D-Printed Seat Bracket."

45. Deloitte, "Made to Order: The Era of Mass-Personalisation," https://www2.deloitte.com/content/dam/Deloitte/ch/Documents/consumer-business/ch-en-consumer-business-made-to-order-consumer-review.pdf (accessed March 14, 2019).

46. Elizabeth Spaulding and Christopher Perry, "Making It Personal: Rules for Success in Product Customization," Bain & Company, September 16, 2013, https://www.bain.com/insights/making-it-personal-rules-for-success-in-product-customization.

47. Paul Brody and Veena Pureswaran, "The New Software-Defined Supply Chain," IBM Global Business Services, July 2013, https://www-935.ibm.com/services/multimedia/The_new_software-defined_supply_chain_Exec_Report.pdf.

48. Giles Kirkland, "Mini Yours Customized: The Next Step in Car Customization," *Fabbaloo*, July 3, 2018, https://www.fabbaloo.com/blog/2018/7/3/mini-yours-customized-the-next-step-in-car-customization.

49. Ali Morris, "Good Design for a Bad World," Dezeen.com, December 4, 2017, https://www.dezeen.com/2017/12/04/dutch-designers-eric-klarenbeek-maartje-dros-convert-algae-biopolymer-3d-printing-good-design-bad-world.

50. "Green Generation: Millennials Say Sustainability Is a Shopping Priority," Nielsen, November 5, 2015, https://www.nielsen.com/us/en/insights/news/2015/green-generation-millennials-say-sustainability-is-a-shopping-priority.html.

51. "This Reusable Straw Company Went from Zero to $5 Million in Less Than a Year. Next Up: Surviving the Growing Pains," *Inc.com*, April 18, 2019, https://www.inc.com/brit-morse/finalstraw-reusable-collapsible-drinking-straw-sustainable-shark-tank-30-under-30-2019.html.

52. Joan Didion, *Where I Was From* (New York: Knopf, 2003).

53. Paul Krugman, *Geography and Trade* (Cambridge, MA: MIT Press, 1991).

54. J-F Arvis, Y. Duval, B. Shepherd, and C. Utoktham, "Trade Costs in the Developing World: 1995–2010," Policy Research Working Paper 6309, World Bank, 2013.

55. Gordon Hanson, "The Effects of Offshore Assembly on Industry Location: Evidence from U.S. Border Cities," in *The Effects of U.S. Trade Protection and Promotion Policies*, ed. Robert C. Feenstra (Chicago: University of Chicago Press, 1997).

56. Brody and Pureswaran, "The New Software-Defined Supply Chain."

57. See, for example, Zhen Chen, "Research on the Impact of 3D Printing on the International Supply Chain," *Advances in Materials Science and Engineering*, Volume 2016, Article ID 4173873, April 17, 2016, https://www.hindawi.com/journals/amse/2016/4173873/#B24.

58. A. Barz, T. Buer, and H.-D. Haasis, "Quantifying the Effects of Additive Manufacturing on Supply Networks by Means of a Facility Location-Allocation Model," Computational Logistics Working Paper, University of Bremen, Germany, 2015, http://www.cl.uni-bremen.de/files/buer/publikationen/Barz_Buer_Haasis_Working%20Paper_12_2105.pdf.

59. Ibid.

60. M. Angeles Villarreal, " U.S.-Mexico Economic Relations: Trends, Issues, and Implications," Congressional Research Service, March 27, 2018, https://fas.org/sgp/crs/row/RL32934.pdf.

61. Susanna Kim, "3.5 Million Manufacturing Jobs Are Coming. Are You Ready?" *GE Reports*, October 3, 2017, https://www.ge.com/reports/us-manufacturing-sector-really-needs-stay-competitive; "2018 Deloitte and The Manufacturing Institute Skills Gap and Future of Work Study," Deloitte and The Manufacturing Institute, 2018, https://www2.deloitte.com/us/en/pages/manufacturing/articles/future-of-manufacturing-skills-gap-study.html.

62. Bennett Greenberg, "Adam Smith's Pin Factory," blogspot.com, November 30, 2017, http://bennettgreenberg.blogspot.com/2013/08/adam-smith-and-pin-factory.html.

63. R. Lanz, S. Miroudot, and H. K. Hordas, "Trade in Tasks," OECD Trade Policy Working Papers, No. 117, OECD Publishing, 2011, http://www.oecd.org/site/tadicite/48707655.pdf.

64. David Bailey, Carlo Corradini, and Lisa De Propris, "'Home-Sourcing' and Closer Value Chains in Mature Economies: The Case of Spanish Manufacturing," *Cambridge Journal of Economics* 42, no. 6 (November 2018): 1567–1584.

65. Author's analysis on the basis of UNCTAD data on services.

66. Joanna Wyszkowska-Kuna, "The Growing Importance of Knowledge-Intensive Business Services in International Trade," *Studia Ekonomiczne* 266 (2016): 249–260, http://cejsh.icm.edu.pl/cejsh/element/bwmeta1.element.cejsh-b5ef4b1d-bf36-465a-8a6f-d3008f8556cd.

67. Freshworks, "About Us," https://www.freshworks.com/company/about/?utm_source=freshdesk&utm_medium=referral&utm_campaign=fdesk_footer_

main&_ga=2.144160245.1570727800.1519450234–1706444160.1519450234&_gac=1.250325876.1519450234.CjwKCAiAlL_UBRBoEiwAXKgW55lbyAOZqGrO3fa-bLTkMnVSRTrziwtA41gt4AK9mijCtPaZLpub37BoC390QAvD_BwE (accessed March 14, 2019).

68. Matthew Miller, "Samba Tech Launches Kast, an Enterprise Mobile Video and Messaging Collaboration Tool," ZDNet, June 15, 2016, http://www.zdnet.com/article/samba-tech-launches-kast-an-enterprise-mobile-video-and-messaging-collaboration-tool.

69. From Kati Suominen, "Accelerating Digital Trade in Latin America and the Caribbean," Inter-American Development Bank Working Paper No. IDB-WP-790, March 2017, https://publications.iadb.org/publications/english/document/Accelerating-Digital-Trade-in-Latin-America-and-the-Caribbean.pdf.

70. Siliconreview Team, "10 Fastest Growing SAP Companies 2017," *The Silicon Review*, April 2017, http://thesiliconreview.com/magazines/10-fastest-growing-sap-companies-2017.

71. Taj Walton, "How Codigo Del Sur Became a Leading Mobile Development Agency on Upwork," Upwork Blog, August 28, 2015, https://www.upwork.com/blog/2015/08/codigo-del-sur-mobile-development-agency-upwork.

72. Ibid.

73. James Manyika, Susan Lund, and Kelsey Robinson, "Connecting Talent with Opportunity in the Digital Age," McKinsey&Company, June 2015, https://www.mckinsey.com/global-themes/employment-and-growth/connecting-talent-with-opportunity-in-the-digital-age.

74. Nicole Amaral, Nick Eng, Carlos Ospino, Carmen Pagés, Graciana Rucci, and Nate Williams, "How Far Can Your Skills Take You?" Inter-American Development Bank, August 2018, https://publications.iadb.org/bitstream/handle/11319/9089/Technical-Note-How-Far-Can-Your-Skills-Take-You.pdf?sequence=1&isAllowed=y.

CHAPTER 3

1. "Modern Spice Routes: The Cultural Impact and Economic Opportunity of Cross-Border Shopping," PayPal, 2014, https://www.paypalobjects.com/webstatic/mktg/2014design/paypalcorporate/PayPal_ModernSpiceRoutes_Report_Final.pdf.

2. Kati Suominen, "Silver Bullet to Fire Up Small Business Exports: Plurilateral Agreement on De Minimis," working paper, April 2017, https://katisuominen.files.wordpress.com/2017/04/de-minimis-plurilateral-suominen-april-2017.pdf.

3. Kati Suominen and Reena Gordon, *Going Global: Promoting the Internationalization of Small and Mid-Size Enterprises in Latin America and the Caribbean* (Washington, DC: Inter-American Development Bank, March 2014).

4. Andrew Bernard, "Firms in International Trade," *Journal of Economic Perspectives* (April 2007): 105–130.

5. Suominen and Gordon, *Going Global*.

6. Elhanan Helpman, Marc J. Melitz, and Stephen R. Yeaple, "Export Versus FDI with Heterogeneous Firms," *The American Economic Review* 94 (March 2004).

7. Mark J. Melitz, "The Impact of Trade on Intra-Industry Reallocations and Aggregate Industry Productivity," *Econovember Metrica* 71 (November 2003): 1695–1725.

8. "Enabling Traders to Enter and Grow on the Global Stage," eBay, 2012, http://www.ebaymainstreet.com/sites/default/files/EBAY_US-Marketplace_FINAL.pdf.

9. A. Fernandes, C. Freund, and M. Pierola, "Exporter Behavior, Country Size and Stage of Development: Evidence from the Exporter Dynamics Database," *Journal of Development Economics* 119 (October 2015): 121–137.

10. Maggie Chen and Min Xu, "Online International Trade in China," background paper for the World Development Report, World Bank, Washington, DC, 2016.

11. Kati Suominen, "Expanding Developing Country Small Businesses' ' Use of Platforms for Trade," report for U.S. Agency for International Development, June 2018 https://pdf.usaid.gov/pdf_docs/PA00TM8V.pdf

12. Kati Suominen, "Ecommerce Development Index," report for the U.S. Agency for International Development, April 2017, https://pdf.usaid.gov/pdf_docs/PA00MP8T.pdf.

13. Kati Suominen, "Accelerating Digital Trade in Latin America and the Caribbean," Inter-American Development Bank Working Paper No. IDB-WP-790, March 2017, https://publications.iadb.org/publications/english/document/Accelerating-Digital-Trade-in-Latin-America-and-the-Caribbean.pdf.

14. Paul Zwillenberg, Dominic Field, and David Dean, "Greasing the Wheels of the Internet Economy," Boston Consulting Group, January 20, 2014, https://www.bcg.com/en-us/publications/2014/technology-industries-public-sector-greasing-wheels-internet-economy.aspx.

15. Paul Resnick, Richard Zeckhauser, John Swanson, and Kate Lockwood, "The Value of Reputation on eBay: A Controlled Experiment," *Experimental Economics* 9, no. 2 (2006): 79–101.

16. Christopher P. Adams, Laura Hosken, and Peter Newberry, "'Vettes and Lemons on EBay," February 2006. Available at SSRN: http://ssrn.com/abstract=880780.

17. James E. Rauch and Vitor Trindade, "Ethnic Chinese Networks in International Trade," *The Review of Economics and Statistics* 84 (February 2002): 116–130.

18. Andreas Lendle and Pierre-Louis Vézina, "Internet Technology and the Extensive Margin of Trade: Evidence from eBay in Emerging Economies," *Review of Development Economics* 19, no. 2 (May 2015).

19. Andrew B. Bernard and Joachim Wagner, "Exports and Success in German Manufacturing," *Weltwirtschaftliches Archiv / Review of World Economics* (1997–2014): 133–157.

20. Alberto E. Isgut, "What's Different About Exporters? Evidence from Colombian Manufacturing," *Journal of Development Studies* 37 (2001): 57–82.

21. For Italy: D. Castellani, "Export Behaviour and Productivity Growth: Evidence from Italian Manufacturing Firms," *Weltwirtschaftliches Archiv* 138 (2002): 605–628; for China: A. Kraay, "Exports and Economic Performance: Evidence from a Panel of Chinese Enterprises," *Mimeo World Bank*, Washington DC, 1999; for Canada: J. B. Baldwin

and W. Gu, "Trade Liberalization: Export-Market Participation, Productivity Growth, and Innovation," *Oxford Review of Economic Policy* 20, no. 3 (2004): 372–392.

22. U.S. International Trade Commission, "Small and Medium-Sized Enterprises: Characteristics and Performance," Investigation No. 332-510, Publication 4189, 2012, https://www.usitc.gov/publications/332/pub4189.pdf.

23. Suominen and Reena Gordon, *Going Global*.

24. Eric Maurin, David Thesmar, and Mathias Thoenig, "Globalization and the Demand for Skill: An Export-Based Channel." *Mimeo*, CERAS-ENPC, 2002.

25. M. V. Jones and D. Crick, "Internationalizing High-Technology Based UK Companies' Information-Gathering Activities," *Journal of Small Business and Enterprise Development* 11, no. 1 (2004): 89–94. R&D for Canadian companies is 10 percent higher after they start exporting than it is for non-exporters. See Baldwin and Gu, "Trade Liberalization."

26. Zwillenberg, Field, and Dean, "Greasing the Wheels of the Internet Economy."

27. Nina Pavcnik, "Trade Liberalization, Exit, and Productivity Improvements: Evidence from Chilean Plants," *Review of Economic Studies* 69 (2002): 245–276.

28. Kati Suominen, "Fueling Digital Trade in Mercosur: A Regulatory Roadmap," Policy report for the Inter-American Development Bank, October 2018, https://publications.iadb.org/en/publication/13102/fueling-digital-trade-mercosur-regulatory-roadmap.

29. "World Development Report 2016: Digital Dividends," World Bank, May 17, 2016, http://www.worldbank.org/en/publication/wdr2016.

30. Louis F. Del Duca, Colin Rule, and Kathryn Rimpf, "eBay's De Facto Low Value High Volume Resolution Process: Lessons and Best Practices for ODR Systems Designers," *Arbitration Law Review* 10 (2014), https://elibrary.law.psu.edu/cgi/viewcontent.cgi?article=1060&context=arbitrationlawreview.

31. For Concilianet website, see https://concilianet.profeco.gob.mx/Concilianet/faq.jsp; for participating companies, see https://concilianet.profeco.gob.mx/Concilianet/archivos/ProveedoresParticipantes.pdf.

32. "Chinese 'Cyber-Court' Launched for Online Cases," *BBC News*, August 18, 2017.

33. Chris Biggs and others, "What China Reveals About the Future of Shopping," Boston Consulting Group, May 4, 2017, https://www.bcg.com/en-us/publications/2017/retail-globalization-china-reveals-future-shopping.aspx.

34. Jon Russell, "FinAccel Takes on Southeast Asia's Lending Industry with Easy Online Credit Service," TechCrunch (June 2, 2016).

35. Anahi Acevedo, "A traves de una alianza con Correo Uruguayo, Mercado Libre lanzo Mercado Envios," *Cronicas*, May 11, 2018, http://www.cronicas.com.uy/empresas-negocios/traves-una-alianza-correo-uruguayo-mercado-libre-lanzo-mercado-envios.

36. Ibid.

37. Neel Patel, presentation at vTex Day, São Paulo, May 30–31, 2017.

38. Daniel Palmer, "Alibaba Turns to Blockchain in Fight Against Food Fraud,"

Coindesk, March 24, 2017, www.coindesk.com/alibaba-pwc-partner-to-fight-food-fraud-with-blockchain.

39. Echo Huang, "Blockchain Could Fix a Key Problem in China's Food Industry: The Fear of Food Made in China," *Quartz*, August 10, 2017, https://qz.com/1031861/blockchain-could-fix-a-key-problem-in-chinas-food-industry-the-fear-of-food-made-in-china.

40. Wolfie Zhao, "Alibaba's T-Mall Is Moving Cross-Border E-Commerce to Block-chain," *Coindesk*, March 1, 2018, www.coindesk.com/alibabas-t-mall-moving-cross-border-e-commerce-blockchain.

41. Sagar Tamang, "Will 5G Truly Transform Our Lives?" *Enterprise Innovation* (August 24, 2017).

42. Joco Bogage, "Etsy Is Growing Up. Here's Why It Needs Congress's Help," *Washington Post*, July 31, 2015, https://www.washingtonpost.com/business/economy/etsy-is-growing-up-heres-why-it-needs-congresss-help/2015/07/31/d1f20e8a-3469-11e5-8e66-07b4603ec92a_story.html?utm_term=.9cf9c4f4b594.

43. KPMG, "Impact of E-Commerce on Employment in India," 2016, https://assets.kpmg/content/dam/kpmg/in/pdf/2016/12/impact-of-ecommerce-on-employment-in-india.pdf.

44. PTI, New Delhi, "E-retail, Allied Sectors to Create 1.45 Million Jobs by 2021 in India: Report," *The Indian Express*, December 6, 2016.

45. "E-Commerce Boosts Inclusive Labor Markets," World Bank Group, March 18, 2016.

46. Michael Mandel, "How E-Commerce Is Raising Pay and Creating Jobs Around the Country," *Forbes*, April 3, 2017, https://www.forbes.com/sites/realspin/2017/04/03/how-e-commerce-is-raising-pay-and-creating-jobs-around-the-country.

47. Mauricio Mesquita Moreira, Juan S. Blyde, Christian Volpe Martincus, and Danielken Molina, "Too Far to Export: Domestic Transport Costs and Regional Export Disparities in Latin America and the Caribbean," Inter-American Development Bank, October 2013, https://publications.iadb.org/en/publication/17434/too-far-export-domestic-transport-costs-and-regional-export-disparities-latin.

48. Richard Morrison, "Where Have All the Startups Gone? New Research from eBay and EIG," Competitive Enterprise Institute, January 19, 2017.

49. See Etsy, "Crafting the Future of Work: The Big Impact of Microbusinesses," 2017 Seller Census Report, https://extfiles.etsy.com/advocacy/Etsy_US_2017_Seller-Census.pdf (accessed March 14, 2019).

50. "Freelancing in America: 2016," Upwork and Freelancer's Union commissioned study conducted by Edelman Intelligence, October 2016.

51. Ebay,"Platform-Enabled Small Business and the Geography of Recovery," Report by eBay, January 2017.

52. Hanne Melin Olbe, "How Online Commerce Can Help Fight Inequality," World Economic Forum, January 19, 2018, https://www.weforum.org/agenda/2018/01/ebay-ecommerce-fight-inequality-hanne-melin.

53. "Advantage India," India Brand Equity Foundation, ibef.org, December 2017, https://www.ibef.org/download/Ecommerce-December-20171.pdf.

54. Burundi Internet General Applications Network, "Use of the Internet in Burundi," unpublished 2010 survey cited in "Contribution by Burundi to the Intergovernmental Group of Experts on E-Commerce and the Digital Economy: First Session," Geneva, October 4–6, 2017, https://unctad.org/meetings/en/Contribution/tdb_ede2017c18_Burundi_en.pdf.

55. Frank Newport, "Americans Big on Idea of Living in the Country," *Gallup*, December 7, 2018, https://news.gallup.com/poll/245249/americans-big-idea-living-country.aspx.

56. "Inside Upwork: A Day in the Life of a Digital Nomad," Upwork Blog, https://www.upwork.com/blog/2016/12/inside-upwork-digital-nomad.

57. P. Mahasuweerachai, B. E. Whitacre, and D. W. Shideler, "Does Broadband Access Impact Migration in America? Examining Differences Between Rural and Urban Areas," *Review of Regional Studies* 40, no. 1 (2010): 5–26. Granted, digital connectivity in remote rural areas creates Internet-based external competition for local entrepreneurs—but such competition is positive for consumers of e-services. See D. Cumming and S. Johan, "The Differential Impact of the Internet on Spurring Regional Entrepreneurship," *Entrepreneurship Theory and Practice*, 34, no. 5 (2010): 857–883.

58. Younjun Kim and Peter F. Orazem, "Broadband Internet and New Firm Location Decisions in Rural Areas," University of Nebraska-Lincoln, College of Business, January 2016, https://business.unl.edu/outreach/bureau-of-business-research/academic-research/documents/kim/broadband.pdf.

59. Kati Suominen, "Women-Led Firms on the Web: Challenges and Solutions," International Centre for Trade and Sustainable Development, October 30, 2018, https://www.ictsd.org/themes/development-and-ldcs/research/women-led-firms-on-the-web-challenges-and-solutions.

60. Khalid Sekkat, Ariane Szafarz, and Ilan Tojerow, "Women at the Top in Developing Countries: Evidence from Firm-Level Data," Institute for the Study of Labor (IZA), Bonn Germany, Discussion Paper No. 9537, November 2015, http://ftp.iza.org/dp9537.pdf.

61. Willem Adema and others, "Enhancing Women's Economic Empowerment Through Entrepreneurship and Business Leadership in OECD Countries," Organisation for Economic Co-operation and Development, 2014, http://www.oecd.org/gender/Enhancing%20Women%20Economic%20Empowerment_Fin_1_Oct_2014.pdf.

62. Gabriela Ramos, "Empowering Women in the Digital Age: Where Do We Stand?" OECD, sixty-second session of the UN Commission on the Status of Women, March 14, 2018, https://www.oecd.org/social/empowering-women-in-the-digital-age-brochure.pdf.

63. Alisa DiCaprio and Kati Suominen, "Aid for Trade in Asia and the Pacific: Thinking Forward About Trade Costs and the Digital Economy," report for the Asian Development Bank for the Global Aid for Trade Review, July 2015.

64. See "World Development Report 2016: Digital Dividends," World Bank, May 17, 2016, http://www.worldbank.org/en/publication/wdr2016.

65. "eBay-Style Online Courts Could Resolve Smaller Claims," *BBC News*, February 16, 2015.

CHAPTER 4

1. "Ericsson Mobility Report: 70 Percent of World's Population Using Smartphones by 2020," Ericsson, June 3, 2015.

2. "Digital 2019: Global Digital Overview," *Datareportal*, January 31, 2019, https://datareportal.com/reports/digital-2019-global-digital-overview.

3. "E-commerce Share of Total Retail Sales in China from 2014 to 2019," Statista, December 2015.

4. eMarketer, "Worldwide Retail Ecommerce Sales Will Reach $1.915 Trillion This Year," August 22, 2016, https://www.emarketer.com/Article/Worldwide-Retail-Ecommerce-Sales-Will-Reach-1915-Trillion-This-Year/1014369.

5. Sarah Steimer, "Baby Boomer Women Remain Invisible to Marketers," *Marketing News*, September 28, 2016.

6. Pamela Lockard, "Facts About Boomer Women and E-commerce," DMN3, May 27, 2015.

7. Ethan Leiber and Chad Syverson, "Online vs. Offline Competition," *Oxford Handbook of the Digital Economy*, July 2010, https://www3.nd.edu/~elieber/research/online_offline.pdf.

8. Louis Columbus, "10 Charts That Will Change Your Perspective of Amazon Prime's Growth," *Forbes*, March 4, 2018, https://www.forbes.com/sites/louiscolumbus/2018/03/04/10-charts-that-will-change-your-perspective-of-amazon-primes-growth/#9f98e6e3feea.

9. Richard Dobbs and others, "Urban World: The Global Consumers to Watch," McKinsey Global Institute, March 2016.

10. Ibid.

11. Youchi Kuo and others, "The New China Playbook," Boston Consulting Group, December 21, 2015, https://www.bcg.com/en-us/publications/2015/globalization-growth-new-china-playbook-young-affluent-e-savvy-consumers.aspx.

12. "E-Commerce Revolution or Revolution in the Fast-Moving Consumer Goods World?" The Nielsen Company, August 2014.

13. "Delhi Retains Its Position as India's No. 1 eCommerce Hub: eBay Census 2012," Delhi eBay, March 20, 2013.

14. Dominique Fong, "Rich, Young Chinese Are Buying Overseas Properties on Their Smartphones," *The Wall Street Journal*, May 9, 2017.

15. "Mobile Web Has Now Overtaken PC in 40 Nations, Including India, Nigeria and Bangladesh," *mobiForge*, October 24, 2014, https://internet.com/internet-news/mobile-web-has-now-overtaken-pc-in-40-nations-including-india-nigeria-and-bangladesh.

16. "Do People Use the Internet for Personal Purposes?" *The Connected Consumer*

Survey 2017, Google Consumer Barometer, https://www.consumerbarometer.com/en/graph-builder.

17. Ibid.

18. James Manyika and others, "Lions Go Digital: The Internet's Transformative Potential in Africa," McKinsey Global Institute, November 2013.

19. "Do People Use the Internet for Personal Purposes?"

20. Brahima Sanou, "ICT Facts and Figures 2016," International Telecommunication Union, June 2016, https://www.itu.int/en/itu-d/statistics/documents/facts/ictfacts-figures2016.pdf.

21. Varsha Bansal, "Flipkart Mobile App Reaches 100 Million Downloads Milestone," ET Bureau, October 31, 2017.

22. Aish Tycoons, "Future of eCommerce in Pakistan," March 16, 2017, http://www.aishtycoons.com/future-of-ecommerce-in-pakistan.

23. "Welcome to Shopee, the Leading Online Shopping Platform in Southeast Asia and Taiwan," https://www.shopee.com.

24. Eurostat, "Internet Users Who Bought or Ordered Goods or Services for Private Use Over the Internet in the Previous 12 Months, EU-28, 2015 (% of Internet Users)," December 2015.

25. Girish Pun, "Effect of Consumer Beliefs on Online Purchase Behavior: The Influence of Demographic Characteristics and Consumption Values," *Journal of Interactive Marketing* 25 (2011): 134–144.

26. Nimisha Jain and Kanika Sanghi, "The Rising Connected Consumer in Rural India," Boston Consulting Group, August 10, 2016.

27. James Medaglio, "Womeconomics: The Global Female Consumer," *U.S. Trust*, Research Analyst, May 12, 2015.

28. "Women: The Next Emerging Market Supporting Women to Fulfill Their Potential," Ernst & Young, 2013, http://www.ey.com/Publication/vwLUAssets/EY_Women_-_The_next_emerging_market/$FILE/EY_Women_the_next_emerging_market.pdf.

29. Kelsey Snyder and Pashmeena Hilal, "The Changing Face of B2B Marketing," Think with Google, March 2015, https://www.thinkwithgoogle.com/articles/the-changing-face-b2b-marketing.html.

30. Sebastian Anthony, "The Humble SIM Card Has Finally Been Hacked: Billions of Phones at Risk of Data Theft, Premium Rate Scams," *Extreme Tech*, July 22, 2013.

31. Saher Asad, "The Crop Connection: Impact of Cell Phone Access on Crop Choice in Rural Pakistan," *Job Market Paper*, March 16, 2016.

32. A report for the GSM Association, "What Is the Impact of Mobile Telephony on Economic Growth?" Creative studio at Deloitte, November 2012.

33. "Women: The Next Emerging Market."

34. "World Development Report 2016: Digital Dividends," World Bank, May 17, 2016, http://pubdocs.worldbank.org/en/165711456838073531/WDR16-BP-Estonian-eGov-ecosystem-Vassil.pdf.

35. Austan Goolsbee and Peter J. Klenow, "Valuing Consumer Products by the Time Spent Using Them: An Application to the Internet," *The Roots of Innovation* 96, no. 2 (2006).

36. O. Nottebohm, J. Manyika, J. Bughin, M. Chui, and A-R. Syed, "Online and Up-coming: The Internet's Impact on Aspiring Countries," *McKinsey & Company, High Tech Practice* (January 2012).

37. Erik Brynjolfsson, Yu (Jeffrey) Hu, and Michael D. Smith, "Consumer Surplus in the Digital Economy: Estimating the Value of Increased Product Variety at Online Booksellers," *Management Science INFORMS* 49, No.11 (November, 2003): 1580–1596.

38. Chuck Martin, "Mobile Millennials: 63% Shop on Smartphones Every Day, 53% Buy in Stores by Chuck Martin," *MediaPost*, August 17, 2016, https://www.mediapost.com/publications/article/282639/mobile-millennials-63-shop-on-smartphones-every.html.

39. Stephanie Lee, "Quantifying the Consumer Surplus from Smartphones," October 19, 2018. Available at SSRN: https://ssrn.com/abstract=3270047 or http://dx.doi.org/10.2139/ssrn.3270047.

40. Katrine Ellersgaard Nielsen, Bruno Basalisco, and Martin H. Thelle, "The Impact of Online Intermediaries on the EU Economy," report prepared for EdiMA, April 2013.

41. Min Jung Kim, "A Thesis Submitted to the Faculty of the Graduate School of the University of Minnesota," *Essays on the Economics of the Smartphone and Application Industry*, September 2013.

42. David Riker, "Internet Use and Openness to Trade," US International Trade Commission Working Paper 2014-12C, December2014, https://www.usitc.gov/publications/332/ec201412c.pdf.

43. "Do People Use the Internet for Personal Purposes?"

44. IPSOS, "PayPal Cross-Border Consumer Research 2015," Paypal Inc., 2015.

45. "Do People Use the Internet for Personal Purposes?"

46. "The Zettabyte Era—Trends and Analysis," Cisco, June 23, 2015, http://www.cisco.com/c/en/us/solutions/collateral/service-provider/visual-networking-index-vni/VNI_Hyperconnectivity_WP.html.

47. "The Relationship Between Local Content, Internet Development and Access Prices: Main Findings and Conclusions," Internet Society (ISOC), the Organisation for Economic Co-operation and Development, and the United Nations Educational, Scientific and Cultural Organization, https://www.oecd.org/internet/ieconomy/50305352.pdf (accessed May 12, 2019).

48. Jeff John Roberts, "Netflix Streams Its Way to Another Blockbuster Quarter, Share Price Soars," *Fortune*, July 15, 2015, http://fortune.com/2015/07/15/netflix-q2-earnings-2015.

49. Rani Molla, "Netflix Makes Up Nearly 30 Percent of Global Streaming Video Subscriptions," *recode*, April 16, 2019, https://www.recode.net/2019/4/16/18410556/netflix-30-percent-global-streaming-video-subscriptions-q1-2019.

50. Chen Zhenghao and others, "Who's Benefiting from MOOCs, and Why," *Harvard Business Review*, September 22, 2015, https://hbr.org/2015/09/whos-benefiting-from-moocs-and-why.

51. Adi Robertson, "Can Online Classrooms Help the Developing World Catch

Up?" *The Verge*, 2015, https://www.theverge.com/2015/2/11/8014563/bill-gates-education-future-of-online-courses-third-world.

52. "How Smartphones Are Transforming Healthcare," *Financial Times*, January 12, 2017, https://www.ft.com/content/1efb95ba-d852-11e6-944b-e7eb37a6aa8e?mhq5j=e2.

53. Ben Kerschberg, "How Crowdsourcing Is Tracking Poverty in the Developing World," *Forbes*, March 21, 2012.

54. See U.S. Census Bureau, Schedule B 2019, https://www.census.gov/foreign-trade/schedules/b/2019/index.html.

55. Robert C. Feenstra and Alan M. Taylor, *Essentials of International Economics*, 2nd ed. (New York: Worth, 2010).

56. Tohmas Karlsson, "Imports, the Extensive Margin and Product Variety: Some Stylized Facts," preliminary draft, *EcoMod2011* 3003, 2011, https://ideas.repec.org/p/ekd/002625/3003.html.

57. Peter K. Schott, "The Relative Sophistication of Chinese Exports," NBER Working Paper No. 12173, April 2006, https://www.nber.org/papers/w12173.

58. Kati Suominen and Reena Gordon, *Going Global: Promoting the Internationalization of Small and Mid-Size Enterprises in Latin America and the Caribbean* (Washington, DC: Inter-American Development Bank, March 2014).

59. Paul Krugman, "Increasing Return, Monopolistics Competition, and International Trade," *Journal of International Economics* 9 (1979): 469–479 1979, http://econ.sciences-po.fr/sites/default/files/file/krugman-79.pdf.

60. Christian Broda and David E. Weinstein, "Globalization and the Gains from Variety," *The Quarterly Journal of Economics*, (May 2006).

61. Jingting Fan, Lixin Tang, Weiming Zhu, and Ben Zou, "The Alibaba Effect: Spatial Consumption Inequality and the Welfare Gains from e-Commerce," *Journal of International Economics* 114 (September 2018): 203–220.

62. Gillion Wong and Loretta Chao, "Alibaba, JD.com Target Rural China for E-Commerce Growth," *Wall Street Journal*, August 30, 2015.

63. See Victor Couture, Benjamin Faber, Yizhen Gu, and Lizhi Liu, "E-Commerce Integration and Economic Development: Evidence from China," July 2017, https://economics.mit.edu/files/14343.

CHAPTER 5

1. Federal Maritime Commission, "U.S. Container Port Congestion & Related International Supply Chain Issues: Causes, Consequences & Challenges," An overview of discussions at the FMC port forums, July 2015, https://www.supplychain247.com/paper/us_container_port_congestion_related_international_supply_chain_issues.

2. Federal Maritime Commission, "U.S. Container Port Congestion."

3. James E. Vance, "History of Ships," *Encyclopedia Britannica*, https://www.britannica.com/technology/ship/History-of-ships (accessed April 20, 2018).

4. Ibid.

5. "Suez Canal," *Wikipedia,* https://en.wikipedia.org/wiki/Suez_Canal (accessed March 2018).

6. Esteban Ortiz-Ospina, Diana Beltekian, and Max Roser , "Trade and Globalization," Our World in Data, https://ourworldindata.org/trade-and-globalization#the-two-waves-of-globalization (accessed May 12, 2019).

7. Jules Hugot and Camilo Umana Dajud, "Trade Costs and the Suez and Panama Canals," Centre d'Etudes Prospectives et d'Information Internationales Working Paper, December 29, 2016.

8. David Donaldson, "Railroads of the Raj: Estimating the Impact of Transportation Infrastructure," *American Economic Review* 108, no. 405 (April 2018).

9. Wolfgang Keller, Ben Li, and Carol H. Shiue, "China's Foreign Trade: Perspectives from the Past 150 Years," NBER Working Paper No. 16550, November 2010, https://www.nber.org/papers/w16550.

10. Gilles Duranton, Peter M. Morrow, and Mathew A. Turner, "Roads and Trade: Evidence from the US," *The Review of Economic Studies* 81, no. 2 (April 23, 2014): 681–724, http://dx.doi.org/10.1093/restud/rdt039.

11. Hugot and Umana Dajud, "Trade Costs and the Suez and Panama Canals."

12. Ibid.

13. "History of Containerization: The Birth of 'Intermodalis'," World Shipping Council, http://www.worldshipping.org/about-the-industry/history-of-containerization (accessed April 20, 2018).

14. "The Impact of Mega-Ships," International Transport Forum, Organisation of Economic Co-operation and Development, 2015, https://www.itf-oecd.org/sites/default/files/docs/15cspa_mega-ships.pdf.

15. Ibid.

16. "The Impact of Mega-Ships."

17. Ananthanarayan Sainarayan, "New Solutions in International Transport and Trade Facilitation," presentation at the UNCTAD E-Commerce Week, April 28, 2017.

18. Chris Barnett, "Boeing: Air Cargo to Expand in Mid-Single Digits Through 2020," *Journal of Commerce,* February 13, 2018, https://www.joc.com/air-cargo/international-air-freight/global-air-freight-demand-likely-remain-strong-2018_20180213.html.

19. See Mauricio Mesquita Moreira, Christian Volpe, and Juan S. Blyde, *Unclogging the Arteries: The Impact of Transport Costs on Latin American and Caribbean Trade* (Cambridge, MA: Harvard University Press, 2009).

20. Greg Knowler, "Evergreen joins Maersk, CMA CGM in Alibaba Direct Booking Deal," *Journal of Commerce,* June 22, 2017.

21. Patrick Berglund, "Alibaba, Maersk, & CMA CGM: A Game-Changer?" *Xeneta,* February 17, 2017.

22. Ralph Jennings, "China Is Developing Ships to Cover the Globe Without Captains," *Forbes,* March 14, 2018, https://www.forbes.com/sites/ralphjennings/2018/03/14/china-is-developing-a-fleet-of-high-tech-ships-with-no-captains/#3f1dd8bd49be.

23. Adam Minter, "Crewless Ships: Safer, Faster, Cleaner, Cheaper Future of Shipping," *Insurance Journal*, May 22, 2017.

24. Ibid.

25. Ibid.

26. "Asia Enters Fully Automated Terminal Era," *Port Technology*, May 15, 2017.

27. Ibid.

28. Bill Mongelluzzo, "LA-LB Terminal Automation a Necessity to Handle Growth," *Journal of Commerce*, May 17, 2016, https://www.joc.com/port-news/port-productivity/la-lb-terminal-automation-necessity-handle-growth_20160517.html.

29. Bruce Barnard, "Europe's Automated Terminals Face Steep Hurdles to Productivity Targets," *Journal of Commerce Port News*, February 4, 2016.

30. Sia-Partners, "The Internet of Things in Transportation: Port of Hamburg Case Study," *Sia Transport*, September 30, 2016.

31. "The Port of Hamburg Gives the Command to 'Cast Off' for the Blockchain," *Hannover Messe*, September 7, 2018, https://www.hannovermesse.de/en/news/the-port-of-hamburg-gives-the-command-to-cast-off-for-the-blockchain-97280.xhtml.

32. Hugh R. Morley, "FMC Proposes Privately Funded Portal to Fight Port Congestion," *Journal of Commerce Maritime News*, December 7, 2017.

33. Sjors Berns, Indra Vonck, Rob Dickson, and Jochem Dragt, "Smart Ports Point of View," Deloitte Port Services, 2017, https://www2.deloitte.com/content/dam/Deloitte/nl/Documents/energy-resources/deloitte-nl-er-port-services-smart-ports.pdf.

34. Gerardo Lazcano Arcos, "Gerardo Lazcano: "La Transformación Digital del Puerto de Valparaíso," *PortalPortuario*, March 23, 2018, https://portalportuario.cl/gerardo-lazcano-la-transformacion-digital-del-puerto-de-valparaiso.

35. "Solving a Data Dilemma, Container Management," Tideworks Technology, October 15, 2018, https://www.tideworks.com/solving-a-data-dilemma.

36. Gaël Raballand, "Why Expanding Africa's Port Infrastructure Is Just a Small Part of the Solution," *Brookings Future Development*, October 15, 2015.

37. Gaël Raballand, Salim Refas, Monica Beuran, and Gozde Isik, *Why Does Cargo Spend Weeks in Sub-Saharan African Ports? Lessons from Six Countries* (Washington, DC: World Bank, 2012).

38. Adam Robinson, "E-Commerce Logistics: The Evolution of Logistics and Supply Chains from Direct to Store Models to E-Commerce," *Cerasis* April 30, 2014.

39. Ethna Hunag, "E-Commerce Drives the Construction of "Mega Warehouses," *More Than Shipping*, February 8, 2017, https://www.morethanshipping.com/e-commerce-drives-the-construction-of-mega-warehouses.

40. Patricia Kirk, "Why Obsolete Warehouses on the 'Last Mile' Are Attracting Institutional Investors," *National Real Estate Investor*, July 21, 2017.

41. "Strategies to Reduce Logistics Costs in the CPG Supply Chain," a Kane Viewpoint, Kane Is Able, Inc., http://cdn2.hubspot.net/hub/396583/file-2128901519-pdf/docs_new/Strategies_to_Reduce_Logistics_Costs_in_the_CPG_Supply_Chain.pdf (accessed May 12, 2019).

42. James Breeze, "E-Commerce 2.0: Last-Mile Delivery and the Rise of the Urban Warehouse," *NAIOP Development Magazine*, Spring 2017.

43. Ibid.

44. Gary Wollenhaupt, "E-Commerce Reshaping Distribution Center Real Estate Strategies," *SDC Supply and Demand Chain Execution*, June 22, 2017.

45. Ibid.

46. Spencer Soper, "This Startup Is the Airbnb of Warehouses and Has Amazon in Its Sights," *Bloomberg News Technology*, May 11, 2017.

47. "Strategies to Reduce Logistics Cost."

48. Breeze, "E-Commerce 2.0."

49. Ibid.

50. Bill Mongelluzzo, "US Distribution and Warehouse Space Scarcer and Pricier," *Journal of Commerce International Logistics*, July 13, 2017.

51. Phil Wahba, "How E-Commerce Is Making Stores Relevant Again," *Fortune*, March 30, 2017.

52. Charles Brewer, "The Last Mile Goes High-Tech," *DHL Commerce*, February 27, 2017.

53. Luigi Ranieri, Salvatore Digiesi, Bartolomeo Silvestri, and Michele Roccotelli, "A Review of Last Mile Logistics Innovations in an Externalities Cost Reduction Vision," MDPI, March 12, 2018, *https://www.mdpi.com/2071-1050/10/3/782/pdf;* "The Last Mile: Finding the Right Workforce System for Urban Logistics," MHI blog, http://s354933259. onlinehome.us/mhi-blog/the-last-mile-finding-the-right-workforce-system-for-urban-logistics (accessed April 30, 2019).

54. C. Nockold, "Identifying the Real Costs of Home Delivery," *Logistics and Transport Focus* 3, no. 10 (2001): 70–71.

55. M. Punakivi and K. Tanskanen, "Increasing the Cost Efficiency of e-Fulfillment Using Shared Reception Boxes," *International Journal of Retail & Distribution Management* 30, no. 10 (2002): 498–507.

56. Payal Ganguly and Vansumita S. Adarsh, "As Rural India Splurges, Young Companies Step in to Connect the Last Mile," *ET Bureau*, November 8, 2014.

57. Eric Jaffe, "Has the Rise of Online Shopping Made Traffic Worse?" *City Lab*, August 2, 2013.

58. M. Jaller, J. Holguin-Veras, and S. Hodge, "Parking in the City: Challenges for Freight Traffic," *Transportation Research Record: Journal of the Transportation Research Board* 2379 (2013): 46–56.

59. "Why Good Movement Matters?" *Regional Plan Association*, June 2016.

60. Ibid.

61. Echo Huang, "In China, a Robot Has Started Delivering Packages to People," *Quartz*, June 19, 2017.

62. Alan Levin, "Amazon's Dream of Drone Deliveries Gets Closer with Trump's Executive Order," *Bloomberg Technology*, October 25, 2017.

63. Martin Joerss, Jürgen Schröder, Florian Neuhaus, Christoph Klink, and Florian Mann, "Parcel Delivery: The Future of Last Mile," McKinsey&Company, September

2016, https://www.mckinsey.com/~/media/mckinsey/industries/travel%20trans-port%20and%20ology/our%20insights/how%20customer%20demands%20are%20 reshaping%20last%20mile%20delivery/parcel_delivery_the_future_of_last_mile.ashx.

64. Sally French, "Drone Delivery Economics: Are Amazon Drones Economically Worth It?" The Drone Girl blog, May 7, 2017, https://thedronegirl.com/2017/05/07/drone-delivery-economics-amazon-drones.

65. John C. Panzar, "Co-Opetition in Parcel Delivery: An Exploratory Analysis," Office of Inspector General, United States Postal Service, RARC Report Number RARC-WP-16-002, November 2, 2015, https://www.uspsoig.gov/sites/default/files/document-library-files/2015/RARC-WP-16-002.pdf.

66. Diane Toomey, "Exploring How and Why Trees 'Talk' to Each Other," *YaleEnvironent360*, September 1, 2016, https://e360.yale.edu/features/exploring_how_and_why_trees_talk_to_each_other.

67. Peter Korsten and Christian Seider, "The World's 4 Trillion Dollar Challenge," IBM Global Business Services Executive Report, 2017, https://www.ibm.com/ibm/files/Y067208R89372O94/11The_worlds_4_trillion_dollar_challenge-Executive_Report_1_3MB.pdf.

68. David Dranove, Christopher Forman, Avi Goldfarb, and Shane Greenstein, "The Trillion Dollar Conundrum: Complementarities and Health Information Technology," NBER Working Paper No. 18281, issued in August 2012, revised in December 2012, http://www.nber.org/papers/w18281.

69. Korsten and Seider, "The World's 4 Trillion Dollar Challenge."

70. See Glen Williams, David Gunn, Eduardo Roma, and Bharat Bansal, "Distributed Ledgers in Payments: Beyond the Bitcoin Hype," Bain Brief, July 13, 2016, https://www.bain.com/insights/distributed-ledgers-in-payments-beyond-bitcoin-hype; and IMDA Singapore, "International Trade and Logistics," November 28, 2016, https://www.imda.gov.sg/industry-development/sectors/infocomm/logistics/international-trade-and-logistics.

71. Alisa DiCaprio, "Digital Trade Needs More Coordination, Leadership," *Asia Pathways*, May 1, 2017, https://www.asiapathways-adbi.org/2017/05/digital-trade-needs-more-coordination-leadership.

72. See, for example, "Maersk and IBM Unveil First Industry-Wide Cross-Border Supply Chain Solution on Blockchain," IBM, news release, March 5, 2017, https://www-03.ibm.com/press/us/en/pressrelease/51712.wss, and Holt Logistics Corp., "Holt Joins Maersk and IBM Global Shipping Platform to Boost Productivity at Packer Avenue Marine Terminal," *CISION*, April 18, 2018, https://www.prnewswire.com/news-releases/holt-joins-maersk-and-ibm-global-shipping-platform-to-boost-productivity-at-packer-avenue-marine-terminal-300632217.html.

73. "Standard-Gauge Railway," *Wikipedia*, https://en.wikipedia.org/wiki/Standard-gauge_railway (accessed February 1, 2017).

74. "Physical Internet: Concept, Research, Innovation," Georgia Tech Physical Internet Center, https://www.picenter.gatech.edu/node/506 (accessed March 15, 2019).

75. "Maersk and IBM Unveil First Industry-Wide Cross-Border Supply Chain Solu-

tion on Blockchain," IBM news release, March 5, 2017, https://www-03.ibm.com/press/us/en/pressrelease/51712.wss.

76. Wolfie Zhao, "Alibaba's T-Mall Is Moving Cross-Border E-Commerce to Blockchain," *coindesk*, March 1, 2018, https://www.coindesk.com/alibabas-t-mall-moving-cross-border-e-commerce-blockchain.

77. "Samsung Jumps on Blockchain Bandwagon to Manage Its Supply Chain," *Bloomberg*, April 18, 2018, https://www.mhlnews.com/transportation-distribution/samsung-jumps-blockchain-bandwagon-manage-its-supply-chain.

78. Ayako Yamaguchi, "Global Value Chains in ASEAN," newsletter, Institute for International Monetary Affairs, April 1, 2018, https://www.iima.or.jp/Docs/newsletter/2018/NL2018No_1_e.pdf.

79. Tim Alper, "From Thailand to Malaysia: Southeast Asian Governments Embracing Blockchain Technology," *Crypto Insider*, October 19, 2017, https://cryptoinsider.com/from-thailand-malaysia-southeast-asia-blockchain-technology.

CHAPTER 6

1. Ratnajyoti Dutta and Mayank Bhardwaj, "Exclusive: Iran Defaults on Rice Payments to India," Reuters, February 6, 2012, https://www.reuters.com/article/us-india-rice/exclusive-iran-defaults-on-rice-payments-to-india-idUSTRE8160CX20120207.

2. George A. Akerlof, "The Market for 'Lemons': Quality Uncertainty and the Market Mechanism," *The Quarterly Journal of Economics* 84, no. 3 (August 1970): 488–500, https://www.jstor.org/stable/1879431.

3. Ann Marie Wiersch and Scott Shane, "Why Small Business Lending Isn't What It Used to Be," Economic Commentary /Cleveland Federal Reserve, August 14, 2013, http://www.clevelandfed.org/research/commentary/2013/2013–10.cfm.

4. ICC Banking Commission, "Rethinking Trade & Finance: An ICC Private Sector Development Perspective," http://store.iccwbo.org/content/uploaded/pdf/ICC_Global_Trade_and_Finance_Survey_2016.pdf (accessed February 25, 2018).

5. "Thomson Reuters 2016 Know Your Customer Surveys Reveal Escalating Costs and Complexity," Thomson Reuters, May 9, 2016, https://www.thomsonreuters.com/en/press-releases/2016/may/thomson-reuters-2016-know-your-customer-surveys.html.

6. "$1.5 Trillion Trade Finance Gap Persists Despite Fintech Breakthroughs," Asian Development Bank, September 5, 2017, https://www.adb.org/news/15-trillion-trade-finance-gap-persists-despite-fintech-breakthroughs.

7. "2016 Trade Finance Gaps, Growth, and Jobs Survey," Asian Development Bank, August 2016, https://www.adb.org/sites/default/files/publication/190631/trade-finance-gaps.pdf.

8. See, for example, Flora Bellone, Patrick Mussoy, Lionel Nestaz, and Stefano Schiavox, "Financial Constraints and Firm Export Behaviour," *The World Economy* 33, no. 3 (2010): 347–373; and Joachim Wagner, "Credit Constraints and Exports: Evidence for German Manufacturing Enterprises," *Working Paper Series in Economics and Institutions of Innovation* 286, Royal Institute of Technology, Centre of Excellence for Science and Innovation Studies. See also Johannes Van Biesebroeck, "Productivity, Exporting

and Financial Constraints of Chinese SMEs," *Mimeo*, Inter-American Development Bank, December 2013.

9. Alisa Di Caprio, Steven Beck, Ying Yao, and Fahad Khan, "2016 Trade Finance Gaps, Growth, and Jobs Survey," *Asian Development Bank Briefs*, no. 64 (August 2016), https://www.adb.org/sites/default/files/publication/190631/trade-finance-gaps.pdf.

10. ICC Banking Commission, "Rethinking Trade & Finance: An ICC Private Sector Development Perspective," 2016, http://store.iccwbo.org/content/uploaded/pdf/ICC_Global_Trade_and_Finance_Survey_2016.pdf.

11. Alisa DiCaprio and Ying Yao, "Drivers of Trade Finance Gaps," Asian Development Bank Institute Working Paper Series No. 678, February 2017, https://www.adb.org/publications/drivers-trade-finance-gaps.

12. Tim Schmidt-Eisenlohr, "Towards a Theory of Trade Finance," *Journal of International Economics* 91, no. 1 (December 2011): 96–112. https://www.economics.ox.ac.uk/materials/papers/5488/paper583.pdf.

13. Ibid.

14. See for example, Mayra Rodriguez Valladares, "Banks Are More Profitable Than Ever But Risks Abound," November 15, 2018, https://www.forbes.com/sites/mayrarodriguezvalladares/2018/11/15/banks-are-more-profitable-than-ever-but-risks-abound/#51fd91717a9f.

15. "More Than $150 Billion in Revenue at Risk for Banks That Cannot Overcome Technical, Adoption Hurdles of Digital Currency," Bain & Company, July 15, 2016, http://www.bain.com/about/press/press-releases/150-billion-dollars-at-risk-for-banks-that-cannot-overcome-hurdles-of-digital-currency.aspx.

16. Alisa DiCaprio, "Digital Trade Needs More Coordination, Leadership," *Asia Pathways*, May 1, 2017, https://www.asiapathways-adbi.org/2017/05/digital-trade-needs-more-coordination-leadership.

17. Chanyaporn Chanjaroen and Darren Boey, "Fraud in $4 Trillion Trade Finance Turns Banks to Digital Ledger," LiveMint, May 23, 2016, http://www.livemint.com/Industry/CXfxl1yePlwTDuokXU3c2K/Fraud-in-4-trillion-trade-finance-turns-banks-to-digital-le.html.

18. Enda Curran, "Standard Bank Starts Legal Action Over Suspected Qingdao Port Fraud," *Wall Street Journal*, July 10, 2014, https://www.wsj.com/articles/standard-bank-starts-legal-action-in-china-over-suspected-qingdao-port-fraud-1404977193.

19. "A New Digital Era for Trade," J.P. Morgan Insights,https://www.jpmorgan.com/country/US/EN/insights/treasury-services/a-new-digital-era-for-trade (accessed February 25, 2018).

20. Alison Kao and Kirk Lundberg, "Tame the Paper in Trade Transactions," Bank of America Merrill Lynch blog, https://www.trade-technologies.com/case-study-baml (accessed May 14, 2019).

21. "Rethinking Trade & Finance: An ICC Private Sector Development Perspective," ICC Banking Commission, 2016, http://store.iccwbo.org/content/uploaded/pdf/ICC_Global_Trade_and_Finance_Survey_2016.pdf.

22. Finbarr Bermingham, "HSBC and IBM Develop Cognitive Trade Finance Tool,"

Global Trade Review, August 16, 2017, https://www.gtreview.com/news/global/hsbc-and-ibm-develop-cognitive-trade-finance-tool.

23. A smart contract "knows" when to execute by using an extrinsic data source that is programmed in a computer. This source is called "oracle," and it tells the smart contract that an event has indeed happened. For example, in trade finance, the registration number associated with an electronic bill of lading can be an oracle. To simplify somewhat, when this oracle indicates that a shipment has arrived at the buyer, funds will automatically move from the buyer's bank to the seller's bank.

24. "Logistics Industry: Next Step to Global Economy's Blockchainization," *Cointeletgraph*, July 15, 2017, https://cointelegraph.com/news/logistics-industry-next-step-to-global-economys-blockchainization.

25. Avi Mizrahi, "BofAML, HSBC and IDA Singapore Develop Blockchain for Letters of Credit," *Finance Magnates*, October 8, 2016, http://www.financemagnates.com/cryptocurrency/innovation/bofaml-hsbc-and-ida-singapore-develop-blockchain-for-letters-of-credit.

26. Peter Lee, "Banking Jumps to Post Blockchain," *Euromoney*, October 24, 2017, https://www.euromoney.com/article/b159v9n3cbm4p2/banking-jumps-to-post-blockchain?copyrightInfo=true.

27. "Leading the Pack in Blockchain Banking: Trailblazers Set the Pace," IBM, September 2016, https://www-01.ibm.com/common/ssi/cgi-bin/ssialias?htmlfid=GBP03467USEN.

28. Anothony Strzalek, "Asean consortium in KYC Blockchain First," *FStech*, October 10, 2017, http://www.fstech.co.uk/fst/Consortium_Completes_First_KYC_Blockchain_PoC.php.

29. "The First Thailand Blockchain Community Initiative," *Kasikorn Bank News*, March 19, 2018, https://www.kasikornbank.com/en/News/Pages/ThailandBlockchain-Community.aspx.

30. Annaliese Milano, "14 Thai Banks Back Blockchain Platform to Digitize Contracts," *coindesk*, March 19, 2018, https://www.coindesk.com/14-thai-banks-back-blockchain-platform-digitize-contracts.

31. Ibid.

32. Samburaj Das, "Butter and Cheese Make the World's First Blockchain Trade Finance Transaction," CCN, September 7, 2016, https://www.ccn.com/cheese-butter-make-worlds-first-blockchain-trade-finance-transaction.

33. Samburaj Das, "Standard Chartered Completes Cross-Border Blockchain Payment in 10 Seconds," CCN, September 29, 2016, https://www.ccn.com/standard-chartered-completes-cross-border-blockchain-payment-10-seconds.

34. See, for example, "How Blockchain Could Disrupt Banking," *CBInsights*, December 12, 2018, https://www.cbinsights.com/research/blockchain-disrupting-banking/?utm_source=CB+Insights+Newsletter&utm_campaign=4776c5a17b-WedNL_12_12_2018&utm_medium=email&utm_term=0_9dc0513989-4776c5a17b-86971753.

35. Eric Piscini, Darshini Dalal, David Mapgaonkar, and Prakash Santhana, "Block-

chain to Blockchains: Broad Adoption and Integration Enter the Realm of the Possible," *Deloitte Insights*, December 5, 2017, https://www2.deloitte.com/insights/us/en/focus/tech-trends/2018/blockchain-integration-smart-contracts.html; and Hong Kong Monetary Authority, "White Paper on Distributed Ledger Technology," November 2016.

36. "Trade Finance: The Landscape Is Changing—Are You?" Accenture, https://www.accenture.com/t20160412T053548Z__w__/us-en/_acnmedia/Accenture/Conversion-Assets/DotCom/Documents/Global/PDF/Dualpub_21/Accenture-Trade-Finance.pdf (accessed February 25, 2018).

37. "Prime Minister Announces Supply Chain Finance Scheme," GOV.UK, October 23, 2012, https://www.gov.uk/government/news/prime-minister-announces-supply-chain-finance-scheme.

38. "Technology Is Revolutionising Supply-Chain Finance," *The Economist*, October 12, 2017, https://www.economist.com/news/finance-and-economics/21730150-squeezed-suppliers-and-big-corporate-buyers-stand-benefit-technology.

39. See, for example, International Finance Corporation, "De-Risking and Other Challenges in the Emerging Market Financial Sector Findings from IFC's Survey on Correspondent Banking," Septemberr 1, 2017, http://documents.worldbank.org/curated/en/895821510730571841/pdf/121275-WP-IFC-2017-Survey-on-Correspondent-Banking-in-EMs-PUBLIC.pdf.

40. "Technology Is Revolutionising Supply-Chain Finance," *The Economist*, October 12, 2017, https://www.economist.com/news/finance-and-economics/21730150-squeezed-suppliers-and-big-corporate-buyers-stand-benefit-technology.

41. David Gustin, "A Disruptive Supply Chain Finance Vendor Fifteen Years Later—Who Is Orbian?" *Spend Matters*, May 9, 2014, http://spendmatters.com/tfmatters/a-disruptive-supply-chain-finance-vendor-fifteen-years-later-who-is-orbian.

42. Tatjana Kulkarni, "12 Banks Join Blockchain Consortium R3 to Create Open-Account Trade Finance Network," *Bank Innovation*, September 26, 2017, https://bankinnovation.net/2017/09/twelve-banks-join-blockchain-consortium-r3-to-create-open-account-trade-fiance-network.

43. See Kati Suominen, *Harnessing Blockchain for American Business and Prosperity: 10 Use Cases, 10 Big Questions, Five Solutions* (Washington, DC: Center for Strategic and International Studies, October 2018), https://wita.org/wp-content/uploads/2018/11/181101_Suominen_Blockchain_v3.pdf.

44. See Ivica Nikolic and others, "Finding the Greedy, Prodigal, and Suicidal Contracts at Scale," Arxiv.org, March 14, 2018, https://arxiv.org/pdf/1802.06038.pdf.

45. Loi Luu and others, "Making Smart Contracts Smarter," Cryptology ePrint Archive, October 2016, https://eprint.iacr.org/2016/633.pdf.

46. Mike Orcutt, "Ethereum's Smart Contracts Are Full of Holes," *MIT Technology Review*, March 1, 2018, https://www.technologyreview.com/s/610392/ethereums-smart-contracts-are-full-of-holes.

47. Hoang Tam Vo, Ashish Kundu, and Mukesh Mohania, "Research Directions in Blockchain Data Management and Analytics," Open Proceedings, March 26–29, 2018, https://openproceedings.org/2018/conf/edbt/paper-227.pdf.

48. Ibid.

49. Ibid.

50. Mark Cartwright, "Trade in Ancient Greece," *Ancient History Encyclopedia,* May 22, 2018, https://www.ancient.eu/article/115/trade-in-ancient-greece.

CHAPTER 7

1. David Reinsel, John Gantz, and John Rydning, "Data Age 2025: The Digitization of the World from Edge to Core," IDC White Paper No. US44413318, November 2018, https://www.seagate.com/files/www-content/our-story/trends/files/idc-seagate-dataage-whitepaper.pdf.

2. Frank Lavin and Peter Cohan, *Export Now: Five Keys to Entering New Markets* (Hoboken, NJ: Wiley, 2011).

3. "Dollar Shave Club Success Story," ReSci, https://www.retentionscience.com/clients/dollar-shave-club (accessed March, 2018).

4. Peter Dahlström, "The Demands of On-Demand Marketing," *The Economist,* December 12, 2013.

5. "Whipping the Supply Line into Shape," *Kellogg Insight,* March 13, 2013.

6. See, for example, Prasanna Kumar, Mervin Herbert, and Srikanth Rao, "Demand Forecasting Using Artificial Neural Network Based on Different Learning Methods: Comparative Analysis," *International Journal for Research in Applied Science and Engineering Technology* 2, no. IV (April 2014).

7. Erik Hofmann, "Big Data and Supply Chain Decisions: The Impact of Volume, Variety and Velocity Properties on the Bullwhip Effect," *International Journal of Production Research* 55, no. 17 (September 2017): 5108–5126.

8. Peter Findlay, "How the World's 5 Billion Low-Income Consumers Decide What to Buy," Southeast Asia A.T. Kearney , Management Agenda, 2011, https://www.atkearney.com/documents/10192/421871/EAXIV_1_How_the_Worlds_5_Billion_Low-Income_Consumers_Decide_What_to_Buy.pdf/9bd5db46-c3e9-4df8-98eb-bdd17cba92cf.

9. Erik Simanis and Duncan Duke, "Profits at the Bottom of the Pyramid," *Harvard Business Review,* October 2014.

10. Antoine van Agtmael, *The Emerging Markets Century: How a New Breed of World-Class Companies Is Overtaking the World* (New York: Free Press, 2007).

11. "Better, Faster Data from Emerging Markets," GeoPoll, https://research.geopoll.com/index.html (accessed March 16, 2019).

12. Tom Foster, "Warby Parker Grew to $250 Million in Sales Through Disciplined Growth. Now It's Time to Get Aggressive," *Inc.,* June 2017.

13. Lauren Thomas, "Amazon and Wal-Mart Might Be Fighting Over Nordstrom Next, Foursquare Says," *CNBC Retail* 23, published 4:38 p.m. ET Wednesday, August 23, 2017; updated 5:23 a.m. ET Thursday, August 24, 2017.

14. Ibid.

15. Danny Vena, "Amazon's AI-Infused Grocery Store Is Open: What Investors Need to Know," Motley Fool, January 23, 2018, https://www.fool.com/investing/2018/01/23/amazons-ai-infused-grocery-store-is-open-what-inve.aspx.

16. Michael Steinhart, "Facial Analytics: What Are You Smiling At?" *Information-Week*, March 14, 2014, https://www.informationweek.com/big-data/big-data-analytics/facial-analytics-what-are-you-smiling-at/d/d-id/1127726.

17. Jenna Bitar and Jay Stanley, "Are Stores You Shop at Secretly Using Face Recognition on You?" *ACLU Speech*, March 26, 2018, https://www.aclu.org/blog/privacy-technology/surveillance-technologies/are-stores-you-shop-secretly-using-face.

18. "Affectiva Automotive AI," Affectiva, https://go.affectiva.com/auto (accessed March 16, 2019).

19. Rebecca Migirov, "The Supply Circle: How Blockchain Technology Disintermediates the Supply Chain," *ConsenSys*, March 9, 2016.

20. Jeff John Roberts, "The Diamond Industry Is Obsessed with the Blockchain," *Fortune*, September 12, 2017.

21. "Walmart, JD.com, IBM and Tsinghua University Launch a Blockchain Food Safety Alliance in China," *New York Times*, Business Day, Markets, December 14, 2017.

22. "Proof of Concept: 4 Organizations Join Forces to Bring Blockchain Traceability to Fish Feed Companies and Pet Foods Suppliers," *Origintrail*, June 15, 2018, https://medium.com/origintrail/proof-of-concept-4-organizations-join-forces-to-bring-blockchain-traceability-to-the-animal-feed-fe8daf933f8f.

23. Tyler Koslow, "GE Files Patent to Improve 3D Printing Security with Blockchain Tech," All3DP, June 29, 2018, https://all3dp.com/ge-aims-to-use-blockchain-tech-to-eliminate-fake-3d-printed-objects.

24. Corey Clarke, "US Navy to Employ Blockchain to Control 3D Printers," 3DPrinting Industry, June 26, 2017, https://3dprintingindustry.com/news/us-navy-employ-blockchain-control-3d-printers-116968.

25. N. Viswanadham, "Mattel's Toy Recalls and Supply Chain Management," Ecosystem Aware Global Supply Chain Management, Lecture at the National Programme on Technology Enhanced Learning (NPTEL), https://nptel.ac.in/courses/110108056/module3/Lecture12.pdf (accessed May 14, 2019).

26. Louise Story and David Barboza, "Mattel Recalls 19 Million Toys Sent from China," *New York Times*, World Business, August 15, 2007.

27. "List of Goods Produced by Child Labor or Forced Labor," United States Department of Labor, Bureau of International Labor Affairs, https://www.dol.gov/agencies/ilab/reports/child-labor/list-of-goods (accessed March 16, 2019).

28. David Floyer, "Defining and Sizing the Industrial Internet," Wikibon, June 27, 2013, http://wikibon.org/wiki/v/Defining_and_Sizing_the_Industrial_Internet; Peter C. Evans and Marco Annunziata, "Industrial Internet, Pushing the Boundaries of Minds and Machines," General Electric, November 2012, https://www.ge.com/docs/chapters/Industrial_Internet.pdf.

29. Y. Daniel Castro and Alan Mcquinn, "Cross-Border Data Flows Enable Growth in All Industries," The Information Technology & Innovation Foundation, February 2015, http://www2.itif.org/2015-cross-border-data-flows.pdf.

30. See 8th Brazilian Industry Innovation Summit, http://www.congressodeinovacao.com.br/o-congresso (accessed May 14, 2019).

31. Kah Chai Tan, "Big Data Initiatives Need Innovative Thinking to Make Things Happen," APAC CIO Outlook, http://www.apacciooutlook.com/ciospeaks/big-data-initiatives-need-innovative-thinking-to-make-things-happen-nwid-718.html (accessed March 16, 2019).

32. P. R. Sanjai, "With New Analytics Arm, Tata Aims to Make Better Sense of Data," LiveMint, September 30, 2015, https://www.livemint.com/Companies/PCgvCZILu-JKV68UKVHZRJO/With-new-analytics-arm-Tata-aims-to-make-better-sense-of-da. html.

33. James Manyika and others, "Big Data: The Next Frontier for Innovation, Competition, and Productivity," McKinsey Global Institute, May 2011, https://www.mckinsey.com/business-functions/digital-mckinsey/our-insights/big-data-the-next-frontier-for-innovation.

34. Matthieu Pélissie du Rausus and others, "Internet Matters: The Net's Sweeping Impact On Growth, Jobs, and Prosperity," McKinsey Global Institute, May 22, 2011, http://www.mckinsey.com/insights/high_tech_telecoms_internet/internet_matters.

35. "The Risk Management Safety Net: Market Penetration and Potential," U.S. Department of Agriculture, Analysis of the Federal Crop Insurance Portfolio, September 2017.

36. "AWS Case Study: Travelstart," Amazon Web Services, https://aws.amazon.com/solutions/case-studies/travelstart (accessed March 16, 2019).

37. See, for example, "Grab Becomes the Largest Tableau Online Customer in Asia Pacific with More Than 1,000 Interactors," Tableau3, April, 2017, https://www.tableau.com/about/press-releases/2017/grab-becomes-largest-tableau-online-customer-asia-pacific-more-1000.

38. "AWS Case Study: WebMotors," Amazon Web Services, https://aws.amazon.com/solutions/case-studies/webmotors (accessed March 16, 2019).

39. Lisa Zyga, "Physicists Provide Support for Retrocausal Quantum Theory, in Which the Future Influences the Past," Phys.org, July 5, 2019.

CHAPTER 8

1. World Development Indicators, World Bank, 2019, https://datacatalog.world-bank.org/dataset/world-development-indicators.

2. See Enterprise Surveys, World Bank Group, http://www.enterprisesurveys.org (accessed May 14, 2019).

3. World Development Indicators, World Bank.

4. See Sanna Ojanpera, "Mapping Broadband Affordability in 2016," Geonet, October 30, 2018, https://geonet.oii.ox.ac.uk/blog/mapping-broadband-affordability-in-2016; and Arturo Muente-Kunigami, "How Affordable Is Broadband?" World Bank blog, October 23, 2014, https://blogs.worldbank.org/ic4d/how-affordable-broadband.

5. Abdi Latif Dahir, "Google's High-Altitude Internet Balloons Could Soon Connect Rural Kenya," QuartzAfrica, July 11, 2018, https://qz.com/africa/1325552/googles-project-loon-to-use-balloons-to-beam-the-internet-in-kenya.

6. Sean Farrell, "Facebook's Solar-Powered Internet Plane Takes Flight," The Guard-

ian, July 21, 2016, https://www.theguardian.com/business/2016/jul/21/facebook-solar-powered-internet-plane-test-flight-aquila.

7. Jayne Miller, "The Evolution of Submarine Cable Connectivity in Africa," Telegraphy Blog, February 22, 2017, http://blog.telegeography.com/the-evolution-of-submarine-cable-connectivity-in-africa; see also Nicole Starosielski, "In Our Wi-Fi World, the Internet Still Depends on Undersea Cables," *The Conversation*, November 3, 2015, http://theconversation.com/in-our-wi-fi-world-the-internet-still-depends-on-undersea-cables-49936.

8. Agency Staff, "Google Is Laying Fibre Optic Cable in Africa to Ease Access to the internet," *Business Day*, March 15, 2017, https://www.businesslive.co.za/bd/companies/2017-03-15-google-is-laying-fibre-optic-cable-in-africa-to-ease-access-to-the-internet.

9. Billy Duberstein, "Why Google is Spending Big on Undersea Cables," The Motley Fool, February 1, 2018, https://www.fool.com/investing/2018/02/01/why-google-is-spending-big-on-undersea-cables.aspx.

10. "World Development Report 2016: Digital Dividends," World Bank, May 2016, http://www.worldbank.org/en/publication/wdr2016.

11. E. J. Malecki, "Digital Development in Rural Areas: Potentials and Pitfalls," *Journal of Rural Studies* 19, no. 2 (2003): 201–214.

12. Kati Suominen, "Ecommerce Development Index," report for the United States Agency for International Development, April 2017, https://pdf.usaid.gov/pdf_docs/PA00MP8T.pdf.

13. Kati Suominen, "Expanding Developing Country Small Businesses' Use of Online Platforms for Trade," report for the United States Agency for International Development, July 2018, https://pdf.usaid.gov/pdf_docs/PA00TM8V.pdf.

14. Leila Ben-Aoun Peltier and Adel Ben Youssef, "Does Internet Speed Matter? Impact of Internet Speed on E-Applications Adoption by Firms in Luxembourg," Université Nice Sophia Antipolis, http://unice.fr/laboratoires/gredeg/contenus-riches/documents-telechargeables/evenements-1/papiers-3en/ben-youssef.pdf (accessed March 16, 2019).

15. Kati Suominen, "Accelerating Digital Trade in Latin America and the Caribbean," Inter-American Development Bank Working Paper No. IDB-WP-790, March 2017, https://publications.iadb.org/publications/english/document/Accelerating-Digital-Trade-in-Latin-America-and-the-Caribbean.pdf.

16. U.S. International Trade Commission, "Digital Trade in the U.S. and Global Economies, Part 2," U.S. ITC Publication 4485, 2013, https://www.usitc.gov/publications/332/pub4485.pdf.

17. Robert Colburn, "First Successful Transatlantic Telegraph Cable Celebrates 150th Anniversary," The Institute, July 11, 2016, http://theinstitute.ieee.org/tech-history/technology-history/first-successful-transatlantic-telegraph-cable-celebrates-150th-anniversary.

18. Kenechi Okeleke and Jan Stryjak, "Closing the Coverage Gap: Digital Inclusion in Latin America," GSMA Connected Society, https://www.gsma.com/publicpolicy/wp-

content/uploads/2016/09/GSMA2015_Report_ClosingTheCoverageGap-DigitalInclu-sionInLatinAmerica.pdf (accessed March 16, 2019).

19. Ibid.

20. Ibid.

21. Melvin P. Vaz, "Erwanda Project," Global Information/Communications Technology, April 4, 2013, http://documents.worldbank.org/curated/en/491851474497141969/pdf/000020051-20140625071025.pdf.

22. Alex Ntale, Atsushi Yamanaka, and Didier Nkurikiyimfura, "The Metamorphosis to a Knowledge-Based Society: Rwanda," World Economic Forum: The Global Information Technology Report, 2013, http://www3.weforum.org/docs/GITR/2013/GITR_Chapter2.2_2013.pdf.

23. Alliance for Affordable Internet, 2008–2018, http://a4ai.org/affordability-report/data/?_year=2017&indicator=INDEX.

24. Herbert Kanale, "Myanmar to Reach 28% Internet Penetration and 15 Million Users," Internet in Myanmar, October 12, 2017, https://www.internetinmyanmar.com/internet-penetration-sept-17.

25. Doug Bock Clark, "Myanmar's Internet Disrupted Society—and Fueled Extremists," *Wired*, September 28, 2017, https://www.wired.com/story/myanmar-internet-disrupted-society-extremism.

26. Filippo Belloc, Antonio Nicita, and Maria Alessandra Rossi, "Whither Policy Design for Broadband Penetration? Evidence from 30 OECD Countries," ScienceDirect, *Telecommunications Policy* 36, no. 5 (June 2012), https://www.sciencedirect.com/science/article/pii/S0308596111002163.

27. Ibid.

28. Stephen Ezell and John Wu, "How Joining the Information Technology Agreement Spurs Growth in Developing Nations," Information Technology & Innovation Foundation, May 22, 2017, https://itif.org/publications/2017/05/22/how-joining-information-technology-agreement-spurs-growth-developing-nations.

29. Patrick Gillespie, "Argentina Tried a Trump-Like Tariff—and It Went Horribly Wrong," *CNN Business*, December 19, 2016, http://money.cnn.com/2016/12/19/news/economy/tariffs-trump-argentina/index.html.

30. Daniel Knowles, "So Near and Yet So Far," *1843* (*The Economist*), December-January 2018, https://www.1843magazine.com/dispatches/so-near-and-yet-so-far.

31. Homa Zaryouni, "Korean Beauty Brands Have Highest Digital IQ," *Daily Insights*, September 11, 2015, https://www.l2inc.com/daily-insights/korean-beauty-brands-have-highest-digital-iq.

32. "E-Commerce Statistics," eurostat Statistics Explained, December 2018, http://ec.europa.eu/eurostat/statistics-explained/index.php/E-commerce_statistics.

33. James Stamps and David Coffin, "Digital Trade in the U.S. and Global Economies, Part 2," United States International Trade Commission, August 2014, Pub. No. 4485, https://www.usitc.gov/publications/332/pub4485.pdf.

34. "World Development Report 2016: Digital Dividends."

35. Suominen, "Ecommerce Development Index."

36. Alisa DiCaprio and Kati Suominen, "Aid for Trade in Asia and the Pacific: Thinking Forward About Trade Costs and the Digital Economy," report for the Asian Development Bank for the Global Aid for Trade Review, July 2015.

37. See Kati Suominen, "How the Global Fund for Ecommerce Is Helping Entrepreneurs in Developing Countries Enter the Digital Era," *GE Reports*, April 12, 2016, https://www.ge.com/reports/kati-suominen-how-to-help-entrepreneurs-in-developing-countries-enter-the-ecommerce-era.

38. MangoTango, "Ecommerce Readiness and Opportunities in Cambodia," report for the Mekong Business Initiative and British Chamber of Commerce of Cambodia, January 2017.

39. Global Findex Database, globalfindex.org (accessed May 15, 2019).

40. "Vodafone M-Pesa and MTN Mobile Money Agree to Interconnect Mobile Money Services," Vodafone M-Pesa, April 21, 2015, http://www.vodafone.com/content/index/media/vodafone-group-releases/2015/m-pesa-mtn.html.

41. "Fintech Innovation Propels B2B Money Transfer Market to $218 Trillion by 2022," Juniper Research, March 26, 2018, https://www.juniperresearch.com/press/press-releases/fintech-innovation-propels-b2b-money-transfer.

42. Author interview with a leading Latin American ecommerce platform, April 2018.

43. Ibid.

44. Matt Higginson, "How Blockchain Could Disrupt Cross-Border Payments," The Clearing House blog, https://www.theclearinghouse.org/banking-perspectives/2016/2016-q4-banking-perspectives/articles/blockchain-cross-border-payments (accessed March 16, 2019).

45. Angelica Mari, "EBANX: The Brazilian Fintech Who Wants to Lead the Cross-Border Online Payments Market," *Forbes*, September 20, 2017, https://www.forbes.com/sites/angelicamarideoliveira/2018/09/20/ebanx-the-brazilian-fintech-who-wants-to-lead-the-cross-border-online-payments-market/#444ee7cc2427.

46. "The Economic Impact of Online Payments: Breaking Barriers Across Europe," Deloitte, May 2013, https://www2.deloitte.com/content/dam/Deloitte/uk/Documents/about-deloitte/deloitte-uk-economic-impact-of-online-payments-tmt.pdf.

47. Hamilton McNutt, Shelley Spencer, and Marcella Willis, "Making the Journey from Cash to Electronic Payments: A Toolkit for USAID Implementing Partners and Development Organizations," USAID Global Development Lab and NetHope, 2016, https://www.usaid.gov/sites/default/files/documents/15396/USAID_NetHope_ePayment_Toolkit_2016.pdf.

48. CPMI and World Bank Group, *Payment Aspects of Financial Inclusion* (Basel, Switzerland: BIS; Washington, DC: World Bank Group, 2016).

49. Daisuke Nakao, "Effective Implementation of the Risk-Based Approach," *ACAMS Today*, March 7, 2016, https://www.acamstoday.org/effective-implementation-risk-based-approach.

50. Suominen, "Expanding Developing Country Small Businesses' Use of Online Platforms for Trade."

51. David Humphrey, Magnus Willesson, Ted Lindblom, and Goran Bergendahl, "What Does It Cost to Make a Payment?," *Review of Network Economics* 2, no. 2 (2003): 159–174.

52. Bhaskar Chakravorti, "India's Botched War on Cash," Huffpost The Blog, December 15, 2016, https://www.huffingtonpost.com/bhaskar-chakravorti/indias-botched-war-on-cas_b_13647026.html.

53. Ibid.

54. Utpal Bhaskar, "Budget 2018 Extends Sops to MSMEs in Push to Formalize Indian Economy," LiveMint,February 2, 2018, http://www.livemint.com/Politics/VKga4L-GtJwU212xTmelp6J/Budget-2018-Arun-Jaitley-announces-relief-for-MSMEs.html.

55. See, for example, Erica de la Harpe, "India Cuts Out Cash for Online Payments," *World Finance*, December 12, 2016, https://www.worldfinance.com/strategy/india-push-banking-online.

56. Kaustav Roy, Disha Kohli, Rakeshkumar Kathirvel, Senthil Kumar, Rupaksh Sahgal, and Wen-Bin, "Sentiment Analysis of Twitter Data for Demonetization in India—A Text Mining Approach," *Issues in Information Systems* 18, no. 4 (2017): 9–15.

57. Sean Creehan, "Demonetization Is Catalyzing Digital Payments Growth in India," Pacific Exchange Blog, Federal Reserve Bank of San Francisco, April 12, 2017, https://www.frbsf.org/banking/asia-program/pacific-exchange-blog/demonetization-is-catalyzing-digital-payments-growth-in-india.

58. See D. L. Birch and J. Medoff, "Gazelles," in *Labor Markets, Employment Policy and Job Creation*, ed. L. C. Solmon and A. R. Levenson, 159–167 (Boulder, CO: Westview, 1994).

59. Yasuyuki Motoyama and Samuel Arbesman, "The Ascent of America's High-Growth Companies," Ewing Marion Kauffman Foundation, http://www.kauffman.org/what-we-do/research/2012/09/the-ascent-of-americas-high-growth-companies (accessed March 16, 2019).

60. David B. Audretsch, "Determinants of High-Growth Entrepreneurship," OECD/DBA International Workshop, Copenhagen, March 28, 2012, https://www.oecd.org/cfe/leed/Audretsch_determinants%20of%20high-growth%20firms.pdf.

61. Motoyama and Arbesman, "The Ascent of America's High-Growth Companies."

62. "How Digital Are You? Middle Market Digitization Trends and How Your Firm Measures Up," National Center for the Middle Market and Nextrade Group, 2016, http://media.wix.com/ugd/478c1a_5ed9a4ccb406435991b12b93ee21cf83.pdf.

63. Suominen, "Accelerating Digital Trade in Latin America and the Caribbean."

64. Sophie Chapman, "UK Manufacturing Not Utilising Digitisation Enough, Compared to Global Competitors," Global Manufacturing, April 11, 2018, https://www.manufacturingglobal.com/technology/uk-manufacturing-not-utilising-digitisation-enough-compared-global-competitors.

65. Ana Paula Cusolito, Raed Safadi, and Daria Taglioni, *Inclusive Global Value Chains* (Washington, DC: World Bank and OECD, 2016), https://openknowledge.worldbank.org/bitstream/handle/10986/24910/9781464808425.pdf.

66. James Manyika and others, "Digital America: A Tale of the Haves and Have-

Mores," December 2015, https://www.mckinsey.com/industries/high-tech/our-insights/digital-america-a-tale-of-the-haves-and-have-mores.

67. Suominen, "Ecommerce Development Index."

68. Diego Comin, "The Evolution of Technology Diffusion and the Great Divergence," Brookings Blum Roundtable, August 8, 2014.

69. Diego Comin and Bart Hobijn, "An Exploration of Technology Diffusion," *American Economic Review* 100 (December 2010), http://www.dartmouth.edu/~dcomin/files/exploration_technology.pdf.

70. See Qualcomm website "The 5G Economy," https://www.qualcomm.com/invention/5g/economy; and "The 5G Economy: How 5G will Impact Global Industries, The Economy, and You," MIT Technology Review (March 1, 2017), https://www.technologyreview.com/s/603770/the-5g-economy-how-5g-will-impact-global-industries-the-economy-and-you.

71. "South Korea Telecoms, Mobile, Broadband and Digital Media Statistics and Analyses 2018," BusinessWire, October 3, 2018, https://www.businesswire.com/news/home/20181003005694/en/South-Korea-Telecoms-Mobile-Broadband-Digital-Media.

72. *Growing United: Upgrading Europe's Convergence Machine* (Washington, DC: World Bank, 2019), http://documents.worldbank.org/curated/en/250311520359538450/pdf/123956-REVISED-volume-2-GrowingUnitedvonlinelinks.pdf.

73. Ibid.

74. *World Development Report 2019: The Changing Nature of Work* (Washington, DC: World Bank, 2019), http://documents.worldbank.org/curated/en/816281518818814423/pdf/2019-WDR-Report.pdf.

CHAPTER 9

1. M. Cali and D. W. te Velde, "Does Aid for Trade Really Improve Trade Performance?" *World Development* 39, no. 5 (2010): 725–740.

2. Diego Rodriguez, "The Five Biggest Logistics Challenges Facing Latin American E-Commerce," *AMI Perspective*, January 16, 2017.

3. "Do People Use the Internet for Personal Purposes?" *The Connected Consumer Survey 2017*, Google Consumer Barometer, https://www.consumerbarometer.com/en/graph-builder.

4. Rodriguez, Diego, "The Five Biggest Logistics Challenges."

5. David Hummels and Georg Schaur, "Time as a Trade Barrier," *American Economic Review* 103, no. 7 (December 2013), https://www.aeaweb.org/articles?id=10.1257/aer.103.7.2935.

6. Simeon Djankov, Caroline Freund, and Cong S. Pham, "Trading on Time," Research Working Paper No. WPS 3909 (Washington, DC: World Bank, 2006), http://documents.worldbank.org/curated/en/761201468175464382/Trading-on-time.

7. Kati Suominen, "Ecommerce Development Index," report for the United States Agency for International Development, April 2017, https://pdf.usaid.gov/pdf_docs/PA00MP8T.pdf.

8. Kati Suominen, "Accelerating Digital Trade in Latin America and the Caribbean,"

Inter-American Development Bank Working Paper No. IDB-WP-790, March 2017, https://publications.iadb.org/publications/english/document/Accelerating-Digital-Trade-in-Latin-America-and-the-Caribbean.pdf.

9. "Digital Trade in the U.S. and Global Economies, Part 2," U.S. International Trade Commission Publication No. 4485, August 2014.

10. Eduardo Galeano, *Open Veins of Latin America: Five Centuries of the Pillage of a Continent* (New York: Monthly Review Press, 1971).

11. Mauricio Mesquita Moreira, Christian Volper, and Juan S. Blyde, *Unclogging the Arteries: The Impact of Transport Costs on Latin America and Caribbean Trade* (Cambridge, MA: Harvard University Press, 2009).

12. "Trading Across Borders Technology Gains in Trade Facilitation," Word Bank, in *Doing Business 2017: Equal Opportunity for All*, http://www.doingbusiness.org/content/dam/doingBusiness/media/Annual-Reports/English/DB17-Report.pdf.

13. Ibid.

14. See for example, Amos Wangora, "Implementation of the Kenya National Single Window System," September 13, 2016, https://www.slideshare.net/Africanalliance/implementation-of-the-kenya-national-single-window-systemkentradeswc2016; GUCE GIE Cameroon, "The Single Form for Foreign Trade Operators," March 14, 2017, https://www.slideshare.net/Africanalliance/the-single-form-for-foreign-trade-operators-guce-gie-cameroon; and "Trading Across Borders Technology Gains in Trade Facilitation."

15. See World Bank's Doing Business website at http://www.doingbusiness.org.

16. Christian Volpe Martincus, "How Does Trade Respond When Borders Are Simplified via Single-Window Systems?" January 31, 2018, https://blogs.iadb.org/integration-trade/en/how-does-trade-respond-when-borders-are-simplified-via-one-stop-systems.

17. See World Bank Group, *Doing Business 2017: Equal Opportunity for All*, http://www.doingbusiness.org/content/dam/doingBusiness/media/Annual-Reports/English/DB17-Report.pdf.

18. Margareta Drzeniek Hanouz, Thierry Geiger, and Sean Doherty, eds., "The Global Enabling Trade Report 2014," *World Economic Forum Insight Report*, 2014.

19. Sung Heun Ha and Sang Won Lim, "The Progress of Paperless Trade in Asia and the Pacific: Enabling International Supply Chain integration," *ADB Working Paper Series on Regional Economic Integration*, October 2014.

20. "Trading Across Borders," World Bank's Doing Business Database, 2019, http://www.doingbusiness.org/en/data/exploretopics/trading-across-borders.

21. Yann Duval, "Trade Facilitation for Sustainable Development in Asia and the Pacific," ITD Workshop on Trade Facilitation for Sustainable Development, Bangkok, August 7–10, https://www.unescap.org/sites/default/files/ITD%20Workshop%20Session%201-2%20TFandSD%20intro%20-%2007%20Aug%202018_Mr.%20Yann%20Duval.pdf.

22. M. H. Abeywickrama and W.A.D.N. Wickramaarachchi, "Study on the Challenges of Implementing Single Window Concept to Facilitate Trade in Sri Lanka: A Freight Forwarder Perspective," *Journal of Economics, Business and Management* 3, no. 9 (September 2015): 883–888, http://www.joebm.com/papers/302-BM00027.pdf.

23. "Russian Anticorruption Pioneer States That a Family Is Plundering Karachay-Cherkessia," CRN Network, http://corruptionresearchnetwork.org/marketplace/resources/Abu%20Dhabi%20Combined.pdf (accessed March 16, 2019).

24. Marc Levinson, *The Box: How the Shipping Container Made the World Smaller and the World Economy Bigger* (Princeton: Princeton University Press, 2007).

25. U.S. Department of Transportation, *Bureau of Transportation Statistics and Federal Highway Administration, Freight Analysis Framework*, Version 4.3.1, 2017.

26. Matt Gersper, "CBP's 10+2 Readiness . . . Beware! It's Strategic, not Tactical!" *Import-Export Institute's GlobalWatch*, September/October 2008.

27. Bernard Kempingski, "Scanning and Imaging Shipping Containers Overseas: Costs and Alternatives," Congressional Budget Office, June 2016.

28. Lorraine Keyes, "Data Analytics: How Data Analytics Can Simplify and Facilitate Trade Within the European Union," Europese Fiscale Studies Post Masters in EU Customs Law, 2015/2016.

29. Customs Now, "W Coast Trade Symposium Recap: E-commerce Is the Hot Topic," Customs and Border Protection, e-manifest, PGAs, PTI, Trade Transformation, May 31, 2017.

30. Ibid.

31. Legiscript.com, "The Internet Pharmacy Market in 2016: Trends, Challenges, and Opportunities," January 2016, https://safemedsonline.org/wp-content/uploads/2016/01/The-Internet-Pharmacy-Market-in-2016.pdf.

32. Hollie Shaw, "Canada Losing Out on More Than $1 Billion in Taxes and Duties on Foreign Online Retail Sales, Study Reveals," *Financial Post*, March 2, 2017.

33. Commission of European Communities, "The Economics of 1992—An Assessment of the Potential Economic Effects of Completing the Internal Market of the European Community," *European Economy* 35 (March 1988), http://ec.europa.eu/economy_finance/publications/pages/publication7412_en.pdf.

34. Mollie Leon, "Benchmark Your Trade Compliance Training Program," Amber Road Powering Global Trade, June 1, 2016.

35. Laure Templer, "Data Analysis for Effective Border Management," World Customs Organization, February 2017.

36. Medha Basu and Nurfilzah Rohaidi, "Exclusive: Singapore's Plans for AI in Border Security: Interview with Sung Pik Wan, Assistant Director-General (Checkpoints) at Singapore Customs," GovInsider, May 14, 2017.

37. Lis Evenstad, "HMRC Builds Blockchain Proof of Concept for UK Border," *ComputerWeekly*, September 15, 2017, https://www.computerweekly.com/news/450426393/HMRC-builds-blockchain-proof-of-concept-for-UK-border.

38. Lewis King, "UK Traders Say Blockchain Can Ameliorate Impending Customs Congestion," *Air Cargo World*, August 16, 2017.

39. Thomas R. Eddlem, "Before the Income Tax," *NewAmerican*, January 18, 2013.

40. See, for example, Katherine Gustafson, "What Is Nexus and How Does It Affect Your Small Business?" Intuit Quickbooks, https://quickbooks.intuit.com/r/taxes/what-is-nexus-and-how-does-it-affect-your-small-business (accessed May 15, 2019).

41. "Australia's New Digital GST Is Rubber-Stamped," *Taxamo*, May 10, 2016, https://www.taxamo.com/blog/australias-new-digital-gst.

42. See Holloway Rae, "De-Minimis Thresholds in APEC,"

43. J. Hintsa and others, "The Import VAT and Duty De-Minimis in the European Union—Where Should They Be and What Will Be the Impact?" Cross-Border Research Association, Lausanne, Switzerland, in co-operation with HEC University of Lausanne and University of Bamberg, final report, October 14, 2014, http://www.euroexpress.org/uploads/ELibrary/CDS-Report-Jan2015-publishing-final-2.pdf.

44. Studies also point out that the savings from increases in *de minimis* levels would enable customs to reallocate resources toward identifying serious threats, from terrorism to counterfeit merchandise, illegal drugs, and unsafe food products.

45. Christine McDaniel, Simon Schropp, and Olim Latipov, "Rights of Passage: The Economic Effects of Raising the DMT Threshold in Canada," C.D. Howe Institute E-Brief, June 23, 2016, https://www.cdhowe.org/sites/default/files/attachments/research_papers/mixed/E-brief_Rights%20of%20Passage_June16.pdf.

46. See Holloway and Rae, "De-Minimis Thresholds in APEC."

47. Jeffrey Rae, "The Economic Impact of Increased *De Minimis* Thresholds on ASEAN Economies," presentation at the ASEAN Regulatory Reform Symposium, Manila, July 23, 2012, http://aadcp2.org/wp-content/uploads/The-Economic-Impact-of-Increased-De-minimis-Thresholds-on-ASEAN-Economies.pdf.

48. Gary Hufbauer and Yee Wong, "Logistics Reform for Low-Value Shipments," Policy Brief PB11-7, Peterson Institute for International Economics, June 2011, https://piie.com/sites/default/files/publications/pb/pb11-07.pdf.

49. These arguments have gained more followers as trade has digitized. In discussions on inter-state taxation in such federal countries as the United States and Brazil, there are two main ways taxes are dealt with—charging the tax at the origin and not at the destination of the sale, and, as is more typical, charging it at the destination. In the latter case, there is contestation over whether the company selling the product has presence via a "nexus" at the destination. Nexus used to be defined in U.S. states as physical presence, such as a store; however, as ecommerce has grown, many U.S. states have argued that nexus means any sales presence or online marketing. See, for example, Gustafson, "What Is Nexus and How Does It Affect Your Small Business?"

CHAPTER 10

1. Francis Fukuyama, *The End of History and the Last Man* (New York: Free Press, 1992).

2. Jason Hassler, "The Power of Personalized Product Recommendations," *Intelliverse* (blog), November 16, 2017, http://www.intelliverse.com/blog/the-power-of-personalized-product-recommendations.

3. "Three-Quarters of Americans Concerned About Identity Theft During Holiday Shopping Season: Markets Insider," *Business Insider,* November 2, 2017, http://markets.businessinsider.com/news/stocks/Three-Quarters-Of-Americans-Concerned-About-Identity-Theft-During-Holiday-Shopping-Season-1006591336.

4. Russell A. Miller, ed., *Privacy and Power: A Transatlantic Dialogue in the Shadow of the NSA-Affair* (Cambridge, UK: Cambridge University Press, 2018).

5. Ibid.

6. J. Walsh, "There's Trouble in the Air Over Transborder Data Flow," *Science* 202, no. 4363 (1978): 29–32.

7. David Reinsel, John Gantz, and John Rydning, "Total WW Data to Reach 163ZB by 2025," *Storage Newsletter*, April 5, 2017, https://www.storagenewsletter. com/2017/04/05/total-ww-data-to-reach-163-zettabytes-by-2025-idc.

8. Ibid.

9. Jamie Carter, "How to Handle the New US-EU Data Regulations," *TechRadar*, May 23, 2016, http://www.techradar.com/news/internet/how-to-handle-the-new-us-eu-data-regulations-1320554/2#.

10. Michael Nadeau, "General Data Protection Regulation (GDPR) Requirements, Deadlines and Facts," *CSO Online*, February 16, 2018, https://www.csoonline.com/article/3202771/data-protection/general-data-protection-regulation-gdpr-requirements-deadlines-and-facts.html.

11. "Consult Hyperion Forecasts Banks to Face Fines Totalling €4.7bn in First Three Years Under GDPR," *AllClear ID*, June 14, 2017, https://www.allclearid.com/business/newsreleases/consult-hyperion-forecasts-banks-face-fines-totalling-e4–7bn-first-three-years-gdpr.

12. "FTSE 100 Companies Could Face Up to £5 Billion a Year in Fines When GDPR Tsunami Hits Our Shores," Oliver Wyman, May 22, 2017, http://www.oliverwyman. com/media-center/2017/may/ftse-100-companies-could-face-up-to-p5-billion-a-year-in-fines-w.html.

13. "Economic Impact Assessment of the European General Data Protection Regulation: Final Report," Deloitte, December 16, 2013, https://www2.deloitte.com/content/dam/Deloitte/uk/Documents/about-deloitte/deloitte-uk-european-data-protection-tmt.pdf.

14. Ibid.

15. Erik van der Marel, Hosuk Lee-Makiyama, and Matthias Bauer, "The Costs of Data Localisation: A Friendly Fire on Economic Recovery," European Centre for International Political Economy, May 2014, http://ecipe.org/publications/dataloc/2014.

16. K. Irion, S. Yakovleva, and M. Bartl, "Trade and Privacy: Complicated Bedfellows? How to Achieve Data Protection-Proof Free Trade Agreements," University of Amsterdam, Institute for Information Law, July 13, 2016, https://ivir.nl/publicaties/download/1807.

17. Nigel Cory, "Cross-Border Data Flows: Where Are the Barriers, and What Do They Cost?" Information Technology and Innovation Foundation, May 2017, https://itif.org/publications/2017/05/01/cross-border-data-flows-where-are-barriers-and-what-do-they.cost.

18. "China Passes Law Aiming at 'Secure and Controllable Internet'," *RT International*, https://www.rt.com/news/271075-china-security-internet-legislature (accessed February 25, 2018); Glenn Kates, "Russia Can Take Inspiration from These Three Coun-

tries to Build a Cyber Firewall," *Quartz*, May 9, 2014, https://qz.com/208102/three-countries-russia-can-take-inspiration-from-for-a-cyber-firewall.

19. "Quantifying the Cost of Forced Localization," Leviathan Security Group, 2015, https://static1.squarespace.com/static/556340ece4b0869396f21099/t/559dad76e4b0899 d97726a8b/1436396918881/Quantifying+t he+Cost+of+Forced+Localization.

20. Ibid.

21. van der Marel, Lee-Makiyama, and Bauer, "The Costs of Data Localisation."

22. "Digital Trade in the U.S. and Global Economies, Part 2," United States International Trade Commission, August 2014, https://www.usitc.gov/publications/332/pub4485.pdf.

23. "Preliminary Assessment: Potential Benefits for APEC Economies and Businesses Joining the CBPR System," Asia-Pacific Economic Cooperation, February 24, 2016, https://static1.squarespace.com/static/5746cdb3f699bb4f603243c8/t/591bbd614 6c3c4823961ecb3/1494990185553/IIS+-+APEC+CBPR+Benefits+Paper+Final+Public ly+Released+Version+-+APEC+Communications+Unit.pdf.

24. Ibid.

25. Mark Scott, "German Privacy Concerns Trip Up High-Tech Ventures," *Politico*, September 25, 2017, https://www.politico.eu/article/german-privacy-concerns-trip-up-high-tech-ventures.

26. The draft regulation also provides an updated list of countries granted adequacy status by the Colombian data-protection authority, which includes Costa Rica, the EU member states, Iceland, Mexico, Norway, Peru, Serbia, South Korea, the United States, and the countries granted adequacy by the European Commission.

27. David Haskel, "Colombia Adds U.S. to List of Data-Transfer-Safe Nations," *Bloomberg BNA*, August 14, 2017, https://www.bna.com/colombia-adds-us-n73014463125.

28. "International Data Flows: Promoting Digital Trade in the 21st Century," testimony by Robert D. Atkinson at the House Judiciary Committee, November 3, 2015, https://itif.org/publications/2015/11/03/international-data-flows-promoting-digital-trade-21st-century.

29. John Shimal, "Facebook Shuts Down 1 Million Accounts per Day but Can't Stop All 'Threat Actors,' Security Chief Says," CNBC, August 24, 2017.

30. Anupam Chander, "How Law Made Silicon Valley," *Emory Law Journal* 63, no. 639 (2014), http://law.emory.edu/elj/_documents/volumes/63/3/articles/chander.pdf.

31. Richard Allan, "Wir arbeiten hart daran, Hassrede zu bekämpfen und haben bereits große Fortschritte erzielt," Facebook, June 19, 2017, https://www.facebook.com/notes/facebook-politik-und-gesellschaft/wir-arbeiten-hart-daran-hassrede-zu-bek%C3%A4mpfen-und-haben-bereits-gro%C3%9Fe-fortschrit/1361657510554965.

32. Eric Goldman, "Congress Is About to Eviscerate Its Greatest Online Free Speech Achievement." *American Constitution Society for Law and Policy*, September 11, 2017, https://www.acslaw.org/acsblog/congress-is-about-to-eviscerate-its-greatest-online-free-speech-achievement.

33. Delegation of the United States to the WTO, "Joint Statement on Electronic

Commerce Initiative, Communication from the United States," April 12, 2018, https://docs.wto.org/dol2fe/Pages/FE_Search/FE_S_S009-DP.aspx?language=E&CatalogueIdL ist=244489,244495,244488,244469,244463,244471,244470,244437,244474,244472&Cu rrentCatalogueIdIndex=6&FullTextHash=371857150&HasEnglishRecord=True&HasF renchRecord=False&HasSpanishRecord=False.

34. Ivana Kottasová, "Europe Just Approved New Copyright Rules That Could Change the Internet," CNN, September 12, 2018, https://money.cnn.com/2018/09/12/technology/eu-copyright-law/index.html.

35. See, for example, "Video Sharing Platforms—Who's Making the Rules and How Do They Apply?" European Audiovisual Observatory, July 12, 2018, https://www.obs.coe.int/en/web/observatoire/home/-/asset_publisher/9iKCxBYgiO6S/content/video-sharing-platforms-who-s-making-the-rules-and-how-do-they-apply-?_101_ INSTANCE_9iKCxBYgiO6S_viewMode=view.

36. Kottasová, "Europe Just Approved New Copyright Rules."

37. "Argentinean Supreme Court Rules in Favor of Google and Yahoo on Civil Liability of Search Engines in María Belén Rodriguez case⊠," Free Internet Project, November 4, 2014, http://thefreeinternetproject.org/blog/argentinean-supreme-court-rules-favor-google-and-yahoo-civil-liability-search-engines-maría.

38. Eriq Gardner, "Music Publisher Gets $25 Million Jury Verdict Against Cox in Trailblazing Piracy Case," *The Hollywood Reporter*, December 17, 2015, https://www.hollywoodreporter.com/thr-esq/music-publisher-gets-25-million-849829.

39. Brian O'Keefe, "The Red Tape Conundrum," *Fortune*, October 20, 2016, http://fortune.com/red-tape-business-regulations.

40. Matthew Le Merle, Raju Sarma, Tashfeen Ahmed, and Christopher Pencavel. "The Impact of U.S. Internet Copyright Regulations on Early-Stage Investment: A Quantitative Study," Booz & Co., 2016, https://www.strategyand.pwc.com/media/uploads/Strategyand-Impact-US-Internet-Copyright-Regulations-Early-Stage-Investment.pdf.

41. "The Economic Impact of Safe Harbours on Internet Intermediary Start-Ups," Oxera, February 2015, https://www.oxera.com/wp-content/uploads/2018/07/The-economic-impact-of-safe-harbours-on-Internet-intermediary-start-ups.pdf.pdf.

42. Paul Starr, "The Great Telecom Implosion," *The American Prospect*, September 8, 2002, https://www.princeton.edu/~starr/articles/articles02/Starr-TelecomImplosion-9-02.htm.

43. "Skype Traffic Continues to Thrive," *TeleGeography*, January 15, 2014, https://www.telegeography.com/products/commsupdate/articles/2014/01/15/skype-traffic-continues-to-thrive.

44. Stephen Sale and Michael Lane, "Communication Services in Western Europe: Trends and Forecasts 2016–2021," *Analysis Mason*, August 2016, http://www.analysysmason.com/Research/Content/Reports/communication-services-WE-Aug2016-RDMV0/sample-TOC.

45. Baker McKenzie, "Brazilian National Cinema Proposes New Regulations for Video on Demand Services," Lexology, February 13, 2017, https://www.lexology.com/library/detail.aspx?g=f363b33d-d052-4a74-8f4c-f744b46a0392.

46. "Report of the Special Rapporteur on the Promotion and Protection of the Right to Freedom of Opinion and Expression, Frank La Rue," United Nations General Assembly, Human Rights Council, Seventeenth Session, May 16, 2011, https://www2.ohchr.org/english/bodies/hrcouncil/docs/17session/A.HRC.17.27_en.pdf.

47. See, for the argument, Javier Pallero and Raman Jit Singh Chima, "Proposals for Regulating Internet Apps and Services: Understanding the Digital Rights Impact of the 'Over-The-Top' Debate," Access.now, August 21, 2017, https://www.accessnow.org/cms/assets/uploads/2017/08/Access_Now_OTT-position%E2%80%93paper.pdf.

48. Min Jung Kim, "Essays on the Economics of the Smartphone and Application Industry," a thesis submitted to the faculty of the Graduate School of the University of Minnesota, 2013, http://conservancy.umn.edu/bitstream/handle/11299/159773/1/Kim_umn_0130E_14389.pdf.

49. "EU Finance Ministers Continue Debate on Digital Tax Scope," *Bloomberg News*, September 2018, https://www.bna.com/eu-finance-ministers-n73014482246.

50. Raul Katz, "The Impact of Taxation on the Digital Economy," a presentation to the ITU Regional Economic and Financial Forum of Telecommunications/ICT for Africa, Abidjan, Côte d'Ivoire, January 19, 2016, http://www.itu.int/en/ITU-D/Regulatory-Market/Pages/Events2016/Abidjan/Ses3_2_Katz_Taxation percent20v4.pdf.

51. Ibid.

52. "Taxing Telecom," AT Kearney, 2013, https://www.atkearney.com/documents/10192/1046683/Taxing+TelecomThe+Case+for+Reform.pdf/88c2d30c-f0d4-4496-b7e3-ab9298d09ced (accessed February 25, 2018).

53. Katz, "The Impact of Taxation on the Digital Economy."

54. Joshi Sujata and others, "Impact of Over the Top (OTT) Services on Telecom Service Providers," *Indian Journal of Science and Technology* 8, no. S4 (February 2015), http://www.indjst.org/index.php/indjst/article/viewFile/62238/48529.

55. See Asia Internet Coalition, "Smart Regulation for OTT Growth," October 2015, https://www.aicasia.org/wp-content/uploads/2015/10/AIC-White-Paper-on-OTT_Final2.pdf.

56. Ibid.

57. Klint Finley, "After Slurping Up AI Researchers, Facebook Offers to Share," *Wired*, November 10, 2017, https://www.wired.com/story/after-slurping-up-ai-researchers-facebook-offers-to-share.

58. For U.S. avocados, see "Florida Avocado Grades and Standards," U.S. Department of Agriculture, https://www.ams.usda.gov/grades-standards/florida-avocado-grades-and-standards (accessed March 17, 2019). For GlobalG.A.P, see "GlobalG.A.P. Retail and Food Service Members," https://www.globalgap.org/uk_en/who-we-are/members/retailers-food-service/index.html (accessed March 17, 2019).

59. Jagdish Bhagwati, *Termites in the Trading System: How Preferential Agreements Undermine Free Trade* (Oxford: Oxford University Press, 2007).

60. Inter-American Development Bank, "Coping with the Spaghetti Bowl of FTAs in LAC and Asia: Effects of FTAs on Company Strategies, *Mimeo*, 2009.

61. "Consumer Market Study on the Functioning of E-Commerce and Internet

Marketing and Selling Techniques in the Retail of Goods," Civic Consulting, September 9, 2011, http://www.civic-consulting.de/reports/study_ecommerce_goods_en.pdf.

62. "A Digital Single Market Strategy for Europe," Communication from the Commission to the European Parliament, the Council, the European Economic and Social Committee and the Committee of the Regions, COM(2015) 192 final, May 6, 2015, http://eur-lex.europa.eu/legal-content/EN/TXT/?qid=1447773803386&uri=CELEX%3A52015DC0192.

63. "The ASEAN Digital Revolution," AT Kearney and Axiata, https://www.atkearney.com/documents/10192/6986374/ASEAN+Digital+Revolution.pdf/86c51659-c7fb-4bc5-b6e1-22be3d801ad2 (accessed February 25, 2018).

64. "The Economic Benefits of Early Harmonisation of the Digital Dividend Spectrum and the Cost of Fragmentation in Asia-Pacific," GSMA and the Boston Consulting Group, May 9, 2012, https://www.gsma.com/spectrum/resources/the-economic-benefits-of-early-harmonisation-of-the-digital-dividend-spectrum-and-the-cost-of-fragmentation-in-asia.

65. "WTO Wrestles with Relevance in Age of Eecommerce," *Financial Times*, December 13, 2017, https://www.ft.com/content/d9f63c20-e01d-11e7-a8a4-0a1e63a52f9c.

CHAPTER 11

1. "MSME Finance Gap, Assessment of the Shortfalls and Opportunities in Financing Micro, Small and Medium Enterprises in Emerging Markets," World Bank Group, SME Finance Forum, International Finance Corporation, 2017, https://www.smefinanceforum.org/sites/default/files/Data%20Sites%20downloads/MSME%20Report.pdf.

2. Kati Suominen, "Ecommerce Development Index," report for the U.S. Agency for International Development, April 2017, https://pdf.usaid.gov/pdf_docs/PA00MP8T.pdf.

3. "Small Business Lending in the United States," Office of Advocacy, U.S. Small Business Administration, 2012, https://www.sba.gov/sites/default/files/files/sbl_12study.pdf.

4. Daniel Paravisini, Veronica Rappoport, Philipp Schnabl, and Daniel Wolfenzon, "Dissecting the Effect of Credit Supply on Trade: Evidence from Matched Credit-Export Data." NBER Working Paper No. 16975, 2011.

5. Jean-Charles Bricongne, Lionel Fontagné, Guillaume Gaulier, Daria Taglioni, and Vincent Vicard, "Exports and Sectoral Financial Dependence: Evidence on French Firms During the Great Global Crisis," European Central Bank Working Paper 1227, July 2010.

6. See Daria Taglioni, Lionel Fontagné, Guillaume Gaulier, Vincent Vicard, and Jean-Charles Bricongne, "Firms and the Global Crisis: French Exports in the Turmoil," VoxEu.irg, November 5, 2009.

7. *Removing Barriers to SME Access to International Markets* (Paris: Organisation for Economic Co-operation and Development, 2008).

8. "Small and Medium-Sized Enterprises: Characteristics and Performance," U.S. International Trade Commission, Investigation No. 332–510, Publication 4189, November 2010, http://www.usitc.gov/publications/332/pub4189.pdf.

9. "Internationalisation of European SMEs," EIM Business & Policy Research, report study for Entrepreneurship Unit, Directorate-General for Enterprise and Industry, European Commission, 2010.

10. See Kati Suominen and Reena Gordon, *Going Global: Promoting the Internationalization of Small and Mid-Size Enterprises in Latin America and the Caribbean* (Washington, DC: Inter-American Development Bank, March 2014).

11. Emanuele Forlani, "Liquidity Constraints and Firm's Export Activity," working paper, Universie Catholique de Louvain—CORE, April 2010.

12. David Greenway, Alessandra Guariglia, and Richard Kneller, "Financial Factors and Exporting Decisions," *Journal of International Economics* 73, no. 2 (November 2007): 377–395.

13. See Taglioni, Fontagné, Gaulier, Vicard, and Bricongne, "Firms and the Global Crisis"; See also Holger Goerg and Marina-Eliza Spaliara, "Financial Pressure and Exit from the Export Market," CESifo-Delphi Conference on the Economics of Firm Exporting, April 26–27, 2013.

14. For the relationship between labor productivity and access to credit, see Veselin Kuntchev, Rita Ramalho, Jorge Rodríguez-Meza, and Judy S. Yang, "What Have We Learned from the Enterprise Surveys Regarding Access to Finance by SMEs?" World Bank Report No. 68292, version February 14, 2012, http://documents.worldbank. org/curated/en/958291468331867463/What-have-we-learned-from-the-enterprise-surveys-regarding-access-to-finance-by-SMEs. For exporting and access to credit, see Greenaway, Guariglia, and Kneller, "Financial Factors and Exporting Decisions." See also J. M. Campa and J. M. Shaver, "Exporting and Capital Investment: On the Strategic Behavior of Exporters," Discussion Paper No. 469, IESE Business School, University of Navarra, 2002; and A. Guariglia and S. Mateut, "Inventory Investment, Global Engagement and Financial Constraints in the UK: Evidence from Micro Data," GEP Research Paper No. 05/23, Leverhulme Centre for Research on Globalization and Economic Policy, University of Nottingham, 2005.

15. Greenway, Guariglia, and Kneller, "Financial Factors and Exporting Decisions."

16. "Finance," Enterprise Surveys, World Bank Group, 2018, http://www.enterprise-surveys.org/data/exploretopics/finance.

17. "Survey: 77% of Banks in Latin America and the Caribbean Plan to Increase Credit to Small and Medium Enterprises," IDB Group-Felaban, November 19, 2012, http://www.iadb.org/en/news/news-releases/2012-11-19/2012-sme-lending-survey-in-latin-america-and-caribbean,10222.html.

18. "Las Pymes de América Latina y el Caribe: Un negocio estratégico para los bancos de la región, 5ta encuesta regional en América Latina y el Caribe," Inter-American Development Bank, 2012.

19. David McKenzie and Christopher Woodruff, "Experimental Evidence on Returns to Capital and Access to Finance in Mexico," World Bank Working Paper, March 2008, http://siteresources.worldbank.org/DEC/Resources/Experimental_Evidence_on_Returns_to_Capital_and_Access_to_Finance_in-Mexico.pdf; and Abhijit Banerjee and Esther Duflo, "Do Firms Want to Borrow More? Testing Credit Constraints Using

a Directed Lending Program," MIT Working Paper, 2012, http://economics.mit.edu/files/2706.

20. Susan Adams, "How Tala Mobile Is Using Phone Data to Revolutionize Microfinance," *Forbes*, August 29, 2016, https://www.forbes.com/sites/forbestreptalks/2016/08/29/how-tala-mobile-is-using-phone-data-to-revolutionize-microfinance/#4faaa8a42a9f.

21. "Average Small Business Loan Amount in 2018: Across Banks and Alternative Lenders," ValuePenguin, https://www.valuepenguin.com/average-small-business-loan-amount (accessed March 18, 2019).

22. There are various models—Kabbage in Atlanta buys small accounts receivables, StreetShares provides three- to thirty-six-month-term small business loans, and Biz-2Credit matches companies to best-fit lenders.

23. "The Economic Impact of OnDeck's Lending," Analysis Group, November 17, 2015, https://www.ondeck.com/wp-content/uploads/2017/09/Impact-Report.pdf.

24. Usman Ahmed, Thorsten Beck, Christine McDaniel, and Simon Schropp, "Filling the Gap: How Technology Enables Access to Finance for Small- and Medium-Sized Enterprises; *innovations* 10, no. 3/4 (2016), https://www.mitpressjournals.org/doi/pdf/10.1162/inov_a_00239.

25. Mark E. Schweitzer and Brett Barkley, "Is 'Fintech' Good for Small Business Borrowers? Impacts on Firm Growth and Customer Satisfaction," Federal Reserve Bank of Cleveland, February 1, 2017, https://www.clevelandfed.org/newsroom-and-events/publications/working-papers/2017-working-papers/wp-1701-is-fintech-good-for-small-business-borrowers.aspx.

26. Miriam Segal, "Peer-to-Peer Lending: A Financing Alternative for Small Businesses," SBA Office of Advocacy, Issue Brief No. 10, September 10, 2015, https://www.sba.gov/sites/default/files/advocacy/Issue-Brief-10-P2P-Lending.pdf.

27. Schweitzer and Barkley, "Is 'Fintech' Good for Small Business Borrowers?"

28. Julapa Jagtiani and Cathy Lemieux, "Small Business Lending: Challenges and Opportunities for Community Banks," ResearchGate, February 2016, https://www.researchgate.net/profile/Julapa_Jagtiani/publication/305422937_Small_Business_Lending_Challenges_and_Opportunities_for_Community_Banks/links/578e403608aecbca4caac856.pdf.

29. Scott Carey, "What Is Open Banking? What Does It Mean for Banks, Fintech Startups & Consumers?" ComputerworldUK, July 16, 2018, https://www.computerworlduk.com/applications/is-2018-year-that-open-banking-becomes-reality-in-uk-3653824.

30. "Opportunities and Challenges in Online Marketplace Lending," U.S. Department of the Treasury, May 10, 2016, https://www.treasury.gov/connect/blog/Documents/Opportunities%20and%20Challenges%20in%20Online%20Marketplace%20Lending%20vRevised.pdf.

31. Connie Loizos, "For Online Lenders, It's Suddenly Touch-and-Go," TechCrunch, 2016, https://techcrunch.com/2016/05/17/for-online-lenders-its-suddenly-touch-and-go-2.

32. "China's Central Bank Orders Crackdown on Online Lenders to Curb Runaway Credit," *South China Morning Post*, November 22, 2017, http://www.scmp.com/business/banking-finance/article/2120972/chinas-central-bank-issues-orders-rein-peer-peer-lenders; and Angus Whitley, Alfred Liu, and Jun Luo, "Military Drills Help China's Best Bank Toughen Up Its Staff," *Bloomberg Businessweek*, November 15, 2017, https://www.bloomberg.com/news/features/2017–11–15/military-drills-help-china-s-best-bank-toughen-up-its-staff.

33. Karen Gordon Mills and Braydon McCarthy, "The State of Small Business Lending: Innovation and Technology and the Implications for Regulation," Harvard Business School, Working Paper 17-042, 2016, http://www.paydayloanuniversity.com/wp-content/uploads/2017/04/Harvard-SME-Small-Medium-Business-Lending-2017.pdf.

34. "MYbank Deepens Push for Business Big Banks Won't Touch," *Bloomberg News*, July 2, 2017, https://www.bloomberg.com/news/articles/2017–07–02/jack-ma-s-bank-deepens-push-for-business-big-lenders-won-t-touch.

35. Ibid.

36. Angus Whitley, Alfred Liu, and Jun Luo, "Military Drills Help China's Best Bank Toughen Up Its Staff," *Businessweek*, November 15, 2017, https://www.bloomberg.com/news/features/2017-11-15/military-drills-help-china-s-best-bank-toughen-up-its-staff. In evaluations, the IPC model stands out with three others as helping lenders profitably make loans for small businesses with low default rates and psychometrics that evaluate the borrower's integrity, attitudes, beliefs, and other otherwise hard-to-quantify factors. Pioneered by a Harvard spinoff EFL, the test took twenty-five minutes and was paired with traditional lending criteria; an entrepreneur had to fail both methods to be declined a loan. In the pilot in Peru, 7 percent fell into that category. An assessment found EFL a useful tool for banks to expand credit loans to business owners without increasing the bank's portfolio risk; however, applicants with credit scores who were rejected by the bank but accepted by the EFL were deemed high risk and ended up being in arrears. In other words, people who had shoddy repayment histories did no better repaying in this case, while people without borrowing history who applied for a loan did well and repaid—which means EFL, like IPC, can help financing institutions extend credit for the new borrowers.

37. Jaime Novoa, "P2P Lending Platform Lendico to 'Temporarily' Stop Operating in Spain," Novobrief, 2014, https://novobrief.com/p2p-lending-platform-lendico-to-close-in-spain.

38. Markus M. Makela and Markku V. J. Maula, "Cross-Border Venture Capital and New Venture Internationalization: An Isomorphism Perspective," Taylor & Francis Online, February 23, 2007, http://www.tandfonline.com/doi/abs/10.1080/13691060500258877?src=recsys&journalCode=tvec20.

39. Mary Ann Azevedo, "As the Tech Boom Continues, VCs Increasingly Look to Latin America for Returns," crunchbase news, August 25, 2017, https://news.crunchbase.com/news/tech-boom-continues-vcs-increasingly-look-latin-america-returns.

40. S. A. Swanson, "6 Ways a China Office Can Help a Lower-Middle-Market PE Firm," Bluepoint Capital Partners, March 13, 2017, https://www.bluepointcapital.com/news/6-ways-a-china-office-can-help-a-lower-middle-market-pe-firm.

41. Gene Teare, "It's 2017, and Women Still Aren't Being Funded Equally," Tech-Crunch, 2017, https://techcrunch.com/2017/07/16/its-2017-and-women-still-arent-being-funded-equally.

42. See, for example, A. Alesina, F. Lotti, and P. E. Mistrulli, "Do Women Pay More for Credit? Evidence from Italy," *Journal of the European Economic Association* 11 (2013): 45–66; G. Calcagnini, G. Giombini, and E. Lenti, "Gender Differences in Bank Loan Access: An Empirical Analysis," *Italian Economic Journal* 1 (2014): 193–217; and Sarah K. Harkness, "Discrimination in Lending Markets: Status and the Intersections of Gender and Race," *Social Psychology Quarterly* 79, no. 1 (2016).

43. Steve Bertoni, "How Mixing Data and Fashion Can Make Rent the Runway Tech's Next Billion Dollar Star," *Forbes*, August 28, 2014, http://campfire-capital.com/apparel/mixing-data-fashion-can-make-rent-runway-techs-next-billion-dollar-star. Women are also less likely to ask for capital, but that's beside the point—experiments reveal that when a man and a woman with the exact same credentials pitch the exact same company with the exact same script, the man is far likelier to get funded, and likelier to be asked to talk about the company's growth prospects, potential market, and scalability, while women are asked to talk about the risks, downside, and other such "how do you mitigate an impending disaster" questions. See, for a number of studies, Doree Shafrir, "How Ingrained Is Sexism in Silicon Valley? Ask the Women Trying to Get Funding," *The Cut*, April 27, 2017, https://www.thecut.com/2017/04/women-entrepreneurs-talk-about-sexism-in-silicon-valley.html.

44. "Venture Capital Funnel Shows Odds of Becoming a Unicorn Are About 1%," CB Insights, Research Briefs, September 6, 2018, https://www.cbinsights.com/research/venture-capital-funnel-2.

45. Josh Lerner and Joacim Tåg, "Institutions and Venture Capital," *Industrial and Corporate Change* 22, no. 1 (February 1, 2013): 153–182.

46. Mark Van Onabrugge, "A Comparison of Business Angel and Venture Capitalist Investment Procedures: An Agency Theory-Based Analysis," *Venture Capital: An International Journal of Entrepreneurial Finance* 2, no. 2 (November 26, 2010): 91–109.

47. See Ant Bozkaya and William R. Kerr, "Labor Regulations and European Venture Capital," Harvard Business School Working Paper, January 2013, http://www.people.hbs.edu/wkerr/Bozkaya_Kerr_LaborReg%26EurVC_Jan13.pdf, which showed empirically that strong employment protection regulation has inhibited venture capital market growth between 1990 and 2008 in Europe and, in particular, in sectors with higher labor volatility.

48. Joshua Aizenman and Jake Kendall, "The Internationalization of Venture Capital and Private Equity," NBER Working Paper No. 14344, September 2008, http://www.nber.org/papers/w14344.

49. Ibid.

50. Blog del Emprendedor, "Programa Mujeres Pyme," January 30, 2017, https://www.inadem.gob.mx/programa-mujeres-pyme.

51. James A. Brander, Qianqian Du, and Thomas F. Hellmann, "The Effects of Government-Sponsored Venture Capital: International Evidence," NBER Working Paper No. 16521, November 2010.

52. Douglas J. Cumming, Luca Grilli, and Samuele Murtin, "Governmental and Independent Venture Capital Investments in Europe: A Firm-Level Performance Analysis Panel," *Journal of Corporate Finance* 42 (February 2017): 439–459; T. Luukkonen, M. Deschryvere, and F. Bertoni, "The Value Added by Government Venture Capital Funds Compared with Independent Venture Capital Funds," *Technovation* 33, nos. 4–5 (April–May 2013): 154–162.

53. See, for example, Olav Sorenson, Guan-Cheng Li, Valentina A. Assenova, and Jason Boada, "Expand Innovation Funding via Crowdfunding," ResearchGate, December 2016, https://www.researchgate.net/publication/311850636_Expand_innovation_finance_via_crowdfunding.

54. Vanessa Naegels, Neema Mori, and Bert D'Espallier, "An Institutional View on Access to Finance by Tanzanian Women-Owned Enterprises," *Venture Capital*, August 23, 2017, 1–20.

55. Ann Marie Wiersch and Scott Shane, "Why Small Business Lending Isn't What It Used to Be," Economic Commentary, Cleveland Federal Reserve, August 14, 2013, http://www.clevelandfed.org/research/commentary/2013/2013-10.cfm.

56. For excellent criticism, see Anneel Karnani, "Microfinance Misses Its Mark," *Stanford Social Innovation Review*, Summer 2007, https://ssir.org/articles/entry/microfinance_misses_its_mark.

57. Ryan Decker, John Haltiwanger, Ron Jarmin, and Javier Miranda, "The Role of Entrepreneurship in U.S. Job Creation and Economic Dynamism," *Journal of Economic Perspectives* 28, no. 3 (2014): 3–24.

58. Patrick Sarch and Kevin Petrasic, "Banking M&A On Course for a Comeback After Rise in Value in 2018," Lexology, White & Case LLP, November 2, 2018, https://www.lexology.com/library/detail.aspx?g=e293197f-3e41-4de9-aa51-1ffea82cf342.

59. Esther Duflo and Abhijit V. Banerjee, *Poor Economics: A Radical Rethinking of the Way to Fight Global Poverty* (New York: PublicAffairs, 2011).

60. Robert Peck Christen, Richard Rosenberg, and Veena Jayadeva, "Financial Institutions with a Double-Bottom Line: Implications for the Future of Microfinance," CGAP OccasionalPaper 8, July 2004, https://www.cgap.org/sites/default/files/CGAP-Occasional-Paper-Financial-Institutions-with-a-Double-Bottom-Line-Implications-for-the-Future-of-Microfinance-Jul-2004.pdf.

61. Karnani, "Microfinance Misses Its Mark."

62. Brian Warby, "Microfinance and Poverty Reduction: How Risks Associated with Government Policies Affect Whether Microfinance Alleviates Poverty in Latin-America," University of South Carolina Scholar Commons, 2014, https://scholarcommons.sc.edu/cgi/viewcontent.cgi?article=3766&context=etd.

63. Abhijit Banerjee, Emily Breza, Esther Duflo, and Cynthia Kinnan, "Do Credit Constraints Limit Entrepreneurship? Heterogeneity in the Returns to Microfinance," Columbia Business School, November 2015, https://www0.gsb.columbia.edu/faculty/ebreza/papers/BanerjeeBrezaDufloKinnan.pdf.

64. See summary at Poverty Action Lab, "Microcredit Doesn't Live Up to Promise of Transforming Lives of the Poor, 6 Studies Show," Press Release, January 22, 2015, https://

www.povertyactionlab.org/sites/default/files/2015.01.22-Microcredit-EurekAlert%21.
pdf.

65. Dean S. Karlan and Martin Valdivia, "Teaching Entrepreneurship: Impact of
Business Training on Microfinance Clients and Institutions," Econstor, Center discussion paper, 2006, https://www.econstor.eu/bitstream/10419/39347/1/52491091X.pdf.

CHAPTER 12

1. Benjamin Oreskes, "POLITICO-Harvard Poll: Amid Trump's Rise, GOP Voters
Turn Sharply Away from Free Trade," POLITICO, September 24, 2016, https://www.
politico.com/story/2016/09/politico-harvard-poll-free-trade-trump-gop-228600.

2. David Ricardo, On the Principles of Political Economy and Taxation (London: John
Murray, 1817).

3. See, for example, Tom DiChristopher, "Sizing up the Trade Adjustment Assistance Program," CNBC, June 26, 2015, https://www.cnbc.com/2015/06/26/is-aid-to-trade-displaced-workers-worth-the-cost.html.

4. Scott C. Bradford, Paul L. E. Grieco, and Gary Clyde Hufbauer, "The Payoff to
America from Global Integration," Peterson Institute for International Economics,
https://piie.com/sites/default/files/publications/papers/2iie3802.pdf (accessed March
18, 2019).

5. Daren Acemoglu, David Autor, David Dorn, Gordon H. Hanson, and Brendan
Price, "Import Competition and the Great U.S. Employment Sag of the 2000s," working
paper, August 2014, https://economics.mit.edu/files/10590.

6. Ibid.

7. Sam Costello, "Where Is the iPhone Made?" Lifewire, October 13, 2017.

8. Barry Eichengreen, The Populist Temptation: Economic Grievance and Political
Reaction in the Modern Era (Oxford, UK: Oxford University Press, 2018).

9. Guobing Shen and Xiaolan Fu, "The Trade Effects of US Anti-Dumping Actions
Against China Post-WTO Entry," The World Economy 37, no. 1 (January 2014): 86–105.

10. Chad P. Bown, Euijin Jung, and Eva (Yiwen) Zhang, "Trump's Steel Tariffs Have
Hit Smaller and Poorer Countries the Hardest," Peterson Institute for International Economics Blog, November 15, 2018.

11. Joseph Gagnon, "Trump and Navarro's Mistaken Assumptions About Trade Deficits," Peterson Institute for International Economics Blog, November 1, 2018, https://
piie.com/blogs/trade-investment-policy-watch/trump-and-navarros-mistaken-assumptions-about-trade-deficits.

12. "Concluding Remarks by the Chairperson," World Trade Organization, Trade
Policy Review of China, July 2018, https://www.wto.org/english/tratop_e/tpr_e/tp475_
crc_e.htm.

13. United States Trade Representative, "2017 Report to Congress on China's WTO
Compliance," January 2018, https://ustr.gov/sites/default/files/files/Press/Reports/
China%202017%20WTO%20Report.pdf.

14. "Independent Monitoring of Policies That Affect World Commerce," Global
Trade Alert, https://www.globaltradealert.org.

15. Chad P. Bown. "Protectionism Was Threatening Global Supply Chains Before Trump," Peterson Institute for International Economics Blog, November 8, 2018 .https://piie.com/blogs/trade-investment-policy-watch/protectionism-was-threatening-global-supply-chains-trump.

16. Shen and Fu, "The Trade Effects of US Anti-Dumping Actions."

17. Lori Ann LaRocco, "China Tariff Effects Started Showing Up in Shipping Data Months Ago," CNBC, October 28, 2018, https://www.cnbc.com/2018/10/26/china-tariff-effects-started-showing-up-in-shipping-data-months-ago.html.

18. Gary Clyde Hufbauer, Cathleen Cimino, and Tyler Moran, "NAFTA at 20: Misleading Charges and Positive Achievements, NAFTA 20 Years Later," Peterson Institute for International Economics Briefing No. 14–3, November 2014, https://piie.com/publications/briefings/piieb14-3.pdf.

19. Pablo D. Fajgelbaum and Amit K. Khandelwal, "Measuring the Unequal Gains from Trade," *The Quarterly Journal of Economics* 131, no. 3 (August 1, 2016: 1113–1180.

20. Eduardo Porter, "Sizing Up Hillary Clinton's Plans to Help the Middle Class," *New York Times*, July 14, 2015, https://www.nytimes.com/2015/07/15/business/sizing-up-hillary-clintons-plans-to-help-the-middle-class.html.

21. James Sherk, "Workers' Compensation: Growing Along with Productivity," The Heritage Foundation, May 31, 2016, https://www.heritage.org/jobs-and-labor/report/workers-compensation-growing-along-productivity.

22. Veronique de Rugy, "The Pay-Productivity Gap Is an Illusion," Foundation for Economic Education, April 18, 2016, https://fee.org/articles/the-pay-productivity-gap-is-an-illusion.

23. Robert Z. Lawrence, "The Growing Gap Between Real Wages and Labor Productivity," Peterson Institute for International Economics, July 21, 2015, https://piie.com/blogs/realtime-economic-issues-watch/growing-gap-between-real-wages-and-labor-productivity.

24. Ibid.

25. Martin S. Feldstein, "Did Wages Reflect Growth in Productivity?" NBER Working Paper No. 13953, April 2008, https://www.nber.org/papers/w13953.

26. Vladimir Gimpelson and Daniel Treisman, "Misperceiving Inequality," NBER Working Paper No. 21174, May 2015, https://www.nber.org/papers/w21174.

27. Herbert A. Simon, "Automation," *The New York Review of Books*, May 26, 1966, https://www.nybooks.com/articles/1966/05/26/automation-3.

28. Quoted in Timothy Taylor, "Automation and Job Loss: The Fears of 1964," Conversable Economist, December 1, 2014, http://conversableeconomist.blogspot.com/2014/12/automation-and-job-loss-fears-of-1964.html.

29. David Ricardo, *Principles of Political Economy*, 3rd ed., ed. R. M. Hartwell (Harmondsworth, UK: Pelican Classics, 1821 [1971]). See also the excellent article by Joel Mokyr, Chris Vickers, and Nicolas L. Ziebarth, "The History of Technological Anxiety and the Future of Economic Growth: Is This Time Different?" *Journal of Economic Perspectives* 29, no. 3 (Summer 2015): 31–50.

30. "Labor Force Statistics from the Current Population Survey," Bureau of Labor Statistics, last modified January 18, 2019, https://www.bls.gov/cps/cpsaat01.htm.

31. Trevor Gallen, "Lecture 8: Growth Theory IV: Why Are There Still So Many Jobs?" Purdue University, Spring 2016, http://web.ics.purdue.edu/~tgallen/Teaching/Econ_352_Spring_2016/Lecture%208%20-%20Growth%20Theory%20-%20IV.pdf.

32. "Accountants and Auditors," Bureau of Labor Statistics, Occupational Outlook Handbook, last modified April 13, 2018, https://www.bls.gov/ooh/business-and-financial/accountants-and-auditors.htm.

33. Acemoglu, Autor, Dorn, Hanson., and Price, "Import Competition."

34. Maureen Dowd, "Elon Musk's Billion-Dollar Crusade to Stop the A.I. Apocalypse," *Vanity Fair*, April 2017, https://www.vanityfair.com/news/2017/03/elon-musk-billion-dollar-crusade-to-stop-ai-space-x.

35. Catherine Clifford, "Facebook CEO Mark Zuckerberg: Elon Musk's Doomsday AI Predictions Are 'Pretty Irresponsible,'" *Entrepreneurs*, July 24, 2017, https://www.cnbc.com/2017/07/24/mark-zuckerberg-elon-musks-doomsday-ai-predictions-are-irresponsible.html.

36. "Automation Threatens 69% Jobs in India: World Bank," *The Hindu*, November 1, 2016, http://www.thehindu.com/business/Industry/Automation-threatens-69-jobs-in-India-World-Bank/article15427005.ece.

37. "Hype cycle," *Wikipedia*, https://en.wikipedia.org/wiki/Hype_cycle (accessed March 18, 2019).

38. David Autor and David Dorn, "How Technology Wrecks the Middle Class," *New York Times*, August 24, 2013, http://www.collier.sts.vt.edu/engl4874/pdfs/autor_nyt_9_24_13.pdf.

39. David H. Autor, "Polanyi's Paradox and the Shape of Employment Growth,". NBER Working Paper No. 20485, September 2014, http://www.nber.org/papers/w20485.

40. "Digital Trade in the U.S. and Global Economies, Part 1," U.S. International Trade Commission, Investigation No. 332–531, USITC Publication 4415, July 2013, https://www.usitc.gov/publications/332/pub4415.pdf.

41. See, for example, Erik Cannon, "Coding Bootcamps Also Teach You How to Get Rejected 10 Times a Day," freeCodeCamp, September 20, 2016, https://medium.freecodecamp.org/jumping-through-loops-at-coding-bootcamp-c5fa34947419.

42. Chang-Tai Hsieh and Enrico Moretti, "Can Free Entry Be Inefficient? Fixed Commissions and Social Waste in the Real Estate Industry," *Journal of Political Economy* 111, no. 5 (2003), https://faculty.chicagobooth.edu/chang-tai.hsieh/research/jpe%20real%20estate.pdf.

43. Russ Juskalian, "Rebuilding Germany's Centuries-Old Vocational Program," *MIT Technology Review*, June 22, 2018, https://www.technologyreview.com/s/611423/rebuilding-germanys-centuries-old-vocational-program.

44. Dirk Krueger and Krishna B. Kumar, "Skill-Specific Rather Then [sic] General Education: A Reason for US-Europe Growth Differences?" NBER Working Paper No. 9408, January 2003, http://www.nber.org/papers/w9408.

45. See Mokyr, Vickers, and Ziebarth, "The History of Technological Anxiety."

46. "Domestic Niche Players Jump Start Malaysia's B2B E-Commerce Sector," HK-

TDC Research, November 21, 2016, http://economists-pick-research.hktdc.com/business-news/article/International-Market-News/Domestic-Niche-Players-Jump-Start-Malaysia-s-B2B-E-commerce-sector/imn/en/1/1X000000/1X0A845J.htm.

47. "Vende en Amazon USA: ¡ahora es más fácil!" Promexico Blog, July 12, 2018, https://www.gob.mx/promexico/articulos/vende-en-amazon-usa-ahora-es-mas-facil?idiom=es; "Amazon y ProMéxico firman acuerdo para impulsar a pymes mexicanas en el ecommerce," eBanking News, October 2, 2018, https://www.ebankingnews.com/noticias/amazon-y-promexico-firman-acuerdo-para-impulsar-a-pymes-mexicanas-en-el-ecommerce-0042562; and Etivally Calva Tapia, "Así te ayudarán Alibaba, Amazon, eBay y UPS a exportar tus productos," Entrepreneur, October 10, 2017, https://www.entrepreneur.com/article/302430.

48. "Snapchat Can Tout Unique User Behavior That Doesn't Overlap with Instagram and Other Social Media," Bloomberg News, May 3, 2017.

49. Nicholas Thompson and Fred Vogelstein, "15 Months of Fresh Hell Inside Facebook," Wired, April 16, 2019, https://www.wired.com/story/facebook-mark-zuckerberg-15-months-of-fresh-hell.

50. "The 8 Most Active VCs in US Ecommerce Startups," Pitchbook, July 11, 2017, https://pitchbook.com/newsletter/the-8-most-active-vcs-in-us-ecommerce-startups.

51. Benedict Evans, "Winner-Takes-All Effects in Autonomous Cars," August 22, 2017, https://www.ben-evans.com/benedictevans/2017/8/20/winner-takes-all,

52. Lesley Chiou and Catherine Tucker, "Search Engines and Data Retention: Implications for Privacy and Antitrust," NBER Working Paper No. 23815, September 2017.

53. Drake Bennett, "The Brutal Fight to Mine Your Data and Sell It to Your Boss," Bloomberg Businessweek, November 15, 2017, https://www.bloomberg.com/news/features/2017-11-15/the-brutal-fight-to-mine-your-data-and-sell-it-to-your-boss.

54. Ibid.

55. See, for example, Makena Kelly, "Sen. Josh Hawley Is Making the Conservative Case Against Facebook," The Verge, March 19, 2018, https://www.theverge.com/2019/3/19/18271487/josh-hawley-senator-missouri-republican-facebook-google-antitrust-data-privacy.

56. Martin Giles, "It's Time to Rein in the Data Barons," MIT Technology Review, June 19, 2018, https://www.technologyreview.com/s/611425/its-time-to-rein-in-the-data-barons.

57. Elizabeth C. Economy, "The Great Firewall of China: Xi Jinping's Internet Shutdown," The Guardian, June 29, 2018, https://www.theguardian.com/news/2018/jun/29/the-great-firewall-of-china-xi-jinpings-internet-shutdown.

58. See Economy, "The Great Firewall of China"; and Christopher Balding, "How Badly Is China's Great Firewall Hurting the Country's Economy?" Foreign Policy, July 18, 2017, https://foreignpolicy.com/2017/07/18/how-badly-is-chinas-great-firewall-hurting-the-countrys-economy.

59. Gary King, Jennifer Pan, and Margaret E. Roberts, "How the Chinese Government Fabricates Social Media Posts for Strategic Distraction, not Engaged Argument," American Political Science Review 111, no. 3, (2017): 484–501.

60. Paul Carsten and Michael Martina, "U.S. Says China Internet Censorship a Burden for Businesses," Reuters, April 8, 2016, https://www.reuters.com/article/us-usa-china-trade-internet-idUSKCN0X50RD.

61. Office of the United States Trade Representative, "2018 Fact Sheet: Key Barriers to Digital Trade," March 2018, ces/press-office/fact-sheets/2017/march/key-barriers-digital-trade.

62. Charlotte Gao, "China's Great Firewall: A Serious Pain in the Neck for European and US Companies," *The Diplomat*, June 21, 2018, https://thediplomat.com/2018/06/chinas-great-firewall-a-serious-pain-in-the-neck-for-european-and-us-companies.

63. Balding, "How Badly Is China's Great Firewall Hurting the Country's Economy?"

64. Sherisse Pham, "China Kills Qualcomm's $44 Billion Deal for NXP," *CNN Business*, July 26, 2018, https://money.cnn.com/2018/07/26/technology/qualcomm-nxp-merger-china/index.html.

65. Timothy Taylor, "The Economics of Daylight Savings Time," Conversable Economist, March 31, 2016, http://conversableeconomist.blogspot.com/2016/03.

CHAPTER 13

1. Kirk Olson, "4 Questions for YouTube's Head of Culture and Trends," Thinkwith-Google, March 2018, https://www.thinkwithgoogle.com/advertising-channels/video/youtube-brand-culture-trends.

2. Dan Andrews, Chiara Criscuolo, and Peter N. Gal, "Frontier Firms, Technology Diffusion and Public Policy: Micro Evidence from OECD Countries," OECD Future of Productivity Papers, 2015, https://www.oecd.org/eco/growth/Frontier-Firms-Technology-Diffusion-and-Public-Policy-Micro-Evidence-from-OECD-Countries.pdf.

3. José DeGregorio, "Productivity in Emerging Market Economies: Slowdown or Stagnation?" Policy paper, Peterson Institute for International Economics, November 2017, https://piie.com/system/files/documents/2–2de-gregorio20171109paper.pdf.

4. Jason Furman and Peter Orszag, "Do the Productivity Slowdown and the Inequality Increase Have a Common Cause?" presentation, Peterson Institute for International Economics, November 9, 2017, https://piie.com/system/files/documents/4-1furman20171109ppt.pdf.

5. Heather A. Conley, Allie Renison, and Kati Suominen, "Freeing Billions of Bits: A Future Roadmap for U.S.-UK Digital Trade," CSIS Policy Report, forthcoming.

6. Kati Suominen, "The Seoul Consensus," *GE Reports*, August 21, 2015, http://www.gereports.com/post/127167023903/kati-suominen-the-seoul-consensus.

7. Peter F. Cowhey and Jonathan D. Aronson, *Digital DNA: Disruption and the Challenges for Global Governance* (Oxford, UK: Oxford University Press, 2018), https://global.oup.com/academic/product/digital-dna-9780190657932?cc=us&lang=en&.

8. Kati Suominen, *Harnessing Blockchain for American Business and Prosperity: 10 Use Cases, 10 Big Questions, Five Solutions* (Washington, DC: Center for Strategic and International Studies, October 2018), https://wita.org/wp-content/uploads/2018/11/181101_Suominen_Blockchain_v3.pdf.

9. "Regulators Club Together to Form Global 'Fintech Sandbox,'" *Financial Times*,

https://www.ft.com/content/ae6a1186-9a2f-11e8-9702-5946bae86e6d (accessed May 18, 2019).

10. Suominen, *Harnessing Blockchain*.

11. Ibid.

12. Kati Suominen, "How the Global Fund for Ecommerce Is Helping Entrepreneurs in Developing Countries Enter the Digital Era," April 12, 2016, http://www.gereports.com/kati-suominen-how-to-help-entrepreneurs-in-developing-countries-enter-the-ecommerce-era.

13. Dr. Joe Dispenza, "Evolve Your Brain," http://www.drjoedispenza.com/?page_id=Evolve-Your-Brain.

14. Matt Symonds, "The Entrepreneurial Employee—How to Make Intrapreneurship a Win-Win for Everyone," *Forbes*, October 29, 2013, https://www.forbes.com/sites/mattsymonds/2013/10/29/the-entrepreneurial-employee-how-to-make-intrapreneurship-a-win-win-for-everyone/#240b6199c202.

15. Thomas Piketty, *Capital in the 21st Century* (Cambridge: Harvard University Press, 2014).

16. Barry Eichengreen, *The Populist Temptation: Economic Grievance and Political Reaction in the Modern Era* (Oxford, UK: Oxford University Press, 2018).

17. Uri Dadush, Kemal Derviş, Sarah P. Milsom, and Bennett Stancil, "Inequality in America: Facts, Trends, and International Perspectives," Brookings, July 13, 2012, https://www.brookings.edu/book/inequality-in-america.

18. Catherine Stephan, "Ins-and-Outs of the Danish Flexicurity Model," BNP Paribas, Economic Research Department, July 11, 2017, http://economic-research.bnpparibas.com/Views/DisplayPublication.aspx?type=document&IdPdf=30102.

19. Alberto F. Alesina and Silvia Ardagna, "Large Changes in Fiscal Policy: Taxes Versus Spending," NBER Working Paper No. 15438, October 2009.

20. Gustavo A. Marrero, Juan Gabriel Rodríguez, and Roy Van der Weide, "Unequal Opportunities, Unequal Growth," VoxEU, February 8, 2017.

21. Paul M. Romer, "Crazy Explanations for the Productivity Slowdown," *NBER Macroeconomics Annual 1987*, Volume 2, ed. Stanley Fischer, National Bureau of Economics Research, 1987, http://www.nber.org/chapters/c11101.pdf.

22. James Feyrer, "The US Productivity Slowdown, the Baby Boom, and Management Quality," *Journal of Population Economics* 24, no. 1 (January 2011): 267–284, https://ideas.repec.org/a/spr/jopoec/v24y2011i1p267-284.html.

23. Ryan Avent, "The Productivity Paradox," *Medium*, March 16, 2017, https://medium.com/@ryanavent_93844/the-productivity-paradox-aafo5e5e4aad.

24. "Discussing the Era of 'New Collar' Workers with IBM CEO Ginni Rometty," *Wall Street Journal*, January 24, 2019, https://www.wsj.com/video/discussing-the-era-of-new-collar-workers-with-ibm-ceo-ginni-rometty/8865662F-6180-4312-918C-DE47856E1DA8.html.

25. Jeffrey Jones, "Americans Say U.S.-China Tariffs More Harmful Than Helpful," *Gallup*, July 26, 2018, https://news.gallup.com/poll/238013/americans-say-china-tariffs-harmful-helpful.aspx.

INDEX

accounting: technological changes and employment, 233
Acemoglu, Daren, 224, 230
additive manufacturing, 12, 19, 23, 24, 26, 27, 28, 32; robotization, 31; and 3D printing technology, 20
Adidas, 20, 21, 23, 50
Affectiva, 127
Afghanistan: customs, 164; public policy, 268
Africa: ecommerce markets, 149; online shopping in, 70; rural commerce in, 55–56; smartphone users in, 64
agglomeration economies, 29, 34
agricultural industry: technological change and employment, 233–234
Ahold Delhaize, 127
Airbnb, 69, 211
Airbus: blockchain use in, 130; 3D printing use in, 19
air cargo, 22: blockchain use in, 99, and ecommerce, 81; and overcapacity challenge, 81
Air Cargo Advanced Screening program, 167
Akamatsu, Kaname, 17
Akerlof, George, 103
algorithms, 178, 188; for customization, 27; for predictions, 119
Alibaba, 8, 11, 41, 42, 50, 51, 74–75, 131, 266; shipping platform, 82; and urban warehouse space, 89; use of blockchain, 99
Align Technology Inc., 24

alimony payments, 223–224
Alipay, 48, 207
Alliance for eTrade Development, 266
Allocca, Kevin, 250
Amazon, 8, 47, 48, 50, 66, 122, 191; air delivery services, 84; Amazon Prime, 62; Dragon Boat project, 84; experimental supermarket, 126; pay-per-use data services, 133; warehousing, 88–89, 90
Americas Market Intelligence (AMI), 161
angel investors, 199–200, 209, 210, 212
anti-dumping, 227, 228
anti-money-laundering (AML), 104
App Store, 69
Argentina: customs, 162; demand-side policies, 142; knowledge-intensive business services (KIBS) in, 35; public policy, 252; and services outsourcing, 35–36
Argentine Chamber of Electronic Commerce, 161, 162
Aronson, Jonathan, 254
artificial intelligence (AI), 50, 71, 108, 118–119, 121, 234, 238–239; fallacies, 234–237; and political risk prediction, 125; and shipping movement forecast, 86
Asian Development Bank, 104
Asia-Pacific Economic Cooperation (APEC), 172; Cross-Border Privacy Rules (CBPR), 183–184, 252, 253
Asia-Pacific region, 39, 61, 137, 172, 196
augmented reality, 51, 156
Australia, 109; Australia Post, 50; Australian Productivity Commission, 171;

Commonwealth Bank of Australia, 109; public policy, 252, 253, 256, 258
automated payments, 114
automation, 232, 235; in shipping industry, 83, 85–88
Autor, David, 224, 230, 235
Avent, Ryan, 272

B2B: cross-border payments, 146; ecommerce, 66
B2C ecommerce, 39, 49
Babylon, 71
Bailey, Andrew, 209
Bain & Company, 26, 106
Baldwin, Richard, 16
BancAlliance, 204
Banco Santander, 109
Banerjee, Abhijit V., 216
Bangladesh, 49, 113, 266
banks, 103–116, 202–203; Basel III, 106; development banks, as Banks-as-a-Service, 268; Dodd-Frank regulations, 204; loans, and customer satisfaction, 204; open banking, 205; technological change and employment, 233
Bank of America, 107
Bank of America Merrill Lynch, 109
Bank of Taizhou, 207
Bank of Thailand, 110
Barclays, 111
BBVA, 35, 109
Belgium, 253
Bernard, Andrew, 40
Bhagwati, Jagdish, 194
Bharti Airtel, 193
Big 5 OCEAN personality traits, 121
big query, 133–134
bilateral trade agreements, 6, 100, 111, 194, 197
Birch, David, 149–150
Bkash, 49
Black Ball Lines, 78
Blackmores, 50
Blendtec, 44
blockchain, 7, 50–51, 99, 101, 122, 169, 256; barrier to adoption of, 100; in food supply chains, 128–129; garbage-in-garbage-out problem, 111; in parts and components maintenance, 129–130; quality verification of products, 129; revolution, 108–111, 114; in supplier risk identification, 130–131; and technology standards, 255, 257–258

Blue Point Capital, 210
BMG Rights Management, 189
BMW, 28
Boeing, 5, 81, 112; machine-to-machine communications, 132; use of 3D printing in, 21
Bown, Chad, 228
Branson, Richard, 270
Brazil, 112; audiovisual platforms regulations, 191; Brazilian Civil Rights Framework for the Internet, 189; cross-border payments, 146–147; customs, 162; ecommerce market diversification in, 48; Internet "safe harbor" laws, 186; knowledge-intensive business services (KIBS) in, 35; online shopping in, 63; service industry, 34; smartphone shopping in, 64
broadband connections, 140–141, 142; download speeds, 70; free WiFi, and consumer surplus, 69; mobile, 64; in rural areas, 56; usage rates, 70, 139
Broda, Christian, 74
bullwhip effect, 121–122
Burundi Shop, 55–56
Business Development Canada's Women in Technology Fund, 214
business growth, and ecommerce, 45–47

Cainiao, 99
Cambodia, 113
Cambridge Analytica, 121
Canada: customs, 164, 172; public policy, 253, 258
Capital Markets Union, 208
Capitol One, 269
cargo manifests, 164, 166–167
Case Holland, 112–113
Caspar, 49, 73

Caterpillar, 18, 112
chained contracts, 114
Chaldal, 48, 49
Chander, Anupam, 187
Chanel, 24
chief executive officers (CEOs): gender gap
    among, 57–58; importance of, 270
Chile: customs, 162; export superstars in,
    40; public policy, 252, 253, 278; trade
    liberalization in, 47
China, 16–17, 94, 104, 177, 226, 255, 260,
    279; blockchain use in, 50–51; cross-bor-
    der ecommerce, 39; customs, 168; cyber-
    censorship, 245–246; cyber court, 48;
    data protection in, 181; diaspora, 44–45;
    ecommerce market diversification in,
    48; Great Cannon, 245; Great Firewall,
    245; job creation, and ecommerce, 52;
    Millennials, 63; online market of, 39, 63;
    ports, 79, 85; rural online shoppers in,
    74–75; screening of online loan market,
    206; 3D printing's impact on trade, 21;
    total cost of ownership in, 17–18; unfair
    practices, 226–228, 245; WTO trade
    policy review (2018), 227
China Sea Rates, 82
Chiou, Lesley, 243
Chipotle, 126, 129
Chiquita, 98
Cisco, 70
Citigroup, 114
ClearCorrect, 19
Clinton, Bill, 186
Clinton, Hillary, 279
cloud computing, 12, 35, 118, 193
Coca-Cola, 124
Codigo Del Sur, 36
cognitive computing, 118–119; see also arti-
    ficial intelligence (AI)
collaterals, 117, 200, 202, 215
Colombia, 191; customs, 163; public policy,
    253
Comin, Diego, 154–155
comparative advantages, 16–17, 177,
    222–223
Concilianet, 48

Congo, 96, 164
connectivity, 137–138, 139; broadband see
    broadband connections; cross-border
    payments, 145–146; in developing coun-
    tries see developing countries; digital
    connectivity 291n.57; and online pay-
    ments, 143–145, 147; rural area, 139; as a
    source of competitiveness, 140
ConsenSys, 127
consumer surplus, 67–69
copyright, 188; infringement, 189; regula-
    tions, 190
cord-cutting, 190–191
Costa Rica, 34; customs, 163–164; public
    policy, 252, 278
Costco's, 90
Countervailing Duty Law, 228
Couture, Victor, 74
Cowhey, Peter, 254
Cox Communications, 189
credit: and export, 201–202; interest rates,
    202–203; microloans, 203–209, 216–218,
    261; no credit situations, 200–201;
    non-bank lender, 147, 205; peer-to-peer
    business-lending market, 204; shortages,
    200–201; and trade, 201
crewless ships, 82–83, 85
cross-border: data transfer, 197; ecom-
    merce, 39, 70 (see also ecommerce);
    economic exchange problems, 12; online
    payments, 145; payments, 145–146; sup-
    ply chain finance, 113
crowdsourcing, 126–127
cuneiform tablets, as promissory notes, 103
Cusolito, Ana Paula, 152
customization: algorithms for, 27; and 3D
    printing, 26–28
customs, 160–161; border bottleneck and,
    161–165; de minimis approach and, 171–
    174; duties on digital goods, 198; solu-
    tions to problems of, 166–170; taxation
    without representation and, 174–175

Dadush, Uri, 271
Daraz, 65
data, 133–134, 243, 244; big data, 119,

130, 131, 243, 265; data partners, 124;
data pipes, 124; foot traffic data, 125–
126; economic costs of tough rules on,
185; granular data, 125–126; historical
data, 243; national data localization,
181–182; personal data, 177–178;
from port automated operations,
86–87; price data, 67, 68, 122, 124;
proprietorship, 243; territorialization
by governments, impacts of, 185–186;
third-party data, 122, 132; trading of,
178; transfer, limitations across companies, 182–183
data flows, 179–180; and free trade agreements, 184
Davis, James J., 248–249
DBS, 109
DCE, 114
Dealstruck, 203
decentralized networks, 31–32, 98
delivery systems/business, 7, 94–95; all-
electric trucks, 83–84; card on delivery,
145; delivery costs, 93, 94; demand
peaks, 90; droids use in, 94; drones use
in, 94; future of, 101; robots use in, 94;
spot-market deliveries, 91; and urban
warehouse space, 89; widening the delivery window, for cost cutting, 92
demand forecasting, 121–122
demand-side policies, 142
demonetization, 148–149
Denmark, 253, 271
Derviş, Kemal, 271
Despegar, 35
Deutsche Bank, 109
Deutsche Post's DHL, 92, 277
developing countries, 17, 220, 222; automation of terminals, 87–88; cashless transactions, 147–148; developmental impact
of smartphones in, 71; ecommerce usage
rates, 143; firms, ocean analogy, 150–
153; importing in, 46; income levels,
155; intra-industry trade in, 73; last-mile
delivery, 93; leapfrogging technologies,
156; online exports in, 41–42; policies on
owning of platforms, 239–240; and port

automation, 87; prediction of political
crises in, 124–125; rural companies in,
53, 55; technology adoption, 155–156;
use of new technologies, lag in, 154;
women, smartphone shopping of, 66; see
also specific countries
diamonds, authenticity verification, 128
DiCaprio, Alisa, 58, 105
Didion, Joan, 29
Digital 9+ (D9), 184, 253
digital divides, 137, 139; and connectivity,
138
digital light synthesis, 23
digitally deliverable services, 34
digital natives, 28, 49, 125
digital protectionism, 13, 177
Digital Standards for Trade, 116, 266
digital trade wars, 245–248; as investment
barriers, 246–247; standard-setting,
247–248
digital transformation: adoption of, 12,
155–156; and government policies,
153–154; lag in, 151–152; and management, 152; and new problems, 11; pace
of, 10–11
DiGi telecommunications, 193
digitization, 221; disparities in, 139; and
employment, 87
Dispenza, Joe, 270
dispute resolution system, in ecommerce,
48
distribution logistics, 88; and ecommerce,
88; see also delivery systems/business
Dollar Shave Club, 120–121
Domino's Pizza, 91
Donaldson, Dave, 79
Dorn, David, 224, 230, 235
DP World, 98
driverless vehicles, 82–83, 94
drones, 87, 94–95, 101
DropBox, 34
drop-shipping, 89
Drucker, Peter, 88
Duflo, Esther, 216, 217, 218
Duval, Yann, 164
Dynamite Data, 124

EBANX, 146

eBay, 8, 41, 42, 44, 45, 48, 50, 54, 55, 266, 277

ecommerce, 7, 38, 39, 41, 218; access to supplies and import, 43; and business growth/economic progress, 45–47; cross-border, 39; differentiated platforms, 242; and economic geography, 54–57; ecosystem, 47–51, 74; exports, 41–43; and gender, 57–59; and Internet connection speed, 139; and job creation, 51–53; market, diversification, 48; multi-platforms, 240; online shopping (see online shopping); rural, 54–55; seller, 143–144; staying power of online exporters, 41; trust in, 47–48; and variety, 72–75; and warehouse vicinity, 90–91

ecommerce deliveries, 94; delivery trucks, 93; and second time deliveries, 94; and traffic, 93–94

economic freedom, 279–280

economic geography, 53–57

economic divisions, 158

Eichengreen, Barry, 225, 271

electronic bills of lading (eBLs), 107–108

electronic letters of credit, 107

electronic single windows, 163–164

electronic ticketing, 98

ELF, 322n.36

El Salvador, 51

employment levels, 228

equity: crowdfunding, 214; finance, 199, 210–211, 261–262

Erickson, Althea, 52

Estonia, 253

ethnic diasporas, 44–45

eTrade, 259–260, 265

Etsy, 45, 54, 55, 73, 277

Eurasia Group, 125

Europe, 14, 157–158; copyright law, 188; cross-border lending, 208; port community system (PCS), 87; see also specific countries

European Union, 162, 172, 188, 213, 244; data privacy and localization laws, impact on EU GDP, 181; data privacy and transfer rules and copyright law, 248; digital taxes, 192, 248; GDPR see General Data Protection Regulation (GDPR); Internet safe harbor laws, 188; Payments Services Directive 2 (PSD2), 205; Single Digital Market, 195; see also specific countries

Evans, Ben, 242

Everledger, 128

eWallets, 148

export, 39–43; and business growth, 45, 46; developing countries, 41–42; and equity investment, 210; export superstars, 40; impact of online sales on export diversification, 43; online platforms, 41–42; productivity of, 40–41, 45; sunk costs, 40, 41

export credit agencies (ECAs), 260–261

Export-Import (EXIM) Bank, 113

Faber, Benjamin, 75

Facebook, 11, 47, 48, 187, 207, 242; Aquila, 138; fraudsters and spammers, 186; Telecom Infra Project, 194; and telecos, 193–194

Facebook merchants, 144–145, 151

facial analytics, 126–127

factoring, 103, 112, 172

Factory World, 14

Feldstein, Martin, 231

Fiat, 126–127

FinAccel, 49

FinalStraw, 28

financial crisis 2007–2008, 54–55, 200–201

financial services regulations, 208

Finland, 253

FinTech companies, 106, 204, 256; loan guarantee, to SMEs, 260–261

5G, 50, 156, 157

Flat World, 14, 15

Flexe, 90

Flexport, 84–85

Flipkart, 50, 65, 66

Ford, 20, 21

foreign labor costs, 18

Foxconn, 20

Freed, Raymond, 18
freedom of expression, 188
Freelancer (online work platform), 36
free market, 176–177
free trade, 5–6, 47; and policy making, 225; *see also* trade liberalization
free trade agreements (FTAs), 4, 194–195, 251–252; and data flows, 184
freight-forwarding business, 84–85
Freshdesk (Freshworks), 35
Friedman, Milton, 279
Friedman, Thomas, 12, 14
Fukuyama, Francis, 176
Function of Beauty, 27
Fundation, 203
funding, 213; equity finance, 199, 210–211, 261–262; government venture funding, 214; reasons for not getting funds, 212; for startups, 189–190, 263
Funding Circle, 203
Furman, Jason, 250

Gagnon, Joseph, 226
Galeano, Eduardo, 162
Garlinghouse, Brad, 106
Gartner, 132
Gates, Bill, 71, 234
Gateway terminal, 85
gazelles, 149–150
General Data Protection Regulation (GDPR), 180, 183, 253; impacts of, 184; implementation costs and fines, 180–181; subverting of, 184–186
General Dynamics, 112
General Electric (GE), 5; GE Transportation, 86; use of 3D printing in, 19, 21; use of blockchain in, 129
Geocast, 125
geographic distance, and trade, 43–44
geopolitical risks prediction, 125
GeoPoll surveys, 124
Georgia, 275
Germany, 185; online content regulations, 187; public policy, 253, 258; view on privacy, 179; vocational training in, 237
Gimpelson, Vladimir, 231

Global Alliance for Trade Facilitation, 258
Global Digital Transformation Fund, 262–263
globalization, 3–4, 37, 221; fragilities of, 15–16; and privacy, 178; and 3D printing technology, 21; in the twenty-first century, 6–10; and unbundling of production and consumption, 16
Globalization 4.0, 8
global supply chains, 4, 8, 37, 112–114; automated supply chain, 100–101; blockchain (*see* blockchain); finance, 112–113; ; management, 88; and regionalized production hubs, 15; shrinking of, 29–32; standardization and scale economies, 26
global taxation framework model, 191–192
Global Trade Alert, 275
Global Trade Connectivity Network, 111
global virtual logistics highway, 98
Glueck, Jeff, 126
GM, 24–25
Goodman, 89
Google, 138, 244; Project Loon, 138
Goolsbee, Austan, 67, 68
Gordon, Robert, 69, 250
Grab (company), 133
Grameen Foundation, 217
Grasshopper, 123, 144–145, 267; drone delivery, 94
gravity model, 43
growth, obsession about, 270–273
growth capital gap, 209–214
Grubhub, 49
Guatemala, 266
Guobing, Shen, 228
Gurucargo, 85

Haiti, 229–230
Haldane, Andy, 250
Hanjin, 81
Hanson, Gordon, 30, 224, 230
Hastings, Reed, 119
Hawley, Josh, 244
Hayek, Friedrich, 279
Heckscher, Eli, 223

Hegazy, Sara, 20
Hero MotoCorp, 20
Hewlett Packard, 15–16; use of 3D print-
    ing, 24
HiQ, 243
HNA Group, 83
Hong Kong Monetary Authority (HKMA),
    111
HSBC, 108, 109, 110
Huawei, 123, 138
Hufbauer, Gary, 173, 229
Hull, Chuck, 18
Hummels, David, 161
hyperloop, 92

IBM, 19, 96–97, 108, 109, 191
IBM Singapore: use of blockchain in, 99
ICC Banking Commission, 105
iCog Labs, 236
Ideal X, 79
IKEA, 50
IMDA, 110
Import Genius, 131
imports, 225; and ecommerce, 43, 46; and
    economic growth, 46; and online shop-
    ping, 70; substitution experiments, 229
India, 34, 50, 104, 155; demonetization,
    148–149; economic geography in, 55;
    India Post, 93; job creation, and ecom-
    merce, 52; last mile logistics in, 91;
    mobile users in, 64; online shopping in,
    63; rural craftspeople in, 55, 73; rural
    shoppers in, 66; smartphone shopping
    in, 65, 66
Indonesia, 49; data protection in, 182
Industry 4.0, 8
Infocomm Development Authority of
    Singapore, 109
informational asymmetry, 68, 104, 117,
    212, 213
Information Technology Agreement, 142
innovation: Economic Innovation Group,
    54; and exporting, 46; financial inno-
    vations scalability, 207–208; Global
    Innovation Forum, 277; and startups,
    216; in telecoms, 193

Instacart, 68
Instagram, 44, 144, 242
Inter-American Development Bank
    (IADB), 53, 73, 100, 162
inter-industry trade, 73, 74
International Organization for
    Standardization (ISO), 80, 116, 255
International Telecommunication Union,
    248
Internet, 29, 34, 218, 234; and connectiv-
    ity, 137; connectivity, and income, 64,
    65–66; consumer surplus from, 67–69;
    and ecommerce, 43, 55; global traf-
    fic, 119; impact on economic growth,
    139–140; impact on telecoms services,
    190–191; inappropriate use of, 186–187;
    intermediaries, 69, 190; intermediar-
    ies, legal liability of, 188–189; penetra-
    tion rates, 39; restrictions and differing
    national regulations, 198; "safe harbor"
    laws, 186–187; speed, 156; Splinternet,
    177, 194–197; and telecommunications
    services, 191; use, demographics of, 62,
    65
Internet of Things, 15, 78, 86, 131, 156, 193,
    255, 264
interoperability, 97–98, 107, 115, 116, 145,
    196, 208, 251, 253, 257, 273–274
Inthree, 93
intra-industry trade, 73, 74
Invoice Check, 111
IPC lending model, 207, 322n.36
Ireland, 253
Israel, 212

Janetssamoa.com, 144
Japan, 14; and CBPR, 183–184; public
    policy, 252, 278
J. C. Penney, 90
JD.com, 50–51
Jingdong, 94
JIPDEC, 183
job creation, and ecommerce, 51–53; in
    adjacent industries, 52; and technology,
    52; wages, 53
John Deere, 132–133

joint ventures, 100, 114
J.P. Morgan Chase, 107
Jumia, 8

Karnani, Aneel, 217
KBC, 109
Kemp, Leanne, 128
Kenya, 49
Kerchin, 51
Keynes, John Maynard, 279
KiliMall, 48
Kindara, 36
kLab, 141
Klenow, Peter, 67, 68
knowledge-intensive business services
    (KIBS), 34–36
knowledge spillovers, 29–30
know-your-customer (KYC), 104; block-
    chain, 109–110; risk-based approach
    (RBA), 147
Kohl's, 90
KPMG, 52
Krueger, Dirk, 237
Krugman, Paul, 29, 74, 222–223
Kumar, Krishna, 237
KYC.Com, 110

labor:and economic growth, 154; protec-
    tions, 130
LACChain, 100
Last Mile Bridge fund, 260
last mile logistics, 49, 52, 75, 91; and aggre-
    gation technologies, 91; and blockchain,
    100; challenges, 92; in delivery networks
    struggling countries, 91–92; delivery
    window, expanding of, 92; in developing
    countries, 93; and logjam, 92; and postal
    systems, 92
Latin America, 91, 191, 213, 257, 278–279;
    banking sector, 202; business growth of
    companies in, 47; customs and, 161, 162;
    importers, 43; online shopping in, 70;
    rural companies in, 53–54; skill content
    of workers, 37; see also specific countries
Lavin, Frank, 120
Lawrence, Robert, 231

Lazada, 42
Lee, Stephanie, 68–69
Lei, Jun, 247
Lendico, 208
Lending Club, 203, 204–205
letters of credit, 112; electronic, 107
Levinson, Marc, 166
liability: Internet intermediaries, legal lia-
    bility of, 188–189; of platforms of user-
    generated content, 197; rules, impact on
    small companies, 189
Lieber, Ethan, 62
liner services, 81–82; bargaining powers, 84;
    cost savings through technology, 82; and
    ecommerce, 82, 84; supply-side cost sav-
    ings, 83–84; vertically integrated, 98–99;
    see also shipping industry
LinkedIn, 243–244
Lizhi, Liu, 75
local work platforms, 36
L'Oreal, 27
Lutz, Frank, 278
Luxembourg, 253
Lyft, 69

machine learning, 27, 125, 133, 169, 175,
    243; and shipping movement forecast, 86
machine-to-machine communications, 86,
    131–133
Macri, Mauricio, 142
Macy's, 121
"made by you and me" products, 73
Maersk, 5, 98, 99
man-versus-machine: matching technology
    with labor, 234–235; switching speed
    and cost of, 235–236; evolution of work-
    ers, 236–237
man vs machine:
market structure, 239–240
Market Track, 124
Marrero, Gustavo, 271
mass customization: and materials custom-
    ization, 28; of products, 8; and 3D print-
    ing, 26–28
MasterCard, 131
Mattel, 130

Mayer-Schönberger, Viktor, 244
Mayflower, 78
McKinsey & Company, 20, 36, 95, 121, 132
McLean, Malcolm, 79–80
"Me2Me" products, 73
median voter theorem, 276, 278
Mediastream, 35
Medic Mobile, 71
Medoff, James, 149
megaships: impact on goods cost, 81; and
    supply chain risks, 81; see also shipping
    industry
Melitz, Marc, 40–41
Mercado Crédito, 49–50
Mercado Envíos, 49
MercadoLibre, 8, 42, 48, 49–50
Mercado Pago, 49
Merkel, Angela, 179
Mexico, 36, 50, 91–92, 229; Concilianet, 48;
    customs, 162; free trade agreements, 194;
    IT services outsourcing, 36; new wom-
    en's SME program, 214; public policy,
    253, 257, 266
microloans, 203–209, 216–218; guarantees,
    on online loans, 261; innovations in, 203
Microsoft, 191, 236
microtargeting, 120
Migirov, Rebecca, 127
Miller, Russel A, 179
Mills, Karen, 206
Milsom, Sarah, 271
Min, Jung Kim, 69
Mitsubishi UFJ Financial Group, 110
mobile banking, 148
Mobile Farm Manager, 132–133
mobile phones, 66–69, 137
Monetary Authority of Singapore (MAS),
    111
Mongolia, 163
Moore, Gordon, 118
"more of the same" syndrome, 120
Movistar, 140
MTN Group, 145–146
multinational corporations, 4, 17–18
Musk, Elon, 82, 92, 234
mutually consenting traders, 222–226

Myanmar: customs, 164, 165; Internet and
    connectivity, 141–142
Mykkänen, Kai, 196–197

National Center for the Middle Market, 152
Natixis, 109
Navis, 87
Ndabahweje, Anderson Ngbado, 142–143
Netflix, 71, 119–120
the Netherlands, 253, 268
new collar employees, 273
New Trade Theory, 74
New Zealand, 109; New Zealand Post, 92
Nextrade Group, 152
Nigeria, 156–157; cross-border ecommerce
    in, 70; data protection in, 181
Nike: supplier risk, 130; 3D printing use in,
    20, 21, 23
Nippon Yusen K.K., 82–83
Nockold, Charles, 92
Nokia, 66–67
nonbank providers, 147, 205
Nordstrom, 50
Normandie, 78
North American Free Trade Agreement
    (NAFTA), 184, 189, 229, 277
North Korea, 229
NxtPort, 86–87

OCBC Bank, 110
offshore manufacturing, 16–17
Ohlin, Bertil, 223
Olbe, Hanne Melin, 54
OLX, 50
OnDeck, 203, 204, 206, 207
OneTouch, 82
online content, 186–190
online economy, tariffs, 196
online lending, 203–204; regulations related
    to, 206; to small businesses, 206; stakes,
    206
online payments, 7, 143–145, 218; benefits,
    147; companies, 49; and epayments law,
    147
online platforms, 41–42; for advertis-
    ing, 38, 44; big platforms, effectiveness

of, 242–243; staying on top, 241–242; channels for local companies, 240–241; customer reviews, 44; differentiated, 242; promiscuous users, 242; trust, 47–48; work platforms, 36–37

online sales: accidental exporters, 44; and individual shoppers, 48–49; reasons for hesitance to, 149

online shopping, 62; and age, 62; and education level, 62; in emerging markets, 63; from foreign countries, 70; future predictions, 63; and impulse buying, 68; and income, 64, 65–66; by Millennials, 63; negative side-effects of, 68; and race, 62–63; in rural areas, 66, 74–75; smartphones, 64–66; variety in, 72–75; versus offline shopping, 68

Ontario Securities Commission of Canada, 208–209

open trade policies, 9, 229

Orbian, 114

Organisation for Economic Co-operation and Development (OECD), 81, 192, 250

Orszag, Peter, 251

outmigration, 56

outsourcing, 14, 16, 33–34; of services, 35–36

over the top (OTT) services, 191; rules and taxes on digital services, 191–192

Pacific International Lines Ltd.: use of blockchain in, 99

Pagés, Carmen, 37

Pakistan: online sales in, 149; public policy, 267; smartphone shopping in, 65

Panama Canal, 79, 81

Panamax ship, 80

Panzar, John, 95–96

paperless trade practices, 163–164

parcels: through postal systems, 168; trade based on, 101

Patel, Neel, 50

Paulson, Roy, 19–20

Pavcnik, Nina, 46–47

PayPal, 69, 145, 204, 260

pay-per-use data services, 133

peer monitoring, 111

People's Bank of China, 111

Peru: national broadband plans in, 140–141; public policy, 253

Petersen, Ryan, 85

Petróeo Brasileiro/Petrobras, 112

Petrobras, 132

Philippines, 34; customs, 163, 171, 173

Physical Internet, 98, 99

Picketty, Thomas, 270

Pinterest, 144

plurilateral agreement, 197

political risk, 124–125

populism, 225

Porter, Eduardo, 230

ports, 79; Antwerp port, 86–87; automation, 85–88; and city, integration of, 98; data for revenue, 86–87; Durban port, 88; Long Beach port, 166; Los Angeles port, 166; Mombasa port, 88; port community system (PCS), 87; Port of Hamburg, 85–86; Port of Los Angeles, 86; Port of Veracruz, 100; Rotterdam ports; Qingdao port, and automation, 85; Shanghai port, 85; use of blockchain, 99–100; Valparaiso port, 87

postal services, 94; battle of, 95–96; and cost effectiveness, 94; future of, 96

Prahalad, C. K., 122

predictive and prescriptive analytics, 132

Premise, 124

Price, Brendan, 224, 230

PriceSmart Inc, 185

PricewaterhouseCoopers, 50

privacy, 177–178; and data see data; and globalization, 178

privatizations, 176

production: centralization of, 31; global production, inflections, 14; localization of, 32; location of, 29–31; mass production, 22–26; regionalized, 15

productivity: and exporters, 40–41, 45; of firms serviced by Internet intermediaries, 69; growth, 5, 7; and online selling, 47; top and the median workers, gap between, 230–231; total factor produc-

tivity (TFP), and economic growth, 154–155; and wages, gap between, 231
product recommendations, 178
product variety, 72–75
progressive data-sharing mandate, 244
Proméxico, 266
Prophet, Tony, 15–16
Prosper (online lender), 205
protectionism, 3, 13, 77, 88, 175, 225, 259, 276, 277
PSA International: use of blockchain technology in, 99
psychographics, 120–121
public policy, 251; coalition creation for, 251–253; customs, borders, and ports, digitizing for, 257–258; *de minimis* political economy transformation for, 258–259; and digital transformation, 153–154, 262–263; and equity investments, 261–262; eTrade and last-mile delivery for, 259–260; FinTech loans to SMEs, 260–261; funding promotion for women-led tech firms and, 263; impact on fundraising, 213; new politics possibility and, 276–278; regulatory sandboxes for, 255–256; smarter systems for, 264–276; standards for, 255–256; Washington Consensus II, 254–255
public-private partnerships, 265–267

Quickbooks, 233

Rabobank, 109
Rakuten, 50
Randolph, Marc, 119
Rappi, 124
Rauch, Jim, 44
real-life distributional impacts of trade, 224–225
Rent the Runway, 211–212
Reshoring Initiative, 17–18
revenue diversification, 46
reverse factoring, 112
Ricardo, David, 16, 222, 232
Riker, David, 70

Rio Tinto: machine-to-machine communications, 131–132
Ripple, 111, 147
Roadie, 91
Roadrunnr, 91
Robin, Li, 247
robots/robotics, 7, 22, 32, 37; in container terminals, 85; intelligent robots, 30–31; intelligent robots and 3D printing, 30–31
Rodríguez, Belén, 188
Rodríguez, Juan Gabriel, 271
Rolls-Royce, 82, 112
Romer, Paul, 157, 272
Rometty, Ginni, 273
royalties-based financing program, 214
Rucci, Graciana, 37
rural areas: broadband connections in, 56–57; businesses, and connectivity, 139; online shopping, 66, 74–75; relocation of urban firms to, 56–57; rural companies, 53–54; rural ecommerce, 54–56
"Rural Taobao" initiative, 74
Russia, 227; data protection in, 181; last mile logistics in, 91
Rwanda, 156; digital transformation and connectivity, 141; e-Soko program, 141

Sablan, Janet, 144
Safadi, Raed, 152
SAFE Port Act (U.S.) (2009), 166
Salesforce, 133
Samba Tech, 35
Samsung, 99
Samuelson, Paul, 223, 224
sandbox approach, 208–209, 255–256
Santander: One Pay FX service, 147
SAP, 114
Savannah, 78
Savvier postal systems, 92
Schaur, Georg, 161
Schmidt-Eisenlohr, Tim, 105
Schwebel, David, 90
SC Johnson, 123
sea-bound trade (maritime trade): acceleration due to technology, 79; anticipatory shipping technique, 122; cargo, and big

data, 131; congestion in ships and ports, 77–78; driverless and crewless ship, 82–83; *see also* shipping industry

Sea-Land Services, 80

second unbundling, 55

Seed, 212

Sendy, 49

Seoul Consensus *see* Washington Consensus II

services unbundling, 33–37

services vendors, 35

Seychelles Trading Company, 111

Sherk, James, 230–231

Shih, Stan, 17

shipment information technology, 86

shipping costs, 82; and exporters and importers, 82; and SMEs' ecommerce and ecommerce platforms, 82

shipping industry, 100–101; automated ports, 85–88; containerized shipments, 79–80; and liner services, 81; overcapacity, 81; port-city integration, 98; space size, 80–81; suspicious containers, spotting using data analytics, 167; and world's ports, 81 (*see also* ports)

Shopee, 65

Siemens, 237

Silicon Valley, 187

silo-busting, 264–265

Simard, Suzanne, 96

Sime Darby Berhad, 132

Simon, Herbert, 232

Singapore: customs, 163, 164, 169, 175; public policy, 252, 256, 257, 269; SingPost, 92

Single Digital Market, 195

singularity, 118

SkillsFuture Credit, 269

SK Telecom, 156

Skylark Services, 94–95

Skype, 191

small and medium-sized enterprises (SMEs), 195, 215; and exporting, 8, 38, 40, 41, 45, 73; growth of, 45; impact of financial crisis, 200–201; online trade, 41, 42, 44; and working capital, 201

small and medium-sized enterprises (SMEs), finance/credit gap, 199, 219; banks, hard work and difficult for, 207; financial innovations scalability, 207–208; friction in information flows in market, 205; gradual adoption rate, 204–205; problems in getting loans, 202–203; too big to fail concerns, 205–206

small businesses *see* small and medium-sized enterprises (SMEs)

small business investment company (SBIC) program, U.S. SBA, 262, 263

smaller packet sizes products, 123

small loans for microenterprises, 215–216

smart contracts, 109, 110, 114–116, 302n.23

smartphones, 61–62, 75–76; apps, 69; and consumer surplus, 68–69; developmental impact of, 71; and exchange of content, 70–71; shopping, 64–66, 68, 70, 74

Smith, Adam, 33

Snapdeal, 66

social impact bonds, 267–268

social media industry: financial regulations, 208

Societe Generale, 109

Softek, 35

solid deposit modeling, 23

South Africa, 95

South Korea, 143, 156, 229, 257; consumer surplus from Internet in, 68–69; intra-industry trade by, 73

spaghetti bowl problem, 194–195

Splinternet, 177, 274; cost of, 194–197; and WTO, 196; *see also* cord-cutting; data; privacy

Sri Lanka, 113, 144–145; customs, 165; public policy, 267

Stancil, Bennett, 271

Standard Chartered, 107, 109, 111

Starbucks, 28, 125–126

Starr, Paul, 190

startups, 216; blockchain use in, 111; funding for, 189–190, 263; and innovations, 216; tech startups, 58

Stephenson, George, 98

Stewart, Martha, 18
Stolper, Wolfgang, 223, 224
Stratasys, 25
StreetScooter, 92
sub-Saharan Africa, 123; exports, 40; imports, 164
Suez Canal, 79
Sumitomo Chemical, 123
Summers, Larry, 124
super-heavy spenders, 63
supplier risk identification, using block-chain, 130–131
supply-side policies, 142
Sweden: customs, 163, 164; public policy, 253, 268, 278
SWIFT KYC Registry, 109–110
Switzerland, 165
system inefficiencies, 96–97
Syverson, Chad, 62

Taglioni, Daria, 152
Tala Mobile, 71, 203
Tanzania, 165
tariffs, 170–171, 221, 224, 225–226, 230
Tata Group, 123, 132
taxes, 192–193; on digital services, 197–198; inter-state taxations, 314n.49; value-added taxes (VATs), 172, 191
TCS Holdings, 267
technology, 219; adaptability of labor to change, 249; -driven economies, 158; and ecommerce, 50–51; and job creation, 52; labor markets optimization, 236; lags, and workarounds, 144–145; and leisure, 238–239; pace of change, 10–11; as substitutes for labor, 235
telecommunications, 190–191; and Internet rivals, collaboration between, 193–194
Telefonica, 191
Telsa, 83
"10+2" rule, 166–167
Terminal of Manzanillo, 87
terminal operating system (TOS) software, 87
Thailand, 110, 156, 256; customs and, 164, 173; Electronic Transactions

Development Agency, 110; online exports in, 41; Thailand Post, 99
3D printing, 7, 15, 18–21, 37; application of, 19–20; challenges, 23; costs, 27; entry by major players into, 25–26; innovation, impact on, 19; and intelligent robotics, 30–31; and mass customization, 20, 26–28; in mass production, 22–26; materials for, 22; of metal parts, 24–25; and production pace, 20; and rebundling of production, 21; 3D-printable lines in companies, 23–24; trade and globalization, impact on, 21–22; transport costs, impact on, 31–32; and U.S. trade deficit, 32–33; world trade, impact on, 22
3D Systems, 18, 25
Tiffany's, 128
Timmons, Jay, 33
Tinbergen, Jan, 43
TMall, 51, 99
Toptal, 36
total cost of ownership, 17–18
Trace Alliance, 129
Track (software), 131
TracPac, 85
Trade Adjustment Assistance, 223–224
trade costs, 29–30
Trade Facilitation Agreement (TFA), 160
trade finance ecosystem, as inefficient, 106–107
trade finance gap, 103–108, 219
Trade Finance Market, 111
trade in tasks, 34
TradeKey, 42, 131
TradeLens platform, 99
trade liberalization, 4, 5, 14, 16, 72, 78, 223, 224; and cost reduction, 30; and economic growth, 46–47; by gender, 57; see also free trade
trade policy: problems, 197; realignment of, 10; see also public policy
transatlantic corridor, 81
transcontinental railway system, and world trade, 79
Trans-Pacific Partnership (TPP), 6, 177, 184, 245, 252

transport costs, 31; reduction of, 30; and
   3D printing, 31–32
Travelstart, 133
Tribe, Lawrence, 243–244
Trindade, Vitor, 44
Triple E, 80
Trump, Donald, 221, 226
TRUSTe, 183
trusted traders, 47–48, 167
Tucker, Catherine, 243
TurboTax, 233
Turkey, 266; online sales in, 149
Twitter, 11

Uber, 211
Uber Eats, 129
unemployment, 220, 232–233, 236, 237,
   238, 249, 271, 272
UniCredit, 109
Unilever, 65; machine-to-machine communications, 132
United Kingdom, 94, 109, 112; Brexit, 6,
   220; cross-border ecommerce, 39; customs, 169; economic geography, 54–55;
   Financial Conduct Authority (FCA),
   208–209; and FinTechs scale, 208; online
   lending in, 205; open banking practices,
   205; public policy, 252, 253, 256, 257,
   258, 278
United Nations, 137
United States, 14, 34, 86, 120, 166–167;
   airspace companies migration in,
   29; American Airlines, 48; American
   Civil Liberties Union, 127; American
   Communications Decency Act (Section
   230), 186, 187; Committee on Foreign
   Investment in the United States
   (CFIUS), 247; cross-border ecommerce in, 39; customs, 165; Customs
   and Border Protection (CBP), 166;
   Department of the Navy, use of blockchain in, 129; ecommerce market diversification in, 48; Digital Millennium
   Copyright Act (DMCA), 186–187,
   189; economic geography, 54; exit
   from Trans-Pacific Partnership, 177;

Export-Import (EXIM) Bank, 261;
   imports, 72; Internet and economic
   growth, 140; Internet safe harbor laws,
   187–188; Internet "safe harbor" laws,
   186–187; interstate highway system, 79;
   job creation, and ecommerce, 53; last
   mile logistics in, 91; liability protections, 189; manufacturing job losses,
   224–225; Maritime Commission, 77;
   and Mexico, 224; National Federation
   of Independent Business, 189; National
   Security Agency (NSA), and data privacy, 178, 179; new enterprise formation in, 54; online market of, 39; online
   spending by women in, 62; ports, and
   trade growth, 77; public policy, 252,
   253, 255, 258, 271, 277; review of China
   (2017), 227; skill content of workers, 37;
   Stop Enabling Sex Traffickers Act, 187;
   tariff policy, 221; 3D printing and trade
   deficit, 32–33; Trump's steel tariffs, 226;
   use of drones in, 94; view on privacy,
   179; warehousing in, 98; withdrawal
   from Trans-Pacific Partnership, 6, 184
unmanned aircraft system (UAS), 95
U Ohn Maung, 142
UPS brown trucks, 91, 94
Upwork, 36, 54, 56, 58
Urmex, 38
U.S.-Mexico-Canada Agreement (USMCA),
   184, 189, 252
UVP, Inc., 18

Valentine, Leonie, 133
value-added taxes (VATs), 172, 191
van Agtmael, Antoine, 123
Varian, Hal, 67, 69
venture capitals (VCs), 210, 211, 212,
   213–214; and employment protection
   regulations, 323n.47
Vietnam, 113; data protection in, 181, 182
virtual private networks (VPNs), 245, 246
Vodafone Group, 112, 145–146
Volkswagen, 24, 28
Volvo, 19
vTex, 50

wages: of ecommerce workers, 53; and job creation, 53; levels of, 228, 230; and productivity, gap between, 231
Walmart, 5, 48, 50; ecommerce distribution, 90–91; use of blockchain, 128; warehousing, 88, 89
Walsh, John, 179
Warby Parker, 49, 73, 125
warehousing, 88–90; city warehouse space, 89–90; elites, 89; mega warehouses, 88–89; mobile warehouse, 96; and time share, 90; time to market, 89
Washington Consensus II, 254–255
Wave, 111
weakest link identification, 130–131
WebMotors, 133
Weide, Roy Van der, 271
Weinstein, David, 74
Wells Fargo, 109
Western Europe, 79
we.trade blockchain system, 109
What3words, 91
WhatsApp, 193
Whole Foods, 126
Wine Fraud, 128
winner-take-all dynamics, 239, 240, 241–242, 244
women, 323n.43: in developing countries, smartphone shopping, 66; digital divas, 62, 63; in ecommerce, 57–59; underfunding of companies lead by, 211
Woodard, John Benjamin, 93
Workana, 36
worker empowerment and job protection, 268–270
working capital, 199, 201; and economic growth, 154; loans, 199

World Bank, 47, 58, 163, 199
WorldCom, 190
World Customs Organization, 165, 257
World Economic Forum research, 164
world trade, 4, 5, 14, 77; data management, 97; and economic growth, 78; and expanded scale and technological progress in global shipping, 78; growth of, 5, 77; inefficiencies, handling of, 97; and inequality, 230–231; and national economy, 229–230; in services, 33–37; symbiotic system, 97
World Trade Organization (WTO), 4, 6, 176, 251–252; Agreement on Technical Barriers to Trade, 256; and digital issues, 196–197; and Splinternet, 196
World Vision, 131
Wyman, Jennifer, 211–212

xCurrent (software), 147
X Electrical Vehicle, 25
Xi, Jinping, 246–247
Xiaolan, Fu, 228

Yara Birkeland, 82, 83
Yee, Wong, 173
YelpEat24, 94
Yemen, 164, 167
Yiannas, Frank, 128
Ying Yao, 105
Yizhen, Gu, 75
YouTube: advertising, 44; trade in, 70–72
Yunus, Mohammed, 216–217

Zimbabwe, 124
Zuckerberg, Mark, 234